CONTENTS

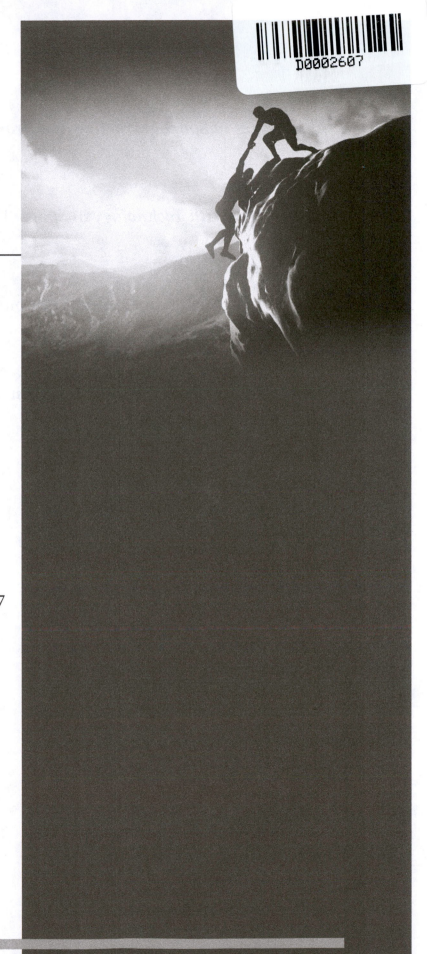

ETHICAL THEORY APPLIED TO SPORT

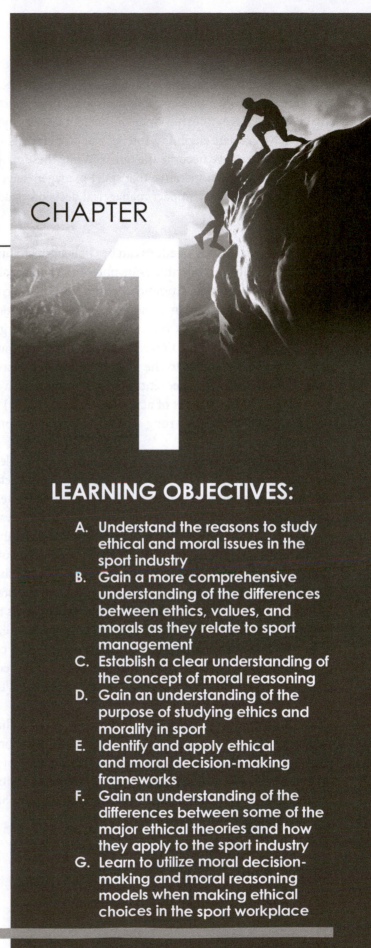

CHAPTER

1

WHY STUDY ETHICS IN SPORT?

The business of sport and the sport industry have grown from $152 billion in 1995 to $498.4 billion in 2015, increasing the need and demand for professionals in the sport industry to be trained to make ethical decisions in the workplace (Cooper, 2000; Plunkett Research Estimate, 2015). The sport industry includes jobs in facility management, recreation, youth program development, youth and high school and college athletics, professional sport, athlete development, international sport, and hundreds of other sport industry positions. Researchers suggest that sport management professionals should study ethics to have an increased capacity to perform their duties, to be able to make informed intellectual decisions about conflicts and problems in the workplace, and to have the ability to grasp the overwhelming philosophical questions that are sometimes hard to answer (Lumpkin, Stoll, & Beller, 2012; McNamee, 2008; Schneider, 2009; Simon, 2010). As mentioned, many ethical challenges exist in the sport industry and over time, sport has seen an increase in the amount of unethical and inappropriate behavior from those that oversee, participate, and regulate not only the games, but the athletes as well. Each year, sport managers witness

LEARNING OBJECTIVES:

A. Understand the reasons to study ethical and moral issues in the sport industry
B. Gain a more comprehensive understanding of the differences between ethics, values, and morals as they relate to sport management
C. Establish a clear understanding of the concept of moral reasoning
D. Gain an understanding of the purpose of studying ethics and morality in sport
E. Identify and apply ethical and moral decision-making frameworks
F. Gain an understanding of the differences between some of the major ethical theories and how they apply to the sport industry
G. Learn to utilize moral decision-making and moral reasoning models when making ethical choices in the sport workplace

crisis, conflict, rule breaking, challenges to personal and professional values, immoral action, and blatant disregard for people, processes, and programs that exist in sport. Ethical issues such as bribery, betting, and gambling have occurred since the ancient Greek Olympics (Taylor & Francis, 2010), while more recent issues such as athlete eligibility, intellectual property rights, transgender equity, power and politics, and athlete misconduct have become the norm. While these are only a few examples of the many issues that occur in the industry, it is imperative that sport managers have a clear understanding of the challenges they may face and how they may impact managerial decision making, leadership, and the success of the industry as a whole.

The philosophical study of ethics can be challenging to understand, and defining the commonly used words to describe ethics can oftentimes be unclear. When speaking of ethics in the context of sport, many terms and definitions are used. Common definitions of the term **ethics** include: the difference between right and wrong, the ability to act in a moral way, taking the correct moral action, and following the values that were set forth during one's youth (DeSensi & Rosenberg, 2003; Lumpkin, Stoll, & Beller, 2003; Schneider, 2009; Simon, 2010). These descriptions and definitions are all valid, but do not clearly identify the specific term "ethics" as it applies to the practice of sport. According to Schneider (2009), *ethics* is an area of philosophy that studies the theoretical basis of moral action and involves theories or principles that determine the rightness or wrongness of actions. Schneider (2009) stated ethics is the formal study of the difference between right action and wrong action and the mental processes involved in individuals making decisions.

Ethical principles are the universal guides that tell people which kind of actions, intentions, and motives are prohibited or permitted in human interactions. Ethics act as "universal rules of conduct," or rules that identify and define what is important. When discussing the term *ethics*, one may say, "ethics are what we believe to be right," while another may say, "ethics are our values and morals." Each of these definitions is partially correct as the study of ethics produces moral decisions and moral actions. The term *ethics*, however, is often confused with the terms *morals* and *values*. In the study of sport ethics, it is important to know each of these terms and how they fit into an individual's decision-making process. As described, the word *moral* or *morals* is included in the definition of ethics. In order to understand the difference, one should know moral philosophies, moral behaviors, and moral outcomes are things that one wishes to achieve. So, if ethics is the set of overarching principles that determine right versus wrong, then a **moral** is the standard of behavior involved in putting those ethical theories into practice. A person can know and understand that it is ethically wrong to cheat on a test, but may act on that instinct to cheat because he or she has no understanding of the moral principle. Simply put, morals involve putting the ethical theories into practice.

Morals is a Latin word that means customs or manners that define a person's character, upbringing, and attitude whereas ethics stresses the larger societal expectations related to action. One's morals are learned based on social systems and societal standards and expectations. Morals are the individual "actions" in everyday behavior. The term **morality** is often interchangeable with morals and it refers to societal rules that govern most forms of everyday interactive behavior (Tangney, Stuewig, & Mashek, 2007). *Morality* is a "system of norms, values and rules that regulate the manner in which human beings treat one another" (Schneider, 2009, p. 4). In sport, managers, athletes, and coaches will often take a moral position on an incident, issue, or topic. This moral stance is what they personally believe and it will dictate the perceived correct or accurate (moral) behavior. Modern sport and its win-at-all-costs mentality have caused many to question the moral actions of some athletes, coaches, and sport managers. Each of these sport figures may have a variety of motives for moral or immoral behaviors. Some of the motives for immoral behavior in sport might include self-promotion, self-interest, lack of respect for rules, lack of understanding of the impact, or other interests related to advancement, winning, power, and/or control.

Ethics, Morals, and Values…What Is the Difference?

TABLE 1.1 *Difference Between Ethics, Morals, and Values*

Ethics	Morals	Values
Overarching sets of philosophical theory or a branch of knowledge that deals with moral principles and codes of conduct An area of philosophical study offering standards or principles that determine the rightness or wrongness of one's actions	Rules that guide behavior or the standards of behavior that are the "norm" Societal rules or norms that govern most everyday behavior	Something having worth or something that is considered worthwhile Something important

If morals are the standards that guide action or behavior, how is a moral different from a value? As indicated in Table 1.1, a moral refers to a "rule that guides behavior or the standards of behavior that are the 'norm,'" whereas a **value** is something that one considers worthwhile, important, or having some type of worth (DeSensi & Rosenberg, 2003). If an individual sees something as having worth or being important, he or she may consider that "action" moral or ethical. There are many variables to consider when discussing the worth of "things" in an individual's life; and many people will confuse a moral with a value. It is human nature to think power, money, and success are worthwhile. Some people will *value* money, a car, a house, or their job. These by definition are nonmoral values (extrinsic). **Nonmoral values** are those that relate to things, places, and events (Burnor & Raley, 2010). **Moral values,** on the other hand, will often reflect personal motives, personality, and personal intentions related to dealing with others. According to Burnor and Raley (2010), moral values typically come into conflict with other values in conflict situations. Some moral values include honesty, honor, truth, respect, sincerity, integrity, justice, duty, cooperation, and family. Moral values that are desirable such as those listed (even in the context of sport) are most often challenged in conflicts related to ethical decision-making.

MORAL DEVELOPMENT AND MORAL REASONING

The ethical decision-making process of sport managers, professionals, athletes, and coaches involves many varieties of factors and must consider an individual's moral compass. One's **moral compass** is the directional assistor in the process of making moral and ethical decisions and judgments. As a population, morals can be developed, acquired, and refined in various sequential stages of life. **Moral reasoning** involves the cognitive processes people employ to make decisions about ethical problems (Schneider, 2009). This type of thinking requires a consideration of moral standards, evidence, and the use of personal opinion and judgment. Good moral reasoning requires impartiality, consistency, and reflective judgment to assist in the process of determining the best course of action or best behavior to pursue. When people are thinking through an ethical scenario, the moral reasoning is the type of thinking, the gathering of information, and the decision-making involved in the scenario. As sport managers are faced with ethical challenges, there are a number of ways that each person may process whether a decision/action is moral or immoral based on a variety of factors. Sport managers will be involved in the moral reasoning process many times throughout their careers. In many cases and situations, sport managers will face a moral dilemma and will be required to employ moral reasoning to determine the best possible outcome. Every individual usually has an ingrained, systematic approach to resolving dilemmas or solving problems; however, resolving ethical issues can present many additional factors that will challenge the decision maker. A sport manager may find it useful to follow a set of guidelines or use applicable decision-making models to assist in processing information and determining the best final outcome.

Ethical Dilemmas

Current day sport managers will be challenged with situations that involve values, conflicts, and morality. Sport managers will be required to make ethical choices. Knowing and recognizing an ethical dilemma will help sport managers make better decisions in the future when faced with ethical challenges. This text will serve to provide answers to the dilemma questions, conflicts, challenges, and results that have been and will likely be faced in this industry. An **ethical dilemma** is an undesirable or unpleasant choice relating to a moral principle or practice (Lumpkin et al., 2012). An ethical dilemma occurs when a person is put in a position and forced to make a decision that questions or challenges values, morals, or personal beliefs. Ethical dilemmas will always involve some type of consequence. When one is faced with an ethical dilemma, no matter what final decision is made, someone or something will be impacted by the outcome. In ethical dilemmas, both positive and negative consequences can occur. One example might include a good friend asking to see the answers on a standardized test. This is an ethical challenge or values conflict if one believe cheating is wrong. There will be a consequence for the act of sharing answers with this friend. There may also be a consequence of NOT sharing answers with this friend. These consequences might include getting caught, losing the chance at a successful test score, facing an angry friend, or losing the friendship altogether, among others.

An ethical dilemma occurs in situations where the course of action is unclear to the decision maker. According to ethics researchers (Rest, 1982; Strategy, 1998), there are three common situations that will exist if an ethical dilemma occurs: (1) there will be a significant values conflict, (2) there will be justifiable options or alternatives to each decision, and (3) there will be significant consequences to each decision. Ethical dilemmas are challenging because of conflicts, alternatives, and consequences that are presented. As sport managers challenged with ethical dilemmas, it is important to decide upon the best alternative to the conflict. This can be challenging for a variety of reasons. One reason is the varying stakeholders that the ethical decision might affect. A **stakeholder** is a person with a vested interest in the organization and its situation. For example, stakeholders who may have an interest in an ethical decision made by an NCAA D1 coach may include the team, the athletic director, the university, the fans, the community, the parents, or the doctors. Each of these stakeholders has a variety of interests and each will have an opinion about what the best option might be to solve this dilemma. Ethical decision-making in regard to dilemmas should involve some type of systematic process of reasoning to assist sport managers who face ethical challenges.

Tashatuvango/shutterstock.com

Developing a procedure to sort out ethical dilemmas is an important key to understanding and processing the ethical dilemmas that sport managers will face. The theory-based concepts discussed later in the chapter will assist in the decision-making process. No matter the organization, an ethical dilemma will occur, and being armed with the proper tools will help each individual succeed in the decision-making process.

Kidder (1995) suggested when facing an ethical dilemma, the following steps should be considered:

1. Identify and recognize the problem or values conflict.
2. Determine who is involved and will be impacted.
3. Gather the facts and the pertinent information.
4. Explore the right versus wrong issues.
5. Discuss significant value consequences for all parties.
6. Apply code of conduct options or standards.
7. Speak with others who can help.
8. Make a list of the options/recommendations and decision.
9. Reflect, evaluate, and revisit the decision.

Applicable Model for Moral Reasoning in Sport

Outside of the context of sport, ethical reasoning is developed in a variety of ways. Children will learn appropriate ethical behavior from parents, family, friends, teachers, church, and their community, among a variety of others. The process of determining moral or ethical reasoning is learned through the understanding of right versus wrong. People learn this concept at a very young age, but identifying and resolving moral issues is a more advanced reasoning process (DeSensi & Rosenberg, 2003). Many researchers throughout history have studied moral reasoning and determined a variety of processes that individuals experience in ethical decision making as they mature from child to adult (Cavanaugh, 1984; Kohlberg, 1987; Piaget, 1932). Each of these specialists in the study of ethical reasoning and moral development asked questions related to understanding how and why people make moral decisions and how and when humans are first exposed to morality and moral reasoning.

Lawrence **Kohlberg** (1987) advanced the study of research on philosophy and ethical reasoning by looking at children and attempting to identify the reasons they made the ethical decisions they did. Kohlberg determined children (and adults) separate their moral decisions into three components or levels: (1) how the decision affects self, (2) how the decision affects others, and (3) how the decision affects the social system or society (Kohlberg, 1987). Using Kohlberg's studies, it is believed children move from different stages of moral reasoning based on how it affects them personally, how it affects others in their life, and how it conforms to the standards of society. Kohlberg (1987) identified three stages of moral decision-making: preconventional (before norms), conventional (normal, or what is normally done), and postconventional (above the normal standard). Many studies looked at a person's ability to make decisions based on independent thinking regarding their personal values and ethical principles. Kohlberg theorized reasoning is learned from others and that people learn moral behavior throughout their lives (DeSensi & Rosenberg, 2003). This model of moral development represents personal growth and moral reasoning in six different stages (see Table 1.2).

TABLE 1.2 *Moral Development Model*

Level I – Preconventional
    Stage 1 – Punishment & Obedience
       • Ethical choice is made to avoid being punished, to be obedient, or based on consequences of the action.
    Stage 2 – Individualism (Self-Interest)
       • Ethical choice is made to satisfy self-interest or in exchange of self-interest.
Level II – Conventional
    Stage 3 – Mutual Expectation & Conformity
       • Ethical choice is made based on immediate sphere of influence or conformity and acceptance of others.
    Stage 4 – Law & Order (Conscience)
       • Ethical choice is made to adhere to laws, rules, and proper authority.
Level III – Postconventional
    Stage 5 – Utility, Duty & Human Rights (Action)
       • Ethical choice is based on rights and duty to act.
    Stage 6 – Universal Principles
       • Ethical choice is guided by quality and worth of all human beings, universal law, and pure conscience.

LEVEL I: PRECONVENTIONAL

Stage 1: *Punishment and Obedience.* In this stage, people make decisions because they want to be obedient to avoid punishment. The moral behavior is learned because there is a punishment attached to the result of the behavior. One example might include a child not coloring on the wall because she does not want to get a spanking from her grandmother. A sport example would be a basketball player who makes the choice not to fight with his teammate because he does not want to run sprints or get cut from the team.

Stage 2: *Individualism and Personal Exchange.* In this case, one will make the ethical decision to satisfy self-interest. When considering stage 2, what is right involves equal exchange, a deal, or an arrangement. The concept of egoism (discussed later in this chapter) is evident in this stage of moral reasoning. Someone using this stage of reasoning will do the right action based on how it will personally or individually affect him or herself. This stage is not about being obedient or avoiding punishment but getting some result out of the decision. An example in the area of sport could be a football player helping the QB with his exam in class because he thinks that by doing so, the QB will throw him the game-winning pass on Saturday.

LEVEL II: CONVENTIONAL

Stage 3: *Mutual Expectation, Influence, and Conformity.* In the third stage, the ethical decision is made based around a person's sphere of influence with a desire to gain approval from those closest to the individual. The ethical decision is made to gain acceptance or approval from friends or to conform to social expectations of those that influence the decision maker. A sport example might include a mother lying to NCAA recruiting officers to help her son stay eligible to play.

Stage 4: *Law, Order, and Conscience.* In the fourth stage, doing right is doing what is considered acceptable in society and obeying laws and rules that are part of the larger social system. The correct behavior is that which abides by the roles and rules of the social system and fulfills expectations of society. A sport example might be that a fan decides not to steal merchandise because it is illegal to steal.

LEVEL III: POSTCONVENTIONAL

Stage 5: *Social Contract and Individual Rights.* In the fifth stage, the ethical decision maker considers the greatest good for the greatest number of people (utilitarianism) and looks at making decisions based on a duty to act. An example might be a coach who pulls her team from the field despite her athletic director's directions because it is 104 degrees and she is concerned for the safety of the players. The individual is concerned with rights and a duty to act in the best interest of the function of society.

Stage 6: *Pure Conscience and Universal Ethical Principles.* In the sixth stage, the individual is guided by pure conscience, universal ethical principles, and the concept of justice. Each ethical decision will not be so concerned with laws and rules but doing what is genuinely good and what is genuinely right. This stage considers equality, respect for all life, and liberty. People who make it to this stage of decision making might include Mother Theresa, Gandhi, and Nelson Mandela. An example of a person making a stage-6 decision is someone who chooses to shoot a suicide bomber to protect the life of an innocent bystander.

WHAT DOES KOLHBERG'S REASONING HAVE TO DO WITH SPORT?

An understanding of an individual's stage of moral development will help gain a more clear understanding of how and why people make ethical decisions. When considering Kohlberg's stages of moral reasoning, it can help to clarify whether an individual is considering consequence or punishment (Level I), how the decision affects others or society (Level II), or perhaps the effect on the greater social system, universal law, or the greater moral good (Level III). In ethical decision making, a sport manager needs to understand the broader social learning theory and recognize many actions and behaviors are learned; and cognitive development, growth, and decision making of others can be dependent on cognitive development of the individual. An understanding of these stages will help sport managers understand the way employees, athletes, coaches, other managers, and even they themselves make ethical decisions. This type of moral development model can be applied to many, if not all, ethical decisions a sport manager will make.

Applicable Example for Moral Reasoning in Sport

Ethical Example Dilemma: Assume you are a football player who runs for a touchdown on the last play of the game and scores for the margin of victory. As your coaches and teammates mob you in celebration, you are torn because you know that you stepped out of bounds during the run, but the referee did not see it.

a. Should you continue celebrating or stop to talk to the referee?
b. If you talk to the referee, will the result of the game change?

Example Answer: Stage 2 – Individualism: If you were to continue celebrating and not tell anyone you stepped out of bounds, you would be using the reasoning of Stage 2 of Kohlberg's model. In this stage of moral reasoning, rules are followed (or in this case broken) to achieve the interest of the individual. In this case "you" would be thinking of the reward for "your" good behavior rather than considering the interests of the other team or the rules of the game.

This could also be argued as a **Stage 1 – Punishment and Obedience** type of reasoning. To avoid being punished by the coach for telling the referee, "you" chose not to mention that you stepped out of bounds.

Stage 3 – Interpersonal Relationships: If you were to continue with the celebration and not talk to the referee because your teammates and coaches would be disappointed, you would be using the reasoning of Stage 3. In this stage of moral reasoning, the individual is concerned with conformity and gaining acceptance of others within his or her sphere of influence.

If you chose to tell the referee that you had stepped out of bounds and therefore followed the rules of the game, you would be using **Stage 4 – Law and Order** reasoning. Your conscience told you that it was the right thing to do even though your coach and teammates would be upset with the decision.

STUDENT EXERCISE:
Choose one of the following scenarios. Consider how you would make an ethical or moral decision. Please attempt to reflect on at least two of the stages of moral development as discussed by Kohlberg in your answer.

1. While your softball team is playing, the opposing team starts taunting your pitcher, heckles every batter, and trash-talks at every opportunity. They win the game 10–2. A few weeks later you have a rematch and your coach and team decide to return the favor and get the crowd involved as well. Would you join the trash-talking and heckling? Explain your answer.
2. During a tennis match without any line umpires your opponent keeps calling balls out that are clearly in bounds. After this happens a half dozen times you decide to take action. What do you do?

MAJOR ETHICAL THEORIES
(RESULTS-BASED ETHICS VERSUS DUTY-BASED ETHICS)

An understanding of moral reasoning will help decision makers manage and handle ethical dilemmas and ethical scenarios. The judgments made by decision makers and the process of making reasoned decisions in sport will challenge most managers in the industry. Many of the conflicts that will be prevalent in sport will involve the use of a variety of tactics and theoretical approaches. These approaches all stem from three categories of ethical theories presented by moral philosophers. Moral philosophers throughout history have provided theories to help understand the decisions humans make and why such decisions are made. These categories of classic theoretical concepts will help to provide a basic understanding of the variety of viewpoints that exist in the study of ethics.

Ethics theorists describe three basic foundations involved in ethical decision making. The three categories are deontological, teleological, and virtue ethical theories. First, **teleological theories** rely on some concept of the good or the humanly desirable (Macdonald & Beck-Dudley, 1994). Teleological theories look at making ethical decisions based on what is the most desirable outcome. In teleological theory, the best course of action is the one that will result in the most good (Schneider, 2009). Teleological theory is a results-oriented approach to decision making (DeSensi & Rosenberg, 2003; White, 1988). When using this ethical theory, one is seeking the best possible outcome. The term *teleo* is a Greek word meaning "end" and the term *logos* is Latin meaning "science" (Beauchamp, 1991). Teleological literally means the "science" of the "end" or result. When making decisions using this type of theory, the decision maker is seeking the best possible outcome, consequence, or end result. When applying this theory to sport, the sport manager will evaluate the outcome, final impact of the decision, or the overall consequence of the ethical decision. One example might include a coach choosing to play or not to play an athlete with a known heart condition. Using this type of ethical theory, the sport manager (coach) will make the decision that will have the best result. If it is known that the player has a heart problem, then the coach will choose not to play the athlete based on their opinion of what will produce the best outcome for the athlete. It is important to note that choosing to "do nothing" is a teleological decision. As managers that are presented with ethical choices (dilemmas) and make the decision based on the result, they are making a teleological ethical decision. In sport, another example might include a high school basketball star who chooses to "hog the ball" because he/she knows that there is a recruiter in the stands and he wants to get the college scholarship. The high school basketball star is concerned with the end result of his/her actions.

There are several types of teleological ethical theories. Each of these theories focuses on the outcome, result, or consequence—but each of the decisions are made for differing reasons. The concept of **egoism** looks at the idea or belief that all actions are motivated by selfish interests (DeSensi & Rosenberg, 2003; Schneider, 2009). Those making decisions based on the teleological theory of egoism will make a decision that results in personal gain, self-promotion, or the end result that benefits oneself. A great sport example is the steroids scandal in Major League Baseball (MLB). Specifically, if Alex Rodriguez made the choice to take steroids to help his personal statistics and gain more exposure from his fans, this would be a teleological (egoistic) ethical decision. In contrast, **altruism** is a theory that suggests each of us acts in the best interest of others while often sacrificing ourselves (Lumpkin et al., 2012). An example of altruism is making the ethical decision to save a drowning child in shark-infested waters. A sport example might include a student-athlete giving her food stipend to a homeless man so he can eat for the week. The primary difference between these two types of teleological theories is self-sacrifice versus selfish interests. When decision makers choose the decision to sacrifice themselves to help others, they are making an altruistic decision. Both of these types of ethical theories consider the end result of the ethical decision being made.

Gustavo Frazao/shutterstock.com

Another type of teleological theory is **pragmatism,** which is the idea that "whatever works, is likely true" and the best possible course of action is the right one (DeSensi & Rosenberg, 2003). A pragmatic coach may think that running excessive sprints is the best warm-up for his team since they always win if they run pregame sprints. **Existentialism** focuses primarily on matters of choice, individuality, subjectivity, freedom, and the nature of existence itself. An existentialist rejects discovering true meaning and does the things that are believed to work most effectively at his or her core. An NBA coach may decide to encourage the team to "tank" because he knows it will provide a better draft pick in the coming year. **Despotism** looks at dominance through threat of punishment and violence to produce the desired result (DeSensi & Rosenberg, 2003). The term *despot* is from the Greeks, meaning "one with power." A sport example of despotism might include an athletic director telling the coach to play the star athlete even though the student is failing classes, and if the coach does not play the star athlete, the coach will be fired. This is an example of dominance through threat and violence that determines an ethical end result. In the **utilitarianism theory**, the only good worth seeking is the one that produces the greatest good for the greatest number of people. The only moral duty one has is to promote the greatest amount of happiness. Utilitarianism holds one person's happiness is just as important as the next person's (DeSensi & Rosenberg, 2003). Utilitarianism can use a cost–benefit analysis to determine the best outcome or result. Sport managers, specifically athletic directors, are commonly faced with utility ethical decisions when evaluating the amount of people who will benefit from the facility or program cut decisions. For example, the athletic director may use utilitarianism to determine the cost–benefit ratio of cutting a football, swimming, wrestling, or rowing program.

In the second type of theory, **deontological theory**, decision makers let things other than consequences determine which actions are morally correct and emphasize the moral nature of specific standards and one's behavior irrespective of the results they produce. Deontological theory considers one has a duty to perform the ethical act. The term *deon* means "duty" and again, *logos* means "science" (Beauchamp, 1991; DeSensi & Rosenberg, 2003; Garner & Rosen, 1967). Unlike results-oriented teleological theories such as utilitarianism, deontology maintains moral standards should determine action. In deontological theory, one considers the respect for people, commitment, rules, allegiance, autonomy, motives, commitment rather than results, and the emphasis on moral obligation and/or duty (Kant, 1785). In deontological ethics, people feel they have a duty to do the right thing even if it produces a bad result.

ISSUES AND ETHICS IN SPORT

There are several types of deontological theories. One example is **absolutism,** which is the view that *good* is objectively real, universal, and constant. In other words, absolutism means that there is a set of rules a person should follow, no matter the situation. For example, is it always wrong to LIE? In absolutism, the answer is yes. An absolutist believes that it is ALWAYS wrong to lie no matter the situation. However, if we consider the example of a murderer seeking the location of his potential victim, would the answer still be yes? Would it be okay to tell the murderer a lie? If the decision is made based on the result or possible outcome (teleological), the answer would be no, it is not always acceptable to lie. In absolutism, the moral obligation to NOT LIE makes the ethical decision to tell the murderer the location of his next victim acceptable and ethical. Another deontological type of ethical decision considers the **Golden Rule.** The "do unto others as you would have them do unto you" approach to ethical decision making does not consider the result of the decision, but the desire to adhere to the general principle of appropriate exchange of behaviors.

One moral philosopher who contributed to the study of duty in ethics was Immanuel **Kant** (1724–1804). Kant, too, determined moral decisions to arise out of a sense of duty rather than to produce a desired result. According to DeSensi and Rosenberg (2003), Kant considered that "keeping one's promises, not lying, respecting one's rents, paying one's debts, not turning one's back on one's friend, and the like are performed because they provide some kind of advantage or gratification, which in turn make them no longer ethical actions" (p. 70). Kant suggested an individual should act so that actions establish a precedent for all future decisions and actions. Kant also looked at the moral character of a person and suggested that an individual should act as if every act is the universal norm and a person should consider the duty associated with all future actions (Lumpkin et al., 2012). Kant theorized that moral and ethical decision-making ultimately exists within each of us and decisions of autonomy will emerge from

Immanuel Kant

mishabender/shutterstock.com

any rational being. In terms of sport managers using Kantian ethics, every moral decision that a sport manager makes will in turn set a precedent for every other decision made down the road.

> *"Two things fill the mind with ever new and increasing wonder, the starry heavens above me and the moral law within me."*
> —Immanual Kant

The third type of approach to ethical decision-making is **virtue ethics**. The word *virtue* means "the qualities, characteristics, attitudes and habits of good people" (Schneider, 2009, p. 27). Virtue ethics considers a decision's effect on individuals and personal relationships. On virtue ethics, philosopher John Gough (1757–1825) suggested most ethical problems could be resolved if individuals seriously considered the idea of developing excellence in character. Gough believed in the "act of being rather than doing" (as cited in Schneider, 2009).

Distinctions: Suppose a person is injured and in obvious need of help.

- A teleological decision maker (utilitarianism) would point out the fact that the consequence of doing something will result in maximum well-being.
- A deontological decision maker (Golden Rule) will act in accordance with the concept of "do unto others."
- A decision maker following virtue ethics will recognize making this decision is a charitable and benevolent act.

Virtue Ethics	Deontological Ethics	Teleological Ethics
Concerned with the **character** of the person	Concerned with the action or the **duty** to act	Concerned with the **results** of the action or actions

APPLICABLE MODEL FOR ETHICAL DECISION MAKING

This chapter has discussed moral reasoning, ethical dilemmas, and the processes in which ethical decisions can and should be made. As business professionals in the sport industry, moral issues will exist, so having a decision-making model to assist with the ethical challenges will help sport managers develop a moral foundation (Josepheson, 1992). In 1984, Gerald F. **Cavanaugh** in his writing, *American Business Values,* utilized Kohlberg's moral development theories and expanded them to create an ethical decision-making framework for business executives. This framework has been referenced and utilized in ethical research to assist decision makers faced with ethical challenges. Cavanaugh (1984) defined ethics as "a system of moral principles and methods for applying them; ethics thus provides the tools to make moral judgements and enables individuals to make effective moral decisions" (p. 137). This decision framework will serve as a personal guide for sport managers and decision makers to evaluate and access alternatives, outcomes, impacts, and consequences of decisions in business. The Cavanaugh decision framework starts with the evaluation of many of the ethical theories already discussed in this chapter: utilitarianism, (Kant) personal rights, justice, and respect. With Cavanaugh (1984), the first step in decision making is to gather all the facts and information involved in the situation. This framework evaluates three concepts: utility, rights, and justice. In the *utility* analysis, the aim is to satisfy the organizational or personal goals (needs) that satisfy the greatest good for the greatest number of people. In evaluation of the *rights,* "a person's right is their entitlement to something which may follow the legal system or may be spelled out in some kind of document" (Cavanaugh, 1984, p. 142). Finally, in the *justice* evaluation, the decisions seek to consider fairness, "democratic principles," and due process.

Cavanaugh (1984) used a variety of ethical theories to build a framework for assisting decision makers to determine the most appropriate ethical decision in business. This information gathering will help to ensure that facts are ascertained and evaluated on each of the three criteria: utility, rights, and justice. To better explain each of the three criteria, consider the sport scenario presented next.

> **SPORT SCENARIO: KLUTCH HELMETS, INC.**
> You are the owner of the football equipment company Klutch Helmets. Your company has just created a new football helmet that is similar to the old style of football helmets (throwbacks). The difference is the new helmets are less expensive to make and manufacture allowing you a much greater profit. The new helmets have been tested by the industry and the league and have been determined to meet the concussion safety standards (just barely). However, through field testing it has been found that if a player is hit at a certain speed and at a certain angle the helmet will crack at impact, causing severe injury. It has also been determined that the players like their lightweight feel and the ease of use. Your company feels since the helmets meet league guidelines that it is safe to put the product on the market. One year later a star football player suffers a severe and long-term head injury putting him in a permanent coma and it is believed the helmet failed to protect his head.

When attempting to solve the ethical dilemma of Klutch Helmets, the first step is to create the ethical question to run through the Cavanaugh framework. In this case the question could be, *Was it ethical for Klutch Helmets to send their product to market?* After asking the question, it is then time to gather all the information possible. In this case, little information is presented, but some of it is crucial. The key information includes using low-quality materials to cut costs, knowledge of possible injury, helmets passed safety standards, players liked the helmet's lightweight feel, and a player's serious injury.

After the question has been asked and the facts have been gathered and analyzed, it is time to run the question through the utility, rights, and justice framework. When looking at the utility criteria, a decision maker seeks to understand what is in the best interest of all involved. So decision makers will consider stakeholders, employees, executives, players, and possibly families. In this example, those who benefit from the helmets going to market are Klutch Helmet employees and managers, players who like the lightweight feel, and those having stake in the business. Those who will be disadvantaged from the helmets going to market include all players that could possibly be injured, the retail stores that sold them (perhaps), and other customers. So, to determine if this decision was ethical, based on utility, it seems that more people would be affected negatively than positively. The decision is NOT ETHICAL based on a utility analysis and the number impacted.

The second criteria evaluated is the consideration of rights. In the example provided, there are several rights to consider. The players have the right to life and the right to safety. The players also have the right to know what could be dangerous gear. On the other hand, Klutch Helmets has the right to privacy, the right to sell in a free market, make money, and get paid. In the case of rights, it is challenging to determine the answer to the question based solely on a rights analysis. *Was it ethical for Klutch Helmets to send their product to market?* The decision maker in this case will need to continue to evaluate the question using the final criteria in the framework, *justice*.

In the justice analysis, a decision maker will seek to determine if the ethical decision was fair, impartial, or just. In the case of Klutch Helmets, it is important to re-evaluate the facts. The helmets were sent to market because they passed the safety standards and the rules were administered fairly; however, the concept of fair blame may come into play. It may not have been the helmet that caused the player's injuries. The decision maker must also consider that Klutch Helmets deserves fair compensation for their product and that the player assumed the risk when playing such a dangerous sport. On the opposing side, the player (or player's family in this case) could point out the helmets were inexpensive and that Klutch acted irresponsibly for putting such a cheap product on the field. In addition, the family could discuss the unfair outcome or result of the injury. In this case, it would seem the decision maker would again be challenged by whether or not this was an equitable or impartial decision.

When a conflict in the possible conclusion is presented, the framework seeks to consider "overwhelming factors." These are situations that will help the decision maker evaluate the three criteria and ideally assist in determining a final ethical decision. Overwhelming factors include: Is one criteria more important than another (life over money)? Was the decision maker coerced or intimidated in the decision? Was there pressure from others? Was force used in the decision? Was the person incapacitated while making the decision? Was all the information available? Was there a conflict in the conclusion or the process? Was there ignorance involved? Each of these questions will be considered with the utility, rights, and justice analysis to make the final determination if the decision was ethical.

UTILITY = WHAT IS GOING TO DO THE GREATEST AMOUNT OF GOOD FOR THE GREATEST NUMBER OF PEOPLE?
Organizational goals should aim at maximizing the satisfaction of the organization's stakeholders.
Those decision makers should consider a cost–benefit analysis and apply it to all parties that are directly or indirectly involved in the issue.
The utilitarian principle should be applied, consideration for the Golden Rule (do unto others…) should be given, and benefits should be taken into consideration.

RIGHTS: WHAT RIGHTS NEED TO BE CONSIDERED? WHO HAS RIGHTS?
Right to Life and Safety: An individual has the right not to have his or her life or safety unknowingly or unnecessarily endangered. An individual has the right to safety.
Truthfulness: The individual has a right not to intentionally be deceived by another. The individual has the **right to know.**
Right to Privacy: The individual has the right to do whatever he or she chooses outside of the workplace. The individual has the right to a private life.
Freedom of Conscience: The individual has the right to refrain from carrying out an order that violates the commonly accepted moral or religious norms.
Freedom of Speech: The individual has the right to criticize conscientiously and truthfully the ethics or legality of the actions of others.   Other rights to consider: **Right to Property, Right to Ownership, Right to Get Paid, Right to Choose, Right to a Fair Trial, Right to Life.**

JUSTICE: IS THE DECISION FAIR, EQUITABLE, AND IMPARTIAL?
Fair Treatment: Persons who are similar to each other in relevant respects should be treated similarly; persons who differ in some respects and perform different jobs should be treated in proportion to the differences between them.
Fair Administration of the Rules: Rules should be consistent, fair, and impartial.
Fair Compensation: Individuals should be compensated for the cost of their injuries by other parties or those responsible for the costs related to the job. **Fair Blame**: Individuals should not be held responsible or accountable for matters in which they have no control. **Due Process**: The individual has the right to fair and impartial treatment when he or she believes rights are being violated.

Steps in Ethical Decision Making

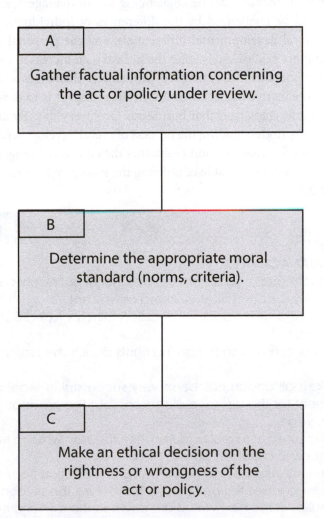

A

Gather factual information concerning the act or policy under review.

B

Determine the appropriate moral standard (norms, criteria).

C

Make an ethical decision on the rightness or wrongness of the act or policy.

CAVANAGH, GERALD F, *AMERICAN BUSINESS VALUES*, 6th Ed., ©2010. Reprinted by permission of Pearson Education, Inc., New York, New York.

Steps in the Ethical Decision-Making Process
1. Gather the information:
2. Ask the question: *Was it ethical for Klutch Helmets to send their product to market?*
3. Ask if it is ethical based on a utility analysis.
4. Ask if it is ethical based on a rights analysis.
5. Ask if it is ethical based on a justice analysis.
6. Determine if there are any overwhelming factors to consider.
7. Make the decision.

Using the Cavanaugh framework, was the decision by Klutch Helmets ethical? Why or why not?

What was the problem with the decision? What portion of the framework most influenced your ethical decision? What could have been done differently? What overwhelming factors did you consider?

Conclusion

The process of ethical decision-making can be challenging for all managers, especially those in the area of sport. Sport managers will be challenged by the differences of individuals, the varying backgrounds, the many influences, the moral developmental differentials, and the personal and professional values of business and self. As more sport professionals enter the industry, an increased capacity for personal ethical decision-making will arise. Sport business is plagued with ethical challenges and issues related to effective problem-solving. One key to effective management in the area of sport is to develop standard processes to address the responsibilities and challenges that businesses face every day. By clearly being able to define ethics and ethical dilemmas, by understanding the process of moral development and moral reasoning, and by implementing a framework for assessing and evaluating the ethical challenges faced in the industry, the current manager in sport will be more capable of utilizing the tools provided in this text to be a more effective decision maker in the future.

GROUP OR INDIVIDUAL ACTIVITY:
Read the following scenarios and determine whether or not each is an ethical dilemma. Be able to explain why it is an ethical dilemma or why not.
1. While searching for a new coach, a qualified minority candidate is excluded from the interview pool.
2. The highest bid for a new venue naming rights deal is the National Rifle Association (NRA).
3. A college basketball coach has been very successful in leading her team to the NCAA tournament for the last several seasons, but the graduation rate of her players is 25% in five years.
4. A star player is accused of sexual assault in the offseason while at home in the summer.
5. A star player receives a DUI just prior to the playoffs.
6. A NASCAR driver intentionally spins out to cause a caution flag.
7. A baseball player greases the ball and his hat before the season opener.
8. Sales of luxury suites in the new venue are down so the owner creates an advertising campaign falsely claiming that "suites are selling fast, BUY NOW."

DISCUSSION QUESTIONS

1. Choose two events you would consider ethical issues in sport history and compare and contrast the decision-making related to these events. Who were the primary players in the decision-making processes? What decisions had to be made? How were they made? What was the ethical outcome of each decision? Why does this matter now?

2. Identify why it is important to know the difference between ethics, morals, and values in sport. Defend your answer with at least one sport example.

3. How does moral development play a role in the decision-making process of some of today's sport leaders or managers? There are many ethical issues that occur in sport. Explain and provide an example of how and why moral development might play a role in these sport manager/leader decisions.

4. How do you determine if something is an ethical dilemma? If it is, how do you solve it?

5. What are the major differences between teleological and deontological theories?

6. Describe at least two examples that will demonstrate the weaknesses with utilitarianism.

USE THE CAVANAUGH DECISION-MAKING MODEL FRAMEWORK AND DO AN ANALYSIS FOR THIS SCENARIO:

Scenario — Sport Facility Reports

You were recently promoted to the facility manager position at a large sport facility. Part of your job is to compile and evaluate the incident reports submitted by fans. Your first week on the job you realize the incident reports have been inaccurate for the last few years. These reports were completed by the fans and they were supposed to be completed by the "manager of duty." You became aware of this issue when a fan brought you a completed form and mentioned "facility negligence" on your first day on the job. After reviewing several prior reports you also realize that many of the reports appeared to have been "tampered with" or "adjusted" in some way. You decide to discuss it with your facility operations manager (your boss) to determine how this issue might be corrected. Your boss says, "Nothing should be done" and suggests that your salary and his are partially determined by the low number of incident reports on file. In fact, he mentions that some of the current incident reports need to be "eliminated or removed" from the records. You need this job because you are helping your brother get back on his feet after losing his job.

CASE STUDY: ETHICAL DECISION-MAKING EXAMPLE FROM THE NBA

Donald Sterling purchased the San Diego Clippers in 2013 for $13 million (Zirin, 2014). His tenure as an owner was tumultuous as evidenced by some of the many incidents with which he was associated during his time as the owner of the Clippers. Table 1.3 summarizes some of the controversy surrounding him.

Despite each of the incidents outlined in Table 1.3, neither the public nor NBA Commissioner David Stern held Sterling accountable for his actions. Sterling was not only accused of each of these incidents, but had settlements against him in most of them yet nothing happened to him with respect to his

role as an owner of an NBA franchise. The practice of allowing Sterling to go unpunished for his actions changed in 2014 when TMZ.com released an audio recording of a private message between Sterling and his girlfriend V. Stiviano. The focus of the conversation was on Stiviano taking pictures with minorities, specifically Magic Johnson (TMZ, 2014). Sterling suggested the situation may lead to the demise of their relationship to which Stiviano responded, "I'm sorry that you still have people around you that are full of racism and hate in their heart. I'm sorry that you're still racist in your heart" (TMZ, 2014, 4:28). Sterling retorted by saying, "I think the fact that you admire him—I've known him well, and he

TABLE 1.3 *Summary of Incidents Involving Donald Sterling as Owner of the Clippers*

YEAR	INCIDENT
1982	Sterling hired a model with no basketball knowledge or experience to be the general manager for his team (Lidz, 2000).
1984	After assuring fans the team was in San Diego to stay, Sterling relocated the San Diego Clippers to Los Angeles without NBA approval in 1984 (Witz, 2014).
2001	Sterling was sued by the city of Santa Monica, California for harassment and threats to evict tenants of his low-income housing after tenants placed potted plants on balconies (Zirin, 2014).
2003	The Housing Rights Center and 19 tenants living in Sterling's complexes sued him for discrimination after he refused to rent to Hispanics and African Americans (Doyel, 2014).
2005	Sterling was ordered to pay $7 million in legal fees and damages for discrimination, but received no punishment from the NBA or public scrutiny (Shreffler, Presley, & Schmidt, 2015).
2006	Sterling is again sued for discrimination for refusing to rent to non-Koreans and not renting to families with children. The case resulted in Sterling paying a $3 million settlement (Shoichet, 2014).
2009	Elgin Baylor filed a civil lawsuit for wrongful termination for discrimination he experienced based on his race and age. The lawsuit brought to light allegations of Sterling wanting a "southern plantation-type structure" for the team (Fenno, 2014).
2011	The Clippers created an advertisement for Black History Month in March, a month after Black History Month. The advertisement included a picture of Sterling and featured Blake Griffin, who is biracial. The advertisement also publicized the organization would be giving away 1,000 free tickets to "underprivileged," implying "underprivileged" equates to Black (Turner & Brayton, 2011).

360b/shutterstock.com

should be admired. And I'm just saying that it's too bad you can't admire him privately, and during your ENTIRE F***** LIFE, your whole life—admire him, bring him here, feed him, F*** HIM, I don't care. You can do anything. But don't put him on an Instagram for the world to have to see so they have to call me. And don't bring him to my games. Ok?" (TMZ, 2014, 8:39).

Unlike previous incidents of racism demonstrated by Sterling, this situation led to detrimental outcomes with respect to his ownership of the Clippers. Rather than ignoring the actions of Sterling as Stern previously had, new NBA Commissioner Adam Silver took four days to dole out punishment. Silver fined Sterling $2.5 million and instituted a permanent life ban from the Clippers and the NBA (Shelburne, 2014). The league felt Sterling's actions undermined the NBA's efforts to promote diversity and pressured Sterling to terminate his ownership of the Clippers. The team was sold to the former CEO of Microsoft for $2 billion (Golliver, 2014).

CASE QUESTIONS

1. Donald Sterling had a history of behavior that was not necessarily illegal, but was morally and ethically questionable. Assume the role of the NBA commissioner and defend your position to uphold Sterling's rights and responsibilities as an owner.

2. Now, take the opposite stance. Defend your position to terminate Sterling's rights and responsibilities as an owner.

3. What is your understanding of why the NBA team owners did not hold Stern accountable for the actions of Sterling? Do you agree with this position? Why or why not?

GLOSSARY

Absolutism is the view that *good* is objectively real, universal, and constant.

Altruism is a theory that suggests that each of us act in the best interest of others while often sacrificing ourselves.

Cavanaugh is a business ethics theorist who created an ethical framework considering the utility, rights, and justice of all parties.

Deontological theory is a theory which holds that things other than consequences determine which actions are morally right.

Despotism looks at dominance through threat of punishment and violence to produce the desired result. The Greek term *despot* means "one with power."

Egoism is the idea or belief that all actions are motivated by self or selfish interests.

Ethical dilemmas are undesirable or unpleasant choices relating to a moral principle or practice.

Ethical principles are the universal guides that tell people which kinds of actions, intentions, and motives are either prohibited or permitted in human interactions.

Ethics is an area of philosophy that studies the theoretical basis of moral action and involves theories or principles that determine the rightness or wrongness of actions.

Existentialism focuses primarily on matters such as choice, individuality, subjectivity, freedom, and the nature of existence itself.

Golden Rule states one should do unto others as you would want to have done unto you.

Kant was a moral philosopher who determined that moral decisions arise out of a sense of duty rather than to produce a desired result.

Kohlberg was an ethical theorist who believed that children move from different stages of moral reasoning based on how actions affect them personally, affect others in their life, and how actions conform to the standards of society.

Moral is a Latin word meaning "customs or manners" that defines a person's character, upbringing, and attitude.

Moral compass is the directional assistor in the process of making moral and ethical decisions and judgments.

Moral reasoning involves the cognitive processes people employ to make decisions about ethical problems.

Moral values are those values that reflect personal motives, personality, and personal intentions related to dealing with others.

Morality is a system of norms, values, and rules that regulate the manner in which human beings treat one another.

Nonmoral values are those values that relate to things, places, and events.

Pragmatism is the idea that "whatever works, is likely true" and the best possible choice.

Stakeholder is a person with a vested interest in the organization and its situation.

Teleological theory is a theory that looks at the best course of action that will result in the most good; a results-oriented approach to decision-making. The term *teleo* is a Greek word meaning "end" and the term *logos* is Latin for "science."

Utilitarianism theory states the only good worth seeking is the one that produces the greatest good for the greatest number of people.

Value is something considered worthwhile or having meaning or worth.

Virtue ethics consider a decision's effect on individuals and personal relationships.

References

Beauchamp, T. L. (1991). *Philosophical ethics. An introduction to moral philosophy* (2nd ed.). New York: McGraw Hill.

Burnor, R., & Raley, Y. (2010). *Ethical choices: An introduction to moral philosophy with cases.* New York: Oxford University Press.

Cavanaugh, G. F. (1984). *American business values* (2nd ed.). Upper Saddle River, NJ: Prentice Hall.

Cavanaugh, G.F. (1990) *American business values* (3rd ed.). New York. American Management Association (p. 195).

Cooper, T. L. (2000). *Handbook of administrative ethics* (2nd ed.). New York: Basel.

DeSensi, J. T., & Rosenberg, D. (2003). *Ethics and morality in sport management.* Morgantown, WV: Fitness Information Technology.

Doyel, G. (2014, April 29). Donald Sterling gets lifetime ban; we should have stopped him sooner. *CBS Sports.* Retrieved from http://mweb.cbssports.com/general/writer/gregg-doyel/24545168/donald-sterling-gets-lifetime-ban-we-should-have-stopped-him-sooner

Fenno, N. (2014, April 26). Elgin Baylor lawsuit among Donald Sterling's past racial issues. *Los Angeles Times.* Retrieved from http://www.latimes.com/sports/sportsnow/la-sp-sn-elgin-baylor-donald-sterling-20140426-story.html

Garner, R. T., & Rosen, B. (1967). *Moral philosophy: A systematic introduction to normative ethics and meta-ethics.* New York: Macmillian.

Golliver, B. (2014, May 30). Shelly Sterling announces agreement to sell Clippers to Steve Ballmer. *Sports Illustrated.* Retrieved from http://nba.si.com/2014/05/30/shelly-sterling-sells-clippers-steve-ballmer-microsoft/

Josepheson, M. (1992). *Making ethical decisions. Sport public relations.* Marina del Rey, CA: The Josepheson Institute of Ethics.

Kant, I. (1785/1964). *Groundwork of the metaphysic of morals.* Translated by H.J. Paton. New York: Harper and Row.

Kidder, R. M. (1995). *How good people make tough choices: Resolving the dilemmas of ethical living.* New York: Fireside.

Kohlberg, L. (1981). *The philosophy of moral development: Moral stages and the idea of justice.* New York: Harper and Row.

Kohlberg, L. (1987). *Child psychology and child education: A cognitive-developmental view.* New York: Longman.

Lidz, F. (2000, April 17). Up and down in Beverly Hills. *Sports Illustrated.* Retrieved from http://www.si.com/vault/2000/04/17/278523/up-and-down-in-beverly-hills-eccentric-multimillionaire-donald-sterling-has-been-a-flaming-success-as-an-la-real-estate-mogul-and-a-dismal-failure-as-the-owner-of-the-clippers

Lumpkin, A., Stoll, S. K., & Beller, J. B. (2003). *Sport ethics: Applications for fair play* (3rd ed.). New York: McGraw Hill.

Lumpkin, A., Stoll, S. K., & Beller, J. M. (2012). *Practical ethics in sport management.* Jefferson, NC: McFarland and Company.

Macdonald, J. E., & Beck-Dudley, C. L. (1994). Are deontology and teleology mutually exclusive? *Journal of Business Ethics, 13*(8), 615–623.

McNamee, M. (2008). *Sports, virtues and vices: Morality plays.* New York: Routledge, pp. 69–86.

Piaget, J. (1932). *The moral development of a child.* Glencoe, IL: Free Press.

Plunkett Research Estimate. (2015). *Sport and recreation business statistics.* Retrieved from https://www.plunkettresearch.com/statistics/sports-industry/

Rest, J. R. (1982). A psychologist looks at the teaching of ethics. *Hastings Center Report, 12,* 29–36.

Schneider, R. C. (2009). *Ethics of sport and athletics: Theory, issues, and application.* Baltimore, MD: Lippincott, Williams, and Wilkins.

Shelburne, R. (2014, April 30). Donald Sterling receives lifetime ban. *ESPN.* Retrieved from http://espn.go.com/los-angeles/nba/story/_/id/10857580/donald-sterling-los-angelesclippers-owner-receives-life-ban-nba

Shoichet, C. (2014, April 18). Racism claims against Clippers owner Donald Sterling: This isn't the first time. *CNN.* Retrieved from http://www.cnn.com/2014/04/27/us/donald-sterling-lawsuits/

Shreffler, M. B., Presley, R., & Schmidt, S. (2015). Getting clipped: An evaluation of crisis management and the NBA's response to the actions of Donald Sterling. *Case Studies in Sport Management, 4*(5), 1–20.

Simon, R. L. (2010). *Fair play: The ethics of sport* (3rd ed.). Boulder, CO: Westview Press.

Strategy, D. M. (1998). Making ethical decisions and taking action. *Ethics in Psychology: Professional Standards and Cases, 3*(20), 235–267.

Tangney, J. P., Stuewig, J., & Mashek, D. J. (2007). Moral emotions and moral behavior. *Annual Review Psychology, 58,* 345–337.

Taylor & Francis. (2010). *Gambling on the Olympics.* Sudbury, MA: International Gambling Studies, 10(1). Retrieved from: http://www.tandfonline.com/doi/full/10.1080/14459791003760882

TMZ (2014, April 25). Clippers Owner Donald Sterling to GF—Don't bring black people to my games, including Magic Johnson. *TMZ.* Retrieved from http://www.tmz.com/videos/0_wkuhmkt8/

Turner, N., & Brayton, J. (2011, March 3). Clippers' Black History ad causes controversy. *NBC Southern California.* Retrieved from http://www.nbclosangeles.com/news/local/Clipper-Black-History-Ad-Causes-Controversy-117289633.html

White, T. I. (1988). *Right and wrong: A brief guide to understanding ethics.* Englewood Cliffs, NJ: Prentice Hall.

Witz, B. (2014, April 27). Vortex of outrage has long trailed Clippers' owner. *The New York Times.* Retrieved from http://www.nytimes.com/2014/04/28/sports/basketball/clippers-owner-donald-sterling-has-public-record-of-bad-behavior.html?_r=2

Zirin, D. (2014, April 26). Donald Sterling: slumlord billionaire. *The Nation.* Retrieved from http://www.thenation.com/article/donald-sterling-slumlord-billionaire/

ETHICAL ISSUES IN SPORT LEADERSHIP

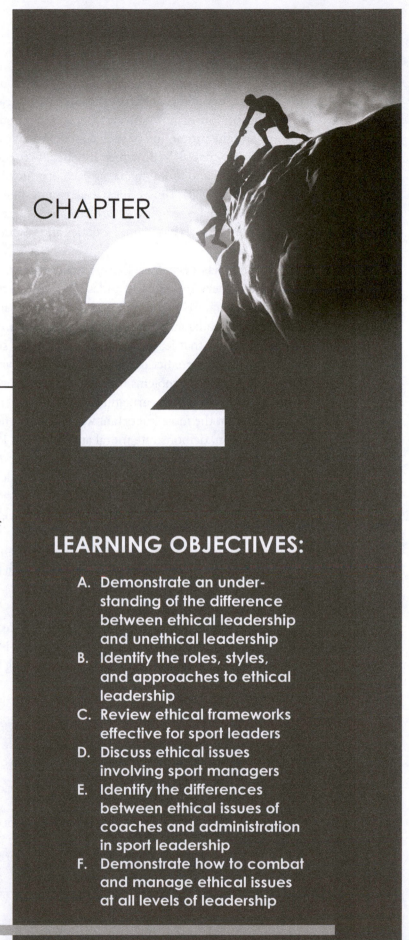

As determined in Chapter 1, sport leaders can be presented with many challenges to their ethics, values, and morals. The sport landscape is constantly evolving; the social, political, personal, and financial influences and expectations can increase the pressures placed on sport leaders. The task of making ethical decisions tests a leader's willingness and ability to guide others. A sport leader is responsible for setting the tone of the organization and also teaching and inspiring followers to act according to a clear set of ethical and moral guidelines. This chapter will serve to identify a leadership framework, recognize leadership roles, identify common issues faced by sport managers, and identify the need for personal, professional, and organizational ethics in the business of sport.

WHAT IS ETHICAL LEADERSHIP?

Leadership has been defined in many ways. Most of the definitions center on the idea that leadership involves the actions associated with leading a group of people or an organization to achieve a

LEARNING OBJECTIVES:

A. Demonstrate an understanding of the difference between ethical leadership and unethical leadership
B. Identify the roles, styles, and approaches to ethical leadership
C. Review ethical frameworks effective for sport leaders
D. Discuss ethical issues involving sport managers
E. Identify the differences between ethical issues of coaches and administration in sport leadership
F. Demonstrate how to combat and manage ethical issues at all levels of leadership

common goal. More specifically, leadership is a process of using one's social influence over others to maximize the achievement of a goal (Kruse, 2013). **Ethical leadership** goes a step further and has been defined as "the demonstration of normatively appropriate conduct through personal actions and interpersonal relationships and the promotion of such conduct to followers through two-way communication, reinforcement, and decision-making" (Brown & Trevino, 2006, pp. 595–596). Ethical leadership requires the leader to be a moral person and moral manager, each of which is characterized by honesty and integrity (Trevino, Hartman, & Brown, 2000). Thus, ethical leaders must demonstrate ethical and moral behavior and influence others (e.g., subordinates, employees, athletes) to act in an ethical manner. Ethical leadership also involves acting in appropriate ways based on the duties and responsibilities set forth by the position they hold.

Ethical leadership has been found to increase trust in management and coworkers, employee satisfaction with their supervisors, job attitudes, and optimism about the future of the organization (Piccolo, Greenbaum, & Eissa, 2012). This means that those who are supervised by leaders can be directly influenced by those that hold leadership positions. In sport, this means that athletes can and are often directly influenced by the coaches that lead them. The perceptions subordinates or employees have of ethical leaders has also been found to predict perceived leader effectiveness, willingness to exert extra effort on the job, and willingness to report problems to management (Brown & Trevino, 2006). This trust is important in the area of sport as leaders seek to earn and keep the respect of their followers, employees, or athletes. Seidman (2015) reported that the most important ways to be an effective ethical leader are to extend trust, offer two-way communication, demonstrate moral authority, and lead with purpose. Each of these traits will help to frame the perception or opinion that the employee, subordinate, or athlete has of the leader. Piccolo et al. (2012) offers five suggestions for an ethical approach to leadership:
1. Broaden an employee's evaluation criteria
2. Craft policies, processes, and stories that highlight ethical commitment and foster an ethical culture
3. Model ethical behavior
4. Publicly celebrate wins that are not exclusively financial in nature
5. Provide employees more autonomy in the workplace and the opportunity to see their work as significant beyond the "bottom line"

By incorporating these suggestions into one's workplace, the positive outcomes of ethical leadership previously identified can be achieved. This is particularly important as ethical leaders establish a vision and influence the behaviors of others, consequently shaping the workplace and impacting a leader's ability to make values-based decisions.

> **STUDENT EXERCISE:**
> Think about an instance when a supervisor, coach, mentor, or advisor did something that you didn't think was a good choice. Did you question this decision? Did you stop and ask if it was the right thing to do? Or did you go along with the decision because this was a leader that you trusted and believed to know what was in the best interest of the team or the organization? Looking back, would you have done something different? Why or why not?

In contrast to ethical leadership, **unethical leadership** is defined as "the organizational process of leaders acting in a manner inconsistent with agreed upon standards of character, decency and integrity which blurs or violates clear measurable and legal standards fostering constituent distrust because of personal self-interest" (Chandler, 2009, p. 71). Unethical leaders are found to make poor decisions, risk great careers, and place themselves in positions where good decisions are hard or impossible to make. They can sometimes be cheats, liars, and often uncaring toward those around them. According to a Harvard Business Review about why leaders lose their way, "many leaders get to the top by imposing their will on others, even destroying people standing in their way. When they reach the top, they may be paranoid that others are trying to knock them off their pedestal" (George, 2011, para. 20). These types of leaders are easy to identify, but can be difficult to remove from power.

Research suggests that people (e.g., employees, fans, audiences) have become numb to the increasing number of issues involving high-level leaders in large organizations (Lebowitz, 2015). The same is true when considering leaders in power positions in sport. Many sport leaders have made poor decisions and retained their leadership position. Some unethical leaders have been fired only to find a similar position at another organization. A few examples include coaches such as Bobby Knight, who was accused of choking a player at Indiana University only to be hired a season later as the head coach of Texas Tech men's basketball; and Pete Carroll, who left his position as the head coach of the football team at the University of Southern California for the same position with the Seattle Seahawks in the National Football League. Shortly after his departure, the USC football team and university would face NCAA sanctions and violations from actions that occurred during his time as the head coach. Unfortunately, these are but a few examples of what has become common practice in sport. It is an issue that current and future sport leaders must consider in their roles with sport organizations.

As we often learn from popular sport media, it is common to encounter unethical behaviors among respected leaders in the industry. Sims (1992) attributes unethical behavior to four factors:

1. People engage in unethical behavior because it is rewarded.
2. The values of top-level management are not congruent with organizational values.
3. An organization appears ethical, but moral actions suggest otherwise.
4. An ethical climate cannot exist in an organization where unethical behavior is justified.

By considering these four factors, managers in sport organizations can take into account the common organizational challenges they may face. In sport, unethical behavior can be rewarded with wins, money, and position advancement. One example may be a coach choosing to have a tutor assist a star athlete with their classwork in order to keep the athlete eligible for the big game. This behavior is not directly rewarded, but by having the ability to play the star player, the team could be rewarded with a win. The same can be said for the differing values from manager to manager or leader to leader. Unethical leadership often occurs when leaders or managers are specifically told how to lead the organization by individuals (e.g., donors, board members, shareholders, owners) who hold influence over the organization. One sport example might include a university alumni association insisting that the coach of a team be fired. This may not be the action the athletic director wants to pursue, but pressure from influential people may serve as an ultimatum for the athletic director that wants to remain in power.

In other instances, the organization appears to be an ethical company, but after unethical information is released, the entire organization is exposed for conflicting moral and value-based behaviors. The best sport example of this scenario is the Penn State scandal involving Jerry Sandusky. Following an investigation, it became evident unethical and immoral behavior was often "pushed under the rug" or looked at as "organizationally acceptable practice" over the course of many years in the football program. While the severe nature of the Sandusky scandal is rare, unethical behavior occurs in many organizations. Often organizations can appear more ethical than they actually are. Finally, some organizations are simply unethical. Just as leaders can be unethical, so can companies. In this case, the leader may face many uphill challenges when working for an organization that simply does not care about being good. The consideration of Sims' (1992) four factors can assist those entering the workplace as leaders and hopefully help organizations overcome ethical leadership issues at the organizational level.

STUDENT EXERCISE:
Research a recent ethical issue faced by a sport manager. On a piece of paper, write down the key problem the leader faced and the decision that was made. Share this situation with a partner and discuss if the decision was ethical based on the principles covered in Chapter 1. Would you and your partner make the same decision or would you choose another course of action? Discuss why or why not.

LEADERSHIP STYLES, THEORY, AND APPROACH

There are many different types of leaders in the sport industry and each of these leaders serve numerous roles for their sport organizations. Leadership, at its core, is the process of influencing others to follow. Sport leaders are a diverse group of people who can be effective or ineffective in a variety of ways. The role of leadership in sport has changed over time. Early conceptions of leadership were that of a leader as a dictator. Today, successful leaders are more accessible and influential in the mentorship and growth of the program, team, or organization (O'Boyle, Murray, & Cummins, 2015). The managerial roles associated with leadership require individuals to have a broad, but complex, set of responsibilities. In sport, to be a successful manager, one must navigate challenges in the process of leading a team to the attainment of organizational goals and objectives. Many theoretical researchers have spent years developing an understanding of leader behavior and the elements of effective leadership in the sport industry. This section will briefly discuss some of the leadership approaches commonly seen in sport.

Historically, leaders have been categorized based on behavioral leadership styles. Goleman (2000) identified six leadership styles needed to be effective. These styles include coercive, authoritative, affiliative, democratic, pacesetting, and coaching. Each style may work differently depending on the influencer or follower, organizational culture, and job tasks. Goleman (2000) indicates that the most effective leader will master all the styles of leadership and use them at the appropriate time. A *coercive* leader will be willing and able to make change happen in the organization. This "do as I say" type of leader will effectively guide others by their willingness to work with all levels and styles of employees. In sport, a coercive leader might be a basketball or football coach who manages a variety of personalities to overcome team challenges or conflicts. The *authoritative* style offers clear expectations and clarity in the position expectations. Goleman (2000) claims an authoritative leadership style is more effective when a business is struggling and is less effective when the team has many experts that are good at their jobs. The *affiliative* leader is one that works effectively with other partners, colleagues, and teammates and is always putting their interests first. In sport, this leader might be a team captain who is always seeking what is best for each player as an individual. A captain who recognizes the strengths of the individuals increases overall team morale. In *democratic* leadership, the leader offers the followers to present their opinions and assist in decision making within the organization. Gill (2016) discusses one of the most effective examples of democratic leadership that took place in the 1988 World Series when coach Tommy Lasorda sent injured batter Kirk Gibson to pinch hit. Lasorda trusted the judgment of others on the team and the Dodgers won the Series. A *pacesetting* leader will show others the way and offer a "do as I do" attitude toward followers. This type of leader can also have high expectations and sometimes seem demanding to the follower. Finally, the *coaching* leader will seek to improve and develop followers to attain their goals and overcome their weaknesses. Each of these types of leaders are effective, and knowledge of these styles will provide useful insight to those seeking to be sport managers in the future.

STUDENT ACTIVITY:
Review the six leadership styles discussed above. Think of three leaders in sport and write down which leadership style you believe they use and why. Be prepared to discuss your answers with the class.

In addition to the knowledge and understanding of the six leadership styles, it is also important to be aware of the theory-based leadership approaches. The four leadership approaches that will be discussed in this section include trait-based, situational, behavioral, and charismatic leaders. One common leadership theory is trait-based. Trait-based leadership theory suggests that leaders inherently possess specific traits that set them apart from their followers (Scott, 2014). In this theory, character traits are used to determine leadership effectiveness and the ability of the leader to guide and motivate others. There are many leaders in the sport industry who have unique personality characteristics that make them effective as leaders. Examples of character traits that make effective leaders include motivation, ability to inspire, integrity, determination, self-confidence, and loyalty (Northouse, 2014). One example of a trait-based leader is Vince Lombardi, who posessed drive, determination, and motivation toward success. Another example of a trait-based leader in sport is Bobby Knight who was recognized for his demanding and oftentimes aggressive leadership style.

According to situational leadership theory, there is not "one way" or a "best way" to approach making decisions. A situational leader may consider the environment, the organization, the followers, or the task before determining the appropriate ethical decision (Lussier & Achua, 2016). Situational leaders are often considered to "flip-flop" as decisions are made in consideration of the "situation." Examples of situational leaders in sport include Pat Summit and John Wooden. Both coaches led a variety of teams toward success using common situational coaching and leadership techniques such as telling, selling, participating, and delegating (Spahr, 2015). In contrast, a behavioral leadership approach seeks to identify what the leader does and how they behave. Two types of behavioral leaders are transformational and transactional leaders. A transactional leader focuses on organization, tasks, group performance, and effectiveness. A transactional leader will seek to get the job done in the most efficient manner possible. This leader might accept things as they have always been if the system is working effectively. To change a system, the transactional leader is likely to implement a rewards system to encourage employees as they adjust to a new system and style of work. On the other hand, transformational leaders seek to make change in the organization, change the status quo, and move the organization forward. This type of behavioral leader has a unique vision and can oftentimes see the big picture before others. An example of a transformational leader might be Adam Silver and his ability to foresee a new vision of the NBA.

STUDENT ACTIVITY:
You and your family have just opened a new event marketing company. You put all your savings into the business and have hired three of your closest friends. In contrast, you are a marketing coordinator of a professional sport franchise and you are losing money fast. You have been directed to increase sales or lose your job.
- Evaluate each situation and discuss how you might lead differently based on the differences in these two situations.

A charismatic leader is a transformational leader. A charismatic leader is one who "has a special personal quality or power making him or her capable of influencing or inspiring large numbers of people through their perceived social relationship to that person" (Lussier & Achua, 2016, p. 322). Some people who might be considered charismatic leaders are Donald Trump, Charles Manson, or Martin Luther King, Jr. In sport, a charismatic leader might be someone like Jackie Robinson, Billie Jean King, or Muhammad Ali. These athlete-leaders inspired cultural change as well as led others toward common goals.

Charismatic leaders inspire followers, but they can also be unethical leaders. Charismatic leaders have been known to use their power for personal gain or to satisfy self-interest. Some sport examples might include Terrell Owens, Pete Carroll, or John Calipari. Some believe these leaders use charisma to their personal and professional advantage. In addition, unethical charismatic leaders can promote their own agenda, be insensitive to the needs of the followers, or even use power for personal gain (Scott, 2014).

RELATIONAL ETHICS APPLIED TO SPORT

Professionals acting as sport leaders can use ethical decision-making models to control and manage a variety of decisions in the business of sport. The universal moral principles presented in Chapter 1, such as utilitarianism, deontological (duty), and teleological (outcome) theories, and virtue ethics are effective guides to assist sport managers in the decision-making process. As a sport leader, many are faced with personal and relational conflicts that require additional reflection for those in power positions. In the case of some sport managers, knowledge of relational ethics will offer additional meaningful assistance in educating and empowering future sport leaders to make appropriate ethical decisions when faced with challenges.

Relational Ethics seeks to determine the right thing to do based on an interdependent relationship with the follower (Bergum & Dossetor, 2005; Pollard, 2015). This approach "looks at people's roles: as practitioner, administrator, team member, teacher, client, student, friend, and global 'neighbor' and examines the relationships created in these environments" (Creed, Zutshi, & Ross, 2007, p. 724). Relational ethics found its roots in a variety of fields where leaders were challenged by the ability to have autonomy in decision-making. In some cases, the decisions they were

© Dean Drobot/Shutterstock.com

trained to make were in direct contrast or conflict with the decisions that might have been appropriate based on previous knowledge of the follower, patient, or client. Studies of relational ethical leadership models are effective in a variety of professional industries (e.g., medicine), but may offer useful guidance for sport managers, as well (Pollard, 2015). The relational framework is important to consider in sport leadership as it utilizes traditional approaches to ethics, but also focuses specifically on the relationships developed between the sport leader and the "follower" (athlete, participant, employee, or client).

A **Relational Leadership Model** seeks to develop a leader's skills in understanding the key components of leadership effectiveness, apply the belief in the model's success, and offer skills necessary to make ethical decisions in leadership situations. The five key criteria used to ensure leaders are effectively leading include inclusivity, empowerment, purpose, ethics, and process (Komives, Lucas, & McMahon, 1998). These criteria are important to consider individually and also as a "process" for making decisions. It might also be important to consider criteria that are the centerpiece of relational ethics such as engagement, mutual respect, and environment (Bergum & Dossetor, 2005). As discussed below, each of these criteria together will assist leaders in making ethical decisions in leader–follower relationships.

A leader who is inclusive encourages an environment that considers diverse points of view and recognition of differences in people (Komives et al., 1998). Engagement involves the leader's ability to actively commit to the relationship. In most cases in sport management, a follower will be engaged in the suggestions or recommendations of their leader. Consider a coach suggesting that a player work more efficiently on form, body position, or technique during the games. Both of these individuals will seek to benefit if the player performs better. This is also an example that can be used in the criteria of mutual respect. If the player respects the coach, the player is more likely to perform. If the coach respects the player, he or she will be more likely to make an ethical decision that will be of mutual benefit to them both. A leader who seeks to empower others will assist in the development of self-esteem and also be willing to share the power with others. Each of these criteria is essential in the practice of relational ethics in sport. See Table 2.1 to review how knowledge of the relational ethics attributes can effectively assist in behaviors and outcomes that offer positive, ethical decision making.

TABLE 2.1 *Leadership Effectiveness Chart*

Atribute	Behavior or Belief	Result Questions
Inclusivity	Leader has a commitment to growth and a "can do" attitude	Does the leader consider diverse points of view? Can the leader recognize the differences in people?
Empowerment	Leader offers assistance to follower self-esteem and is willing to share power	Is the leader sensitive to helping others personally and professionally?
Mutual Respect	Leader will respect and appreciate the ideas and opinions of followers	Does the leader show respect and admiration to the followers?
Environment	Leader offers a safe place for communication	Does the leader provide an effective opportunity for success?
Purpose	Leader will act with intention	Does the leader show support of all others?
Ethics	Leader will have a commitment to social and personal responsibility	Does the leader make moral decisions that are in the best interest of others?
Process	Leader will engage in follower development and growth	Does the leader develop a willingness to engage in the relationship? Does the leader assist in development of followers as individuals?
Engagement	Leader is actively committed to the relationship	Does the leader show a genuine interest in the follower?

ETHICAL DECISION MAKING BY LEADERS

When managers are faced with a complex ethical problem, there are a number of variables that must be considered, including one's personal values and experience, ethical foundations, and moral principles. As discussed in Chapter 1, values are something having worth or something considered worthwhile to an individual. The ethical decision-making frameworks discussed in Chapter 1 will help leaders determine the correct and moral action necessary as they face challenges. Leaders in the area of sport need to be aware of the values they bring to the organization or to the team. The core values of an organization should also be considered when making ethical decisions, as they serve as guiding principles that should never be compromised (Lumpkin & Doty, 2014). The core values of an organization should be deeply ingrained within the organization and guide the company's actions (Lencioni, 2002). An example of a core value in an organization is integrity. When considering the integrity of the organization and the people involved, the reputation of all parties could be affected. According to Morris (1997), a person with integrity will not deviate from his or her values for immediate gain. This is particularly important in the sport industry setting, as an overemphasis on winning and revenue generation oftentimes impedes the decision-making processes of leaders. One example might include an opponent's coach having knowledge of an injury on the other team and the leader choosing not to tell the team to attempt to capitalize on that injury for team gain. This can be challenging for sport leaders as unethical behaviors can often be attributed to pressures and challenges from stakeholders (e.g., fans, alumni, boosters, faculty, advisory boards, etc.). Addressing these pressures requires leaders to have integrity, emotional intelligence, self-awareness, commitment, and authenticity (Lumpkin & Doty, 2014).

In addition to the recognition of personal values, it is also important for sport managers and leaders to consider their personal morals. Morals include customs or manners that define a person's character, upbringing, and attitude while ethics stress the larger societal expectations related to action. It is important to consider each of these variables when making a decision to reduce bias and its influence on the decision (Cooke, 1991). In addition to considering the aforementioned variables, sport managers can also use a variety of approaches to find a solution. When engaging in ethical decision making, Cooke (1991) offers five cautionary points that managers need to consider:

1. Decision making is a process of reasoning through an actual or potential dilemma;
2. Reasonable people may disagree about what ethical course of action is appropriate;
3. Not all ethical situations are clear-cut;
4. There are seldom "quick fixes" to an ethical dilemma;
5. Sound management practice requires the assessment of all relevant information (pp. 250–251).

As leaders, others can often challenge decisions that need to be made within the organization. The easy decision for fans, parents, or the organization may not always be the most ethical. When considering the above factors, leaders can take a long, hard look at the impact of their ethical choices.

STUDENT EXERCISE:
Research a recent ethical issue faced by a sport manager. On a piece of paper, write down the key problem the leader faced and the decision that was made. Share this situation with a partner and discuss if the decision was ethical based on the principles covered in Chapter 1. Would you and your partner make the same decision or would you choose another course of action? Discuss why or why not.

As discussed, sport leaders face a variety of challenges in their ability to make ethical decisions in many situations. Many organizations face challenges with employee conduct, customer relations, adhering to company policy, lack of information, fear of failure, and consistency (Giang, 2015; Squazzo, 2012). In general, managers are often challenged by putting the interests of others ahead of their own personal or professional interests. This continues to be a key challenge that leaders at all levels face. Lumpkin, Stoll, & Beller identified a number of examples of ethical conundrums that happen specifically in the area of sport leadership. Some of these examples include playing concussed athletes, changing athletes' grades to keep them eligible, violating recruiting rules, having tutors complete work for athletes, requiring athletes to spend more than the allowed number of hours dedicated to their sports, and giving cash to players. Each of these situations presents an ethical dilemma which sport leaders need to address. Chapter 1 discusses many of the ethical decision-making models that can be used as a sport manager; however, general decision-making models in leadership can be useful in leadership positions as well. Many researchers (Zinn, 1993; Hums, Barr, & Gullion, 1999) suggest the use of the following step-by-step process when making ethical decisions.

1. Identify the correct problem to be solved.
2. Gather all the information.
3. Explore codes of conduct relevant to the profession or situation.
4. Examine personal values and beliefs.
5. Consult with others who may have experienced similar situations.
6. Generate and evaluate decision options.

7. Seek "win-win" situations if at all possible.
8. Ask the question "How would my family feel if my decision and how I arrived at my decision were printed in the newspaper tomorrow?"
9. Sleep on it. Do not rush to a decision.
10. Evaluate alternatives.
11. Make the best decision possible, knowing it may not be perfect.
12. Evaluate the decision over time.

As future sport leaders, students should take note of the many challenges that occur daily in industry organizations. This above decision-making framework can assist leaders with a step-by-step guide to the basic decision-making process. By gathering information, analyzing options, generating alternatives, and selecting the most appropriate choice, leaders in the sport industry will be more equipped to make clear ethical choices.

THE ROLE OF POSITION IN ETHICAL DECISION MAKING

There are many controversial issues that arise in the sport industry, often from professionals trusted to positively and ethically influence the behaviors of others. The type of ethical issue can change based on the level of sport participation being supervised. Many past researchers suggest that ethical leadership can change depending on the level being managed. Sport managers have historically altered their leadership styles when changing from amateur sport to professional sport (Lumpkin et al., 2003). Sport participants are taught as youth (amateurs) to honor those with more knowledge and experience within the game, and these leaders are elders entrusted to act in positive, productive, and ethical ways. However, there are times when unethical leaders challenge coaches and managers, instructors, team captains, and even high-level commissioners, and officials to act in immoral and unethical ways. The moral dilemmas faced by sport leaders are often driven by the need for domination and the desire to win (Lumpkin & Doty, 2014). Each of these issues will be discussed further as issues presented specifically to leaders in the role of managers, coaches, and administrators.

ETHICAL CHALLENGES FACED BY COACHES AND ADMINISTRATORS

Those in high-ranking positions in sport are often faced with controversy or decision-making challenges. While sport offers many victories, rewards, and benefits to its coaches and administrators, sport leaders face a multitude of issues related to controversy. Some of these challenges faced by sport managers at all levels include (but are not limited to) coaching intimidation, sportsmanship versus gamesmanship, bias, boundary issues, consistency, bribery, scandal, loss of control, conflict of interest, and other legal issues. These and additional issues are essential to review as, even at the top, leaders can be faced with ethical dilemmas and moral challenges. A few of the potential ethical challenges faced by leaders in the sport industry will be discussed below.

Coaching Intimidation

A key issue in leadership at all levels of sport is the ability of coaches and assistant coaches to utilize power and control to intimidate and influence athlete behavior. **Coaching intimidation** is defined as the purposeful means used to control the behavior of others by coaches (Lumpkin, Stoll, & Beller, 2011). Many coaches believe that intimidation can be an effective form of motivating players toward success. Intimidation can come in different forms and is often an abuse of authority, which may result in bullying an athlete or player. Some coaches will abuse their power, insult, threaten, or even physically attack a player in an attempt to produce action or a behavior change.

Svesla Tasla/shutterstock.com

In youth sport, players are in the beginning stages of skill development and many coaches use negative feedback, fear of failure, shaming, name calling, and immense pressure to influence behavior. Many times at the youth level, coaches who use bullying tactics simply have a lack of knowledge or training in being an effective leader. Many high school athletic associations are implementing rules, policies, and training programs to help to educate coaches on effective teaching and motivational practices. Sport psychology researchers have found that sport and leisure activities play a large role in the positive development of young adults (Cote, 2009). As youth and young adults utilize sport as a way to physically and mentally prepare for life, coaches need to recognize the impact of their positive and negative motivational tactics.

Aspen Photo/shutterstock.com

Many coaches at the high school level have been accused of intimidation and bullying. At Somerville High School in New Jersey, the football coach was accused of bullying and tormenting players, angering parents, jeopardizing recruitment, and even facing potential lawsuits for his aggressive behavior. In Tennessee, a high school basketball coach was suspended for belittling his players and acting in an uncivil manner. In Colorado, Hall of Fame Eaton High School baseball coach Jim Danley and his staff were accused of mistreatment of players, threats, and abuse. Administrators overseeing the baseball program managed the number of complaints they received from parents regarding the negative approach that Danley had toward the young athletes (Fernandez, 2015).

At the college level, Coach Mike Rice of Rutgers University crossed the line of coaching intimidation when a video surfaced of him verbally assaulting his players and throwing balls at their heads. At Seton Hall, softball coach Paige Smith was accused of placing sports above academics and allegedly bullying the team with threats of taking away scholarships (Stanmyre, 2013). The University of Louisville head women's lacrosse coach Kellie Young faced allegations of abuse and was creating a culture of fear, and, at the University of Nebraska-Lincoln, basketball coach Connie Yori resigned due to allegations of mistreatment of her players. These examples are just small displays of the excessive lengths to which many college coaches go to motivate student-athletes and the "disturbing culture" that has become acceptable in college sport programs (Himmelsbach, 2013).

In professional sport, coaching intimidation takes on a variety of forms as the athletes are adults and are being paid to do a job. The problem in many professional ranks is the control that coaches and managers have over a player's career and the player's ability to achieve desired success. In professional soccer (football) in the United Kingdom (UK) and Ireland, verbal and physical abuse by coaches has become commonplace. Even those with established playing careers in professional soccer have noted the lack of managerial control and issues related to coaching intimidation in the sport. Mark Quinn, a former player for several professional clubs, described professional football (soccer) as "a sport full of bullies and lunatics" in his autobiography (as cited in Kelly & Waddington, 2006, p. 153). The culture of punishment, physical violence, and threats by managers in professional soccer is the norm. Players either accept it or they get out of the sport.

In the United States, professional coaches have become experts at so-called "trash-talking" as an effective way to intimidate athletes before, during, and after the game. The pressure to win in today's professional sports has created a culture of hyper-anger toward the athletes on the field from the coaches. On many professional teams, **verbal acts of abuse**, or behavior that is verbally harmful, such as name-calling or repeated excessive yelling that serves no purpose, have been banned from many locker rooms. **Physical acts of abuse** such as throwing, punching, and hitting players have resulted in suspensions for professional coaches, but there usually is no termination of the contract. Many coaches in professional sport enjoy the idea of being feared by their players. Coach Mike Keenan, also known as "Iron Mike," is considered one of the most feared coaches in the National Hockey League (NHL). Other coaches to join the notable ranks of scariest coaches include Bill Belichick of the NFL's New England Patriots for his calm demeanor but ability to instill fear and Greg Popovich of the NBA's San Antonio Spurs for his silent but deadly stare (Watkins, 2015). This idea that fear will make players more successful only increases the ability for coaches to intimidate players at all levels of sport.

SPORTSMANSHIP AND GAMESMANSHIP

In participation sport at all levels, the need for fairness, character development, and overall fair play is essential in the goal of enhancing player experiences and enticing today's sport fan to watch. At the same time, it has become common practice in participant sports to challenge rules, criticize officials, harass opponents, and even complain about calls, fouls, and overall game outcomes. In sport, the development of character and appropriate balance between the acceptable and the unacceptable has become a blurred line.

A basic understanding of the differences between sportsmanship and gamesmanship will help sport leaders recognize the impact that a good sport has on the overall outcome of the sport experience. **Sportsmanship** is the emphasis on fairness, fair play, equality, the rules, and athletic excellence (Keating, 1964). A *good sport* shows sportsmanship by respecting the game, showing concern for others' well-being, appreciating the experience, and being gracious in victory and in defeat. A good **sportsman** is a person who can take defeat without complaint and celebrate victory without gloating. A sportsman treats opponents with fairness, generosity, and courtesy while also respecting the game itself. Understanding the differences in sport leaders, and the value of a good sportsman who is modest in victory and has composure in defeat can make ethical decision makers and those participating in sport more valuable assets to the team and to the game.

It can be a difficult task for leaders to determine the difference between sportsmanlike and unsportsmanlike conduct. Those who are *poor sports* in a game might play fairly, but use a variety of standards to judge acceptable play. A poor sport will be more concerned with winning than with the experience. Those who have a difficult time in sport participation may find themselves giving up, acting out, or even turning to normative cheating to try to change the game outcome. A common gamesmanship practice in youth sport is player intimidation. **Player intimidation** is the act of causing the opponent to be fearful, withdrawn, or coerced by words or actions before, during, or after the competition. In this case, a player may physically, mentally, and emotionally try to take the opponent out of the game by challenging them in some way. Intimidation can occur on purpose or on accident.

A **gamesman**, however, will often win the game or contest by means of unsportsmanlike behavior or use other conduct that does not actually break the rules but is crossing a line of acceptability (Butcher & Schneider, 1998). **Gamesmanship** involves an attempt to gain an unfair advantage and is based on a primary concern with winning. Gamesmanship typically involves purposeful acts permitted within the rules of the game that are not explicitly forbidden (Lumpkin et al., 2002). Those participating in gamesmanship will often utilize tactics such as strategic fouling, flopping, talking trash to opponents, taunting or distracting other players, or faking an injury to get a timeout. In a *New York Times* article former NFL player Bob Whitfield indicated, "Everybody cheats. After that initial handshake, anything goes. The code of honor and respect probably ends when they toss the coin" (Vecsey, 2006, para. 7). This mentality has become common at all levels of play from youth to the professional ranks. In sport, there is almost always a winner and a loser; although gamesmanship is not cheating, it is the crossing of a fine line to challenge the ethical rules of sport.

Lumpkin et al. (2011) described **purposeful intimidation** as direct intention, an action to attempt to remove the opposing player from the game. Purposeful intimidation can include the use of psychological tricks, intentional physical injury, trash-talking, or other physical or verbal attempts to offend an athlete. Many athletes who participate in intimidation believe it is the coach's responsibility or the leaders responsibility to teach players to ignore the behavior or the opponents' responsibility to act in a similar manner. **Nonpurposeful intimidation**, or unintentional intimidation can also be a challenge between athletes in sport. Nonpurposeful intimidation could involve a star player making a comment such as "nice work" to an opponent. This star player may not intend to intimidate the other player, but based on previous experience, the opponent may be intimidated or perceived the comments as sarcasm. The ethical challenges in gamesmanship and player intimidation includes knowing the rules, recognizing the unsportsmanlike acts, and determining the appropriate response as a sport manager.

STUDENT ACTIVITY:

Imagine a shoving match under the basket in a high school basketball game that has escalated, but no fouls are called by the referees. One athlete, John, who has taken several shoves, has had enough. The next time he is pushed by his opponent, John grabs him and puts him in a headlock hold. John refuses to let go. The opponent retaliates by throwing John to the ground. Before the referees can break up the scuffle, punches from both players and others on the team have landed.

1. Who is violating sportsmanship rules in this situation?
2. Is the absence of a whistle calling a foul on John or his opponent condoning intimidation? Explain your answer.
3. If you were the coach, how would you attempt to change these behaviors, especially in situations of rival teams?

Bias

Another common leadership issue in coaching is bias. **Bias** has been defined by many as a prejudice in favor of or against one thing, person, or group compared with another, usually in a way considered to be unfair. Common biases in sport include racial and ethnic biases, gender bias, position bias, and performance bias. Each of these are cognitive biases, but unique in their effect on the decision-making process. Bias is very common in sport; so common, in fact, we often have a difficult time recognizing when our bias exists. For example, take a sport fan with a favorite team. This fan is already biased as they are interested and invested in the success of the team. Fans are more likely to watch replays of controversial outomes and rulings and rule in favor of their favorite team based on this "fan" bias (as cited in McNerney, 2011). In addition to the biases already mentioned, leaders must also be aware of other common biases. Pearson (2016), for example, discusses the common biases that exist in coaching:

- **Confirmation Bias** is the ability to look only at what confirms one's intuition and beliefs and ignore those things that contradict them. This type of bias is present when one seeks to identify the information that supports or "confirms" a pre-conceived belief. One sport example might include a coach being of the opinion that the athletic director does not support his/her team. The coach may feel the bias is confirmed when the AD cuts funding for the upcoming year.
- **Self-Serving Bias** is when one seeks to see the positive events as a personal success and attributes the negative ones to other external factors. This might happen when a coach has determined his players are good and can win the game but later claims the referees were mentally "out to get them" or trying to "get in their heads".

- **Information Bias** is the tendency to seek more information even though it may not have any influence on the outcome. In coaching, an assistant might gather many unrelated facts on the opponents just to gather them. The facts might not be relevant to the potential success of the team or player.
- **Planning Fallacy** is the habit of underestimating how much time it will take to get the job done or completed. A coach may believe it is not necessary to prepare for a competitor they have already played. This type of bias also occurs in situations where coaches or sport leaders underestimate the amount of work that goes into planning for an upcoming game, event, or match.

Each of these types of bias are important to recognize as a leader in sport. Many people form preconceived opinions and make decisions based on these notions. All bias can have a negative effect on the outcome and success of sport programs, coaches, and leaders. Bias can also lead a coach or sport manager to make unethical decisions in an effort to overcome the bias situation.

The attempt to overcome a bias can be a challenge for sport leaders. It is important to find ways to recognize and overcome such bias in any leadership position. The most common approach to overcome any bias is to recognize that it exists. Changing focus, recognizing prejudices, and evaluating one's own perception can be effective ways to pinpoint any biases that exist. Stafford (2017) suggests the "consider the opposite" strategy. This strategy was used in a study to assist participants in overcoming the **bias assimilation effect**. This is the process in which one's bias perception is further supported by more information. People will assimilate to their preconceived beliefs. For example, if protesters attend an "anti-gun" rally and are presented with more information to support their anti-gun stance, the bias will be perpetuated. The same is true on the opposing side. The "consider the opposite" strategy suggests that a person's perception or bias can be changed once they are offered strong alternatives, facts, and information supporting the opposing position. As future decision makers in sport, a "consider the opposite" strategy could be a very effective tool to ethical decision making. For example, a coach may have a strong opinion about the conservative opinions of Tim Tebow because he/she only knows the information presented in the media. As the coach does research, considers the facts, and speaks to Tebow himself, the coach may be able to remove the initial bias and take an informed position on Tebow as a person and athlete.

There are many more controversial issues that coaches face in sport. As professionals who are trusted to influence the behaviors of others, coaches face ethical challenges and moral dilemmas often. Some of these biases can easily be remedied; however, challenges will continue to occur.

CONFLICT OF INTEREST

Corbett (2009) discusses the conflicts that can occur in sport related leadership positions. Sport managers, coaches, and administrators seek to belong to many organizations in their respective areas. It can be concerning when coaches, employees, and directors of sport organizations also sit on national boards, committees, or national governing bodies. This conflict of interest is common and can present a variety of ethical issues for the participants or the organizations. In addition, many sponsors or industry partners who have business relationships with a sport organization also act as board members or boosters. This becomes even more common in sport organizations with low operating budgets that seek to have leaders perform a variety

of duties for the program. For example, at a high school, a coach may also act as the history teacher. This presents a conflict if the coach is dealing with athletes who may also be students in the history class.

SCANDALS

Scandals have become all too commonplace in the sport industry. Across all levels of sport, the industry faces a variety of challenges that are controversial and scandalous. A **scandal** is defined as any circumstance, action, or conduct that causes moral or legal disgrace to an organization or its constituents (Merriam-Webster, 2017). Two of the most notable scandals in recent years involve the International Olympic Committee (IOC) and the Federation Internationale de Football Association (FIFA). These organizations have both faced a long history of corruption and scandal involving high level, high ranking executives associated with the organizations. The issues involving FIFA will be addressed in the case study for this chapter, so this section will focus on the IOC scandals.

During the 1998 Salt Lake City bid process to host the Olympic Games, it was revealed that members of the IOC accepted financial bribes (Ingle, 2016). The IOC leadership committee and members pledged to clean up the bidding process, yet continue to face allegations of bribery as recent as the 2020 bid for the games in Tokyo, Japan. Additionally, during the 2016 Brazil Olympic Games, IOC member Patrick Hickey was arrested for reselling tickets to the Games (MacDonald, 2016).

The IOC has had a storied history when it comes to corruption and scandal, dating back to the first modern Olympic Games in Athens, Greece when Pierre de Courbertin only wanted to promote mens athleticism and leave the women out. The Paris Games in 1900 faced racism allegations, and other Olympic contests have rarely been without issue. In 1936, the awarding of the Olympic Games to Berlin, Germany, controlled by Adolf Hitler, was a controversial move followed by many years of boycotts or potential boycotts of the athletic events. In more recent years, before the 1988 Summer Games, in Seoul, South Korea the government was accused of removing many citizens from their homes to make way for new stadiums and Olympic infrastructure. During the planning of the Summer Games in 2008 in Beijing, the IOC was plagued with controversy surrounding the environment, the treatment of the citizens in the community, and the rising costs of the Olympic infrastructure requirements (Lane, 2016). Year after year the Olympics makes an impact on sport in the community, but the IOC continues to be plagued with scandal and corruption. These types of administrative level scandals are not unusual or rare as there have been many other scandals throughout sport history (see Table 2.2).

TABLE 2.2   Leader (Coach/Administrator) Sport Scandals

League/Team	Sport Leader	Scandal/Unethical Behavior
NBA	Tim Donaghy	Tim Donaghy, a senior NBA referee, was involved in a federal investigation in which he admitted to betting on thousands of games and also impacting referee calls to change the outcome of games he officiated.
FIFA	Sepp Blatter	Sepp Blatter was riled with 17 years of allegations of bribes, kickbacks, and governments paying for votes to host future World Cup events.
USC	Coach Sarkisian	Sarkisian had repeated issues with alcohol and showed up drunk at a USC booster event. Sarkisian was also accused of beating his players.
Penn State	Jerry Sandusky/Joe Paterno and Penn State Administration	Jerry Sandusky was charged and convicted of 52 counts of sexual abuse. Paterno and Penn State suffered the consequences of unethical and ineffective leadership of the football program.
NHL	Rick Tocchet	Assistant Coach accused of operating an illegal NHL gambling ring.
NFL	Bill Belichick	Coach of the New England Patriots accused of deliberate violations of NFL rules by videotaping opponents during games and practices; a scandal famously called "Spygate."
NFL	Tom Brady	The "deflategate" controversy in which gameday footballs were not properly inflated as required by game rules.

As the sport industry continues to grow into a multi-billion dollar entity, the unethical behavior of sport managers and sport leaders is also likely to grow. The number of instances and occasions in which sport figures and leaders have made unethical decisions increases by the day. Tiger Woods, Greg Hardy, and Ray Rice regarding domestic violence, Lance Armstrong and the Russian Olympic Committee involved in doping scandals, Michael Phelps opening up about marijuana use, FIFA and the IOC involved in bribery scandals, sexual assault accusations against athletes at Baylor University and other universities, and Roger Clemens and the steroid scandal just to name a few. Leaders in the sport industry have in the past and will continue to face ethical challenges. One essential key is for students seeking careers in the industry to learn to manage in a values-based ethical sport environment.

PROMOTING CHANGE IN SPORT LEADERSHIP

Sport leaders in the future will be faced with a variety of personal, professional, and organizational challenges. As sport changes, leaders must learn to adapt and change with the game, the athlete, the fan, and the organization. Nash (1990) suggests the ethical leader must have the personal motivation to do the right thing. As the economic growth of sport continues, ethical dilemmas and decision-making processes will only become more complex. As an ethical sport leader today, the leader must be able to address current ethical issues, but also anticipate potential dilemmas and decisions within the sport industry and respective organizations. It is important to promote an ethical climate and organizational culture, set ethical standards as a manager, and model those standards and expect employees to model them for each other.

Many researchers believe the sports economy needs better policing, more policies and procedures to force leaders to act in an ethical manner, and a new structure forcing leaders to act with integrity (Cortsen, 2016; Stoldt, Dittmore, & Brandvold, 2012). The need for a strong system to control the current sport industry structures will become essential for the moral and ethical responsibility of future sport leaders regarding all challenges they face. Mandatory guidelines for scandals, lack of fan interest in corruption and bribes, and the ability to minimize conflicts of interest will be essential for the future of leaders in sport. Decisions will not be easy and they will not always be popular. Thus, it is important to understand why unethical behavior occurs in sport organizations. Decision makers at all levels must consider the challenges they will face and make conscious ethical decisions for the future of sport organizations. As leaders are challenged with ethical decisions, it is key for them to reflect on the ethical decision-making models addressed in this text.

DISCUSSION QUESTIONS

1. What is ethical leadership? How can a sport manager determine if a leader is ethical?

2. Is there a difference between personal ethical leaders, professional ethical leaders, and organizational ethical leaders? Explain your answer.

3. Discuss the commercialization of the sport product and how it has changed leaders in sport at all levels (i.e., youth, intercollegiate, and professional).

4. Discuss the difference between gamesmanship and sportsmanship. Provide at least two examples of each.

5. What are the most important attributes of an effective leader? Why?

6. What are some of the challenges faced by sport managers at all levels? Discuss the importance of each.

7. How can bias affect a coach's ability to make fair decisions? Explain your answer.

8. What are the different types of bias and why is it important to recognize them? How can a sport manager overcome a bias?

CLASS DISCUSSION: SPYING AND ESPIONAGE IN SPORTS

The New England Patriots team and Coach Bill Belichick were caught videotaping signals of a New York Jets practice in 2007. This issue became known as "Spygate."

- Should one team try to spy on another team's practice to gain valuable information for the next game? When does it go too far? Is this cheating? Why or why not?

Businesses develop trade secrets and make every effort to protect those secrets from their competitors.

- Do you think this is the same as in the world of business? How can teams protect themselves?

CLASS ACTIVITY

As a sport leader, you will be involved in numerous situations that require some form of leadership competence. Work in groups to consider the role of the leader described in the situations below. Discuss the type of leader in each scenario and consider the variety of ethical leadership approaches discussed in the chapter. After identifying the type of leader being used in each case, discuss the advantages and disadvantages of their specific leadership style.

Scenario #1

Rachel, the executive director of a sport management firm, has been in meetings all day with two co-chairs of a county sport commission. She has created a great bond with these two chairs and they respect and admire her work. They feel that she has a mission that is radically different from the status quo. She is an inspiring leader of this firm and has really created social relationships with all members of the sport commission community. They really LIKE her style.

What type of leadership approach is Rachel using? What are the advantages and disadvantages of Rachel's approach as a leader? Is she an ethical leader? Why or why not?

Scenario #2

Following a Health and Safety Committee (HSC) visit, a MarksSpace concession vendor that serves alcohol and food has been warned they are suffering from inadequate safety procedures. MarksSpace has been mandated to take steps to remedy the problem and is given one month. The guidelines for remedying the problems and issues are available in HSC policy and procedures manuals. John, the Chief Operating Officer, has determined that asking employees for their opinions will be helpful in determining the appropriate next steps. John encourages employees to share their ideas and wants each employee to come up with creative ways to achieve the goals detailed in the HSC policies.

What type of leader is John? What are the advantages and disadvantages of John's type of leadership? Is John an ethical leader? Why or why not?

Scenario #3

A sport team has contacted your sport marketing firm to come up with a new logo that represents a change in the direction the team wishes to go. The new logo and associated corporate branding are set to coincide with the launch of the re-branding in two month's time at the start of the new season. If it does not meet this deadline, the client will run the risk of falling behind its rivals whom it has suffered against in recent years. The supervisor insists that we push through by clarifying tasks and assign each employee new project roles. He plans to give everyone who meets the deadlines a 2% raise and a bonus for timely completion.

What type of leadership approach is the supervisor using? What are the advantages and disadvantages of this approach?

CASE STUDY: FIFA LEADERSHIP CORRUPTION AND SCANDAL

FIFA was founded in 1904 and oversees and governs the play of international soccer. Over the course of the past few years, FIFA has been the source of several scandals involving racketeering, bribes, and an FBI investigation into corruption among its president and senior executives. The ethical issues related to these allegations began when World Cup revenues began to skyrocket. The World Games played in Germany in 2006 generated $749 million in revenue for FIFA while the gross revenue for Brazil's World Cup in 2014 was an estimated $15 billion, the majority of which came from broadcast rights (Manfred, 2015). The discrepancy in the amount of money and the continued rumors that FIFA was involved in World Cup bribery scandals caused concern for leaders inside and outside the organization.

The president of FIFA, Sepp Blatter, held his position from 1998 to 2015 and had a reputation of being understanding and committed to the success of the organization, its growth, and global recognition. However, FIFA was riled with allegations of referees taking bribes, club owners taking kickbacks, and governments paying for votes to host future World Cup events. The controversy grew after a lawsuit was filed by MasterCard, who had been a longtime sponsor of the World Cup, following the malacious findings from the book, *Foul! The Secret World of FIFA: Bribes, Vote Rigging and Ticket Scandals* (McMillian & Gandz, 2015). President Sepp Blatter continued to deny any wrongdoing, but in 2010 after awarding the World Cup 2018 to Russia and the 2022 to Qatar, FIFA was under a much larger microscope. In 2014, the United States Federal Bureau of Investigation (FBI) got involved and launched their own investigation and eventually even the police in Switzerland, where FIFA is headquartered, announced they were conducting a "criminal inquiry" into the widespread issues (McMillian & Gandz, 2015). Reports claimed that FIFA executives accepted over $150 million in bribes for World Cup location bids, participated in over two decades of corruption from the senior leadership and coerced votes for the re-election of Sepp Blatter to his position as president of FIFA. Only four days after his re-election, he resigned as President. In 2015, over 14 high-ranking FIFA officials and executives (excluding Blatter) were indicted.

CASE QUESTIONS

1. Do you think the sponsors of the World Cup games should have exposed the bribery scandal? Explain your answer.

2. In instances of long-standing cultural norms, can it be easy for new leaders to change the unethical practices of a large organization such as FIFA?

3. Do you think that Sepp Blatter should have been held responsible for the corruption of the organization? Why or why not?

GLOSSARY

Bias is a prejudice in favor of or against one thing, person, or group compared with another, usually in a way considered to be unfair.

Coaching intimidation can be defined as the purposeful means used to control the behavior of others by coaches.

Confirmation bias is the ability to look only at what confirms one's intuition and beliefs and ignore those things that contradict them.

Ethical leadership is the demonstration of normatively appropriate conduct through personal actions and interpersonal relationships and the promotion of such conduct to followers through two-way communication, reinforcement, and decision-making.

Gamesman is a person who competes in a game or contest by means of unsportsmanlike behavior or uses other conduct that does not actually break the rules but is crossing a line of acceptability.

Gamesmanship involves an attempt to gain an unfair advantage and is based on a primary concern with winning.

Information bias is the tendency to seek more information even though it may not have any influence on the outcome.

Physical acts of abuse are physical acts such as throwing objects or punching and hitting that serve no productive training or motivational purpose.

Planning fallacy is the habit of underestimating how much time it will take to get the job done or completed.

Player intimidation is the act of causing the opponent to be fearful, withdrawn, or coerced by words or actions before, during, or after the competition.

Purposeful intimidation is direct intention, an action to attempt to remove the opposing player from the game.

Relational ethics seeks to determine the right thing to do based on an interdependent relationship with the follower.

Relational Leadership Model (RLM) ensures leaders are effectively leading through inclusivity, empowerment, purpose, ethics, and process.

Self-serving bias occurs when a person seeks to see the positive events as a personal success and attributes the negative ones to other external factors.

Scandal is any circumstance, action, or conduct that causes moral or legal disgrace to an organization or its constituents.

Sportsman is a person who can take defeat without complaint and celebrate victory without gloating; treats opponents with fairness, generosity, and courtesy while also respecting the game itself.

Sportsmanship is the emphasis on fairness, fair play, equality, the rules, and athletic excellence.

Unethical leadership behavior is defined as "the organizational process of leaders acting in a manner inconsistent with agreed-upon standards of character, decency and integrity which blurs or violates clear measurable and legal standards fostering constituent distrust because of personal self-interest."

Verbal acts of abuse are behaviors that are verbally harmful, such as name-calling or repeated excessive yelling that serve no purpose.

References

Bergum, V. & Dossetor, J. (2005). *Relational ethics: The true meaning of respect*. Hagerstown, MD: University Publishing Group.

Brown, M. E., & Treviño, L. K. (2006). Charismatic leadership and workplace deviance. *Journal of Applied Psychology*, *91*, 954–962.

Butcher, R., & Schneider, A. (1998). Fairplay as respect for the game. *Journal of the Philosophy of Sport*, 25(22). 1–22.

Chandler, D. J. (2009). The perfect storm of leaders' unethical behavior: A conceptual framework. *International Journal of Leadership Studies*, 5(1), 69–91.

Cooke, R. A. (1991). Danger signs of unethical behavior: How to determine if your firm is at ethical risk. *Journal of Business Ethics*, 10(4), 249–253.

Corbett, R. (2009). Conflict of interest: The organization's 'achilles heel.' *Sport Law & Strategy Group*. Retrieved from http://www.sportlaw.ca/2009/01/conflict-of-interest-the-sport-organizations-achilles-heel/

Cortsen, K. (2016, May 9). Scandals and the business of sports: implications for new approaches in the sports industry. Sport Management Perspectives. Retrieved from http://kennethcortsen.com/scandals-business-sports-implications-new-approaches-sports-industry/

Cote, J. (2009). Understanding adolescents' positive and negative developmental experiences in sport. *The Sport Psychologist*, 3(23), 3–23.

Creed, A., Zutshi, A., & Ross, J. (2007). Relational ethics, global business and information and communications technology: Interconnections explored. *IRMA International Conference*. Retrieved from http://www.irma-international.org/viewtitle/33172/

Fernandez, B. (2015, September 12). Eaton baseball coaches accused of bullying players. *The Greeley Tribune*. Retrieved from http://www.greeleytribune.com/news/18152196-113/eaton-coaches-accused-of-bullying-players#

George, B. (2011). Why leaders lose their way. *Harvard Business Review*. Retrieved from https://hbr.org/2011/06/why-leaders-lose-their-way.html

Giang, V. (2015, June 2). 7 biggest leaders share how they solved the biggest moral dilemmas of their careers. Fast Company. Retrieved from https://www.fastcompany.com/3046630/7-business-leaders-share-how-they-solved-the-biggest-moral-dilemmas-of-their

Gill, E. (2016). What is democratic/participative leadership? How collaboration can boost morale. St. Thomas University. Retrieved from http://online.stu.edu/democratic-participative-leadership/

Goleman, D. (2000). Leadership that gets results. Harvard Business Review. Retrieved from https://hbr.org/2000/03/leadership-that-gets-results

Himmelsbach, A. (2013, October 6). Louisville lacrosse coach accused of abusive tactics. *USA Today*. Retrieved from http://www.usatoday.com/story/sports/college/lacrosse/2013/10/05/louisville-cardinals-womens-lacrosse-kellie-young/2930285/

Hums, M. A., Barr, C. A., Barr, & Gullion, L. (1999). The ethical issues confronting managers in the sport industry. *Journal of Business Ethics*. 20(1), 51–66.

Ingle, S. (2016, May 11). Toyko Olympic Games corruption claims bring scandal back to the IOC. *The Guardian*. Retrieved from https://www.theguardian.com/sport/2016/may/11/tokyo-olympic-games-2020-ioc-international-al-olympic-committee-corruption-bid-scandal

Kruse, K. (2013). What is leadership? *Forbes*. Retrieved from https://www.forbes.com/sites/kevinkruse/2013/04/09/what-is-leadership/#729f224e5b90

Keating, J. W. (1964). Sportsmanship as a moral category. *Ethics*, 75(1), 25–35.

Kelly, S., & Waddington, I. (2006). Abuse, intimidation and violence as aspects of managerial control in professional soccer in Britain and Ireland. *International Review for the Sociology of Sport*, 41(2), 147–164.

Komives, S., Lucas, N., & McMahon, T. (1998). Exploring Leadership for College Students That Want to Make A Difference. San Francisco: Jossey-Bass. (68–72).

Lane, C. (2016, May 21). Corruption is killing the Olympic games – or should. *The New York Post*. Retreived from http://nypost.com/2016/05/21/corruption-is-killing-the-olympic-games-or-should/

Lebowitz, S. (2015, June 26). The danger of working for an unethical boss. Business Insider. Retrieved from http://www.businessinsider.com/unethical-leaders-can-make-you-look-bad-2015-6

Lencioni, P. (2002). The five dysfunctions of a team. San Francisco, CA: Jossey-Boss.

Lumpkin, A., & Doty, J. (2014). Ethical leadership in intercollegiate athletics. *The Journal of Value-Based Leadership, (7)2.*

Lumpkin, A., Stoll, S. K., & Beller, J. (2002). *Sport ethics: Applications for fair play* (3rd ed.) New York: McGraw Hill Education.

Lumpkin, A., Stoll, S. K., & Beller, J. (2011). *Practical ethics in sport management.* Jefferson, NC: McFarland.

Lussier, R. N., & Achua, C. F. (2016). Leadership: Theory, application and skill development (6th ed.). Boston, MA: Cengage Learning.

Manfred, T. (2015, March 20). FIFA made an insane amount of money off Brazil's $15 billion World Cup. Business Insider. Retrieved from http://www.businessinsider.com/fifa-brazil-world-cup-revenue-2015-3

McDonald, C. (2016) The 2016 Rio Olympics were a great sporting event, and an ethical mess. Canadian Business. Retrieved from http://www.canadianbusiness.com/blogs-and-comment/rio-2016-ethics-roundup/

McMillian, C., & Gandz, J. (2015). FIFA: The beautiful game and global scandal. *Ivey Publishing* [Case W15398-PDF-ENG]

McNeary, S. (2011). Cognitive biases in sports: The irrationality of coaches, commentators and fans. Scientific America. Retrieved from https://blogs.scientificamerican.com/guest-blog/cognitive-biases-in-sports-the-irrationality-of-coaches-commentators-and-fans/

Nash, N.L. (1990). *Good intentions aside.* Boston, MA: Harvard Business School Press.

Northouse, P. G. (2010). Leadership: Theory and practice (5th ed.). Thousand Oaks, CA: Sage Publications Inc

O'Boyle, I., Murray, D., & Cummins, P. (2015). Leadership in Sport. Foundations in sport management. New York: Routledge.

Pearson, C. (2016). Thinking errors and the coaching process: how to help your leaders make better decisions. *Institute of Coaching.* Retrieved from http://www.instituteofcoaching.org/blogs/thinking-errors-and-coaching-process-how-help-your-leaders-make-better-decisions

Piccolo, R. F., Greenbaum, R., & Eissa, G. (2012). Ethical leadership and core job characteristics: Designing jobs for well-being. In Reilly, N., Sirgy, M. J., & Gormann, A. Work and quality of life: Ethical practices in organizations. New York, NY: springer.

Pollard, C. L. (2015). What is the right thing to do: Use of relational ethical framework to guide clinical decision-making. *International Journal of Caring Services, 8(2),* 362–368.

Scott, D. (2014). Contemperary leadership in sport organizations. Human Kinetics: Champaign, IL.

Seidman. D. (2015, April 16). 6 key traits of an ethical leader. Retrieved from http://chiefexecutive.net/6-key-traits-ethical-leader/2/

Sims, R. R. (1992). The challenge of ethical behavior in organizations. *Journal of Business Ethics, 11(7),* 505–513.

Stafford, T. (2017, January 31). How to get people to overcome their bias. *BBC.* Retrieved from http://www.bbc.com/future/story/20170131-why-wont-some-people-listen-to-reason

Stanmyre, M. (2013, October 14). Bullying accusations in high school sports blur lines between good coaching and abusive tactics. NY Nation Media. Retrieved from http://www.nj.com/hssports/blog/football/index.ssf/2013/10/bullying_accusations_in_high_school_sports_blur_lines_between_good_coaching_and_abusive_tactics.html

Spahr, P. (2015). What is situational leadership? How flexibility leads to success. St. Thomas University. Retrieved from http://online.stu.edu/situational-leadership/

Squazzo, J. D. (2012). Etical challenges and responsibilities of leaders. Retrieved from https://www.ache.org/abt_ache/JF12_F3_reprint.pdf

Stoldt, G.C., Dittmore, S., & Branvold, S. (2012). *Sport Public Relations: Managing Stakeholder Communication.* Human Kinetics: Champaign, IL.

Treviño, L. K., Brown, M., & Hartman, L. P. (2003). A qualitative investigation of perceived executive ethical leadership: Perceptions from inside and outside the executive suite. Human Relations, 55, 5–37.

Trevino, L., Hartman, L.P., & Brown, M. (2000). Moral person and maoral manager: How executives develop a reputation for ethical leadership. California Management Review: (42)4.

Vecsey, G. (2006, September 23). When gamesmanship blurs to cheating. *New York Times*. Retrieved from http://www.nytimes.com/2006/09/23/sports/football/23vecsey.html?_r=0

Watkins, J. (2015, October 28). Top ten scariest active coaches. Athlon Sports. Retrieved from http://athlonsports.com/overtime/top-10-scariest-coaches-nick-saban-harbaugh-popovich-coach-k-frank-martin-ryan-matta

Zinn, L. M. (1993). Do the right thing: Ethical decision making in professional and business practice. *Adult Learning* 5, 7–8, 27.

ETHICAL ISSUES AFFECTING YOUTH, COLLEGE, AND PROFESSIONAL SPORT

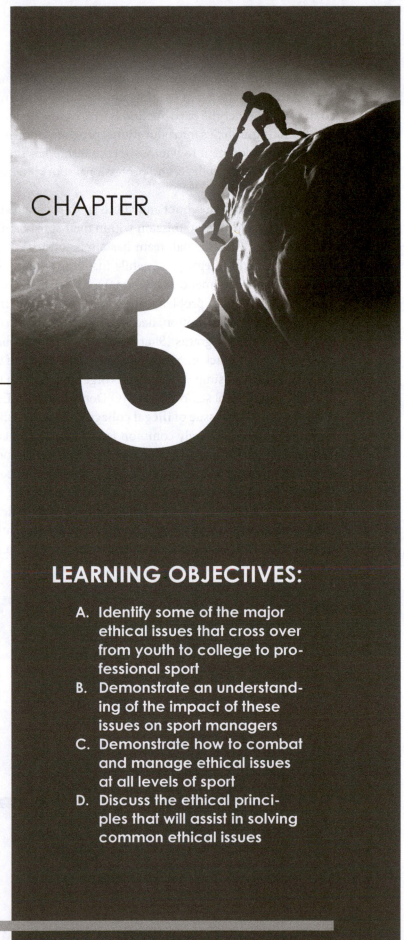

In the United States, over 17 million youth participate in team sports, according to the Sport and Fitness Industry Association (Lee, 2015). In 2015, the National Collegiate Athletics Association (NCAA) reported 482,533 college student-athletes participated, which was up nearly 2.1% over the previous year. The U.S. Department of Labor (2016) reports over 13,000 professional (paid) athletes and sport competitors competing on the field, on the court, or in the rink in the United States. These numbers represent the large percentage of the U.S. population that is currently involved in organized sport participation. As interest in sport participation continues to grow, so have the ethical issues surrounding each of these industry segments. As sport managers, it is important to consider all levels that may present ethical issues in sport programming and how to manage each area with sound ethical decision-making practices.

ATHLETE EXPLOITATION

Youth sport participation and interest in sport fandom for young generations has made it necessary

LEARNING OBJECTIVES:

A. Identify some of the major ethical issues that cross over from youth to college to professional sport
B. Demonstrate an understanding of the impact of these issues on sport managers
C. Demonstrate how to combat and manage ethical issues at all levels of sport
D. Discuss the ethical principles that will assist in solving common ethical issues

to consider the ethical issues surrounding programs at all levels, but particularly the youth level. **Athlete exploitation**, or the act of treating athletes unfairly in order to profit or benefit from their skill has become common. Whether the participation is in private schools offering campus programs or teams, public schools incorporating athletics into educational programs, non-school youth leagues, or coaches teaching skills and character development to youth, sportsmanship has seemed to be replaced by a myriad of ethical issues in youth, high school, college, and professional sport programs.

It is common for high school and youth sport programs to emphasize and encourage development of character and the educational mission within their sport organizations. The Rockland Rockets Amateur Athletics Union (AAU) basketball team has a mission to "educate and empower today's youth with confidence, commitment and integrity . . . while instilling a code of ethics built on honesty, responsibility and team work" (Mission Statement, 2016, para. 1). However, AAU basketball programs such as the Rockland Rockets have seen a variety of problems and ethical issues over the years. Andrew Sharp of SB Nation wrote of the 25-year history of corruption, deceit, and conflict of interest involved in the operation and management of **AAU basketball** programs (Sharp, 2011). Many AAU basketball coaches have been involved in scandals related to bribes, black market deals, and fraud. Many of the issues with AAU teams stem from the fact that the organization is simply a grassroots organization with the broad scope of overseeing basketball programs after the high school season is over (O'Donnell, 2015). This lack of oversight in AAU programs has also led to the larger ethical issue of **illegal college athletic recruiting**. A 2012 *New York Times* article reported that it has become increasingly common for middle school athletes to receive college scholarship offers before they even step foot on a high school basketball court or football field. This type of behavior is currently acceptable by the NCAA, as it only has rules that limit contact with students as young as the seventh grade (Tierney, 2012). AAU programs are circumventing the rules and finding ways to access athletes without "breaking any official policies." Exploitation is not limited to the high-profile programs such as basketball and football, as young athletes in gymnastics, figure skating, swimming, and wrestling are also commonly being recruited at younger and younger ages (Murphy, n.d.).

Seamartini Graphics/shutterstock.com

Mistreatment of young athletes by adults has been a problem for decades. As the professional sport product becomes more commercialized, an increasing number of coaches and parents are pushing youth to specialize in one sport. **Sport specialization** is the focus on one specific athletic talent of an athlete while excluding all others; the goal of sport specialization is to assist the young athlete to become more dominant in one sport (e.g., a student only playing football to fully develop the skills needed for that sport). Youth sport might not be as successful as it is today without the support of parents, yet intense training or **overtraining** (reaching a performance plateau from an increased training load) by parents and coaches can result in many issues for the young athlete. Some of the consequences of early specialization in youth sport include, but are not limited to, anger, loss of interest, overuse injury, and, most importantly, sport dropout (Baker, 2003). A recent study by the Sport and Fitness Industry Association noted that youth dropout rates have continued to increase over the past few years, and a primary reason is the increase in youth sport specialization. Parents and coaches are putting an increased amount of pressure on kids to be more competitive in their respective sport (Woo, 2015). This emphasis on winning and transitioning kids from youth to college has become a common ethical concern. Overly aggressive parents have increased the stress levels of young athletes and of coaches alike. A Michigan State University study indicated that over 70% of kids drop out of youth sports by the age of 13, and the primary reason is parents and coaches (Bruneau, 2014). This aggressive behavior by adults to increase the mental and physical demands on youth has become a cause for concern. As athletes approach the college level, parents and coaches often become obsessive. A 2013 HBO Sports documentary shed light on the pressure that parents place on their children as they approach college. The documentary shows overbearing parents of prospective college and professional athletes and the struggle the kids face managing the pressure or embarrassment they feel from their parents (Strauss, 2013). Featured athlete Todd Marinovich describes how he was groomed to be a Michigan State Spartan and discusses the extreme pressure he felt to be the next football prodigy. Marinovich was drafted by the National Football League (NFL) and quickly developed a drug problem. Marinovich places some of the blame on the increased pressure he felt from his father and the immediate demands he felt in the league. Each year young athletes face an array of challenges from parents on the sidelines who have dreams of their young athletes making it to the professional ranks. In 2015, Sean "Diddy" Combs allegedly tried to hit an assistant football coach with a dumbbell because the coach was yelling at his son during a UCLA Bruins practice. This pressure to win combined with an overly aggressive parent has become a problem in sport today.

Former athletes across a variety of sports have historically made accusations of being exploited in many ways during their athletic careers in college (Crandall, 2015). In business, exploitation is determined by the amount of money or wage an employee earns that is significantly less than the contribution the employee provides the organization. In athletics, **athlete exploitation** is the difference in the amount of money earned by the program from athletic performance that is

Jose Gil/shutterstock.com

---

significantly less than the scholarship and housing money provided to the athlete (Berri, 2014). Former college athlete Abram Booty has attempted to create a movement against college athlete exploitation with the support of many former college athletes. Booty, a former college and professional athlete turned high school football coach wrote and produced a movie entitled *Work Horses: The Truth Beyond the Glory* which tells the fictional story of athlete exploitation and abuse of athletic talent at the college level (Soloman, 2015b). This has been a consistent theme in recent years as many former athletes have spoken out in support of providing college athletes adequate compensation for their skills (See Pay for Play Debate, Chapter 12).

BURNOUT AND ELIMINATION

As athletics have become more competitive at youth levels, competition has become more valued by those that are successful, and avoided by those who are not. Those that are involved in youth sport programs have seen a significant decline in children participating in sport. By the age of 12, more than half of all youth have already opted out of participation in a sport in which they had previously participated (Aspen Institute, 2013). It is common for young athletes (6–12) to feel burnout from the amount of work and expectations from both parents and coaches. **Burnout** is a symptom of overuse, exhaustion, and fatigue caused by increased and repetitive participation. Lumpkin, Stoll, and Beller discuss burnout as "too much, too often and too soon" in youth sport (2003, p. 121). Burnout and **sport exhaustion** are common in youth participation as young athletes participate in year-round training, have increased specialization in one sport, or often play through injury. These symptoms have led to a decrease in individual youth sport participation and an increase in sport dropout. According to the Sports and Fitness Industry Association (SFIA) "fewer than one in three children ages 6 to 12 engage in high calorie-burning sport or fitness activities three times a week" (Aspen Institute, 2015). This change in youth behavior may also be attributed to factors involving poor coaching techniques, limited skills, lack of exposure to exercise, and household income.

Sport elimination, on the other hand, is often an outcome of an overemphasis on competitive youth sport. Young athletes will often be eliminated from the team as they are not meeting the highly skilled expectations of the coach and parents. This will often cause children to disengage in sport activities or dropout of the sport altogether. **Sport dropout** can happen for a number of reasons. Dropout refers to the reasons in which athletes choose to separate from participation in the sport. Researchers of youth sport participation claim that a lack of skills, lack of enjoyment in the sport, or the pressure to win has caused youth to drop out of sports altogether. According to the National Alliance for Sport, 70% of children drop out of organized sport by the age of 13 (Miner, 2016). Children prefer playing on losing teams over sitting on the benches of winning teams (Overman, 2014). Children learn early that their more skillful teammates play in the most games and at preferred positions while receiving more praise and attention. This can become an ethical issue when goals and outcomes of the team or program are favored over teaching skill and/or skill development. Coaches often support this by limiting the number of students accepted to the team or by playing only the more talented athletes. These and other factors often ensure that better competition will be available and the more highly skilled players will move on to the college level from youth sport.

In college sport, athletes often burn out due to their sudden lack of skill as compared to their peers. College athletes have also been found to grow tired, bored, or disinterested in sport altogether once reaching college (Lumpkin et al., 2003). Some athletes outgrow sport as their interests change and new talents are discovered. Many athletes who consider practice to be work, and certainly not fun, have to endure all types of **physical**, **verbal**, and emotional abuse. College athletes may drop out or quit for a variety of reasons, such as academics, changing interests, injury, stress, friends, or increased expectations (Lumpkin et al., 2003). Those accustomed to being stars may have difficulty adjusting to less playing time, increased competition, or participation in a losing program. There are a variety of other reasons why burnout occurs both physical, psychological, or social.

Physical burnout includes the "repercussions of overuse, overtraining, and overspecialization" (Lumpkin et al., 2003 p. 122). Each of these physical demands is unique to the college athlete; however, physical burnout can involve not listening to the demands of the body or focusing too much on one's specific sport. Sport can also take a mental toll on a college athlete. The psychological demands of college can be increased by the demands of the athletic program. **Psychological burnout** is "the mental and emotional pressures from demands for improved performances and winning" (Lumpkin et al., 2003, p. 125). As athletes approach the college level, the expectations of athletes to continually improve and offer superior performances can challenge an athlete's mental state. Researchers suggest that college athletes are often questioned, berated, punished, and pressured which can lead to a lack of self-confidence, disengagement, and lack of interest in sport altogether (Coakley, 2015). In addition to these two types of burnout, athletes can also suffer from **social burnout**. Social burnout is an overall lack of interest in life, potentially inside and outside of sport. The social organization of high-performance sport may constrain an adolescent's identity, social development, or even prevent them from having meaningful control over their lives (Coakley, 2015).

STUDENT ACTIVITY:
What are the ethical dilemmas associated with the dropout phenomenon in sport? How does the emphasis on winning contribute to sport dropout? Should youth who lack skills be cut from sport teams? Why or why not?

Burnout can also happen in professional sport as athletes are competing at a much higher level. Professional sport leagues require advanced levels of training and often increase both physical and mental expectations. The increased level of competence and autonomy in professional sport can change an athlete's perception of themselves within the game. This autonomy can lead to dissatisfaction with themselves and also a disinterest with the game itself (Lonsdale, Hodge, & Rose, 2009). A 2008 study of elite athletes discusses that the pressures that professional athletes endure in sport can include inadequate time to recover from injury, a 24-hour commitment to the job, and feelings of entrapment, stress, and perfectionism (Gustafsson, Hassman, & Johansson, 2008). These common stressors can cause elite athletes to leave their sport early and can also increase the psychological effects of their personal and social lives. Common signs and symptoms of burnout in professional athletes are aggressiveness, mood swings, aggravation, setting unrealistic goals, and lack of interest in social activities (Belz, 2013). A common perception is that athletes at the professional level worked hard to get in the game, yet burnout can happen even with these elite professionals. Andre Agassi, a professional tennis star, admitted in his autobiography that he played tennis even though he hated the game. Agassi also admitted to having a crystal meth addiction during a low point in his tennis career, showing how professional athletes can feel burnout from work expectations as well (Agassi, 2009).

CHEATING

Cheating in a variety of forms has become a common problem in sport today. **Cheating** is generally defined as dishonest or unfair acts to gain a competitive advantage. Common forms of cheating in youth, college, and professional sport include academic fraud, corruption, blood doping, the use of performance enhancing drugs, game fixing, gambling, bribes, and a variety of other forms of immoral behavior. Cheating has become so common in both amateur and professional sport that unfair advantages are often considered "part of the game."

Youth sport has recently seen an increase in cheating among athletes, coaches, parents, and sport managers. Many of the challenges relating to youth sport lie in recognizing that the adults are the ones who are often doing the cheating. One frequent scandal in youth sport involves the eligibility of young athletes. For instance, the eligibility of young athletes was altered following a scandal involving the alleged falsifying of age documents in competitive gymnastics. In 2008, the Chinese Olympic gymnastics team was found to have falsified birth documents and passports to have young girls qualify for the Olympic team. The International Olympic Committee (IOC) was notified, but had limited power to verify the ages of all the athletes involved in the Games (Flumenbaum, 2011). This type of cheating and document fraud has become somewhat commonplace in many youth sport programs. Thus, teaching moral values to young sport participants has become increasingly challenging for sport managers.

As the youth grow older, a common form of cheating in some sports is the use of performance enhancing drugs (PEDs). PEDs such as steroids will be discussed later in this chapter, yet it should be noted that steroids are a common form of cheating in high school sport. Other high school cheating scandals include using **ringers**, or ineligible players, to keep the team competitive and stealing playbooks or plays from other coaches.

TABLE 3.1 *Cheating in Professional Sport*		
League	Athlete	Cheating Scandal
MLB	Chicago White Sox	In 1919, eight members of the team threw the World Series against the Cincinnati Reds, as they had money bet on the Reds team to win. This is also known as the "Black Sox Scandal."
Boston Marathon	Rosie Ruiz	Was the first woman to cross the finish line in the 1980 Boston Marathon with a time of 2:31:56, and it was later found that she took a shortcut (the subway) to the finish line.
MLB	Ryan Braun	Reports of positive drug tests and violation of the league's PED policy, which resulted in a 2013 suspension.
FIFA/EUFA	Sepp Blatter	Former president of FIFA confirmed widespread corruption and cheating was prevalent in determining matches for EUFA and FIFA.
Boxing	Mike Tyson	Mike Tyson bit the left ear of Evander Holyfield in a 1997 fight that ended in a disqualification.

FRAUD

The unethical behavior of student-athletes in the classroom has become a recent issue for sport managers. The problem of academic fraud has been perpetuated by the advent of the Internet and the ease of access to information for students. Academic organizations and faculty utilize **plagiarism** policies and computer software such as *Turnitin.com* and *SafeAssign* to try to discourage students from fraudulent academic misconduct. In the face of the commercialized sport product in many high-profile basketball and football programs (see commercialization below), college sport has become a breeding ground for corrupt academic behaviors. In many cases, athletics take precedence over academics and student-athletes are "trained and groomed" to find exceptions to standard academic procedures. Academic scandals have become the norm in many big-time college sport programs. One such academic scandal happened at the University of Minnesota, where a men's basketball tutor was found responsible for writing over 400 academic papers for student-athletes (Benford, 2007).

Suzanne Tucker/shutterstock.com

Another example of unethical behavior surrounding student-athletes occurs when athletes are placed in classes that never meet in person or in classes that have minimal academic requirements, often called **paper classes**. This and other academic misconduct on the part of the institution or on the part of the student only leads to the further exploitation of the student and their academic experience. While many believe that improper academic conduct is an important ethical issue, it was recently proven in college basketball that getting to the BIG game might be worth the risk. In 2016, Syracuse University and the University of North Carolina met at the NCAA Final Four Men's Basketball Tournament while both academic programs were facing academic fraud violations. In 2015, the coach of the Syracuse team, Jim Boeheim, had been suspended for nine games after it had been revealed that university employees had been writing papers for the athletes. At the University of North Carolina, reports indicate over 1,500 athletes were directed to take "paper classes," classes in which students wrote one paper and no attendance was required (New, 2016). Many educational institutions have been involved in academic fraud, and in some cases the administrators, athletic departments, tutors, advisors, coaches, and professors were also at fault (see Table 3.2).

TABLE 3.2	*Recent Examples of University Academic Fraud*	
Year	**University**	**Academic Fraud Scandal**
1995–2015	University of North Carolina at Chapel Hill	Reports of nearly 20 years of unethical conduct on the part of the athletic department. Most recently, more than 188 cases of students taking "paper classes" and getting assistance in writing academic papers (New, 2014).
2001–2015	Syracuse University	The NCAA investigation showed that Syracuse had academic fraud cases dating back to 2001. The report found that Syracuse failed to control its athletic programs, follow its own drug testing policy, and manage its prevalent academic misconduct (Solomon, 2015a).
2015	University of Texas at Austin	Some members of the basketball team were found to have received special attention prior to enrollment, and one student-athlete allegedly took pictures of math tests and shared answers but still managed to pass the class and graduate with honors (Hair, 2015).
2014	Weber State University	A math instructor violated the NCAA code of conduct by assisting five football student-athletes with test and quiz hints, notes, and answers (James, 2014).
2004–2011	Texas Southern University	Reports of impermissible benefits, academic issues, and lack of institutional control primarily with the football and basketball programs (Dennie, 2012).

In 2015, the president of the **Fédération International, de Football (FIFA)**, Sepp Blatter, was banned from the ethics committee and was the subject of a national corruption scandal involving bribes and kickbacks. FIFA is responsible for governing the international football (soccer) competition and ensuring fair play, world rankings, and statistics in football (soccer). **Corruption** is defined as the dishonest or fraudulent conduct by those in powerful positions, which typically involves bribery, while **corruption in sport** is any illegal, immoral, or unethical activity that attempts to deliberately distort the result of a sporting contest for the material gain of one or more parties involved in that activity (Gorse & Chadwick, 2010). The corruption scandal involved the process by which FIFA awarded the 2022 World Cup to Qatar. The allegations were that the bidding process was corrupt and that the awarding committee took bribes and payments to award the games to Qatar. This occured after investigations that the **International Association of Athletics Federations (IAAF)**, which governs track and field world rankings, was also reported to have taken bribes to cover up positive drug tests by its athletes. Each of these examples depicts the international scale on which cheating and corruption can exist in sport.

Constantine Pankin/shutterstock.com

ISSUES AND ETHICS IN SPORT

DRUG USE

The use of Performance Enhancing Drugs (PEDs) has increasingly become a problem in sport due to the high level of competition and the pressure to win. PEDs are commonly defined as substances taken to improve performance, including **human growth hormone (hGH), and stimulants** (Drug Free Sport, 2015). In all levels of sport today, winning becomes most important and many athletes may consider using drugs to enhance their performance and gain unfair advantages over their opponents. The disproportionate emphasis on winning or the pressure to win can supersede skill development or focus on participation in many sports. Athletes from youth to professional sport have been known to use stimulants, depressants, and anabolic steroids to enhance performance in their game. Athletes are seeking to enhance their strength, energy, and endurance in a variety of ways. There are many types of drugs that fall into the PED category.

Ergogenic aids are broadly defined as techniques, supplements, or substances used for the purpose of enhancing athletic or physical performance (Thein, Thein, & Landry, 1995). Ergogenic aids are prohibited by the rules of many leagues and organizations in an attempt to maintain competitive balance. Ergogenic aids can assist athletes in enhancing performance but can also increase the athlete's image of self and of their skill.

Stimulants are also common PEDs that can "increase heart rate, blood pressure, metabolism; feelings of exhilaration, energy, increased mental alertness, reduced appetite; weight loss; heart failure; nervousness and insomnia" (Hales, 2009, p. 354). Stimulants can be drugs such as Amphetamines (speed), Ephedrines (found in cold medicines and nasal sprays), Cocaine, Nicotine, and Caffeine. Some athletes in sport use stimulants to increase performance in the game and consequently increases in motivation and confidence in performance abilities often result.

katatonia82/shutterstock.com

Depressants are drugs designed to relax. Athletes often use depressants to recover from intense pressure or the adrenaline rush brought on by competition. Depressants commonly used include alcohol, sleeping pills, and tranquilizers (Hales, 2009).

Another common type of PED is **anabolic steroids**. Anabolic steroids are synthetic varieties of testosterone, which contribute to the development of secondary sex characteristics, including muscular strength. The side effects of anabolic steroids can include heart disease, liver and kidney damage, and cancer (Hales, 2009).

In college sport, the use of PEDs is considered to be less common as the NCAA has a Doping and Drug Enforcement Task Force designed to combat drugs in college athletics. Recent research suggests that rates of Performance Enhancing Drugs (PEDs) and other substances among college athletes range from 5 to 31%. Many of these performance enhancing substances can pose a serious threat to the health and well-being of college athletes (Momaya & Fawal, 2015). College athletes are faced with a variety of physical and social challenges that may cause the increase in use of PEDs. Common PEDs used by NCAA athletes include hGH, hCG, Clenbutrol, and SARMs, which are all designed to bulk up the athlete.

In 1986, Brian Bosworth tested positive for steroids and was suspended from play in the Orange Bowl between Oklahoma and Arkansas (Volsky, 1986). At that time, Bosworth was one of the first athletes to be suspended by the NCAA who had recently implemented drug-testing policies for players in championship games. Bosworth came out publically against his disappointment with the NCAA and their 90-day suspension policy, yet did not play in the game. One recent example involves former University of Florida quarterback Will Grier, who tested positive for banned substances and was suspended for a year by the NCAA (Trahan, 2015). This has been a controversial subject, as the NCAA does random testing while schools are allowed to administer their own drug testing system. According to Trahan (2015), had Florida tested Grier he would have likely only been banned for one game. The inconsistency in college testing policy has created a culture of college athletes' disinterest and disenchantment with the NCAA and its policies.

In professional sport, cheating has become common practice. Some of the most common forms of cheating include drug use, stealing of other teams' signs and signals, lying, and blood doping. **Blood doping** is an illicit method of injecting oxygenated blood into an athlete for the purpose of enhancing the athlete's performance (Karriem-Norwood, 2014). In many cases the athlete will see an increase in their muscles' ability to perform and blood doping can also improve overall athletic stamina. Blood doping had become a common problem, in the Tour de France and has recently been banned by the International Olympic Committee (IOC). Athletes have also reportedly started using a method of injecting DNA into the body to restore function, reverse muscle degeneration, and enhance performance called **gene doping**. The **World Anti-Doping Agency (WADA)** was established in 1999 to fight against, monitor, and regulate doping in sport. Each year, WADA is faced with new challenges when athletes try to gain a competitive advantage by using new technologies, science, or new drugs that are undetectable to current medical professionals.

In professional sport, one of the most notable PED users in football was Lyle Alzado who admitted using steroids during his entire career. Alzado came clean of his life-long use in a *Sports Illustrated* interview in 1991 and died a year later (Puma, n.d.). PED use in professional sport has a long history and can be traced back to the beginning of many of the players in all professional leagues. Most notable is the Major League Baseball (MLB). Star athletes in the MLB had successful careers as strong hitters. In 1927, Babe Ruth became the first professional baseball player to hit 60 home runs in a season. Roger Maris broke it 34 years later when he hit 61 home runs. In 1998, Sammy Sosa and Mark McGwire were in a home run race throughout the entire MLB season. In 2001, Barry Bonds hit 73 home runs during the season. The "Steroids Era" in MLB was the time from the 1980s through the late 2000s where many MLB players were accused of using PEDs. The ban on steroids in Major League Baseball brought about a government investigation and fan backlash in the sport history record books. In recent years, the steroid problem is not gone from baseball but has made consistent strides. A 2016 *Sports Illustrated* story claims that in 2003 when all members of each 40-man roster were tested "96 of the 1,438 samples (from roughly 1,200 players) tested positive, a rate of 6.7% compared to the seven players suspended in 2016, that's less than 1% of all players on major league rosters" (Jaffe, 2016, para. 4).

STUDENT ACTIVITY:
Is taking a substance for medical reasons ethical if it gives a competitive advantage? What penalty, if any, should be assessed against the athlete who takes stimulants? What ethical issues are associated with the use of depressants by athletes?

GAMBLING

Gambling has been a part of sport since its inception. In more recent years, gambling has become a problem at all levels of sport. **Gambling,** by law, is defined as a stake or the risk of something of value upon the outcome of a contest of chance or of an event (US Legal, 2016). Gambling poses major ethical dilemmas for sport leagues, fans, players, coaches, and society in general. In youth sport, gambling is uncommon, but in recent years has seen an increase due to the competitive nature of youth programs. A 2012 ESPN Outside the Lines (OTL) report found that youth sport gambling was growing in popularity in some pee-wee leagues across the nation. One OTL investigation found that in a South Florida Little League football program, men were betting tens of thousands of dollars on the young athletes and the outcome of the games. One parent reported that a Little League Super Bowl pot could reach $75,000 (Lavigne, 2013). These youth were also occasionally paid for their performance on the field. Many of those participating in the gambling ring were arrested, and among them were some of the team coaches. In the same ESPN report, it was determined that many Florida-based low-income families were being paid to have their children participate in some of the Little League programs. Gamblers would find parents in need of money and pay them to allow the children to participate (Lavigne, 2013).

Gambling in youth sport is illegal and adults typically know the dangers of sport gambling; however, the increase in sport gaming and access to the Internet has seen an increase in youth involved in online gambling. According to Jacobs (2000) a growing number of youth are participating in gambling in the United States. Gambling has become increasingly popular in youth ages 12 to 17 (Jacobs, 2000; Pitt, Thomas, Bestman, Daube, & Derevensky, 2007). Many young adults are seeking to establish their own identity and have increased access to gambling online. This increased access and exposure have changed the perceptions, attitudes, and consumption of gambling products for youth. The esport community has seen an increase in online video gambling. As young adults become more interested in the esport phenomena, the need for regulation and oversight increases. Gamers are becoming increasingly involved in the community and therefore interested in virtual gambling opportunities. Walker (2016) states that there are limited resources preventing teenagers and children betting and gambling on esports. The lack of oversight from the gambling industry, the growing interest in gaming by youth, the "normalization of gambling" among kids, and the advances in technology are all contributing to the growing esports betting problem (Walker, 2016).

The problem gambling that has become increasingly challenging in youth sport is also a concern in college and professional sport. **Problem gambling** is a type of behavior that causes disruptions in any major area of life. Problem gambling has a strong history in sport as many coaches, athletes, and sport administrators have been removed from their positions due to problem gambling. The NCAA strongly opposes gambling in all forms, both legal and illegal, on sports. Sports wagering has become a serious problem that threatens the well-being of the student-athlete and the integrity of college sports. The explosive growth of sports wagering has caused a noticeable increase in the number of sports wagering-related cases processed by the NCAA. Greenberg (2014) reminds us that the NCAA prohibits fantasy sport for athletes and considers it "gambling" or "betting" although the 2006 Internet Gambling Prohibition and Enforcement Act categorizes fantasy sports as a game of skill. The Internet has also increased the ability for athletes to access gaming sites and gambling opportunities. Fantasy sports have provided student-athletes the ability to get involved in organized gambling and often as easy marks. When student-athletes gamble, could be breaking the law and jeopardize their eligibility with the NCAA and their universities, as the NCAA defines gambling as putting something at risk with the opportunity to win something in return (Greenberg, 2014). When student-athletes become indebted to bookies and cannot pay off their debts, alternative methods of payment are introduced that threaten the well-being of the student-athlete or undermine an athletic contest—such as point-shaving. Nearly 70% of male student-athletes reported gambling in 2014 versus 47% among females (College Gambling, 2014). In addition, in 2014 about 35% of males and 10% of females admitted to wagering on a sporting event, which is a direct violation of NCCA bylaws regarding sports wagering. 20% of males and 5% of females bet on collegiate sporting events, even though if caught they would be banned from playing at an NCAA school for the rest of their lives (College Gambling, 2014).

As problem gambling is a concern, pathological gambling is a serious and often financially deteriorating issue. **Pathological gambling** is a chronic disorder that results in the loss of control over gambling. Pathological gambling can include preoccupation, tolerance, withdrawal, loss of control, commission of illegal acts, and lying (Fong, 2005). College athletes have been known to gamble on the stock market, lottery, fantasy sports, and poker and video games. Unfortunately, gambling by college athletes can result in significant debt and often leads to other serious consequences including being forced to leave school due to gambling-related hardships. Pathological gambling has been known to co-exist with other psychiatric disturbances such as depression, mania, and panic disorders. A growing number of college students are involved in gambling and suffering the consequences of long-term gambling addictions.

Professional sport athletes and managers have also been involved in illegal gambling practices. Athletes gamble for a variety of reasons and in a variety of ways. Gambling has become a large industry in the United States with an estimated $57 billion spent on gambling in 2006 alone (Vacek, 2011). Since the beginning of professional sport in America, some form of gambling has been evident. The most famous professional sport gambling scandal (mentioned above in Table 3.3) involved eight members of the Chicago White Sox team. In 1919, the team played in the World Series against the Cincinnati Reds and rumors surfaced that some of the team had bet against themselves and thrown the series. Gambling was an issue that had surfaced in baseball and multiple sources were investigating many accusations of cheating and fraud within the game. The eight men, one of whom was the infamous "shoeless" Joe Jackson, had reportedly agreed to lose the World Series in exchange for $100,000 (Andrew, 2014). The scandal later became know as the Black Sox scandal of 1919 and each player eventually came clean and admitted their involvement in a gambling game fix. Each of these players was ruled permenantly ineligible to play in the game by then MLB Commissioner Judge Kenesaw Mountain Landis (Andrew, 2014). This bold move helped clean up the gambling problem in early baseball history, but gambling still prevailed in baseball and other US professional sports. In football, Heisman Trophy winner and notable champion Paul Hornung was banned from the 1963 season for reportedly betting on college and professional games. Pete Rose received a lifetime ban from the game of baseball for his involvement in MLB betting, yet no evidence was found that he ever bet on his own team. In the National Hockey League (NHL) a series of gambling rings were reported involving bookies who represented multiple star players (Craig & Oklobzija, 2014). Each of these incidents involving players and mangers provides evidence that gambling and betting on sport is an ethical issue that needs to be handled and contained by sport managers. Ethical decision-making models can be used to assist sport managers in determining the correct action related to gambling issues in the sport industry.

STUDENT ACTIVITY:
Discuss the common issue of wagering money in office pools during the March Madness championships. Is it ethical to bet money on college athletes? Should gambling outside their sport be accepted for college or professional athletes? Why or why not? Is fantasy sports considered gambling? Explain your answer.

COMMERCIALIZATION

Commercialization is the process of making money from the production and introduction of a product or service into the market. The commercialization of the sport industry from youth to college to professional leagues has seen enormous growth over the past century. The consequent increase in revenue at every level of sport must be considered when discussing ethical issues in the industry. In youth sport, the commercialization is evident in the live broadcast of the Little League World Series on ESPN. In 2014, air-time increased even more for the league as Philadelphia, Pennsylvania, pitcher Mo'ne Davis became the first girl to throw a shutout (Fenno, 2014). Youth sport has also seen an increase in the naming rights money that has become so common in other sport industries. In 2016, the Aspen School District in Aspen, Colorado, listened to proposals to exchange large donations for the commercial naming rights of their public school venues and facilities. In Westminster, Colorado, the Westminster North High School accepted a naming rights deal with First Bank as part of a $1.2 million deal with the public school system (Blevins, 2016). This type of fundraising has become increasingly popular, but has also contributed to the discussion of the public school system commercializing the youth sport product. Lumpkin, Stoll, and Beller (2011) suggested that, although youth sport is modeled after college and professional games, youth sport has remained "somewhat insulated" from the negative side of the commercialized sport industry.

In college athletics, the commercialization of the NCAA March Madness tournament, the increasing amounts of money made by the football bowl games, and the showcasing of the athletes as professional players has perpetuated the conversation about college sport as a moneymaking machine (Critelli, 2011). According to many researchers, the college sport entertainment industry has grown exponentially over the past several decades (Benford, 2007; Shulman & Bowen, 2001; Sperber, 1990). The NCAA, which promotes the protection of the amateur status of the student-athlete, earned $1 billion in the 2016 March Madness Tournament from television adds, media rights, corporate sponsorships and ticket sales (NCAA.org). The NCAA does distribute a large percentage (96%) of the March Madness revenue back to its Division I member institutions for championships, yet the non-profit organization still makes billions. In a recent deal with CBS Sports and Turner Broadcasting, the NCAA agreed to accept $10.8 billion for 14 years to televise the NCAA March Madness Tournament. This evidence of commercialization in college sport leaves those supporting the young college players to wonder if this is corruption of the young athletes, negligence on the part of the institution, or simply ethical sport commerce.

Another common ethical issue in college sport is the "one and done" scenario in college basketball. The NCAA and the NBA have determined that a basketball athlete must complete at least one year of college to be eligible for the NBA draft. This rule has recently seen much controversy as athletes play one year for a college and then head off to the NBA. Recently, Louisiana State University (LSU) forward Ben Simmons, who completed his first year of college at LSU, was not considered for the Wooden Award based on his poor academic record at LSU. Students like this are not going to college to get an education, but simply to showcase their skills on the national college basketball stage and then prepare for the next NBA draft. According to Benford (2007), faculty, administrators, and sport organizations have spent over a century trying to address the issues with college sport. The Carnegie Foundation, the NCAA, The Knight Commission, the Drake Group, and many others have made numerous attempts to reform college athletics and a nation's obsession with the commercialized sport product.

Corporations have also become dominant in the commercialization of the sport industry. Organizations are making big plays to get their name on or near the athletes at the youth, college, and professional levels. Large companies spend billions recruiting youth and college athletes and marketing and endorsing professional athletes. This commercialized interest in being associated with sport has increased the ethical issues related to corporate organizations involved in sport. The growth of sponsorship and endorsement deals in college and professional sport have added to the moneymaking power of sport organizations. Companies such as Nike and Adidas have become more and more involved in college campus programs to increase their brand image and exposure. In 2001, 80 students and faculty at Stanford signed a petition expressing their unhappiness with the relationship between Nike and the Stanford Athletic Department (Alexander, 2001). The main claim by the faculty and students was that Nike was adding to the commercialization of college sports. Nike and Stanford officials claimed it was a business deal and that no ethical issue was present. Nike has staked their claim in the college sport realm ever since Sonny Vaccaro convinced Nike to pay college coaches to put the athletes in Nike shoes, which later evolved into the paying of the university athletic departments for corporate sponsorship deals. This opened the door for corporations and organizations to become more and more involved in the college sport spectacle.

In professional sport, the demand and desire for athletes to gain exposure through endorsements has increased corporate involvement. Athletes and their access to endorsement deals have grown larger and

Aspen Photo/shutterstock.com

Helga Esteb/shutterstock.com

larger. This increase has drawn more and more interest from fans and organizations seeking to be involved. High-profile athletes such as Tiger Woods, who has $65 million in endorsements from Nike, Rolex, and Upper Deck, to Serena Williams with $24.6 million from Chase and Pepsi continue to remain at the top of the endorsement charts. One current athlete who is challenging the commercialized endorsement business is Stephen Curry. Curry, of the Golden State Warriors, has proven to demand more control over his endorsement partnership decisions. In 2016, it was reported that Nike rejected his interest in a shoe displaying a religious verse. Curry, who had a previous relationship with the brand, has recently re-signed a deal with Under Armour to develop a shoe that represents him and his faith (Welch, 2016). Corporations and organizations such as Nike have powerful influence in the industry and taking a pass on a star player shows the perceived domination they have in the industry. The Steph Curry shoe, the Curry 3, although popular, has not garnered the same interest as his previous jersey sales (Owusu, 2017). Under Armour, seeking to become a top competitior in the marketplace, is still grasping to top NIKE in the competitive area of the NBA.

The growth of sponsorships in NASCAR can possibly be attributed to the 75 million fans of the sport worldwide. NASCAR has continually increased its popularity and in turn increased the interest of corporations to become involved in the sponsorship of the sport, its cars, and its athletes. Corbett and Lekush (2003) discussed how the sport has grown for sponsors due to its "emotional connections, intense competition, and uniquely American product" (p. 17). The fans associate with the drivers and then purchase and use the products of these drivers. NASCAR sponsorships have become so strong that organizations such as Pfizer, Hills Bros. Coffee, and M&M's are making bold brand statements to guarantee their position and placement on the cars. The NASCAR model of sponsorship is successful, but could it work for other sports? This is a constant conflict and ethical consideration between the owners and those who measure the effectiveness and the impact of the brand association in the sport. Those involved in achieving marketing and sales goals for

NASCAR claim that "NASCAR performs for its sponsors like no other sport. It builds bonds between fan and sponsor" (Corbett & Lekush, 2003, p. 22). This is an important example as this is the goal of many professional sport organizations today and achieving this bond increases the value of the fan/brand relationship. The ethical question, however, remains: Does the commercialization of the sport product at any level (youth, college, or professional) take away from the game itself? Or does the branding, imagery, and excessive advertising create a more enriching experience for fans?

STUDENT EXERCISE:
Over the years, NASCAR has dramatically increased its branding by using sponsors and advertisers on its cars and drivers. In recent years, the National Basketball Association (NBA) has approved the use of advertising on jerseys on the players. Utilizing Cavanaugh's Ethical Decision Making Model from Chapter 1, evaluate and determine if the NBA's use of advertising on jerseys is an ethical problem and who might be affected by the decision to do so.

BULLYING IN SPORT

The culture of hazing has increasingly become a problem across campuses and in student organizations in nearly every educational setting from high schools to colleges across the nation. The act of **hazing** is anything committed against someone joining or becoming a member in any organization that is humiliating, intimidating, or demeaning that could endanger the health and safety of that person (Wilfert, 2007). In many states, hazing has become illegal but hazing laws can vary from state to state. Some states, such as Colorado, have hazing laws that include "any forced and prolonged physical activity, consumption of food or substance and or deprivation of sleep" (stophazing.org, 2015). Hazing often involves physical abuse, alcohol, personal hygiene, public humiliation, beatings, and assault (Insidehazing.com). Hazing has been defined in many ways, but the power of tradition, athletic rites of passage, and social acceptance have created many customs that can be harmful and dangerous to athletes from youth to professional sport. In today's society, athletes are seeking the acceptance to belong and in the process have become the victims of many malicious and demeaning crimes. There is a growing need for the education of athletes old and young regarding the dangers of societal influence, socialization, and victimization.

There are many misconceptions about hazing and bullying in sport. According to an Alfred University study, over 80% of college recruits have been subject to some form of hazing (Goetschius, 1980). It is common that hazing stems from many of the traditions that exist in society that perpetuate a hazing culture. According to the novel *Dogs are Barking* by Mark Taylor, the Duntroon Royal Military College has had a culture of torture developed from years of intolerable rites and rituals of the freshmen recruits. In recent years, administrators have become more aware as some states can hold an education professional with knowledge of the incidents liable, if the hazing involves students at an educational institution and there was no reasonable attempt to prevent the acts (Villalba, 2007).

A culture of acceptance has become common in athletic locker rooms at all levels. Following a football practice in 2000, high school athlete Brian Seamons was grabbed and taped to a bathroom towel bar by his fellow teammates. Seamons also had his genitals taped and his girlfriend was brought into the locker room by another player on the team. Seamons reported this incident to the coach and the principal. The school district suspended the team from the final game. Following the suspension, Seamons was instructed by the coach to apologize to the team for reporting the incident to school administration (Roche, 1993).

Bullying has also been reported in professional sport across multiple leagues. A culture of bullying was determined in the National Football League (NFL) in 2014 when then Miami Dolphins offensive linesman Johnathan Martin reported being harassed and tormented by his teammates. One teammate in particular, Richie Incognito, was accused of abusive name-calling, racial slurs, and improper physical touching (ESPN, 2014). This type of behavior has become common in locker rooms where a culture of male dominance has become normalized. There has been a long line of intimidators in sport that have influenced the way that others are treated in their respective sports (see Table 3.3). Sport managers and other organizational decision makers need to advocate for the safe and effective workplace free of harassment and bullying.

TABLE 3.3	Bullying Examples in Professional Sport (Rush, 2013)	
League	Athlete	Bullying
NASCAR	Dale Earnhardt Sr.	Dale Sr. was known as the "intimidator" and for his criticizing words and crushing hits to opponents on the track.
NBA	Kermit Washington	Known for his famous punch to the face of Rudy Tomjanovich; Kermit was a beast on the court.
NHL	Todd Bertuzzi	Bertuzzi reportedly had a bounty on the head of Avalanche player Steve Moore. Bertuzzi punched and hit Moore down to the ice and Moore suffered a paralyzing hit. Moore never played hockey again. Bertuzzi continued to play in the NHL for 10 years.
MLB	Ty Cobb	Cobb is known for a bad attitude and for intentionally hitting the bases with his spikes up.
Boxing	Floyd Mayweather	Known for his tough exterior, Mayweather does not want anyone, not even his managers and promoters, to talk back to him.

CONCUSSIONS

In 2013, the National Football League (NFL) reached a $765 million settlement with 4,500 former NFL players who had filed a **class-action lawsuit**. The court ruled on the behalf of the large group of plaintiffs who had common interest in receiving compensation for concussions or traumatic head injuries suffered during their NFL playing years. The ruling and settlement determined that the long-term effects of concussions can include Alzheimer's disease, dementia, cognitive issues, and/or other long-term brain trauma (Breslow, 2014). Concussions in the NFL in recent years have become increasingly visible due to this lawsuit, and the impact of these head injuries is being studied in great detail. In several recent NFL concussion studies, it has been determined that concussions are on the rise. The NFL reported during the 2015 regular reason that concussions increased 58% over the previous year, which is cause for serious concern for both the league and players alike (Vinton, 2016). The National Football League Players Association (NFLPA), the players' union that plays a role in protecting the health and safety of its members, has demanded educational programs and a protocol to increase player safety in the league (Sharp, 2015). The impact of the lawsuits and the increase in regular-season-reported concussions has generated a national conversation around youth and their involvement in high impact sports such as football.

According to a 2013 report by the Institute of Medicine, little is known about the impact of concussions in youth (considered ages 5 to 21; Heitz, 2013). Little research has been done on the impact of concussions on the young brain or the trauma that high impact sport programs can cause in a child's future. According to *USA Today*:

> There are 1.3 million high school and 2.8 million youth football players in this country (compared to 1,700 players in the NFL). The vast majority of high school and youth football games are played without medical personnel [on] the sidelines. It's sobering to note that only 42% of high schools in the United States have athletic trainers and those trainers obviously can't attend all of a given school's athletic events or practices (Reed, 2015, para. 9).

A federal report by the Institute of Medicine recognized that although football has the highest concussion rate, it is not the only sport where there is a cause for concern regarding concussions. Other male youth sports that have high numbers of concussion rates include: soccer, ice hockey, wrestling, and lacrosse. Although female concussions are more rare, the most common high school and college sports for female concussions are basketball, lacrosse, and soccer. It is also reported that the young athletes who have reported one sport-related concussion had a higher chance of suffering from another concussion in their sport career (Heitz, 2013).

Although there are a variety of studies looking at the impact of concussions, it is important as sport managers to seek and find solutions. Many reports have discussed the importance of the players reporting their symptoms to coaches and coaches responding to these reports. Also, it is crucial that both coaches and officials respond to any and all rules and procedures regarding concussion protocol no matter what the level of play.

STUDENT EXERCISE:
Over the years, there have been many cases of concussions in the NFL. Research a recent NFL case and answer the following questions:
1. How did the coach respond to the concussion?
2. Was the concussion reported during the game or after the game?
3. Do players typically report when they are having concussion symptoms? Why or why not?
4. Is it ethical for a coach to put a player back in the game if they suspect a player is injured? Explain your answer.

ROLE OF RELIGION IN SPORT

Religion and religious practice and participation on the court or on the field are ethical concerns for managers involved in sport at all levels in today's society. The subject of religion comes up in youth sport as many advocates for religious programming have made claims that sport has taken the place of religious practice for some (Briggs, 2013; Cook, 2014). In some cases, church elders have blamed the increased level of youth participating in sport as reason for the lack of attendance in church or church-related functions. The perception that sport has become a replacement for religion is an important ethical consideration for sport managers. As indicated previously, many young athletes feel increased pressures to participate despite their interest in individual or team sports. According to the US Department of Labor Bureau of Labor Statistics, the average teen spends 42 minutes on sport on the weekdays and nearly an hour on sports on the weekends. In contrast, the average teen spends less than 40 minutes per week on religion or religious based activities (2015). These percentages may be related to sport participation but also may be a result of an increase in youth involvement in online media and communication.

As college athletes become more independent, religion may or may not play a larger role in their everyday lives. In some cases, claims have been made that religion can cause a disruption in the collegiate sport experience. College athletes dedicate an average of 15–20 hours in the off-season and upward of 40–60 hours a week on their respective sport during their season (Isidore, 2014). This time commitment may leave little room for other activities, which can include religious attendance and practice. Some college athletes have gone the extra mile to include religion in their athlete training programs. **Athletes in Action**, a religious organization with the mission to "build spiritual movements everywhere through the platform of sports" has assisted student-athletes to organize across campuses and build faith in a common religious goal (Athletes in Action, 2016). Many argue that the involvement of religion in sport can cause conflict among the team or disrupt team unity. Christian athlete Reid Monaghan discusses that adding prayer before, during, and after competition can have adverse effects on team unity. As superstitious rituals become commonplace in sport, Reid claims, "It's dangerous as Christian athletes to mix God up into our routine as if we are using him as a means to our athletic ends. Some of us pray before practices and games almost as if God will give us good luck if we do so. As if God is a lucky rabbit's foot and our prayers are mere chants to get us wins on game day. God is not our good luck charm and neither are our prayers" (Monaghan, 2016, para. 5). College athletes across the nation may not have the same views as those stated above; however, many believe that sport and church teach many of the exact same skills and values. Religion teaches dedication, determination, humility, suffering, and ritual. Arguably, sport teaches these same core values. Some religious college athletic programs have issues trying to prioritize the religious beliefs, especially those programs grounded in faith like Texas Christian or Notre Dame that may have mandatory "church days" and "require" student-athletes to attend. At one school with no religious affiliation, East Mississippi Community College, coach Marcus Wood leads a weekly Bible study for players while Coach Buddy Stephens regularly leads the team in the Lord's Prayer (Korman, 2017). Many schools now offer a Fellowship of Christian Athletes (FCA) program for religious students. The practice of attending this meeting is not required by these athletes, but is strongly encouraged by the program and the coach. The convergence between athletics and religion can often present challenges for programs. Those programs with religious affiliations can sometimes face conflicts between practice of religion and sport. In 2012, a Jewish school basketball team in Texas was reportedly forced to forfeit a game that was scheduled during the Sabbath. This was a challenge for administrators who refused to change the time of the championship games (Jennings, 2012). This type of management of sport has become increasingly concerning, as individuals have rights to religious freedoms, but sport, sport managers, and sport programs are not legally required to comply.

In international sport, religious headgear such as turbans and hijabs have been banned by the International Basketball Association (Waldron, 2014). FIBA, the governing body overseeing international basketball competition, has recently been reviewing their policies over religious headwear after athletes began to speak out about their religious freedoms and social media movements have been commanding change. Some other governing bodies like the NCAA and the IOC have made exceptions for athletes to wear their religious headgear during active competition. Most recently, USA Basketball and the WNBA have led campaigns for rights against the ban of religious headwear in all basketball competitions. When Sepp Blatter was the President of the Federation of Football International (FIFA), he banned praying before and after all FIFA matches (King, 2009). This decision, of course, was met with controversy from athletes and fans alike, yet Blatter held strong that religion was to remain out of his sport program.

FUTURE FOR EVENT MANAGERS

Sport managers in the future will be faced with a variety of challenges that will cross over youth, high school, college, and professional sport. Sport has grown on an international level as well, and future sport managers will face a variety of issues and ethical challenges. Common issues that are currently challenging each of these levels of sport programs will require sport managers to consistently change and adapt to the environment. As interest in sport participation continues to grow, ethical issues surrounding each of these industry segments will grow as well. For sport managers, it is important to consider all levels of ethical issues that may be present in sport programming and think carefully about how to manage each area with sound ethical decision making.

DISCUSSION QUESTIONS

1. Discuss the commercialization of the sport product and provide at least two examples of commercialization not discussed in the chapter.

2. How has cheating and fraud changed the college game? Professional game? Explain your answer.

3. Describe two ways athletes are exploited. Is the exploitation ethical? Why or why not?

4. Is steroid use or blood doping cheating in professional sport? Explain your answer.

5. Is there an issue with the commercialization of the sport product in youth sport programming? If yes, provide an example. If no, explain why not.

6. Should religion be allowed to be openly practiced in sport participation at all levels? Why or why not?

CASE STUDY: LITTLE LEAGUE BASEBALL

Little League Baseball has been the source of several scandals in youth sport. The ethical issues date back to 1974 following Taiwan's fourth consecutive Little League championship. Controversy arose following Taiwan's repeat success as they practiced year-round and had out-of-district players on the roster. In 1975 foreign teams were banned from reaching the series while Little League worked to strengthen rules surrounding the issues presented by Taiwan's continued success (Associated Press, 2015).

Despite the stricter rules with respect to out-of-district players, the winner of the 1992 World Series, Zamboanga City Little League of the Philippines, was found to have assembled a national all-star team, which included eight players from outside the Zamboanga City league's boundaries (Associated Press, 1992). The actions of the team led to the first forfeiture of a championship in Little League history. The forfeit gave Long Beach Little League of California the championship.

More recently, Little League Baseball encountered boundary issues from Jackie Robinson West, a team based out of Chicago. The team was forced to vacate its wins from the 2014 season including the Great Lakes Regional and United States championship following the discovery that the team had falsified a boundary map and, with the help of neighboring districts, built an all-star team (Farrey & McDonald, 2015). Officials associated with the team, including the team's manager Darold Butler and District Administrator Mike Kelly, signed documents to make players eligible who should not have been. The review of the situation led to the suspension of Butler from Little League activity and the removal of Kelly from his position (Farrey & McDonald, 2015).

The decision of Little League Baseball to strip the team of their wins received criticism from influential individuals, including the Mayor of Chicago and former President of the United States, Barack Obama. Chicago Mayor Rahm Emanuel stated it was unfair for the league to punish children for the actions of adults and unsuccessfully pushed for Little League to reconsider their decision (ESPN, 2015). Obama, who hosted the team at the White House following its winning of the championship, called the actions of the adults associated with the team dirty and said the actions of the "dirty dealing" adults should not take away from the accomplishments of the young men on the team.

CASE QUESTIONS

1. In instances in which forfeiture is required, should the second place team automatically win or should additional competition of some sort be required? Explain your answer.

2. While the actions of the adults involved with each of the aforementioned Little League teams were clearly unethical, was it just and fair for the athletes to be punished? Why or why not?

CASE STUDY: THE 2000 PARALYMPICS

The 2000 Paralympics in Sydney, Australia, were the source of much controversy, specifically with respect to Spain's gold medal-winning basketball team in the intellectual disability tournament. Following the games, Spanish sports daily *Marca* published a picture of the basketball team celebrating on the court (Tomlinson, 2013). Readers saw the publication and recognized some of the athletes, whom they knew were not mentally disabled.

Shortly thereafter, Carlos Ribagorda, a member of the basketball team, claimed he and other Spanish athletes in other sports such as track and field, table tennis, and swimming were not mentally deficient (Zaccardi, 2013). It was revealed only two players on the twelve-man roster had IQs below 70 as required, while the other ten posed as mentally disabled with the help of fake medical certificates (Tomlinson, 2013). Ribagorda also disclosed he was not asked to complete an intelligence test and the only test he was asked to complete at his first training session was six press-ups (DeLessio, 2015).

As a result of the controversy, the team was ordered to return their gold medals and intellectually disabled basketball was removed from the Paralympic program after the 2000 Games (Zaccardi, 2013). Over 13 years after the incident, a Madrid court found Fernando Martin Vicente, the former head of the Spanish Federation for Mentally Handicapped Sports, guilty of fraud and ordered him to pay a fine of $7,300 and return nearly $200,000 in government subsidies, which the Spanish Federation for Mentally Handicapped Sports received for the athletes with disabilities (Zaccardi, 2013).

CASE QUESTIONS

1. Identify the ethical dilemmas in this case study.

2. Is this cheating, fraud, or something else? Explain your answer.

3. Should intellectually disabled basketball have been removed as a sport from the Paralympic games based on the actions of the Spanish basketball team? Why or why not?

4. As a policy-maker, what protocols would you employ to prevent violations like those by the Spanish national team?

GLOSSARY

AAU basketball is a U.S. amateur basketball sports organization.

Anabolic steroids are synthetic varieties of testosterone, which contribute to the development of secondary sex characteristics, including muscular strength.

Athlete exploitation is the act of treating athletes unfairly in order to profit or benefit from their skills.

Athletes in Action is a religious organization with the mission to "build spiritual movements everywhere through the platform of sports."

Blood doping is the illicit method of injecting oxygenated blood into an athlete for the purpose of enhancing the athlete's performance.

Burnout is a symptom of overuse, exhaustion, and fatigue caused by increased and repetitive participation.

Cheating is commonly defined as dishonest or unfair acts to gain a competitive advantage.

Class-action lawsuit involves charges brought to court by one or more plaintiffs on the behalf of the large group who had common interests.

Commercialization is the process of making money from the production and introduction of a product or service into the market.

Corruption is the dishonest or fraudulent conduct by those in powerful positions, which typically involves bribery.

Corruption in sport is defined as any illegal, immoral, or unethical activity that attempts to deliberately distort the result of a sporting contest for the material gain of one or more parties involved in that activity.

Depressants are drugs designed to relax, and commonly include alcohol, sleeping pills, and tranquilizers.

Ergogenic aids are broadly defined as techniques, supplements, or substances used for the purpose of enhancing athletic or physical performance.

Fédération International, de Football (FIFA) is responsible for governing the international football (soccer) competition and ensuring fair play, world rankings, and statistics in football (soccer).

Gambling by law is defined as the process of risking something of value in hopes for an outcome of a contest of chance or of an event that will maximize that risk.

Gene doping is injecting DNA into a person's body to restore function, reverse muscle degeneration, and enhance performance.

Hazing is anything committed against someone joining or becoming a member in any organization that is humiliating, intimidating, or demeaning that could endanger the health and safety of that person.

International Association of Athletics Federations (IAAF) is the organization that is responsible for governing international track and field competitions, statistics, and world rankings.

Overtraining happens when an athlete reaches a performance plateau from an increased training load; overtraining can result in loss of strength and even injury.

Paper classes are classes that never meet in person and/or that have minimal academic requirements to help student-athletes stay eligible.

Pathological gambling is a chronic disorder that results in the loss of control over gambling, and can include preoccupation, tolerance, withdrawal, loss of control, commission of illegal acts, and lying.

Physical burnout includes the repercussions of overuse, overtraining, and overspecialization.

Plagiarism is the copying of another's work without attribution.

Psychological burnout is the mental and emotional pressure from demands for improved performances and winning.

Social burnout is an overall lack of interest in life, potentially inside and outside of sport.

Sport dropout refers to the reasons in which athletes choose to separate from participation in a sport such as loss of interest, overuse, injury, or lack of interest.

Sport elimination is an outcome of an overemphasis on competitive youth sport where young athletes are eliminated from the team as they are not meeting the highly skilled expectations of the coach and parents.

Sport specialization is a focus on one specific athletic talent and excluding all others to assist a child to become more dominant in one sport.

Stimulants are a common PEDs that can "increase heart rate, blood pressure, metabolism; feelings of exhilaration, energy, increased mental alertness, reduced appetite; weight loss; heart failure; nervousness and insomnia."

Title IX is the Education Amendment to the Civil Rights Act of 1964, passed in 1972, which states that no one on the basis of sex shall be excluded from participation in, denied benefits of, or be subject to discrimination under any educational institution receiving federal financial assistance.

World Anti-Doping Agency (WADA) is an international agency established in 1999 to fight against, monitor, and regulate doping in sport.

References

Agassi, A. (2009). Open: An Autobiography. Random House: NY, New York.

Alexander, M. (2001, April 30). Corporate sponsorship of athletes raises ethical issues in campus debate. *Stanford News*. Retrieved from https://news.stanford.edu/pr/01/nike52.html

Andrew, E. (2014, October 9). The Black Sox scandal, 95 years ago. *History.com*. Retrieved from http://www.history.com/news/the-black-sox-baseball-scandal-95-years-ago

Aspen Institute. (2013). Project play playbook: Reimagining youth sport in America. SIFA: Retrieved from http://youthreport.projectplay.us/appendices/main-content-citations

Associated Press. (1992, September 18). Scandal turns Philippines into Little League chumps. *Deseret News*. Retrieved from http://www.deseretnews.com/article/248215/SCANDAL-TURNS-PHILIPPINES-INTO-LITTLE-LEAGUE-CHUMPS.html?pg=all

Associated Press. (2015, February 11). Little League World Series scandals at a glance. *Fox Sports*. Retrieved from http://www.foxsports.com/mlb/story/little-league-scandals-at-a-glance-021115

Athletes in Action. (2016). Mission. Retrieved from http://www.goaia.org/about

Baker, J. (2003). Early specialization in youth sport: A requirement for adult expertise? *High Ability Studies, 14* (1).

Belz, J. (March 27, 2013). When enough is enough: Warning signs of burnout in elite athletes. All About Performance. Retrieved from https://allaboutperformance.wordpress.com/2013/03/27/when-enough-is-enough-uncovering-warning-signs-of-burnout-in-elite-athletes/

Benford, R. D. (2007). The college sports reform movement: Reframing the edutainment industry. *The Sociological Quarterly*, 48, (1), 1–28.

Berri, D. (2014, November 14). Exploitation is everywhere is college basketball. *Time*. Retrieved from http://time.com/3586037/exploitation-is-everywhere-in-mens-college-basketball/

Blevins, J. (2016, March 29). Aspen school district may sell naming rights for public school buildings. *The Denver Post*. Retrieved from http://www.denverpost.com/business/ci_29696396/aspen-district-may-sell-naming-rights-public-school

Breslow, J. M. (2014, September 19). NFL concussion problem still has not gone away. PBS. Retrieved from http://www.pbs.org/wgbh/frontline/article/the-nfls-concussion-problem-still-has-not-gone-away/

Briggs, D. (2013, April 13). The Final Four, travel teams and empty pews. Research on sports and religion. Retrieved from http://blogs.thearda.com/trend/featured/the-final-four-travel-teams-and-empty-pews-research-on-sports-and-religion/

Bruneau, K. (2014, June 14). Youth sports and the problems with parents. *Democratic & Chronicle USA Today*. Retrieved from http://www.democratandchronicle.com/story/lifestyle/her/blogs/moms/2014/06/16/youthsports-and-the-problem-with-parents/10573497/

Coakley, J. (2015). Sports in society: Issues and contraversities (8th Ed.). McGraw Hill: New York, NY.

College Gambling. (2014). National Center for Responsible Gaming. Retrieved from http://www.gamblinghelp.org.sections/college/inside.html

Cook, B. (2014, February 24). Why God is losing to youth sports. Retrieved from http://www.forbes.com/sites/bob-cook/2014/02/24/why-god-is-losing-to-youth-sports/#2cdbc5d109b3.

Corbett, J., & Lekush, J. M. (2003). NASCAR sponsorship: Putting your company in the driver's seat. *Journal for Integrated Communications*. 2002–2003 (17–22).

Craig, G., & Oklobzija, K. (2014, July 24). Hockey and gambling have history. USA Today. Retrieved from http://www.usatoday.com/story/sports/nhl/2014/07/24/hockey-gambling-thomas-vanek-jaromir-jagr/13135711/

Crandall, D. (2015, October 12). How college athletes are being exploited. Attn. Retrieved from http://www.attn.com/stories/3601/how-college-athletes-are-being-exploited

Critelli, M. J. (2011, April 5). The good, the bad and the ugly about the commercialization of amateur sports. *Huffpost Sports*. Retrieved from http://www.huffingtonpost.com/michael-j-critelli/amateur-sports_b_844686.html

DeLessio, J. (2015, January 22). The 5 ballsiest cheaters in team-sports history. *The New York Times*. Retrieved from http://nymag.com/daily/intelligencer/2015/01/5-ballsiest-cheaters-in-team-sports-history.html

Dennie, C. (2012, October 10). The NCAA committee on infractions has spoken: Texas Southern University. B, G & S. Retrieved from http://www.bgsfirm.com/college-sports-law-blog/the-ncaa-committee-on-infractions-has-spoken-texas-southern-university

Drug Free Sport. (2015). Performance Enhancing Drugs. *The National Center for Drug Free Sport*. Retrieved from http://www.drugfreesport.com/drug-resources/performance-enhancing-drugs-steroids.asp

ESPN. (2014, February 15). Incognito, others tormented Martin. ESPN.com Retrieved from http://www.espn.com/nfl/story/_/id/10455447/miami-dolphins-bullying-report-released-richie-incognito-others-responsible-harassment.

ESPN. (2015, February 13). Chicago mayor's attempts fail. *ESPN*. Retrieved from http://espn.go.com/chicago/story/_/id/12316478/chicago-mayor-rahm-emanuel-asks-little-league-return-team-title

Farrey, T (2008). *Game On: The All-American Race to Make Champions of Our Children*. ESPN Books. NY: New York.

Farrey, T., & McDonald, J. (2015, February 12). Little League punishes Chicago team. *ESPN*. Retrieved from http://espn.go.com/chicago/story/_/id/12308988/little-league-strips-chicago-team-us-championship-suspends-coach

Fenno, N. (2014, August 13). Mo'ne Davis legacy isn't done with this Little League World Series. *Los Angeles Times*. Retrieved from http://www.latimes.com/sports/la-sp-mone-davis-baseball-20140823-story.html

Fernandez, B. (2015, September 12). Eaton baseball coaches accused of bullying players. *The Greeley Tribune*. Retrieved from http://www.greeleytribune.com/news/18152196-113/eaton-coaches-accused-of-bullying-players#

Flumenbaum, D. (2011, May 25). Scandal of the ages: Documents reveal underage Chinese gymnast. *The Huffington Post*. Retrieved from http://www.huffingtonpost.com/david-flumenbaum/scandal-of-the-ages-docum_b_118842.html

Fong, T. W. (2005). The bio psychosocial consequences of pathological gambling. *Psychiarty*, 2(3) 23–30.

Goetschius, S. C. (1980). Alfred University Hazing Study. Retrieved from www.alfred.edu/news/html/hazing_study.html

Gorse, S., & Chadwick, S. (2010, July/August). Conceptualising corruption in sport: Implications for sponsorship programmes. *The European Business Review*, 40–45.

Greenberg, M. (2014, September 8). If you're an NCAA athlete, you can't get in on the fantasy football fun. DC Inno. Retrieved from http://dcinno.streetwise.co/2014/09/08/ncaa-athletes-cant-play-fantasy-football/

Gustafsson, H., Kenttä, G., Hassmén, P., & Johasson, M. (2008). A qualative analysis of burnout in elite athletes. *Psychology of Sport & Exercise*, 9(6), 800–816.

Gustafsson, H., Kenttä, G., Hassmén, P., & Lundqvist, C. (2007). Prevalence of burnout in competitive adolescent athletes. *The Sport Psychologist*, 21, 21-37.

Hair, K. (2015, June 22). Academic fraud cases of 2015. Sports Analytics. Retrieved from https://wepicksports.com/academic-fraud-cases-of-2015/

Hales, D. (2009). An invitation to health: Choosing to change. Cengage Learning: Retrieved from http://college.cengage.com/health/course360/personal_health_1111764875/hales_0538736550_ch11.pdf

Head, J. (2017, January 25). When Sports and Religion Collide. Retrieved January 29, 2017, from http://bleacherreport.com/articles/127040-when-sports-and-religion-collide

Heitz, D. (2013, November 21). Dangerous concussions on the rise in youth sports. Retrieved from http://www.healthline.com/health-news/children-concussions-rising-in-youth-sports-112113

Insidehazing.com (2016). https://www.insidehazing.com

IOC. (2016). International Olympic Committee. Retrieved from https://www.olympic.org/ioc

Isidore, C. (2014, March 31). Paying college athletes, a long, tough job. CNN Money. Retrieved from http://money.cnn.com/2014/03/31/news/companies/college-athletes-jobs/

Jaffe, J. (2016, May 5). Explaining MLB's recent wave of PED bans, and what league can do. Sports Illustrated. Retrieved from http://www.si.com/mlb/2016/05/05/ped-suspensions-steroids-dee-gordon-turinabol

James, E. (2014, November 19). Weber State math instructor assists with academic dishonesty. NCAA.org. Retrieved from http://www.ncaa.org/about/resources/media-center/news/weber-state-math-instructor-assists-academic-dishonesty

Jennings, R. (2012, February 28). Jewish HS teams appeal turned down. ESPN. Retrieved from http://www.espn.com/dallas/story/_/id/7622886/sabbath-conflict-ends-hoop-dream-jewish-high-school-team

Karriem-Norwood, V. (2014, August 18). Blood doping. Retrieved from http://www.webmd.com/fitness-exercise/blood-doping

King, D. (2009, July 12). Keep God out of football: FIFA tells soccer superstars. Dailymail.com Retreived from http://www.dailymail.co.uk/news/article-1199121/Brazils-football-superstars-told-Keep-faith-football.html

Korman, C. (2017, July 14). Last Chance U season 2 review: Not everyone can find redemption. *USA Today*. Retrieved from: http://ftw.usatoday.com/2017/07/last-chance-u-season-2-review-overview-netflix-east-mississippi-junior-college-football

Lavigne, P. (2013, December 19). Adults bet thousands on youths. ESPN. Retrieved from http://www.espn.com/espn/otl/news/story?id=6451796

Lee, A. (2015, February 24). 7 charts show the state of youth sport and why it matters. Retrieved from http://www.aspeninstitute.org/about/blog/7-charts-that-show-the-state-of-youth-sports-in-the-us-and-why-it-matters

Lonsdale, C., Hodge, K., & Rose, E. (2009). Athlete burnout in elite sport: A self-determination perspective. *Journal of Sport Sciences, 27*(8), 785–795.

Lumpkin, A., Stoll, S. K., & Beller, J. (2003). *Sport ethics: Applications for fair play* (3rd ed.) New York: McGraw-Hill Education.

Lumpkin, A., Stoll, S. K., & Beller, J. (2011). *Practical ethics in sport management.* Jefferson, NC: McFarland.

Miner, J.W. (2016, June 1). Why 70% of kids quit sports by age 13. Retrieved from https://www.washingtonpost.com/news/parenting/wp/2016/06/01/why-70-percent-of-kids-quit-sports-by-age-13/?utm_term=.50dfe3979bc8

Mission Statement. (2016). Rockland Rockets Basketball. Retrieved from http://www.rocklandrockets.com/page/show/24007-mission-statement

Momaya, A., & Fawal, M. (2015). Performance Enhancing Substances in Sports: A Review of Literature. *Sports Medicine, 45*(4), 517–531.

Monaghan, R. S. (2016, December 19). How not to pray, before, during and after competition. Athletes in Action. Retrieved from http://athletesinaction.org/underreview/how-not-to-pray-before-during-and-after-competition#.WNAikhShjkM

Murphy, S. (n.d.). Dark side of youth sports. Retrieved from http://www.momsteam.com/team-of-experts/six-problems-in-youth-sports?page=0,0

New, J. (2014, October 23). Two decades of paper classes. *Inside Higher Ed*. Retrieved from https://www.insidehighered.com/news/2014/10/23/report-finds-academic-fraud-u-north-carolina-lasted-nearly-20-years

New, J. (2016a, January 14). NCAA establishes 'best practices' for mental health of college athletes. Retrieved from https://www.insidehighered.com/news/2016/01/14/ncaa-establishes-best-practices-mental-health-college-athletes

New, J. (2016b, April 1). Fraud and the Final Four. *Inside Higher Ed*. Retrieved from https://www.insidehighered.com/news/2016/04/01/two-teams-facing-charges-academic-fraud-meet-ncaa-basketball-tournament

NCAA (2016). About NCAA. Retrieved from http://www.ncaa.org/student-athletes/current

NFLPA. (n.d.). Retrieved from https://www.nflpa.com/

O'Donnell, R. (2015, January 05). Kobe Bryant brings three misconceptions about AAU basketball into focus. *SB Nation*. Retrieved from http://www.sbnation.com/nba/2015/1/5/7490697/kobe-bryant-aau-basketball-criticism-misconceptions

Overman, S. J. (2014). *The youth sport crisis: Out-of-control adults, helpless kids*. Denver, CO: Praeger.

Owusu, T. (2017, February 13). Under armour's Steph Curry 3 shoe sa;es are flagging. Retrieved from https://www.thestreet.com/story/13999918/1/under-armour-s-steph-curry-3-shoe-sales-are-flagging.html

Pitt, H., Thomas, S. L., Bestman, A., Daube, M., & Derevensky, J. (2017). Factors the influence children's gambling attitudes and consumption intentions: Lessons for gambling, harm prevention research, policies and advocacy strategies. *Harm reduction Journal, 41*(11).

Puma, M. (n.d.) Not the size of the dog in the fight. ESPN.com Retrieved from http://www.espn.com/classic/biography/s/Alzado_Lyle.html

Reed, K. (2015, November 15). Game over for concussion debate. *USA Today*. Retrieved from http://www.usatoday.com/story/opinion/2015/03/06/youth-sports-avoidance-behavior-column/24383229/

Roche, V. (1993). Football hazing penalty splits tiny Utah town: Student is threatened after his complaint ends his teams season. Los Angelas Times. Retreived from http://articles.latimes.com/1993-11-22/news/mn-59668_1_football-hazing

Rockland Rockets. (2016). Rockland Rockets basketball program. Retrieved from http://www.rocklandrockets.com/page/show/24007-mission-statement

Rush, N. (2013, November 14). 25 biggest bullies in sport history. Athlon Sports & Life. Retrieved from https://athlonsports.com/overtime/25-biggest-bullies-sports-history

Schwarb, A.W. (2015, October 29). Number of NCAA college athletes climbs again. NCAA.org

Sharp, A. (2011, July 20). David Salinas, college basketball and a scandal the NCAA will probably just ignore. Retrieved from http://www.sbnation.com/hamsandwich/2011/7/20/2285146/david-salinas-college-basketball-scandal-ncaa

Sharp, K. (2015, August 18). NFLPA gets concussion lawsuit dismissed. *SB Nation*. Retrieved from http://www.sbnation.com/nfl/2015/8/18/9173377/nflpa-former-nfl-players-concussion-lawsuit-dismissed

Shulman, J. L., & Bowen, W. G. (2001). *The game of life: College sport and educational values*. Princeton, NJ: Princeton University Press.

Solomon, J. (2015a, March 7). What Syracuse's NCAA case revealed about academic fraud. *CBS Sports*. Retrieved from http://www.cbssports.com/collegefootball/writer/jon-solomon/25096871/what-syracuses-ncaa-case-revealed-about-academic-fraud

Solomon, J. (2015b, December 9). Ex-NCAA stars plan movie about exploitation of college athletes. *CBS Sports*. Retrieved from http://www.cbssports.com/college-football/news/ex-ncaa-stars-plan-movie-about-exploiting-college-athletes/

Sperber, M. (1990). *Beer & Circus: How big time college sport has crippled undergraduate education*. New York, NY: Henry Holt and Company.

Sports Illustrated (2017). FIBA to review discriminatory 'ban' on headgear. Time Inc. Retrieved from https://www.si.com/2014/07/25/ap-bko-fiba-headgear-rules

Stophazing.org (2015). Prevention through education: Colorado. Retrieved from http://www.stophazing.org/colorado/

Strauss, C. (2013, December 3). New HBO sports documentary shines light on obsessive sports parents. *USA Today*. Retrieved from http://ftw.usatoday.com/2013/12/peter-berg-hbo-state-of-play

Thein, L. A., Thein, J. M., & Landry, G. L. (1995). Ergogenic aids. *Physical Therapy, (5)*, 426–39.

Tierney, M. (2012, June 2). Not yet in high school, but able to receive college scholarship offers. *New York Times*. Retrieved from http://www.nytimes.com/2012/06/03/sports/ncaabasketball/seeking-recruiting-edge-colleges-court-middle-schoolers.html?pagewanted=all&_r=0

Tomlinson, S. (2013, October 14). Man that led shameful Spanish basketball team who pretended to be disabled to win Paralympic gold found guilty of fraud. *Daily Mail*. Retrieved from http://www.dailymail.co.uk/sport/othersports/article-2459172/Spanish-basketball-team-pretended-disabled-win-Paralympic-gold-guilty-fraud.html

Trahan, K. (2015). Will Greirs PED suspension is another example of why college athletes need a union.

Vice Sports. Retrieved from https://sports.vice.com/en_us/article/will-griers-ped-suspension-is-another-example-of-why-college-athletes-need-a-union

U.S. Department of Health and Human Services. (2008). *2008 Physical Activity Guidelines for Americans.* Retrieved August 11, 2014, from http://www.health.gov/paguidelines/pdf/paguide.pdf

U.S. Department of Labor. (2015). Labor and statistics. Retrieved from http://www.bls.gov/ooh/entertainment-and-sports/athletes-and-sports-competitors.htm

US Legal. (2016, March 17). Law and legal definition of gambling. Retrieved from https://definitions.uslegal.com/g/gambling/

Vacek, H. (2011). The history of gambling. Center for Christian Ethics at Baylor University. Retrieved from https://www.baylor.edu/content/services/document.php/144593.pdf

Vecsey, G. (2006, September 23). When gamesmanship blurs to cheating. *New York Times*. Retrieved from http://www.nytimes.com/2006/09/23/sports/football/23vecsey.html?_r=0

Villalba, D. (2007). Review of selected California legislation: Matt's Law. McGeorge School of Law: University of the Pacific McGeorge law Review.

Vinton, N. (2016, January 30). Concussions are on the rise in the NFL: League releases data that shows a 58% increase in regular season concussions. *New York Daily News*. Retrieved from http://www.nydailynews.com/sports/football/concussions-rise-nfl-league-data-reveals-article-1.2513828

Volsky, G. (1986). Bozworth tells of steroid use. New York Times. Retrieved from http://www.nytimes.com/1986/12/27/sports/bosworth-tells-of-steroid-use.html

Walker, A. (2016, April 29). The Greens call for stronger regulations around gambling in video games. *Allure Media*. Retrieved from https://www.kotaku.com.au/2016/04/the-greens-call-for-stronger-regulations-around-gambling-in-video-games/

Waldron, T. (2014). Muslim basketball player speaks out against internsational federations ban on religious headwear. Think Progress. Retrieved from https://thinkprogress.org/muslim-basketball-player-speaks-out-against-international-federations-ban-on-religious-headwear-3d0c9e2ebde5

Welch, D. (2016, March 15). Nike rejects Stephen Curry's bible verse sneaker, Curry pursues deal with Under Armour instead. *World Religion News*. Retrieved from http://www.worldreligionnews.com/religion-news/christianity/nike-rejects-stephen-currys-bible-verse-sneaker-curry-pursues-deal-with-under-armour-instead

Wilfert, M. (2007). Building new traditions: Hazing prevention in college athletics. Indianapolis, IN. NCAA. Retrieved from https://www.ncaa.org/sites/default/files/hazing%20prevention%20handbook%2057315.pdf

Woo, T. (2015, August 11). Study shows major drop in American youth sport participation. *Sports Illustrated*. Retrieved from http://www.si.com/more-sports/2015/08/11/american-youth-sports-participation-drop-decline-statistics-study

Zaccardi, N. (2013). Spanish official fined for fielding athletes without disabilities at Paralympics. *NBC Sports*. Retrieved from http://olympics.nbcsports.com/2013/10/08/paralympics-scandal-spain-disabilities-sydney-2000/

VIOLENCE AND SPORT

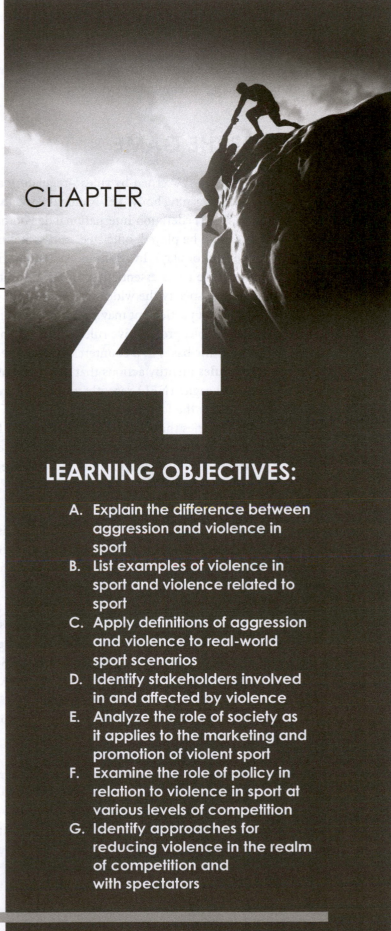

"Umpire attacked at baseball game in South Korea"[i]
"Brazilian referee decapitated after stabbing player"[ii]
"Punch lands Ducks' Blount in hot water"[iii]
"The malice at the Palace"[iv]

The headlines above represent only a handful of actual events involving violence and sport. From the seemingly absurd (see Caldwell, 2008) to acts so gruesome (see BBC, 2013) they would make Eli Roth[1] squirm, the realm of sport—from youth to professional—has been described as a "war without shooting" (Orwell, 1945).

The "war" of sport has consequences both in competition and in greater society. This chapter will examine the difference between physical sport and violence in sport. Students will have the opportunity to examine violence in sport at various levels of competition (e.g., youth/interscholastic, college, professional) as well as the social ramifications of violence involving athletes, spectators and fans, officials, coaches, and

---

1. Described as a "mastermind of some of the grisliest horror films in the business," (Spangler, 2015) Eli Roth is an actor, director and producer known for his work on films including *The Green Inferno*, *Cabin Fever*, and *Hostel*.

LEARNING OBJECTIVES:

A. Explain the difference between aggression and violence in sport
B. List examples of violence in sport and violence related to sport
C. Apply definitions of aggression and violence to real-world sport scenarios
D. Identify stakeholders involved in and affected by violence
E. Analyze the role of society as it applies to the marketing and promotion of violent sport
F. Examine the role of policy in relation to violence in sport at various levels of competition
G. Identify approaches for reducing violence in the realm of competition and with spectators

sport administrators. Finally, students will consider the role of ethics in decision making related to policy in promoting, reducing, or eliminating violence in sport.

RULES OF THE GAME

Sport competitions are governed by rules—regulatory and constitutive (Shogan, 2007). **Regulatory rules** are legislated by a governing body [i.e., National Basketball Association (NBA), National Collegiate Athletic Association (NCAA), Federation International de Football Association (FIFA)]. **Constitutive rules** address how the game should be played, officiated, and sometimes consumed by fans (e.g., fans should not throw objects onto the field of play). In addition, constitutive rules are descriptive, prescriptive, and proscriptive in nature. **Descriptive rules** essentially provide illustrative information about the field of play. For example, descriptive rules specify the width of a soccer goal or the length of a football field. **Prescriptive rules** include "actions that a participant may perform when engaged in a particular game" (Shogan, 2007, p. 26). In baseball, for example, prescriptive rules dictate when a batter can "walk" to first base or how the player should run around the bases in a counterclockwise direction. Finally, and most importantly for this chapter, **proscriptive rules** identify actions that a participant cannot perform in the realm of competition. The National Football League (NFL) recently voted to make "chop blocks" illegal. A **chop block** is a tackling technique that targets the legs, knees, and/or ankles of a football player; the block has resulted in player injury, including injuries that could end a professional football career (Stites, 2016). In short, proscriptive rules are intended to reduce or eliminate violence at all levels of sport (Shogan, 2007). The following section examines perspectives on violence in sport and violence related to sport.

Violence Versus Aggression

What images come to mind when the term "violence" is mentioned? For many, violence evokes images of destruction, physical harm, use of weapons, injury, or even death. According to the *Merriam-Webster Dictionary*, violence is defined as "an exertion of physical force so as to injure or abuse; intense, turbulent, or furious and often destructive action or force" (violence, n.d.). Terry and Jackson (1985) defined **violence** in sport as behavior that occurs outside the rules of the sport and causes harm to a participant. Thus when applying the term violence in a sport context, images such as Mike Tyson biting Evander Holyfield's ear during a boxing match, Chicago Blackhawks star Andrew Shaw screaming homophobic slurs at opposing players and officials, or when world tennis star Monica Seles was stabbed by a fan during a professional tennis match. These examples are clear instances of violence, but what about a hard tackle in football? A bumper tap in a NASCAR race that may lead to a wreck? Or a "body check" in hockey? Are these acts violent, or are they merely perceived as an aggressive action to help an individual or team establish a competitive edge (Burton, 2005)?

Aggression is defined as "the forceful and sometimes overly assertive pursuit of one's aims and interests" (aggression, n.d.). In sport, **aggression** might be perceived as an action to impose physical harm, but may not necessarily be considered violent within the rules of a particular sport competition. In professional hockey, for example, players may "body check" opponents to gain an advantage over the puck. The body-to-body contact is aggressive, but is it violent? Does it violate the proscriptive rules of the game? Even within this example and those listed in the previous paragraph, it can be difficult to know whether an action in the field of competition is violent or an act of aggression. This also begs the question, are aggressive acts always violent? If not, at what point does an aggressive act, intended to gain a competitive advantage, turn violent?

Leonard (1988) identified two types of aggression—instrumental and reactive. **Instrumental aggression** is task-oriented and applied without emotion. Consider basketball players as they line up along the lane during a free throw. As the shooter prepares to release the ball, the players lower their bodies and widen their stances, often extending their arms in a defensive position to prevent the opponent from grabbing the rebound. When the ball is released from the shooter's hands, the basketball players use their bodies to gain a positional advantage. Often the player who exhibits the most aggression gets the rebound. This is an example of instrumental aggression as it is task-oriented and rarely involves emotion as these actions fall within the prescriptive rules of the game.

Reactive aggression, on the other hand, involves emotion and the intent to harm a competitor. To illustrate reactive aggression, examine the 2006 FIFA World Cup Final. In the much-anticipated showdown between France and Italy, French soccer star and team captain Zinedine Zidane spent much of the second half "trash-talking" with Italian defender Marco Materazzi. In the 110th minute of the match, shortly before the penalty shootout, Materazzi made a derogatory reference about Zidane's sister. Zidane retaliated with a headbutt to Materazzi and was subsequently given a red card and removed from the game. France lost to Italy on penalty kicks, 5 to 3. In short, Zidane was angered (emotion) by the comments of Materazzi. The emotion inspired by the comments provoked Zidane to retaliate (react) against and harm Materazzi.

SMALL GROUP ACTIVITY:
Think about the definitions of violence, aggression, and proscriptive rules. In the context of sport, complete the following:
- Give an example of an action in the realm of sport competition that you perceived to be violent.
  - o Describe the factors that contributed to the violence.
  - o Explain how players, officials, and fans reacted to the violent act.
  - o Discuss if the act was perceived to be a violation of a proscriptive rule. If so, how do you know? If not, why not?
- Give an example of an action in the realm of sport that you perceived to be aggressive, but not necessarily violent.
  - o Describe the factors that contributed to the aggression.
  - o Explain how players, officials, and fans reacted to the aggressive act.
  - o Discuss if the act was perceived to be a violation of a proscriptive rule. If so, how do you know? If not, why not?

While this chapter focuses primarily on violence, it is important to be able to distinguish between violent and aggressive activity in sport and in social sport settings. The next section explores violence in and outside of competition.

Violence in Competition

Violence has long been an issue in sport competition and in off-the-field settings still associated with sport (e.g., spectator violence, riots due to winning or losing a game). Thus, researchers have sought to better understand the types of violence that occur in both settings. First, consider violence in competition.

Smith (1983, p. 34) identified four types of sport violence:

1. **Brutal body contact:** Conforms to the rules of the sport and comprises all significant contact performed within the official rules of the game.
2. **Borderline violence:** Violates the rules of the game, but is widely accepted as part of the sport.
3. **Quasi-criminal violence:** Practices that violate the formal rules of the game, public laws, and even informal norms among players. May or may not be perceived as acceptable by officials, players, or spectators.
4. **Criminal violence:** Violates the official rules of the sport, the law of the land, and players' informal norms. Not accepted by officials, players, or spectators.

According to Smith, these types of on-the-field violence are identified by their escalation or level of violence and examples of violence within each typology (Figure 4.1).

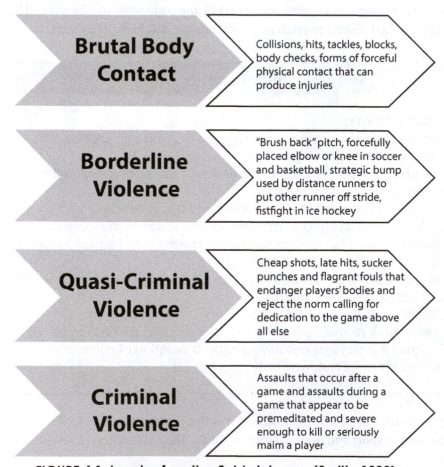

Brutal Body Contact — Collisions, hits, tackles, blocks, body checks, forms of forceful physical contact that can produce injuries

Borderline Violence — "Brush back" pitch, forcefully placed elbow or knee in soccer and basketball, strategic bump used by distance runners to put other runner off stride, fistfight in ice hockey

Quasi-Criminal Violence — Cheap shots, late hits, sucker punches and flagrant fouls that endanger players' bodies and reject the norm calling for dedication to the game above all else

Criminal Violence — Assaults that occur after a game and assaults during a game that appear to be premeditated and severe enough to kill or seriously maim a player

FIGURE 4.1. Levels of on-the-field violence. (Smith, 1983)

TECHNOLOGY TIME-OUT

Using your smartphone, tablet, or laptop computer, find one example of each type of violence defined above that has occurred at any level of sport (youth/interscholastic, college, and/or professional) in the last 5 years. Complete the following:

1. Apply the appropriate types of violence to your real-world examples. Fill in the "real-world example" column in the chart below with your corresponding examples.
2. Explain why the type of violence you selected applies to the example you identified.
3. Describe the consequences of the violent behavior for the athlete/fan/official.
4. Based on the definitions of aggression and violence, do you perceive the acts to be aggressive, violent, or both? Explain why. What factors did you consider when determining the difference between an aggressive or violent act?
5. If you could reclassify the violence typologies to include your understanding of aggression versus violence, how would you do so?
6. Discuss what you learned from this exercise.

TECHNOLOGY TIME-OUT CHART

TYPE OF VIOLENCE	DEFINITION	REAL-WORLD EXAMPLE
Brutal body contact	Physical practices common in certain sports and accepted by athletes as part of sport participation.	
Borderline violence	Practices that violate the rules of the game but are accepted by most players and coaches as consistent with the norms.	
Quasi-criminal violence	Practices that violate the formal rules of the game, public laws, and even informal norms among players.	
Criminal violence	Practices that are clearly outside the law to the point that athletes condemn them without question and law enforcement officials may prosecute them as crimes.	

Identifying an aggressive action versus violence in the realm of competition may be difficult, unless it rises to the level of quasi-criminal or criminal violence. Prior research on the violent nature of sport has failed to appropriately account for context (Raney & DePalma, 2006). Still, others argue that violence is aggression in its severe form, meaning it is possible to have aggressive acts that are not necessarily violent (Cox, 2002).

Sport managers must be able to identify and hold accountable athletes, officials, and spectators who violate regulatory and constitutive (e.g., prescriptive, proscriptive, descriptive) rules of the game.

But what happens when an athlete violates rules *outside* of competition? What happens when fans and spectators engage in violent acts as they relate to a competition or the outcome of a competition? What role does sport play in the perpetuation and perception of violence outside of competition? The next section will help answers these questions.

VIOLENCE OUTSIDE OF COMPETITION

At the beginning of this chapter, headlines from real media outlets describing violence at sport events were introduced. They described violence committed by athletes and/or officials in the realm of competition. The headlines could have easily read like this:

> *"Lamb leg thrown at football match"[v]*
> *"Riots erupt in Vancouver after Canucks loss"[vi]*
> *"93 are dead after a crush at soccer game in England"[vii]*
> *"George Huguely V sentenced to 23 years for Yeardley Love murder"[viii]*
> *"Manny Pacquiao's contract terminated by Nike following homophobic comments"[ix]*
> *"Parent rage at youth hockey game ends in death"[x]*

Each of these headlines depicts a violent event that occurred at a sport venue between fans and spectators or a violent event in the personal lives of athletes. Many may also recall the names of other popular athletes, venues, or fan affiliations connected to violent events.

QUICK RECALL EXERCISE;
First, select a level of play—youth/interscholastic, college, or professional (including international competitions). Next, in a small group (three or four students), you have one minute to identify violent events that involve athletes or fans/spectators outside the field of competition at the level you selected (i.e., youth/interscholastic, college, or professional). If necessary you may use your smartphone, tablet, or laptop computer, but before you do, see how many your group can identify without technical assistance.

Small to Large Group Discussion
Based on your findings, answer the following questions.
1. How many violent events could you identify?
2. What event incited the violent act?
3. Could the violent act have been prevented? If so, how? If not, why not?
4. What did you learn from this exercise?

Athletic Violence

As noted in the previous exercise, off-the-field violence occurs in many forms and at every level of competition. These incidents often reflect problems in society. The following paragraphs will address some of the more prevalent social issues involving athletes outside the realm of competition.

Domestic Violence

Domestic violence has long been considered a social issue in the United States and abroad. Defined as "a pattern of behavior used to establish power and control over another person through fear and intimidation, often including the threat or use of violence," domestic violence affects millions of people every year. Physical assaults and psychological, sexual, and economic abuse are all forms of domestic violence. Statistics suggest that every 9 seconds a woman is assaulted or beaten in the United States (NCADV, 2016). To put this into context, by the completion of this chapter and participating in the activities (approximately 1 hour), 400 women will have experienced physical violence. One in three women and one in four men will experience physical violence by an intimate partner in their lifetime (NCADV, 2016). Look around the classroom. Of the 20 men in the room, 5 are likely to be victims of domestic violence.

Despite the fact that domestic violence has been identified as a complex social issue affecting individuals of every gender, race, socioeconomic status, sexual orientation, and other factors for hundreds of years, rarely does it gain media attention. Recently, however, high-profile athletes including Ray Rice (formerly Baltimore Ravens), Aroldis Chapman (New York Yankees), Johnny Manziel (formerly Cleveland Browns), and Greg Hardy (formerly Dallas Cowboys) have found themselves in the spotlight for documented acts of domestic violence. One of the most well-known policies addressing domestic violence issues stems from the documented footage involving Ray Rice. The new policy was outlined in a letter to National Football League (NFL) team owners from NFL commissioner Roger Goodell. The commissioner's letter outlined actions to "reinforce and enhance" policies relating to domestic violence including punishments levied against players and/or team personnel:

> "Effective immediately, violations of the Personal Conduct Policy regarding assault, battery, domestic violence or sexual assault that involve physical force will be subject to a suspension without pay of six games for a first offense, with consideration given to mitigating factors, as well as a longer suspension when circumstances warrant. Among the circumstances that would merit a more severe penalty would be a prior incident before joining the NFL, or violence involving a weapon, choking, repeated striking, or when the act is committed against a pregnant woman or in the presence of a child. A second offense will result in banishment from the NFL; while an individual may petition for reinstatement after one year, there will be no presumption or assurance that the petition will be granted. These disciplinary standards will apply to all NFL personnel" (Farmer, 2014).

As a result of the NFL's more stringent policy, the governing bodies of other professional sport leagues and intercollegiate athletics have created and implemented policies punishing players for engaging in acts of domestic violence, while also providing programs and support for survivors of domestic violence.

Discrimination

Many are familiar with the term discrimination. To refresh, **discrimination** is the practice of "unfairly treating a person or group of people differently from other people or groups of people" (discrimination, n.d.). Discrimination can take many forms, including (but not limited to) treating people differently due to age, disability, national origin, race, religion, or sex. Moreover, discrimination can take many forms. As you will learn in the chapter on Diversity and Inclusion, sport organizations and national governing bodies are adopting policies to prevent discrimination and encourage inclusion. Still, in sport, racism in the form of athletes and fans using racial slurs against other athletes of color has become commonplace. There have been attempts to circumvent sexism with the enactment of Title IX and other gender equity policies. Men and women who are (or are thought to be) homosexual are often not hired for jobs in coaching or athletic administration due to negative stereotypes associated with gay, lesbian, bisexual, and transgender people. Persons with disabilities may have trouble accessing facilities or opportunities for sport participation despite efforts to create laws to enhance opportunities for sport engagement.

Often people who report discrimination or other unethical behavior are labeled as "whistleblowers" (see Whistleblowers.gov). While the law protects whistleblowers from retaliation by an employer, it does not necessarily protect the whistleblower from social or psychological consequences. One infamous bullying scandal in the NFL involving Jonathan Martin and Richie Incognito. Martin accused teammate Incognito of bullying by imposing mental abuse through derogatory language about Martin's playing ability, family, and race. When Martin reported the abuse, both he and Incognito faced inquiry from the team and media. Martin was reviled for not being "man enough" to stand up against Incognito's "typical football player" banter. Today, Martin's professional football career is over. Incognito currently plays for the Buffalo Bills.

1-MINUTE REFLECTION
When you consider the definition of "discrimination," do you perceive discrimination to be violent? Why or why not? How might homophobic comments, racial slurs, and other derogatory language be perceived as violent?

Hazing

Hazing is anything committed against someone joining or becoming a member in any organization that is humiliating, intimidating, or demeaning that could endanger the health and safety of that person (as discussed in Chapter 3). Not surprisingly, hazing and bullying have somehow become common practices on sport teams in an attempt to forge teammate relationships and establish a hierarchy. According to the National Study of Student Hazing (Allan & Madden, 2008), more than half of respondents had experienced hazing as a member of a club or team. Another study suggests that 80% of NCAA athletes experience some form of hazing during their college athletic career (Doyle, 2015). Excessive alcohol consumption, humiliation, isolation, sleep-deprivation, and sex acts were identified as the most common hazing practices. The consequences of hazing can have catastrophic short- and long-term consequences, including:

- Physical, emotional, and/or mental instability
- Sleep deprivation
- Loss of sense of control and empowerment
- Decline in grades and coursework
- Relationships with friends, significant others, and family suffer
- Post-traumatic stress syndrome
- Loss of respect for and interest in being part of the organization
- Erosion of trust within the group members
- Illness or hospitalization with additional effects on family and friends
- Death (HazingPrevention.org, 2016).

Despite the fact that 71% of students hazed identified suffering from the aforementioned consequences, nearly 95% of hazing incidents go unreported. Perhaps this is because hazing in sport is perceived as commonplace and part of the experience regardless of the consequences. Moreover, hazing often involves other forms of violence, including physical assault, rape, psychological torment, and verbal harassment.

CLASS REFLECTION
Schneider (2008) proposed that athletes who compete in violent sports "may have an affinity for violence and thus are attracted to violent sport" (p. 179). The class should be divided so that half the students argue in support of this statement; the other half must argue against this statement.

FAN VIOLENCE AT SPORT VENUES

Despite the potential consequences for athletes, fans, and officials, violence and aggression have become hallmarks of the most-popular, modern spectator sports (Jewell, Moti, & Coates, 2011) both on and off the field of competition. Violence and aggressive behavior occurs not only between players, but also between fans and spectators.

Alcohol

"Dollar beer nights." "Thirsty Thursdays." Many professional and collegiate sport organizations use the draw of alcohol to lure a crowd. Even the nearly $8 beer at Fenway is likely to entice a fan to "have a good time." However, much of the violence perpetrated by fans and spectators at sport events or in reaction to sport events is due to alcohol consumption and intoxication. A team of researchers from the University of Minnesota found that 1 in 12 fans attending professional sport events in the United States will leave the stadium legally drunk (Neporent, 2011). Not only do intoxicated fans pose a threat to the general public when leaving the stadium, but inside they may be more likely to engage in verbal and physical altercations. Simply perform a Google search for "intoxicated fan" it is likely that stories detailing fans falling multiple stories from a stadium balcony to the concrete below, theft, lawsuits against sport organizations because intoxicated fans assaulted and caused injury to other spectators, and any number of images and videos capturing fan-on-fan violence.

At the collegiate level, the NCAA states that the "Illegal use and abuse of alcohol is contrary to the mission of the NCAA and destroys such fundamental values as respect, fairness, civility, honesty, and responsibility" (CCSAP, n.d.). Within this resolution, colleges and universities were also encouraged to: (1) prohibit the sale of alcoholic beverages during all preseason, regular season, conference, and post-season collegiate events; (2) promote only the legal and responsible use of alcohol; (3) prohibit on-site alcohol advertising; (4) prohibit media advertising of alcoholic beverages exceeding 6% alcohol by volume (ABV); (5) limit advertisements of alcoholic beverages under 6% (ABV); and (6) provide programs and resources for the education, prevention, and treatment of alcohol abuse (CCASP). However, many NCAA Division I institutions disregard this "encouragement" from the NCAA as alcohol sales are important alternative revenue streams for cash-strapped as well as well-to-do athletic departments (ESPN, 2014). Even the NCAA disregarded its own messaging when, in January 2016, the Division I board approved a waiver allowing alcohol sales at baseball and softball national championship series.

Projectiles and Stampedes

Intoxicated or not, sport fans also engage in violent acts like throwing objects onto the field of play or rushing the court or field after a triumphant victory. In a 2016 game against the Cincinnati Bengals, Pittsburgh Steeler quarterback Ben Roethlisberger was carted off the field after sustaining an injury. Cincinnati fans threw garbage, including full water bottles, at Roethlisberger as he left the field. Ice hockey fans are notorious for their ingenuity in tossing projectiles onto the ice. Infamous objects include an octopus, rats, catfish, and umbrellas. While fans might throw objects out of tradition (think hat trick in hockey) or poor sportsmanship, any item thrown into the field of competition poses a danger to players, officials, and other fans.

Similarly, fans who "rush the field" or "storm the court" pose additional risks. Often these fan surges have the potential to injure other fans who lose their footing and may be trampled by the crowd. In 1989, 98 people died and hundreds were injured from an incident at a FC soccer match at Hillsborough Stadium where too many fans were let into the game (Gordon, n.d.). Additionally, large crowds may prevent security from reaching players, officials, or other fans who may be in harm's way. Large crowds in a sport venue pose significant security risks and may create situations in which more violence can erupt.

FAN VIOLENCE OUTSIDE OF SPORT VENUES

In addition to violence in the realm of competition and in the sport venue, violence also occurs outside of sport venues, often in reaction to the outcome of sport events. In 2011, the Vancouver Canucks were swept by the Boston Bruins in the Stanley Cup Final. More than 20,000 Canucks fans took to the streets, setting fire to storefronts, looting, and turning over police cars. Public transportation was suspended and hospitals were overrun with injuries sustained from the riot. Fans at West Virginia University had such a long history of setting fire to furniture, specifically couches, following major victories in football and basketball, that the city council had to ban outdoor upholstered furniture so that fans could not set it on fire (Volk, 2015). In addition, couch burning became a felony in the city of Morgantown.

The popularity and spectacle of sport also often draw tens if not hundreds of thousands of people to a single space, the venue, and surrounding areas. As such, sport events become targets of terrorism. In 1972 at the Munich Olympics, a Palestinian militant group took nine Israeli national team members and representatives hostage. Eleven Israeli athletes and coaches were murdered (two during the initial storming of the Olympic Village, and nine during a botched rescue attempt). The 1996 Olympics in Atlanta were marred by the detonation of three bombs in Centennial Olympic Park; two people were killed and more than 120 were injured. On April 15, 2013, two bombs exploded near the finish line of the Boston Marathon killing three spectators and injuring more than 260 people. Given the scope of mega-events like the Olympics or the Boston Marathon, it can be difficult for event organizers and security officials to ensure the safety and security of all participants and spectators.

SMALL GROUP ACTIVITY

In a small group (three or four students), pick an issue of violence discussed in this chapter. Identify the level of sport (youth/interscholastic, college, or professional) for which you would like to create a new policy. In your small group, draft a policy that you believe would help reduce the aspect of violence you identified. Consider the stakeholders involved, the practicality of implementation and the potential consequences for implementation.

MARKETING AND PROMOTING VIOLENCE IN SPORT

Violence in sport is attractive to many fans and has been identified as a motivator and predictor for watching and attending sport events (Greenwell, Hancock, Simmons, & Thorn, 2015; Greenwell, Thorn, & Simmons, 2015; Paul, Weinbach, & Robbins, 2013). Violence in sport and violent aspects of sport are attractive to fans and spectators because violence adds excitement to the event (Goldstein & Arms, 1971; Raney & Kinnally, 2009). People are also motivated to watch sport because they enjoy the violence (Andrew, Koo, Hardin, &

Greenwell, 2009). Some research suggests that fans enjoy violence because it offers spectators the opportunity to, in some way, release their own hostility and anger (Bryant, Zillman, & Raney, 1998). For example, studies have shown that attendance at National Hockey League games is higher when there are greater instances of fighting (Paul, 2003). Aggressive driving in NASCAR is appealing to some fans as it might lead to wrecks or fights between drivers (Von Allmen & Sollow, 2012). While fans of mixed martial arts (MMA) seek the excitement of a fighter submitting or knocking an opponent unconscious.

1-MINUTE REFLECTION

From a sport management perspective, is it ethical to market and promote the violent aspect of sport? Why or why not? Defend your answer.

CONCLUSION

Violence in sport occurs at every level of competition. Athletes, officials, and fans and spectators can perpetuate violence; however, they also have the opportunity to reduce violence. Sport managers will be tasked with creating an environment that is safe for all. Part of creating that environment is to understand the components of violence and aggression, as well as the contexts that can contribute to violent incidents. It is important to consider how to address issues with players, fans, and officials to maintain the integrity of the game and enhance the fan experience.

DISCUSSION QUESTIONS

1. Explain the difference between aggression and violence in sport.

2. What are the different rules of the game and how do they differ between the varying leagues?

3. What are the four types of violence in competition? How are they different? Provide an example of each.

4. What type of ethical reasoning could explain violence that happens within the rules of the game? Outside of the game?

5. Is hazing an ethical issue? Provide an example of a hazing situation not discussed in the text. Was the situation ethical? Why or why not?

6. Describe a time in which violence happened at a sporting event. Was it an ethical concern?

7. Can athletes, officials, fans and spectators perpetuate violence? How?

CASE STUDY: ATTACK AT THE RINK

On January 6, 1994, Shane Stant attacked Nancy Kerrigan with a collapsible baton during a practice round at Cobo Arena in Detroit, Michigan. At the time of the attack, Kerrigan was considered the United States' best female figure skater and a gold medal favorite for the Olympics in Lillehammer, Norway (Longman, 1994). The day after the attack, Tonya Harding, another United States Olympic hopeful, skated in and won the national championship in Detroit, securing her spot on the Olympic team. The days following the attack were filled with media coverage and speculation about what occurred.

Less than a week after the attack, the FBI began investigating Harding's ex-husband Jeff Gillooly and bodyguard Shawn Eckardt after Portland minister Eugene Sanders told investigators he heard a recording of the two men discussing the attack with the actual attacker Shane Stant (Muldoon, 2014). In a confession to the FBI, Eckardt implicated Harding, Gillooly, and his friends Stant and Derrick Smith. Eckardt and Smith were arrested on January 12, 1994, and Stant surrendered to the FBI in Phoenix, Arizona, two days later (Muldoon, 2014). One week later Gillooly turned himself into authorities following the issuing of an arrest warrant. Throughout the entire investigation Harding maintained her innocence. In a prepared statement, Harding said, "Despite my mistakes and my rough edges, I have done nothing to violate the standards of excellence in sportsmanship that are expected in an Olympic athlete" (Crossman, 2013).

The investigation took an interesting turn when Kathy Peterson, owner of the Dockside Saloon, found trash bags in her restaurant's dumpsters that were not hers. She went through the trash to determine who was taking advantage of the services

Tinseltown/shutterstock.com

for which she paid and found Gillooly's name and address, a check from the United States Figure Skating Association, and an envelope with doodles on it (Crossman, 2013). The envelope was a key piece of evidence as the handwriting was Harding's and notes were from the conversation she had with her ex-husband planning the attack on Kerrigan. The envelope contained the arena's name and phone number, which Gillooly claimed Harding used to call and get the practice time of Kerrigan.

Although Kerrigan did not skate in the national championships because they occurred a day after the attack, she was given the second spot on the Olympic team (Crossman, 2013). With the aftermath of the attack and subsequent investigation, the question was whether or not Harding should be allowed to compete in the Olympics. The United States Olympic Committee (USOC) scheduled a hearing to determine if Harding should be removed from the team. Harding sued to block the meeting. She later dropped the lawsuit, which led the USOC to concede and allow her to skate in the Olympics (Crossman, 2013). The Olympic television ratings soared as the drama surrounding the two was intense. Harding ended up getting eighth place, while Kerrigan skated for gold, but earned the silver medal (Muldoon, 2014).

Just weeks after the Olympics, Harding pled guilty to conspiracy to hinder prosecution. She was placed on probation, ordered to pay $160,000 in fines and forced to resign from the U.S. Figure Skating Association (Muldoon, 2014). Despite pleading guilty to hindering the prosecution, as evidenced in the ESPN 30 for 30 film, *The Price of Gold*, Harding reaffirmed her claim she knew absolutely nothing about the attack. While the documentary focused on Harding and provided her with the platform to maintain her innocence, her animosity toward Kerrigan was still evident as she called her a "crybaby that didn't win the gold" (Holmes, 2014).

CASE QUESTIONS

1. What type of violence is depicted in this situation? Explain your answer.

2. Discuss your perspective on whether or not the USOC should have given Nancy Kerrigan the number two spot on the Olympic team despite not being able to qualify for the team.

3. Should the USOC have allowed Harding to skate in the Olympics? Defend your answer.

4. Discuss the role of the media in the Kerrigan/Harding saga, including the ESPN 30 for 30 film, *The Price of Gold*.

GLOSSARY

Aggression might be perceived as an action to impose physical harm, but may not necessarily be considered violent within the rules of a particular sport competition.

Borderline violence violates the rules of the game, but is widely accepted as part of the sport.

Brutal body contact conforms to the rules of the sport and comprises all significant contact performed within the official rules of the game.

Chop block is a tackling technique that targets the legs, knees, and/or ankles of a football player; the block has resulted in player injury, including injuries that could end a professional football career.

Constitutive rules address how the game should be played, officiated, and sometimes consumed by fans (e.g., fans should not throw objects onto the field of play).

Criminal violence violates the official rules of the sport, the law of the land, and players' informal norms. Not accepted by officials, players, or spectators.

Descriptive rules essentially provide illustrative information about the field of play.

Discrimination is the practice of "unfairly treating a person or group of people differently from other people or groups of people."

Domestic violence has long been considered a social issue in the United States and abroad. Defined as "a pattern of behavior used to establish power and control over another person through fear and intimidation, often including the threat or use of violence."

Hazing is nything committed against someone joining or becoming a member in any organization that is humiliating, intimidating, or demeaning that could endanger the health and safety of that person.

Instrumental aggression is task-oriented and applied without emotion.

Prescriptive rules include "actions that a participant may perform when engaged in a particular game" (Shogan, 2007, p. 26).

Proscriptive rules identify actions that a participant cannot perform in the realm of competition.

Quasi-criminal violence is a practice which violates the formal rules of the game, public laws, and even informal norms among players. May or may not be perceived as acceptable by officials, players, or spectators.

Reactive aggression involves emotion and the intent to harm a competitor.

Regulatory rules are legislated by a governing body [i.e., National Basketball Association (NBA), National Collegiate Athletic Association (NCAA), Federation International de Football Association (FIFA)].

Violence involves behavior that occurs outside the rules of the sport and causes harm to a participant.

References

Abrams, J. (2012, March 20). The malice at the palace. *Grantland*. Retrieved from http://grantland.com/features/an-oral-history-malice-palace/

Aggression. (n.d.). *Merriam Webster's collegiate dictionary*. Retrieved from http://www.merriam-webster.com/dictionary/aggression

Allan, E. J., & Madden, M. (2008). *Hazing in view: College students at risk*. Retrieved from http://www.stophazing.org/wp-content/uploads/2014/06/hazing_in_view_web1.pdf

Al-Samarri, R. (2016, February 17). Manny Pacquiao's contract terminated by Nike following homophobic comments. *MailOnline*. Retrieved from http://www.dailymail.co.uk/sport/boxing/article-3451652/Nike-terminate-Manny-Pacquiao-contract-following-homophobic-comments.html

Andrew, D. P. S., Koo, G., Hardin, R., & Greenwell, T. C. (2009). Analyzing motives of minor league hockey fans: The introduction of violence as a spectator motive. *International Journal of Sport Management and Marketing, 5*(1), 73–89.

BBC. (2013, July 7). Brazil referee decapitated after stabbing player. *British Broadcasting Corporation*. Retrieved from http://www.bbc.com/news/world-latin-america-23215676

Bryant, J., Zillmann, D., & Raney, A. A. (1998). Violence and the enjoyment of media sports. *MediaSport*, 252–265.

Burton, R. W. (2005). Aggression and sport. *Clinics in Sports Medicine, 24*(4), 845–852.

Caldwell, J. (2008, March 24). Lamb leg thrown at football match. *BBC News*. Retrieved from http://news.bbc.co.uk/2/hi/uk_news/northern_ireland/7311282.stm

CBC News. (2011, June 15). Riots erupt in Vancouver after Canucks loss. Retrieved from http://www.cbc.ca/news/canada/british-columbia/riots-erupt-in-vancouver-after-canucks-loss-1.993707

CCSAP. (n.d.). Alcohol advertising and NCAA sporting events. Retrieved from http://ccsap.wsu.edu/position-statements/alcohol-advertising/alcohol-advertising-and-ncaa-sporting-events/

Cox, R. H. (2002). *Sport psychology: Concepts and applications* (5th ed.). Toronto: McGraw Hill.

Crossman, M. (2013, December 19). Harding-Kerrigan 20 years later: Remembering the stunning, life-changing attack. *Bleacher Report*. Retrieved from http://bleacherreport.com/articles/1887592-harding-kerrigan-20-years-later-remembering-the-stunning-life-changing-attack

Discrimination. (n.d.). *Merriam Webster's collegiate dictionary*. Retrieved from http://www.merriam-webster.com/dictionary/discrimination

Doyle, K. (2015, December 28). Hazing is still common in collegiate and youth sport. *The Huffington Post*. Retrieved from http://www.huffingtonpost.com/entry/hazing-youth-college-sports_us_56814d6de4b06fa688809254

ESPN. (2014). Schools eye beer sales for help. Retrieved from http://espn.go.com/college-football/story/_/id/11392186/colleges-turning-beer-sales-stadiums-alternative-revenue-stream

Farmer, S. (28 August, 2014). NFL sets new penalties on domestic violence, sexual assault violations. *Los Angeles Times*. Retrieved from http://www.latimes.com/sports/nfl/la-sp-nfl-domestic-violence-20140829-story.html

Flaherty, M. P. (2012, August 30). George Huguely V sentenced to 23 years for Yeardley Love murder. *The Washington Post*. Retrieved from https://www.washingtonpost.com/local/crime/george-huguely-sentencing/2012/08/30/517821a4-f2b8-11e1-adc6-87dfa8eff430_story.html

Goldstein, J. H., & Arms, R. L. (1971). Effects of observing athletic contests on hostility. *Sociometry, 34*, 83–90.

Gordon, D. (n.d.). ESPN Films: 30 for 30 Hillsborough. Retrieved from http://www.espn.com/30for30/film?page=hillsborough

Greenwell, T. C., Hancock, M., Simmons, J. M., & Thorn, D. (2015). The effects of gender and social roles on the marketing of combat sport. *Sport Marketing Quarterly, 24*(1), 19–29.

Greenwell, T. C., Thorn, D., & Simmons, J. M. (2015). How is violence used to promote mixed martial arts? *International Journal of Sport Marketing and Sponsorship, 16*, 249–260.

HazingPrevention.org. (2016). Hazing and its consequences. Retrieved from http://hazingprevention.org/home/hazing/hazing-and-its-consequences/

Holmes, L. (2014, January 14). Complicating the Tonya and Nancy narratives, 20 years later. *NPR*. Retrieved from http://www.npr.org/sections/monkeysee/2014/01/16/263073794/complicating-the-tonya-and-nancy-narratives-20-years-later

Jewell, R. T., Moti, A., & Coates, D. (2011). A brief history of violence and aggression in spectator sports. In R. T. Jewell (ed.) *Violence and aggression in sporting contests: Economics, history, and policy.* Springer: New York.

Leonard, W. M. (1988). *A sociological perspective of sport* (3rd ed.). New York, NY: Macmillan Publishing Company.

Lohr, S. (1989, April 16). 93 are dead after a crush at a soccer game in England. *The New York Times.* Retrieved from http://www.nytimes.com/1989/04/16/world/93-are-dead-after-a-crush-at-soccer-game-in-england.html

Longman, J. (1994, January 6). Jealousy on ice. *The New York Times.* Retrieved from http://www.nytimes.com/packages/html/sports/year_in_sports/01.06.html

Maisel, I. (2009, September 4). Punch lands Ducks' Blount in hot water. *ESPN.* Retrieved from http://espn.go.com/ncf/news/story?id=4444898

Mazza, E. (2014, May 1). Umpire attacked at baseball game in South Korea. *Huffington Post.* Retrieved from http://www.huffingtonpost.com/2014/05/01/umpire-attacked-south-korea_n_5244923.html

Muldoon, K. (2014, January 6). Tonya Harding–Nancy Kerrigan 20 years later: The highlights in a timeline. *Oregon Live.* Retrieved from http://www.oregonlive.com/tonya-harding/2014/01/tonya_harding-nancy_kerrigan_2.html

NCADV. (2016). Statistics. National Coalition Against Domestic Violence. Retrieved from http://www.ncadv.org/learn/statistics

Neporent, L. (2011, January 19). Study finds one in 12 are drunk at major sporting events. *ABC News.* Retrieved from http://abcnews.go.com/Health/tailgaters-drunk-sporting-events/story?id=12646946

O'Donnell, K. (Reporter), & Brokaw, T. (Anchor). (2000, July 10). "Parent Rage" at youth hockey game ends in death. [Television series episode]. *NBC Nightly News.* Retrieved from https://highered.nbclearn.com/portal/site/HigherEd/browse/?cuecard=2308

Orwell, G. (1945). The sporting spirit. Retrieved from http://www.orwell.ru/library/articles/spirit/english/e_spirit

Paul, R. J. (2003). Variations in NHL attendance: The impact of violence, scoring, and regional rivalries. *American Journal of Economics and Sociology, 62*(2), 345–364.

Paul, R. J., Weinbach, A. P., & Robbins, D. (2013). American Hockey League attendance: A study of fan preferences for fighting, team performance, and promotions. *International Journal of Sport Finance, 8*(1), 21–38.

Raney, A. A., & Depalma, A. J. (2006). The effect of viewing varying levels and contexts of violent sports programming on enjoyment, mood, and perceived violence. *Mass Communication and Society, 9*(3), 321–328.

Raney, A. A., & Kinnally, W. (2009). Examining perceived violence in and enjoyment of televised rivalry sports contests. *Mass Communication and Society, 12*, 311–331.

Schneider, R. C. (2008). Violence in sport: Ethically acceptable boundaries. In R. C. Schneider (Ed.), *Ethics of sport & athletics* (pp. 173–208). Philadelphia, PA: Lippincott, Williams, & Wilkins.

Shogan, D. (2007). *Sport ethics in context.* Toronto, Ontario: Canadian Scholars' Press, Inc.

Smith, M. D. (1983). What is sport violence? A sociolegal perspective. In J. H. Goldstein (Ed.), *Sports Violence* (pp. 33–46). New York, NY: Springer-Verlag New York, Inc.

Spangler, T. (2015, October 22). Eli Roth on Netflix's 'Hemlock Grove' season 3: 'It had even me shocked.' *Variety.* Retrieved from http://variety.com/2015/digital/news/eli-roth-netflix-hemlock-grove-season-3-1201624414/

Stites, A. (22 March, 2016). NFL removes exemptions and bans all chop blocks. *SB Nation.* Retrieved from http://www.sbnation.com/nfl/2016/3/22/11262136/chop-blocks-nfl-rule-change-competition-committee

Terry, P. C., & Jackson, J. J. (1985). The determinants of control of violence in sport. *Quest, 37*(1), 27–37.

Violence. (n.d.). *Merriam Webster's collegiate dictionary.* Retrieved from http://www.merriam-webster.com/dictionary/violence

Volk, P. (2015). West Virginia fans burn couches so often, outdoor furniture is now illegal. *SBNation.* Retrieved from http://www.sbnation.com/2015/4/9/8378219/west-virginia-couch-burn-outdoor-furniture-ban

Von Allmen, P., & Solow, J. (2012). The demand for aggressive behavior in American stock car racing. In *Violence and Aggression in Sporting Contests* (pp. 79–95). New York: Springer.

Whistleblowers.gov. (2016). The whistleblowers protection program. Retrieved from http://www.whistleblowers.gov/

ENDNOTES

i. Mazza (2014) reported an angry fan attacked a baseball umpire for a possible blown call.

ii. Soccer fans decapitated a referee after the referee stabbed a player for failing to leave the field after an ejection (BBC, 2013).

iii. University of Oregon football standout LeGarrette Blount punched a Boise State University (BSU) football player shortly after a loss to BSU (Maisel, 2009).

iv. Indiana Pacers player Ron Artest leapt into stands with teammates Jermaine O'Neal and Stephen Jackson to fight fans who threw a drink onto Artest (Abrams, 2012).

v. The leg of a lamb was thrown at a soccer official during the match between Ballymena United and Distillery, teams of the NIFL Danske Bank Premiership (Caldwell, 2008).

vi. Following the Vancouver Canucks' elimination loss in the National Hockey League Stanley Cup finals, dozens of fans were injured during violent riots and looting in downtown Vancouver (CBC News, 2011).

vii. Known as the "Hillsborough Disaster," 93 people were killed and nearly 200 were injured when fans surged forward in overly crowded stands during a soccer match in Sheffield (Lohr, 1989).

viii. University of Virginia (UVA) men's lacrosse player George Huguely was found guilty of murdering UVA women's lacrosse player and ex-girlfriend, Yeardley Love, following a domestic violence dispute (Flaherty, 2012).

ix. In a television interview during his campaign for political office, Manny Pacquiao claimed homosexuals are "worse than animals." His homophobic remarks resulted in termination of his contract with Nike and other sponsors (Al-Samarrai, 2016).

x. During a pick-up youth hockey game in Boston, two fathers engaged in a physical altercation leaving one father dead and the other in police custody (O'Donnell & Brokaw, 2000).

ISSUES AND ETHICS IN SPORT

POWER AND POLITICS

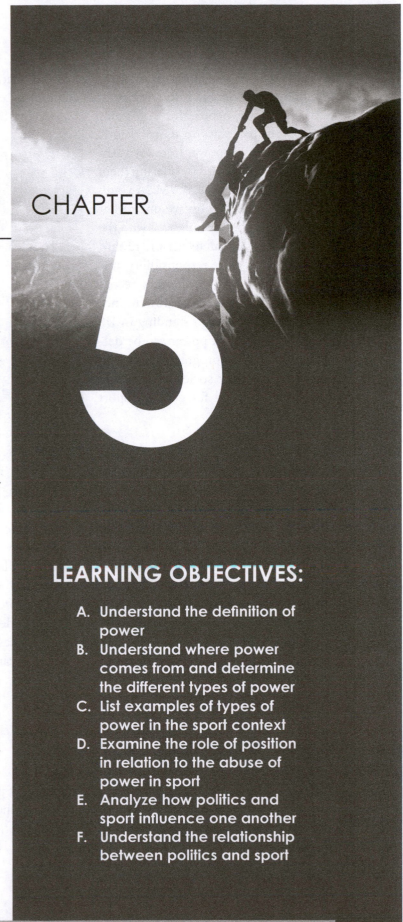

CHAPTER

5

As the purity of the game of sport continues to change, so does the intersection and interaction of sport and politics. Power plays a significant role in both sport and politics and the two can often collide at a variety of levels. This chapter will examine the different types of power, power positions, and the association and underlying roles that politics has on sport. The abuse of managers in power positions will be analyzed and students will gain knowledge and understanding of the role of decision making related to position, politics, policy, and power.

WHAT IS POWER?

Power is defined as one actor's ability to influence another actor to carry out any tasks that he or she wishes (Etzioni, 1961). By definition, the perception of power may be perceived as negative. There are many instances in sport when someone has abused personal or professional power. One example might include the Penn State scandal involving Jerry Sandusky. In this case, Sandusky was charged and convicted of sexual abuse of athletes and other children involved in the Penn State athletic program. This was a clear abuse of power. Another example of negative leadership involving the abuse of power could be the scandals that

LEARNING OBJECTIVES:

A. Understand the definition of power
B. Understand where power comes from and determine the different types of power
C. List examples of types of power in the sport context
D. Examine the role of position in relation to the abuse of power in sport
E. Analyze how politics and sport influence one another
F. Understand the relationship between politics and sport

affected the Federation International de Football Association (FIFA). In 2016, FIFA admitted it accepted tens of millions of dollars in bribe money from countries in exchange for hosting the World Cup. These examples support why people think of "power" in a negative light. While power can oftentimes be abused, there are also positive ways to use power. A coach may use his power to reward athletes who practice hard by offering them additional playing time. A YMCA youth sports director may observe one of her young coaches performing well with the elementary basketball teams and reward the coach with more responsibility. It is important that sport managers recognize the different types of power since sport holds such a high standing in US society. The abuse of power can be detrimental for sport programs as well as within current day society. Power can and should be used for good by sport managers.

Oleg Golovnev/shutterstock.com

As mentioned above, power is loosely defined as the ability of one to overcome another. Power can be examined as the resistance between two actors. Emerson (1963) states, "The power of actor A over actor B is the amount of resistance on the part of B which can potentially be overcome by A" (p. 32). So, if there is a small amount of resistance that B has to overcome to surpass A, then A has weak power over B. If there is a large amount of resistance that B has to overcome to surpass A, then A has strong power over B. Consider an offensive and defensive lineman. Each lineman resists, and whoever can push the other one back has more power and can impact the game in a greater manner. Sometimes, a defensive lineman is so good, such as defensive lineman for the Houston Texans (2016) J.J. Watt, it takes two offensive linemen to stop him. In his case, the offensive line needs two actors to overcome the resistance of the other. As a sport manager, power can and will play a pivotal role in the daily duties of all "actors" in the industry.

TYPES OF POWER

There are many varieties of power. The different types of power include legitimate, reward, coercive, expert, informative, and referent. When going through each of these types of power, it is important to consider both good and bad examples of each type of power. Remember, power is not always bad. Power used correctly has the capability to improve sport organizations and society as a whole.

Legitimate Power

Legitimate power is the power that comes from the position held or the title one person holds over another. Legitimate power comes from within the organization and can be as simple as a name being placed on an organizational chart. This type of power comes from one's formal position within an organization or within society. The higher up someone is on the organizational chart, the more legitimate power he or she has. The athletic director has legitimate power over his or her associate athletic director for facilities and operations. In turn, that associate athletic director for facilities has legitimate power over the coordinator of facilities and operations, who has legitimate power over the intern. The athletic director may give a task to the associate athletic director for facilities and operations and expect this person to use his or her legitimate power to help complete the assigned projects and tasks. Other examples of those with legitimate power include doctors, lawyers, police officers, and business owners.

Reward Power

Reward power comes from the ability to reward an individual or group. Reward power oftentimes comes with legitimate power, as reward power gives an individual the ability to give a raise or increase benefits over another. The YMCA director of sports may believe the youth sport coordinator is meeting organizational objectives and give him a raise or additional opportunities. Even on the field, a player may be rewarded with a starting position because of his or her hard work. When considering power in ethical decision making, some people make ethical decisions based on the rewards they may receive or think they may receive.

Coercive Power

Coercive power is the opposite of reward power. Instead of granting someone a reward, coercive power is the ability to punish someone or take something away. Coercive power comes from the power of fear. If a leader threatens to take away compensation, playing time, or any other benefit from the employee, then the leader is using coercive power. Chris Kluwe, punter for the National Football League (NFL) Minnesota Vikings and an advocate for LGBT rights, is a great example of the use of coercive power. While Kluwe's coaches used homophobic slurs in practice, Kluwe was using his football position and social media platform to send pro-LGBT messages to his fans. The coaches and general managers told him to stop "making noise" about the issue, but Kluwe refused. Kluwe was released from the Vikings after a successful season in which he was in the upper half of punters in the league (Kluwe, 2014). The Vikings management exercised their coercive power to take away Kluwe's job for advocating for LGBT rights.

Expert Power

Expert power comes from the actor's own knowledge and skill. As with all forms of power, it can be both good and bad. When thinking of expert power, an example could be an elite athlete like a star quarterback or pitcher. It is not a coincidence that those who are the best in their sport usually get paid the most. Elite athletes are being paid for their expert skills in their positions, which can help an organization succeed. Leaders in the industry like top athletic directors or conference commissioners command expert power because they have the knowledge and skill to be good at their jobs. One example could be the expert power of Adam Silver. Silver, who worked his way through the National Basketball Association (NBA) holding numerous power positions such as deputy commissioner, chief operating officer, chief of staff, and special assistant to the commissioner, exerts his expert power today with extensive knowledge of the league and its operations.

Informative Power

Informative power is similar to expert power, but it comes from the ACCESS to knowledge and skill, not necessarily possessing the knowledge and skill. When Billy Beane, general manager of the Oakland Athletics, started using data analytics to put a competitive baseball team together with a low budget, he had the informational power that few could understand. In fact, after his Oakland A's marvelous run in 2001, he was offered a five-year $12.5 million contract to become the Boston Red Sox general manager, but turned it down (Bryant, 2010). He, along with scout Paul DePosta, devised a way to measure player's contributions outside of home runs and runs batted in. They changed the way professional sport was analyzed. For a brief time, his team was the team able to use this method and thus commanded a tremendous amount of power. With access to the formulas, data, and methods, it was attractive for other teams such as the Boston Red Sox to come calling for his informative power.

Referent Power

Referent power is synonymous with charisma. This type of power comes from people's ability to attract other individuals with their personality. Famous people like Oprah Winfrey and Barack Obama are said to have referent power. People know who they are and listen to them based on their perceived power. In sport, people with big personalities such as Rex Ryan, former coach of the New York Jets and the Buffalo Bills in the NFL, Russell Wilson, quarterback for the Seattle Seahawks, or Abby Wambach, an American soccer player, are also individuals that have referent power. Anytime they are on the sideline, on the field, or attending a press conference they are smiling, clapping, and leading players with a strong sense of charisma. Unlike the other forms of power, this is difficult to attain without having a charismatic and strong personality. Leaders can succeed without this form of power, although it can be more challenging to achieve similar success. Take, for example, New England Patriots head coach Bill Belichick. He is not the most charismatic coach, but he commands power due to other types of power he possesses. Belichick has position and expert power from success on the field and legitimate power from his ability and expert knowledge of the game of football.

All types of power—legitimate, reward, coercive, expert, information, and referent power—are used daily in sport. Sport managers use different types of power in different situations to influence others. As a sport manager and a leader, it is best to recognize which type of power is being used and make sure it is the appropriate form of power. The next section will cover some of the instances when people in positions of power within the sport world have used their power in an inappropriate way, allowing power to corrupt them and their ability to make effective decisions as managers.

ABUSE OF POWER IN SPORT

Jerry Sandusky and Penn State

The Jerry Sandusky Penn State scandal could be considered one of the worst scandals in all of sport. Not only did Jerry Sandusky, the defensive coordinator for the Penn State University Nittany Lions football team, abuse his power, but the head football coach, Joe Paterno, did as well. Together, these two men created a culture of negative leadership and power that stemmed from the football team and circumvented and evaded both the athletic director and president of the university at the time.

Jerry Sandusky originally garnered his power as the linebackers coach for the football team under Joe Paterno in 1970. During his tenure coaching linebackers, Penn State was nicknamed "Linebacker U" in honor of the ability to develop great linebackers at the university. Sandusky was promoted to defensive coordinator and the program continued to create success on the football field by boasting one of the best defenses every year. Sandusky was defensive coordinator from 1977 to 1999, and during that time Sandusky acquired expert power. He was known by the football team, athletic department, university, and community because of the success he had as a defensive coordinator, which gave him immense power. However, Sandusky gained more power within the community through his formation of The Second Mile, an organization that helped young people achieve their potential and develop life skills. Through The Second Mile, Sandusky gained referent power, which allowed him even more power within the community. He was helping the youth of America, an act seen as righteous by many. Through "Linebacker U" and The Second Mile, Sandusky created the immense power that would lead to the worst scandal in Penn State's storied history.

Joe Paterno had a similar rise to power through the success of the football program at Penn State. Paterno took over an abysmal Nittany Lion program in 1966 after a 5–5 season. In his first two decades of coaching, Paterno led the program to four undefeated seasons and two national championships, the first coach to have earned such an achievement. Paterno acquired expert power through his ability to lead a successful football team, but he gathered reward power through donations to Penn

Richard Paul Kane/shutterstock.com

State University. In 1997, Paterno donated $200,000 to open up the Paterno Library and then he donated over $4 million shortly after for faculty positions, scholarships, and two more campus buildings (Murphy, 2012). His contributions can be seen as a reward to the university.

While a coach at Penn State University, Sandusky was caught sexually molesting young boys in the university athletic facilities. One instance that clearly highlights the abuse of power by Sandusky and Paterno happened after Sandusky was retired from football. Two janitors and employees of Penn State saw Sandusky and a little boy in the locker room showers on campus. The two janitors consulted and decided not to report the incident because, as one of the janitors described it in the Freeh Report, going against Paterno (and the football team) would be like "going against the President of the United States . . . football runs this University" (Freeh, 2012, p. 65). This mentality in regard to the head football coach being as powerful as the president of the United States prevented the janitors from reporting the incident.

In 2001, Athletic Director Tim Curley and Penn State President Graham Spanier were made aware of Sandusky's sexual abuse of young boys. Mike McQuery, a graduate assistant for football, reported the information to university authorities. Curley and Spanier had legitimate power in the organization, as they were ranked above all coaches at the university; however, because Paterno's and Sandusky's power had grown over time, instead of reporting the incident, Curley and Spanier let the two coaches' power control the decision making and tried to sweep the scandal under the rug.

Colorado Rockies Stadium

While Sandusky used his power gained through sport to influence the masses, the Colorado Rockies stadium financing shows how power can be gained through the association with sport. George Sage (1993) wrote an article on how major stakeholders used power to deceive the City of Denver into using taxpayer money to build a stadium for the Colorado Rockies. In June 1990, Major League Baseball (MLB) announced it would add two new franchises to the National League in 1993. Against its wishes, MLB did not want to expand, but were forced to expand due to legal issues and public pressure from Colorado Senator Tim Wirth and Florida Senator Connie Mack. MLB took the opportunity to create unprecedented demands for expansion teams. Teams would have to pay $95 million to buy into the league, which was $88 million higher than in 1977, two decades earlier. Further, MLB wanted organizations that had natural grass fields and in instances of shared stadiums, gave priority scheduling to baseball.

Multiple organizations in Denver that had desperately wanted an MLB franchise for over a decade were interested in making a bid to be one of the two expansion teams. Denver already had a stadium, Mile High Stadium, with natural grass, but priority scheduling would be given to the Broncos, and not the new organization. That meant the city was going to be forced to build an entirely new stadium if the city wanted an organization. However, potential owners would not be attracted to spending hundreds of millions of dollars to possibly acquire a team. The owners would need assurance that an organization would be awarded to Denver, so a stadium needed to be built first to help convince MLB to expand in the city. Without an owner to pay for the stadium, the public would have to pay for most of the stadium using sales taxes. The proposal was for the taxpayers, in the six surrounding counties of the stadium, to pay one-tenth of one percent of the sales tax. For the proposed $139 million stadium, the taxpayers would pay $97 million. The plan would also specifically state that the stadium district board would make every effort to attain as much money from private sources as possible. They predicted 30% of the total cost would come from private sources, or $42 million (Sage, 1993). The public was allowed to vote on whether to approve the proposal or not, but not without influence from some of the key stakeholders.

With a vote on the line to approve the sales tax plan for the new stadium, local politicians and businesses were the biggest supporters of the plan. It is not surprising that these two entities were the initiators of this project because they had the most to gain. With their legacies at stake, the act of bringing a professional organization to any city begins with politicians. In fact, it was Senators from Colorado and Florida who were

Evan Meyer/shutterstock.com

first to pressure MLB into granting two expansion teams and the same two locations would ultimately be awarded the teams. Many politicians have a desire to be the ones responsible for bringing in a historic franchise to a major city. They also do not want to be known as the ones who allowed a sport organization to get away, so they use their power to bring in major sport organizations. Local businesses stand to gain a tremendous amount of profit from the new sport organization. Not only would paying customers come to Denver for a handful of Broncos games during the year, they would also come for 81 baseball games in the summer season. The sport organization could provide boosted revenues and potential sponsorship opportunities.

The politicians and local businesses used a number of tactics to convince the public that spending $97 million and raising sales tax on a new stadium was a great idea. The foundation of their argument was the financial and "intangible" benefits the stadium would bring into the city. To build their argument, the city had an economic impact report conducted. An **economic impact** report is created to see the financial implications for an event or organization. Economic impact reports are staples in an Olympic bid, for example. They allow the local people, local businesses, event hosts, and other organizations to understand how much money will be made or lost in the city and community due to an event. A few common issues in economic impact reports led to the deception of the people of Denver. Unfortunately, economic impact reports are widely unreliable and often show a stadium shifts expenditures and economic resources instead of generating new financial activity. Second, stadiums tend to benefit the wealthy, while burdening the low-income citizens, the ones hurt most by the sales tax proposal. Third, economic impact reports are usually conducted by a third-party entity for the organization that wants to implement the stadium/event. There have been instances where these third-party entities will stretch the report to favor the organization that ordered the report to please the people paying for the report. For this case, the economic impact report showed a $25 million influx of direct revenue for the Denver area, while the overall impact to the area would be $93 million. In addition, the study projected 650 jobs would be added from the stadium (Sage, 1993). The proponents of the stadium boasted about this large revenue generation prospect, as well as spoke about the "intangible benefits," such as civic pride and neighborhood redevelopment.

Another tactic proponents of the stadium used, in addition and in coordination with the economic impact report, was using the *Rocky Mountain News*, Denver's largest newspaper. The *News* was a strong supporter of the stadium, urging people to go out and vote to approve the tax. The news outlet used the economic impact report as ammunition and spoke of the intangible benefits such as civic pride, fan interest and public image for the city. In addition, the *News* criticized those who opposed it, calling them "shortsighted" and "envy-wracked" (Sage, 1993, p. 116).

On August 14, 1990 the tax proposal passed 54% to 46% in the majority of the counties. Two counties, including Denver County, voted the proposal down. However, four of the six other counties approved the vote. Less than 24 hours later, it was reported that the *Rocky Mountain News* was interested in ownership of the expansion team. There were major legal and ethical concerns over this piece of news. Many believed the newspaper had used its legitimate power to help their own interests and trick the people of Colorado to vote to approve the stadium.

The abuse of power did not end with the vote. Originally, the stadium was going to cost $139 million, with $97 million coming from taxpayers and $42 million coming from private donations. Those were the figures given to the voters before the election. However, when the lease was negotiated, the total cost of the project was $180 million, due to loan interest, which was hidden from the public. Instead of the original estimated price of $97 million, the city was then responsible for $156 million. Additionally, private donations only accounted for $24 million, which was half of the 30% that was supposed to come from private donations.

Stories like this happen more often than they should: political figures, local organizations, and team owners use their power to influence the public to fund their stadiums. In the 1950s, only one baseball team, the Cleveland Indians, played in a publicly owned stadium. The number of publicly funded stadiums has only increased. By 1992, 21 of 26 MLB teams had a publicly funded stadium (Sage, 1993). However, a recent trend in stadium finance is the ability of policy makers and public services to allocate public funds for a stadium without a vote from the people paying for the stadium (Kellison & Mondello, 2014). Recall the Colorado Rockies example; the decision to use taxpayers' money was voted on by the counties affected by the vote. Today, many in the public do not even get the chance to vote. Take for instance Scott Walker, governor of Wisconsin, who signed legislation to approve spending $250 million of taxpayers' money on a new arena for the Milwaukee Bucks (Johnson, 2015). A new ownership group, including one of Walker's top campaign fundraisers, took over the Milwaukee Bucks in 2015 and demanded the taxpayers be responsible for paying for a new stadium. If not, the ownership group would move the organization to another city. Walker quickly signed legislation for the state of Wisconsin to spend the money for a new stadium without consulting the taxpayers who would be paying for the stadium.

This new trend of forcing taxpayers to pay for stadium construction and renovations highlights the abuse of power caused by sport managers and politicians alike. It is not just MLB and NBA team owners demand-ing money from the public to pay for their stadiums. From 1997 until 2015, 20 new NFL stadiums opened with $4.7 billion coming from taxpayers' money (Isidore, 2015). Unfortunately, new stadiums rarely create citywide economic benefits (Lee, 2013). The finances are shifted around the city, but oftentimes do not offer financial benefits that warrant subsidies from the public. However, politicians and local businesses use their various forms of power to convince the public to pay millions and billions of dollars for stadiums.

POLITICS IN SPORT

As noted above, politicians often use the power sport brings to promote a personal agenda. It may be to push an agenda with a malicious intent, like the 1936 Berlin Olympic Games, or drive a peaceful agenda, like the 1995 Rugby World Cup. While there are many more cases of politicians using sport to further their own agendas, these two stories stand out as being two of the more important events in history influenced by sport.

Hitler's Propaganda Olympics

In 1931, Berlin was awarded the 1936 Summer Olympic Games. The International Olympic Committee (IOC) voted to give Germany the Olympics as a symbol that the country was returning to the world community after World War I. Two years after the IOC awarded Germany the Olympic Games, the leader of the Nazi Party, Adolf Hitler, became chancellor of the country. His dictatorship was built on the persecution of Jews, Romani, homosexuals, persons with disabilities, and anyone who was not Aryan. Hitler and his followers used the 1936 Olympics to showcase this idea (The Nazi Olympics, 2016).

Hitler believed that not all races were equal and those of German blood, the Aryan race, were the members of the superior race. He believed the Aryan race should be pure and not be mixed with Jews, Roma, Africans, or Slavs. This idea was promoted throughout the streets of Germany with posters, signs, newspapers, and other

Everett Historical/shutterstock.com

mediums condemning non-Aryan races. Even in sport, the Nazi Party determined an Aryan-only policy would be instituted in 1933. Jewish and Romani athletes were not allowed to participate with German athletic organizations. Many of Germany's best Jewish and Romani athletes fled Germany to the United States or surrounding countries just to be able to participate in sports.

Hitler had two main goals for the 1936 Olympic Games: show the strength of the Aryan race and convince the world Germany was a peaceful nation following World War I. Hitler and the Nazi Party promoted the idea of Aryan racial superiority through the Olympics. Hitler wanted success for his Aryan athletes to show the military strength of Germany. If they were the most physically fit and at the peak of athletic ability, they would be the best military in the entire world. In addition to showing the world his Aryan race was superior physically, Hitler knew he had to convince the world Germany was a peaceful nation, despite the opposite being true. The anti-Jewish posters and Nazi propaganda were taken down temporarily for the Games, and the newspapers toned down their harsh criticism of other races. The Nazi Party wanted to show the world they were a peaceful people, if only for two weeks. Despite the attempts, movements started to boycott the games, particularly from the United States, Great Britain, and France. However, those movements did not live long, as reporters and journalists who went to Germany saw no anti-Jewish rhetoric.

Hitler's propaganda Olympics were a success. His German athletes were victorious on the fields and they captured the most medals. Visitors, reporters, and athletes also were convinced the Nazi Party stood on a platform of peace toward those of Jewish descent and other non-Aryan races. The Olympics were used by Hitler to put Germany back on the world map after the destructive World War I. After the Games, the anti-Jewish posters and newspaper stories came out again, even stronger. Hitler had used the Games to generate support from the Germans due to the high amount of pride in their athletes and home country. He would use the momentum from the Olympic Games to start World War II and the Holocaust.

Nelson Mandela and Rugby

Not all stories of politics, sports, and power are negative. A prime example of a politician mixing sport and politics for the betterment of a nation is the 1995 Rugby World Cup. In 1948, the National Party gained power in South Africa. They built their platform on the policy of **apartheid**, which literally means separateness. Their initial goal was to separate White South Africans and Black South Africans. They also separated many Black South Africans to suppress their ability to organize and challenge the status quo. The National Party was able to accomplish the segregation by enacting a number of Land Laws.

The Land Laws mandated that 80% of the country's land be available to the White minority. Black South Africans were forcibly removed from lands and their land was sold to White farmers in extreme circumstances. Further, Pass Laws were introduced to require non-White individuals to carry a pass authorizing their presence in restricted areas. In 1952, Black South Africans started to resist through organized protests. The African National Congress (ANC) was the main resistance organization, led by Nelson Mandela. The ANC joined the South Indian National Congress to burn their pass books in organized meetings. The government found out about the meetings and arrested 150 people for high treason. In 1960, police opened fire in a Black township of Sharpesville on a group of Black South Africans who arrived at a police station without passes. The "act of resistance" led 67 Black South Africans to be killed and 180 wounded. Understanding that non-violent demonstrations were ineffective, the ANC formed armed resistance. By 1961, most resistance leaders had been captured and sentenced to execution or long prison sentences, including Nelson Mandela, who was incarcerated from 1962 to 1989 (Apartheid, 2010).

Even after Mandela's incarceration, relations between White South Africans and Black South Africans worsened and the world noticed. In 1976, thousands of Black students protested against the language requirements. The police fired upon the Black South African students with tear gas and bullets. The world, having seen police officers

shooting at students and children, took action against South Africa. The United Nations Security Council, in 1976, imposed a mandatory embargo on all firearm sales to South Africa. The United Kingdom and United States followed suit by imposing economic sanctions on South Africa.

In the sport world, international organizations imposed their own sanctions against South Africa for their apartheid (Jeffery, 2002). In 1961, FIFA suspended the Football Association of South Africa for practicing racial discrimination. Three years later, South Africa was banned from competition in the 1964 Tokyo Olympics for their actions. The United Nations, in 1968, became involved and called for boycotts of all South African teams that participated in racial segregation. South Africa would be banned from the International Cricket Council in 1970, causing England and Australia to cancel their South African tours. In possibly the greatest blow to the country, a British Lions rugby tour in South Africa was cancelled in 1986. Rugby, one of the most popular sports in South Africa, was being taken away from the people of South Africa due to their racial segregation.

The international community's pressure continued to grow until 1989. The National Party's leader, Pieter Botha, was forced to resign. F. W. de Klerk would take charge of South Africa and create change in the country. With Mandela and the African National Congress's (ANC) help, apartheid would come to an end by 1994. The same year, more than 22 million South Africans voted to elect the next party to lead the nation. Nelson Mandela was elected as the country's first Black president, with de Klerk serving as his first deputy. White South Africa was afraid of what would be the result of Mandela becoming president. The man had just served 27 years in prison. How would he retaliate against the White South African people? Instead of retaliation, Mandela wanted to unite the people of South Africa. Instead of apartheid and racial differences as a foundation for the nation, he wanted to unite them under one flag. Mandela knew exactly how he would accomplish this goal; he would use the power of sport and the 1995 Rugby World Cup.

Mandela asked the nation to support the national rugby team, the Springboks, for their upcoming competitions (Effron, 2013). This was a controversy as the Springboks stood for more than the racial divide. For the White South Africans, the Springboks stood for pride and identity, while the Black South Africans saw the

Springboks as a symbol of the apartheid. Mandela wanted to tear down this paradigm about the Springboks and South African teams that practiced racial segregation. Mandela believed the 1995 Rugby World Cup, hosted by South Africa, was the perfect opportunity. The whole world would be watching South Africa and that gave South Africans a sense of pride that could be channeled through their national rugby team.

For Mandela's plan to unify Black and White South Africans through sport, he needed the support of the Springboks. A month into his term as president, Mandela invited Springbok captain and White South African François Pienaar to meet with him. Pienaar, who had grown up hearing Mandela's name associated with being a terrorist and criminal, met with Mandela. The South African president urged Pienaar and his teammates to be ambassadors for peace on the field and off of the field. He wanted Pienaar and the Springboks to stand for racial unity with the slogan "One team, one nation" (Zavis, 2009, para. 17). If Pienaar could get the Springbok players to promote peace, Mandela could get the Black South Africans to support the Springboks, even when the majority of them hated the Springboks. It was a gamble for Mandela as the nation would be thrust into a civil war if he failed.

The gamble to utilize the Springboks to promote peace between Black and White South Africans paid off. The Springboks went undefeated in their pool, gaining support from the citizens of South Africa. On June 24, South Africa watched their team play against the New Zealand national team in the championship. The stadium watched as Mandela walked out to shake the players' hands in a green and yellow Springbok shirt (Nelson Mandela, 2009). Many were shocked to see the first Black president in the colors that had represented oppression and discrimination toward Black South Africans. He wore the colors with confidence as a symbol for Black and White South Africans to forget the past and come together for the finals against the heavily favored New Zealand All Blacks. Few had given South Africa a chance at winning the 1995 Rugby World Cup, but on June 24, South Africa shocked the world with an upset victory against the All Blacks. Both Black and White South Africans came together to celebrate in the streets over the Springbok victory. Mandela's gamble paid off and the nation came together to help ease the pain of the past 40 years. Of course, racial tensions were never totally set to rest. However, Mandela used the Springboks to transform a nation on the brink of a ruthless and bloody civil war into a nation celebrating together in the streets for their one nation.

SMALL GROUP ACTIVITY

Using the examples above, think about some recent issues in sport that have involved politics or politicians. Complete the following:

- Give an example of the situation and how it involves power and politics.
  - o Describe the factors that contributed to the political involvement.
  - o Explain how players, officials, and fans reacted to the situation.
  - o Discuss if you think it was appropriate for the political involvement. Why or why not?
- Give an example of an action in politics that involved a sport, team, league or athlete.
  - o Describe the factors that contributed to the situation.
  - o Explain how media, politicians or other fans reacted to the political involvement.
  - o Discuss if the involvement was necessary. Why or why not?

NFL and the Concussion Research

Ethical issues related to power and politics are happening every day in sport. More recently, in the National Football League (NFL), a 91-page report was released detailing the NFL pulling funds from a major U.S. government research study on football and brain disease (Fainaru & Fainaru-Wada, 2016). The NFL, who has continued to face criticism of their concussion protocol and policies, pledged to give $16 million to the National Institutes of Health (NIH) for the brain disease research project. The NIH is an agency in the U.S. government that is responsible for health research. The $16 million was part of a $30 million unrestricted gift the NFL gave the NIH in 2012. Robert Stein, a Boston University researcher and expert on neurodegenerative disease, was the lead researcher on the project. The NFL pressured the NIH to remove Stein from the study due to claims of Stein being biased against the NFL. The NFL was accused of pressuring the government and major decision makers to use the researcher of their choice. The notion was that Stein, who had spoken against the NFL's treatment of players with brain trauma, would not be able to do fair research as his agenda may be to make the NFL look bad. The primary advocate for Stein's removal came from the co-chairman of the NFL's committee on brain injuries, Dr. Richard Ellenbogen. Dr. Ellenbogen was one of the researchers who applied for the $16 million grant from the NFL, but was ultimately denied in favor of Stein. The NIH refused to pull Stein from the research study and told the NFL that the $16 million they had pledged would have to be funded by an alternative source: the taxpayers. The NFL was happy to let the taxpayers pay for the project they had pledged to fund. This is a prime example of sport managers mixing sport and politics. To avoid these types of scenarios, sport managers should go through the ethical decision-making models when making any decisions, such as the NFL and the decision to pull funding for the study on brain damage from football.

Sport, power, and politics often mix in today's society. Whether it is politicians trying to lure professional sport teams to their city to maintain a personal legacy or country leaders using international events to promote their own agenda, sport and politics continue to mix. Sport managers need to be prepared to understand the evolving political environment and its place within the sport industry. Sport, power, and politics are not only for political figures or figureheads of large sport organizations. Sport managers need to understand the power provided through the association with sport. It is important to not only understand what type of power a sport manager uses (reward, legitimate, coercive, referent), but how to use that power appropriately. Sport managers may have large events influenced by the politics in society. For instance, the 2014 Sochi Olympics became a tremendous platform to discuss the treatment of the LGBT community. Sport organizations used the Games to support the LGBT community and show the Russian government that equal and nondiscriminatory treatment of LGBT individuals was necessary. When power, politics, and sport mix, influential events happen and can have major influence on the world.

DISCUSSION QUESTIONS

1. What is the definition of power?

2. What are the different forms of power? Provide examples of each form.

3. What forms of power did Jerry Sandusky and Joe Paterno have at Penn State, and how did they use those forms of power over others?

4. Who has power in stadium financing situations? Why? Who doesn't have power? Why?

5. How did Adolf Hitler use sport to push his social and/or political agenda?

6. How did Nelson Mandela use sport to push his social and/or political agenda?

7. How can power be used for good?

8. What are some policies that could be put in place to ensure college coaches do not get too much power?

9. Are all forms of power equal? Are some inherently good and some inherently bad? Explain your answers.

CASE STUDY: NARCO SOCCER

Money laundering is a practice in which money generated from one source is made to look like it originated from another source. The practice typically occurs when criminals attempt to disguise the origins of money obtained through illegal activities (Layton, n.d.). Because drug traffickers deal almost exclusively with cash in their illegal actions, they are especially reliant on money laundering. Such was the case of the head of the Medellín Cartel, Pablo Escobar, who was considered the most powerful drug lord in Colombia from the mid-1970s to the early 1990s (Krupp, 2010). Escobar chose to launder his money through Colombia's Atlético Nacional soccer team.

Although Escobar, commonly referred to as the "King of Cocaine," grew up poor, he was considered one of the wealthiest men in the world by the time he was 35, with his cartel earning an estimated $420 million per week, or $22 billion a year (Macias, 2015). His wealth was attributed to the fact that he supplied 80% of the world's cocaine, including roughly 15 tons of cocaine that came into the United States every day (Bowden, 2015). Although he was exceptionally dangerous and obviously involved in illegal activity, many Colombians loved his generous nature, as he handed out cash to the poor, built homes for the homeless, constructed 70 community soccer fields, and built a zoo (Macias, 2015).

While many were appreciative of Escobar's generous behavior, the illegal nature of his business eventually caught up to him. On June 19, 1991, Escobar surrendered to authorities that wanted to end the war between the state and the country's drug

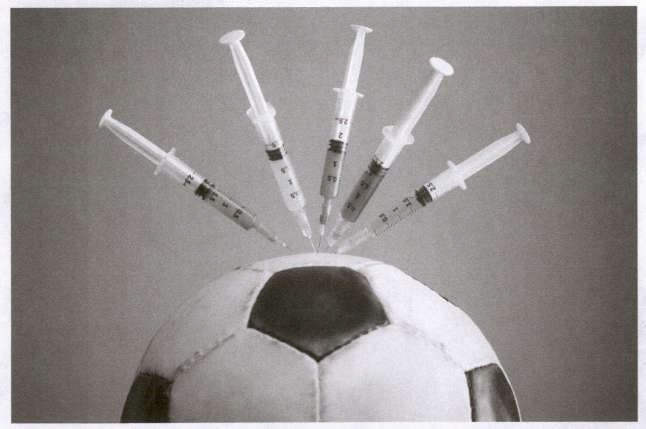

Diego Cervo/shutterstock.com

traffickers (Ambrus, 1993). A condition of his surrender required authorities to allow him to serve his time in "La Catedral," a luxurious prison he financed himself (Vincent, 2015). Just 13 months after surrendering to authorities, on July 22, 1992, Escobar and nine of his top lieutenants fled authorities in the attempt to transfer them from the luxurious prison to a regular jail (Ambrus, 1993). After 18 months in hiding, a 20-minute shootout during the attempted capture of Pablo Escobar led to his death.

Prior to his death, Pablo's involvement with the Colombian soccer team provided funds to recruit foreigners, while retaining the best local players (Krupp, 2010). For the first time, the team was not only winning, but also competing at the international level. One reason for the success of the team was Andrés Escobar (of no relation to Pablo), who was regarded as the gentleman of the game. Many of the athletes, including Andrés, recognized not only who was funding their team, but also the source of the funds—the Medellín Cartel. The power of the cartel continued to pressure the athletes to not only

win, but to do whatever was requested of them. This was evidenced by the fact that the athletes visited Pablo in prison for lunch, and would play soccer for him on a pitch built at La Catedral (Wilson, 2014).

The billion-dollar drug war led to roughly 20,000 homicides a year in Colombia, with a peak of 28,000 in 1992 (Vincent, 2015). While many hoped the death of the most powerful drug lord in the world would lessen the violence throughout Colombia, anarchy ensued because of the omnipresent social and political problems, evidenced by Colombia having the highest murder rate in the world (Wilson, 2014). The violence off the pitch found its way to the game when Andrés Escobar scored a lone goal against the United States that led to the elimination of his team from the World Cup. A mere 10 days later, he was shot dead in a parking lot. The motivation for his murder was reportedly revenge for heavy betting losses on Colombia at the World Cup (Wilson, 2014). Given the political and social tensions pervading Colombia, the murder of Andrés Escobar depicts the influence power and politics can have on sport.

CASE QUESTIONS

1. Identify three ethical dilemmas in this case. Explain the components of each dilemma.

2. Discuss whether or not Colombia's Atlético Nacional should have used Escobar's money to recruit and retain players.

3. Extend your understanding of this case to corporate social responsibility. If a person or organization is supporting the community, but the way in which that support is given may be ethically questionable, does it matter?

4. Explain how each of the six types of power could apply to this case.

5. How does political power play a role in this case?

GLOSSARY

Apartheid is the racial segregation and discrimination that was present in South Africa and can be literally defined as separateness.

Coercive power is the ability to punish.

Economic impact reports are created to see the financial implications for an event or organization.

Expert power comes from the actor's own knowledge and skill.

Informative power is the actor's access to knowledge and skill.

Legitimate power comes from one's formal position within an organization or society.

Money laundering is a practice in which money generated from one source is made to look like it originated from another source.

Power is one actor's ability to influence another actor to carry out any tasks that he or she wishes; the ability of one to overcome another.

Referent power is someone's ability to attract other individuals with their charismatic personality.

Reward power is power derived from the ability to provide rewards.

References

Ambrus, S. (1993). Colombia drug lord Escobar dies in shootout. *Los Angeles Times*. Retrieved from http://articles.latimes.com/1993-12-03/news/mn-63509_1_pablo-escobar

Apartheid. (2010). *History*. Retrieved from http://www.history.com/topics/apartheid

Bowden, M. (2015). *Killing Pablo: The hunt for the world's greatest outlaw*. New York: Penguin Putnam Inc.

Bryant, H. (2010, January 15). The revolutionary. *ESPN*. Retrieved from http://espn.go.com/espn/otl/columns/story?id=4357166

Effron, L. (2013, December 5). Nelson Mandela: 'A South African Lincoln'. *ABC News*. Retrieved from http://abcnews.go.com/International/nelson-mandela-1995-rugby-world-cup-south-africa/story?id=12789149

Emerson, R. M. (1963). Power-dependence relations. *American Sociological Review, 27*(1), 31–41.

Etzioni, A. (1961). *A comparative analysis of complex organizations*. New York: The Free Press, Macmillian.

Fainaru, S., & Fainaru-Wade, M. (2016, May 24). Congressional report says NFL waged improper campaign to influence government study. *ESPN*. Retrieved from http://espn.go.com/espn/otl/story/_/id/15667689/congressional-report-finds-nfl-improperly-intervened-brain-research-cost-taxpayers-16-million

Freeh, L. (2012). Report of the special investigative counsel regarding the actions of the Pennsylvania state university related to the child sexual abuse committed by Gerald A. Sandusky.

Isidore, C. (2015, January 30). NFL gets billions in subsidies from US taxpayers. *CNN Money*. Retrieved from http://money.cnn.com/2015/01/30/news/companies/nfl-taxpayers/

Jeffery, S. (2002, May 30). Timeline: Sporting boycotts. *The Guardian*. Retrieved from http://www.theguardian.com/world/2002/dec/30/zimbabwe.politics

Johnson, J. (2015, August 12). Scott Walker approves spending $250 million on Milwaukee Bucks arena. *The Washington Post*. Retrieved from https://www.washingtonpost.com/politics/scott-walker-approves-spending-250-million-on-milwaukee-bucks-arena/2015/08/12/5cd72d54-4055-11e5-9561-4b3dc93e3b9a_story.html

Kellison, T. B., & Mondello, M. J. (2014). Civic paternalism in political policymaking: The justification for no-vote stadium subsidies. *Journal of Sport Management, 28*, 162–175.

Kluwe, C. (2014, January 2). I was an NFL player until I was fired by two cowards and a bigot. *Deadspin*. Retrieved from http://deadspin.com/i-was-an-nfl-player-until-i-was-fired-by-two-cowards-an-1493208214

Krupp, S. (2010). *Colombia: The rise and fall of narco-soccer*. Retrieved from http://clas.berkeley.edu/research/colombia-rise-and-fall-narco-soccer

Layton, J. (n.d.). *How money laundering works*. Retrieved from http://money.howstuffworks.com/money-laundering.htm

Lee, J. (2013, November 25). Taxpayers on the hook for stadium costs. *USA Today*. Retrieved from http://www.usatoday.com/story/news/nation-now/2013/11/25/stadiums-taxpayers/3663541/

Macias, A. (2015, September 21). 10 facts reveal the absurdity of Pablo Escobar's wealth. *Business Insider*. Retrieved from http://www.businessinsider.com/10-facts-that-prove-the-absurdity-of-pablo-escobars-wealth-2015-9.

Murphy, J. (2012, January 24). Joe Paterno: A life—a fundraiser supreme. *Penn Live*. Retrieved from http://www.pennlive.com/specialprojects/index.ssf/2012/01/joe_paterno_a_life_-_a_fundrai.html

Nelson Mandela. (2009). *History.com*. Retrieved from http://www.history.com/topics/nelson-mandela

Sage, G. H. (1993). Stealing home: Political, economic, and media power and a publicly-funded baseball stadium in Denver. *Journal of Sport and Social Issues, 2*(17), 110–124.

The Nazi Olympics Berlin 1936. (2016, January 29). *United States Holocaust Memorial Museum*. Retrieved from https://www.ushmm.org/wlc/en/article.php?ModuleId=10005680

Vincent, I. (2015, October 18). The real 'Narcos': My life inside Pablo Escobar's cocaine kingdom. *New York Post*. Retrieved from http://nypost.com/2015/10/18/the-real-narcos-i-covered-pablo-escobars-cocaine-kingdom/

Wilson, J. (2014, July 2). Andrés Escobar murder: Colombia prepares for biggest ever World Cup match on 20th anniversary of death. *The Telegraph*. Retrieved from http://www.telegraph.co.uk/sport/football/teams/colombia/10938692/Andres-Escobar-murder-Colombia-prepare-for-biggest-ever-World-Cup-match-on-20th-anniversary-of-death.html

Zavis, A. (2009, December 15). A reporter remembers when Nelson Mandela united South Africa behind a rugby team. *Los Angeles Times*. Retrieved from http://articles.latimes.com/2009/dec/15/entertainment/la-et-mandela15-2009dec15

ETHICAL ISSUES IN THE BUSINESS OF SPORT AGENCY

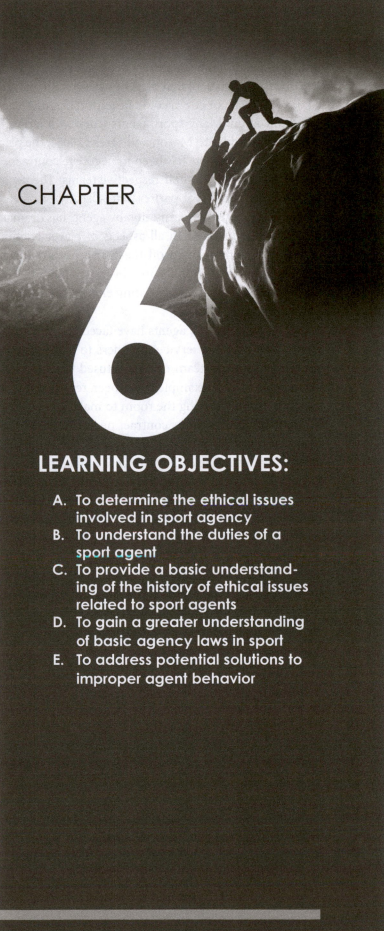

CHAPTER

6

LEARNING OBJECTIVES:

A. To determine the ethical issues involved in sport agency
B. To understand the duties of a sport agent
C. To provide a basic understanding of the history of ethical issues related to sport agents
D. To gain a greater understanding of basic agency laws in sport
E. To address potential solutions to improper agent behavior

The business of sport agency got its start in the early 20th century when athletic talent began appearing on the field and on the radio. Agents began selling themselves to athletes with a promise of increased profits and exposure. Players of the time, like Harold "Red" Grange and Babe Ruth, worked with friends and colleagues who had backgrounds in law to secure more lucrative deals with teams. The benefit of these relationships was that agents could help athletes find more money while maintaining personal relationships and building trust with players. Those acting as agents began to see the value in developing relationships with players, and it became a key element in the growth of the sport agency industry. Once the value of the high-profile athlete began to be recognized, athletes became pressured to seek agents to negotiate with teams and team owners and eventually to seek more lucrative contracts and endorsement deals. This demand and need for more agents in sport led to an increase in unethical and dishonest behavior on the part of many sport agents.

The term **agent** has been loosely defined in the sport industry as any person who represents a player or athlete or acts on behalf of that player or athlete. Ruxin (2010) indicates that an agent can be anyone. This means a friend, relative, or coach could be a sport agent. An agent could also include a lawyer or a representing firm or organization. Many sport agents work with large corporations or organizations that represent multiple players. According to Mason and Slack (2003), the primary **fiduciary duty** (legal duty to act in the athlete's best interest) of agents has been to negotiate contracts, match the services of players to clubs, and to broker deals for players with their respective teams. The negotiation of a **contract**, or primary binding agreement between two persons or parties that is legally enforceable, is a key duty of the player-agent relationship. The demand for player representation by agents has dramatically increased over the years as agents have become more actively involved in all aspects of player relations. Athletes have become more reliant on agents as "trusted advisors for many off-the-field aspects of their careers" (Masteralexis, Masteralexis, & Snyder, 2013, p. 69). Agents today fulfill a broad variety of duties, such as negotiating salaries, bonuses, and benefits; marketing a player's image; negotiating endorsements; and even managing player finances.

Over the past century, agents have faced a number of issues that have challenged their positions and confronted their role as service providers to the athletes. Many of these problems began in the early years of sport agency when team owners refused to work with agents and would enact barriers to try to regulate agent behavior. For example, it has been reported that Vince Lombardi showed his disinterest and distrust of agents by simply leaving the room to make a call to trade Jim Ringo to the Philadelphia Eagles when Ringo brought an agent into his contract negotiation (Shropshire & Davis, 2008). Lombardi was not alone in his distaste for agents, as most teams refused to negotiate with players who were represented by lawyers negotiating as agents in the early years of the industry. This limited the power of agents and hindered their ability to help. The lack of interest by teams and the limitations in the agency market caused some sport agents to seek alternate means to successfully represent athletes in both individual and team sports. The alternative methods often resulted in the unethical, dishonest, and corrupt behavior that has plagued the sport agency industry for the past century.

The role of a sport agent is to coexist in a mutually beneficial relationship with an athlete to assist in their professional career. Over the years, the highly lucrative business of professional sport has caused more and more questionable and illegal behavior on the part of many sport agents. The most common ethical issues that have occurred in sport agency include legal incompetence, improper ethical practices, conflict of interest, bribes, overcharging, "illegal" player contact, and overly aggressive tactics to recruit and retain players and coaches.

In 1987, Ed Hookstratten, who was the general counsel for the Los Angeles Rams at the time, discussed his dislike and embarrassment in the type of player agent representation he saw coming into his office (Neff, 1987). Over the years, the agent industry has had many of its own discuss their aversion for the practices inside and outside the agency spectrum. Today's top sports agents speak of tarnished reputations, increased player benefits, and the daring efforts to build and develop long-term relationships with prospective clients. According to Forbes, **Scott Boras** is one of the top agents with over 30 years of negotiating experience and $2.2 billion in current baseball contracts (Forbes, 2016). Boras, who claims he is always doing what is in the best interest of the game and his clients, was accused of providing over $70,000 in cash over 5 years to a top Dominican Republic baseball prospect (Fusfeld, 2010). This payment was a direct violation of Major League

Baseball Players Association (MLBPA) union rules. The reputation of a sports agent can grow quickly with the signing of one high-profile athlete, but most agents work tirelessly fighting for clients without the glory of signing the one "winning" player. The average agent certified by a players association(s) has only one or two clients (Brandt, 2010). Josh Luchs, a former NFL certified player agent, confessed to *Sports Illustrated* that he was taught how to effectively and illegally pay players at the beginning of his 20-year career as an agent. Luchs claims he paid high-profile athletes with money, gifts, or guarantees of a contract in the NFL to convince players to sign with him. A common way for an agent to gain a foothold in the business is by getting involved with a single school. Drew Rosenhaus, who has negotiated over $2 billion in National Football League (NFL) contracts, is a prime example. Rosenhaus graduated from the University of Miami and had developed relationships at the school to assist him in signing Ray Lewis, Warren Sapp, and other athletes who attended the school (Dohrmann, 2010).

Agents across all of the four major American professional sports talk of the irony of their "sleazy" profession, yet the industry and player representation continue to grow. Those who are making the money and working with the high-profile athletes are often the most powerful but also the worst offenders. Again, Scott Boras is discussed as one of the best agents in the industry but is arguably the most hated and has often been called "the man who doesn't have a soul . . . so he sells his clients" (*Sports Business Journal* as cited in Shropshire & Davis, 2008, p. 68). Some agents have determined the industry to be so cutthroat that they have decided to get out. Former NFL sport agent Andrew Brandt left the industry for a variety of reasons. In a 2013 *Sports Illustrated* article, Brandt discussed the shady process that exists in athlete representation because there are so many agents and relatively few top players. Brandt described how the industry has given the players the **buying power,** allowing them to dictate fees paid to an agent, create an environment for abuse, and create an atmosphere of tolerance for enticements such as money, trips, cars, women, club visits, game tickets, and more (Brandt, 2013). The reputation of the industry, the ruthless nature of sport agents and the ethical challenges that agents face have tarnished both those interested in pursuing careers in agency and those formally involved in the industry.

REGULATION OF AGENTS

The number and variety of legal challenges related to agents over the years has increased the need for regulation of the industry. The NCAA, the players associations of the major professional leagues, and state and national governments have implemented several legal processes to try to combat agent issues. This regulation has become necessary over the years to control the growing number of unethical agent practices. Regulation of agents began in California with a player-agent federal register. The National Collegiate Athletics Association (NCAA) and some state legislatures have enacted the **Uniform Athlete Agents Act (UAAA)** which regulates the relationship between agents, student-athletes, and educational institutions (Ruxin, 2010). This specific state regulation sets rules and is designed to protect players from unethical and dishonest agent behavior. Under UAAA, agents must register in each state in which they are working as an agent (Sharp, Moorman, & Claussen, 2007). In addition, the **Sports Agent Responsibilities and Trust Act (SPARTA)** is a federal statute instituted in 2004 to supplement the requirements of UAAA and prevent bribery and illegal gifts by agents. This federal regulation allows states to prosecute the unethical behaviors of agents. Both of these laws are limited in focus and cannot regulate all activities of agents once an athlete is no longer associated with the NCAA. Many agents believe they have power and control over young athletes and that these laws do not apply to them. In 2008 after National Basketball Association (NBA) player Michael Beasley was sued by his agent Joel Bell of Bell Sports for wrongfully terminating his agreement, Beasley quickly filed a counterclaim that his "agent" illegally provided money and gifts to his mother in an attempt to manipulate and control the young ballplayer's future decisions. Beasley and his mother alleged that Bell Sports was in violation of the UAAA and SPARTA while he was still NCAA eligible (Heitner, 2011). The case was eventually dismissed, but indicates that athletes do have some power and laws can help to regulate and control unethical agent behavior. However, these state and national regulations have not stopped much of the unethical behavior by sport agents.

Throughout the 1940s and 1950s, many of the major leagues began to grow financially, which added more incentive for players to demand rights, salaries, and the assistance of an agent. In 1946, the **American Baseball Guild (ABG)** was organized to help baseball players negotiate higher salaries, reform treatment of athletes, and attempt to remove the **Reserve Clause**. This clause obligated players to be bound to a team beyond the expiration of their contract. As players sought for rights in baseball, no real successful players association began in Major League Baseball until the development of the Major League Baseball Players Association (MLBPA) in 1966. In football, leagues developing and folding added to the strength and viability of the NFL. The collapsed American Football League (1936–1937) and the All-American Football Conference (1946–1949) helped the NFL gain the strength and structure that became its big-time growth (Staudohar, 1991). This increase in NFL power convinced two Cleveland Browns players to form the National Football League Players Association (NFLPA) in 1956. During this same time, the National Basketball Players Association (NBPA, 1954), and National Hockey Players Association (NHLPA, 1967) were formed to represent player rights (NHLPA, 2017). Each of these **players associations** served to confront team owners about salaries and achieve some type of fair labor practices. Some league associations were more successful than others, and players recognized the need for adequate representation.

Agents representing players in the four major professional leagues in the United States are also regulated by these respective players associations. Each of the players associations in the NFL, NBA, NHL, and MLB has a general application process that requires documentation of an applicant's education, experience, licenses, and a potential professional client list (Ruxin, 2010). From attending new agent seminars to requiring agents to pass a written exam, the NFLPA has a history of having some of the strictest agent regulations. The NFLPA has limited commission percentages, requires a $2,500 payment, and an advanced degree and agents must pass a background check (Dohrmann, 2010; Sharp et al., 2007). While not as strict, the NBPA requires the payment of an annual fee of $1,500 and agents must also pass an extensive background check to represent players (Sharp et al., 2007). In Major League Baseball, the players association is unique in that the player completes a form to indicate their selection for representation. Only then can the agent apply for certification to represent an MLB athlete. The MLBPA has a long history of disputes between players and management; however, agents representing baseball athletes have greater flexibility in no fees, no background check, and no special training (Sharp et al., 2007). In the NHL agents must have a player to represent in order to obtain certification and can lose the certification if they go a year without representing any hockey player (Ruxin, 2010). The NHLPA requires agents to complete its Agent Certification Program and has strict requirements related to conflict of interest in agent behaviors. Both state regulators and players associations have worked to ensure that players are protected and that an agent's behavior can be managed and controlled.

HISTORY OF ETHICAL ISSUES IN AGENCY

One of the first recorded player-agent relationships was between **Charlie C. (aka: C.C. or "Cash and Carry") Pyle** and Harold ("Red") Grange in 1925 (Masteralexis et al., 2013; Ruxin, 2010). Grange was a star halfback at the University of Illinois, known as the Galloping Ghost, and Pyle recognized his unique and financially worthy talents. Pyle reportedly convinced Grange to play in the NFL and assisted him in negotiating a deal with team owner George Halas of the Chicago Bears. Pyle reportedly negotiated not only $3,000 a game for Grange, but also bargained for endorsement money and movie contracts (Berry, Gould, & Staudohar, 1986 as cited in Masteralexis et al., 2013). Thus began the interest in players seeking assistance and advice from professionals in contract negotiations and other related financial deals. Professional sport was growing at a rapid pace and the labor (players) was seeking new and innovative ways to capitalize on talents on and off the field.

By 1935, Congress had enacted the **National Labor Relations Act (NLRA)** to protect the rights of employees, to encourage collective bargaining, and to regulate labor and management practices in the United States economy. This law assisted athletes to realize the importance of their rights as paid employees. During this time in professional sport, players received no healthcare benefits, no minimum wage, and earned very minimal salaries (Masteralexis, Barr, & Hums, 2012). The average player salary in Major League Baseball in 1935 was $7,000 a year (Staudohar, 1996). Most players were not highly regarded by teams, and many teams and leagues refused to work with players who were represented by agents. One prime example is the **reserve system** that existed in MLB at the time. This restrictive system was a gentleman's agreement between owners that bound players to their teams and ultimately gave the teams in the league the power to retain all players. This barrier to player movement kept salaries low and limited the ability of an agent to help a player. It was not until the development of strong players' unions and the addition of the players' rights through lawsuits that athlete representation began to fully flourish.

The duties of an agent in professional team sports began to take shape in the 1960s when players in these associations started demanding higher salaries, better benefits, and union rights. All of the leagues had become more commercialized with the addition of media and television contracts, and teams began bringing in much larger revenues. Each of the major professional leagues in the United States started to see players band together to fight for labor rights and advocate for increased bargaining power. This increased the need for agents and contributed to the growth of agency issues that had been building over the past 50 years.

Many of the ethical issues with sports agents began in the 1960s when leagues grew more commercialized and players sought more financial control. The number of cases reported involving **corruption**, or dishonest or fraudulent conduct by agents, dramatically increased as the number of competing leagues grew and many legal challenges developed with a newer commercialized professional sport product. One notable high-profile issue in the transition of player-agent relations was NHL hockey player Bobby Orr's trust in his long-time agent Alan Eagleson. Ruxin (2010) recalls:

> Perhaps no one epitomizes the impact of the evolution of the agent's impact on team sports and players, for better or worse, than Orr. In 1966, Orr's lawyer-agent negotiated a record rookie contract ($25,000) and 5 years later the first $1 million hockey contract ($200,000 guaranteed for 5 years). When that deal expired, the Bruins tried to offer Orr a multi-year deal that included an 18.5% ownership interest in the team. His agent turned it down and persuaded Orr to accept a contract with the Blackhawks (apparently without discussing the ownership offer with Orr).

Orr lost money and potential team ownership based on the negotiations of his agent and longtime friend. Orr expressed that his relationship with Eagleson was like they were brothers and he trusted Eagleson with his business and financial decisions. This type of agent control over not only contracts, but also future financial investments, can be seen over and over again throughout agency history. One scandal involved sportswriter-turned-agent Richard Sorkin who reportedly stole $1.2 million of his 50 NHL and NBA clients' money in the 1970s (Neff, 1987). Former Syracuse University basketball player Dennis Duvall was one of his victims; he allowed Sorkin to manage his finances and pay his bills. Duvall lost an estimated $30,000 of his own money to Sorkin's mismanagement of his finances. Sorkin was later sentenced for the $1.2 million in his clients' losses (Ruxin, 2010). Around this same time, well-known athletes such as Los Angeles Lakers center Kareem Adbul-Jabbar and Jack Clark of the St. Louis Cardinals lost millions of dollars in investments and real estate deals because of agents mismanaging their finances. It was even reported that Clark asked some teammates to borrow money to help him pay his rent (Neff, 1987). The player-agent relationship is typi-cally one of an unequal balance of power as athletes are dependent on attorneys, agents, or experts in contract negotiations. Athletes who are experts in their sport often have limited ability to deter-mine the best option related to agent decisions. This dependency has increased agents' wrongdoing, such as abuse of power, financial mismanagement, and a variety of other unethical behaviors by play-er-agents (King Jr., 1989). Even so, athletes have been and continue to be dependent on the expertise and experience of their agents.

SPORT AGENCY AND CHANGE

As the professional game has seen major changes to negotiations, collective bargaining, and the addition of free agency, the role of agents has become increasingly about money, financial benefits, and working the system to manage high-profile athletes. A more common agency issue in recent years relates to the "improper behavior" of agents in their communication with and mismanagement of college athletes. Agents spend a lot of time trying to create relationships with athletes, their families, and coaches. Dishonest individuals can potentially ruin the careers of prominent professional prospects. Marcell Dareus from the University of Alabama, AJ Green from the University of Georgia, and Reggie Bush from the University of Southern California have all been penalized for reportedly receiving money, gifts, or "extra benefits" from agents seeking to represent them (Masteralexis et al., 2013). Many agents will also go to extreme lengths to get to know or learn about an athlete and their daily routine. University of California running back Marshawn Lynch reported that he was often followed on his way to class and that **agent "runners"** (those that provide simple services to agents) were targeting him to try to win him over or control his future career decisions (FitzGerald, 2007). Agents fear losing potential prospects and educational institutions have limited power over the unruly and sneaky attempts that agents often utilize. Agents use a variety of tactics to earn the respect of potential clients. Ruxin (2010) described how an agent bought season ticket seats next to a prospective client's family

in order to gain access to the player. This attempt at developing close relationships with friends or family members is a common practice for potential high-profile athletes. Friends and influential family members often report receiving free tickets, having agents join family meals, and even agents dating members of the family to try to get close to athletes.

Ethical decision-making is essential and plays a key role in the sport agency industry. Overly aggressive recruiting and war-like practices to gain a competitive advantage are common in sport agency. Many sports agents have a legal background that provides them with specific knowledge of contract requirements, financial dealings, and negotiations. This experience gives agents **authoritative power**, power that appears legitimate and comes from a perceived expert, over players who have limited or no knowledge of the sport business. This abuse of power has also perpetuated many agents' overly aggressive tactics in recruiting athletes to represent and sustaining the representation relationship. According to Evans (2010), many agents are not concerned with what is in the best interest of the athlete, but what outcome will produce the most lucrative financial deal for the agent. Some agents convince prospects that they will negotiate the best possible deal; while in many cases the money is predetermined. In the NFL, for example, the league sets first-year salaries and agents are really only involved in basic negotiations. In the rookie pool, agents are typically only helpful in negotiating bonuses or endorsement deals (Evans, 2010).

> An agent who touts that he or she can get an NFL draftee the most amount of money is not being entirely truthful with the client, because the funds are coming from a finite pool that is largely

predetermined based on draft number; perhaps the agent could negotiate for a contract that offered more than the team originally intended, but each team still has a salary cap (Evans, 2010, p. 102).

The recent **Collective Bargaining Agreement** (CBA) in the NFL between the employer, players, and the union regarding pay, hours, and working conditions "has pre-fabricated contracts that a trained monkey" could negotiate (Brandt, 2013, para. 1).

One of the most common issues in sport agency today is conflict of interest. **Conflict of interest** refers to a situation in which an agent is faced with competing demands of two or more clients (Ruxin, 2010). As sport agency has grown, so has the number of agents representing multiple athletes. Agents such as Scott Boras and Drew Rosenhaus represent multiple clients in the same sport. Each of these agents is required to act in the best interest of each of his clients; however, assisting multiple athletes in the same sport can cause several conflicts. The job that an agent does representing one client may have a significant impact on other clients. This conflict can worsen when clients represented by the same agent are seeking a similar, or the same, position. One recent example is college football coaches Ed Orgeron and Steve Sarkisian who were both represented by Gary Uberstein and seeking the same position at the University of Southern California. Uberstein defended his position of representing both coaches by stating that agents only bring the clients, and organizations choose the best fit and make the hiring decisions. However, the conflict still existed (Dave, 2013). In Major League Soccer (MLS), it was common practice for agents to represent both players and coaches until

2008 when the MLS issued a ban on this behavior citing "conflict of interest that could damage the integrity of the league" (Ruxin, 2010, p. 83). In the NFL and the NHL, agents are required to inform each client of **dual representation** (representation of other athletes, coaches, or management) and policies on representing coaches and players have resulted in a variety of lawsuits against agents. Again, these types of regulations reinforce the continued interest and effort of governing bodies to attempt to manage and control the behavior of agents and protect the investment of their coaches and athletes on the field and on the sidelines.

Billion Photos/shutterstock.com

Professional sports alone in the United States today account for $32 billion in revenues, and athletes and coaches pay roughly 15 to 25% commissions to their sport agents. This financial benefit only increases the frequency of agents acting to gain a share of growth in the sport industry. Currently there are more than 700 agents registered with the NFLPA, of which only half actually represent clients (Brandt, 2013). The NFLPA reported that between 1999 and 2002 NFL players lost an estimated $42 million to fraudulent agents (Masteralexis et al., 2013). A number of athletes have recognized this trend and with greater frequency are moving to the **Elam Model** when dealing with fees and prospective agents. As rookie contracts in the NFL have become predetermined, athletes like Matt Elam, first-round pick of the Ravens, have begun negotiating

ISSUES AND ETHICS IN SPORT

contracts without an agent. Elam reportedly saved $203,000 in agent fees and other players took notice (Brandt, 2013).

Today, in most cases, especially those of high-profile athletes, salaries continue to increase and large agencies are recognizing the new trends. In recent years, many agents who once worked alone building lasting relationships with young athletes have failed to compete with the mega-firms that guarantee more money, the development of talent, and high-dollar endorsement deals. This transition has caused a decline in the number of active agents in the sport agency business. Much of the decline in recent years is also due to the limitations and availability of athletes and, again, the strict regulations by players associations. Large industry competitors like William Morris Endevoer (WME), Creative Arts Agency (CAA), and Roc Nation Sports are changing the sport agency outlook by offering a multitude of services and innovative competitive advantages for athletes.

New large-scale agencies specialize in managing and representing professionals in sport and entertainment. CAA, for example, works with athletes and entertainers assisting not only in contract negotiations, but also in opportunities for clients off the field in areas including licensing, endorsements, speaking, philanthropy, video games, and digital content. According to their website, "CAA Sports represents more than 800 of the world's best athletes in baseball, football, hockey, basketball, soccer, tennis, and golf, in addition to icons in individual sports, Olympians, coaches, broadcasters, and other sports personalities" (CAA Sports, 2016). There is a common perception that larger agencies and the more powerful, well-known agents will offer a greater benefit for the players. As player salaries and endorsement opportunities continue to grow, agents like Scott Boras help to perpetuate this idea. Boras, who assisted Alex Rodriguez with two contracts in excess of $250 million in 2001 and 2008, will act to serve many more functions to capitalize on the ever-growing athlete revenues. Agents like Boras have also learned to work around many of the regulations, policies, and procedures put in place to protect players and athletes. Agents have learned that negotiating contracts, no matter the length, provides up-front payment of fees. Agents have also taken notice of guaranteed up-front money, duration of the contract, overall payment, and bonus structures. The contract experts can manipulate contracts to benefit themselves and leave the athlete facing the long-term consequences.

SOLUTIONS TO AGENCY ISSUES

Understanding athlete representation, the sport agency industry, and the ethical challenges they face are essential to effective sport management. The current legislation that attempts to manage ethical issues in sport agency offers limited help to the players. Although many regulations have been set in place to help the athletes navigate unethical behavior of agents, researchers have suggested a variety of options might improve how agents are monitored, controlled, and managed as sport moves through the 21st century. Willenbacher (2004) suggests a National Sports Agent Registry to help control agent behavior and implement stronger penalties for agents who violate the national regulations, while others suggest a non-profit corporation to ensure that current state and national regulation is implemented and legal and ethical standards are enforced. This organization, called the Sport Agent Accountability Board (SPAAB), would register, certify, and discipline all agents and agency firms at a national level to ensure a uniform and fair system in sport agency (Masteralexis et al., 2013). Some researchers have suggested the creation of a new sport agent law to better protect both amateur (youth and college) and professional athletes. The new federal law would protect the principal relationship, employ universal laws of fairness and consistency, and attempt to minimize the conflict of interest in current agency relationships (Edelman, 2013). Even agents like Scott Boras have made suggestions that Congress make better efforts to enforce SPARTA and UAAA, that professional teams report any perceived wrongdoings, and that institutions promote more education for athletes and their families (Willenbacher, 2004).

Today, in attempts to combat unethical agent behavior, researchers and state and national organizations are seeking solutions to protect the player-agent relationship. An important aspect of this process is the education of athletes at a younger age to encourage and acknowledge the importance of understanding the process. It is also key that uniform processes be implemented to help reduce confusion on the part of the athlete. The ability for sport managers to assist high-profile athletes to navigate the current agent selection process will help to empower athletes to make informed decisions. Ideally, increased agent regulation and policy will help to limit and potentially eliminate the unethical behaviors of those trying to capitalize on young talent.

STUDENT ACTIVITY:
Research two sport agents who have been in the news in the past 10 years regarding ethical issues. What are the problems that these agents are facing? What is the primary concern for the athletes? Are there any legal issues that still need to be resolved in these cases?

STUDENT EXERCISE:
Joshua Minder is in his fourth year at UC Berkeley (Cal), and is seeking to be drafted by the NFL. He has been a starter since his freshman year and is a great prospect. Joshua has been approached by several students and family members about making sure he finds an agent. He has heard some names from other teammates, but is very concerned about improper conduct. Joshua isn't sure if an agent will be helpful to him or not.
1. What are the main concerns for Joshua in his career at this point?
2. What issues does Joshua need to be concerned about with a possible agent?
3. Will an agent help Joshua in his potential to be drafted by the NFL?

DISCUSSION QUESTIONS

1. What are some of the common issues related to agency in sport?

2. Discuss the reasons that athletes began to seek assistance from agents in the early development of American sport leagues.

3. How are agents regulated in sport? Who is responsible for agent behavior?

4. What is the NLRA and how does it play a role in sport agency?

5. Research agent responsibilities in one state. What are the policies and procedures required to become an agent?

6. What are benefits of agents in sport? Drawbacks?

7. Should the NCAA have the ability to make policies related to agency? Why or why not?

8. What role do players associations have in the regulation of agents?

9. What are some ethical issues not discussed in this chapter that might happen in the sport industry?

10. Do you think that agents are effectively regulated in sport? How might regulation help to manage the ethical challenges faced in the sport industry?

CASE STUDY: CAN JAY Z BE AN ETHICAL AGENT?

One significant new player in the sport agency industry is Shaun Carter (Jay Z) with his agency Roc Nation Sports, which launched in the spring of 2013. Jay Z started the company with his continued interest in sports and to have the ability to work with athletes in a different capacity. The organization's mission states, "Roc Nation Sports focuses on elevating athletes' careers on a global scale both on and off the field" (Roc Nation, 2012). "Roc Nation conceptualizes and executes marketing and endorsement deals, community outreach, charitable tie-ins, media relations, and brand strategy" (Roc Nation, 2012, para. 2). Roc Nation Sports and Jay Z have been accused of potentially **poaching** some of the athletes whom they represent. Athletes represented by Roc Nation Sports include the National Basketball Association's (NBA) Kevin Durant; Women's National Basketball Association's (WNBA) Skylar Diggins; Major League Baseball's (MLB) Robinson Cano and C. C. Sabathia; the National Football League's (NFL) Geno Smith, Dez Bryant, Victor Cruz, Ndanukong Suh, and Hakeem Nicks; and Boxing's Andrew Ward (Roc Nation, 2016). The accusation was confirmed in 2015 when Jay Z and Roc Nation Sports were sued for allegedly convincing athletes to "nullify their agreements" with their former agents in exchange for the opportunity to be represented by him and his agency (Heitner, 2014, para. 2). Former boxing promoter Joe DeGuardia sued Jay Z for $20 million

claiming Jay Z "intentionally interfered with an Exclusive Promotional Agreement" by attempting to lure young fighter Demetrious Andrade to Roc Nation Sports (Abramson, 2015, para. 2). If Jay Z is found to have committed these acts without disclosure, Jay Z may find himself liable and other agents could continue to claim damages against Jay Z for interfering in contractual relationships. This type of "poaching," or stealing other clients' business and players, is common practice in sport agency.

CASE QUESTIONS

1. What is the logic behind Jay Z getting involved in sport agency? Evaluate Jay Z's decision to expand into sport, and explain why it may or may not prove successful.

2. Discuss the ethical issues that Jay Z is facing as a sport agent and the impact of his decisions.

3. How can Roc Nation Sports achieve and sustain success in the sport industry?

4. Does Jay Z, as a certified agent, present a conflict of interest in the industry?

5. Can Jay Z continue to attract young athletes to his agency with the promise of fame and fortune? Why?

CASE STUDY: JOHNNY NEEDS AN AGENT

Johnny Manziel was the star quarterback for the Texas A&M football program. Known as "Johnny Football" to the fans in College Station (location of Texas A&M) Manziel became a leading National Football League (NFL) prospect when he won the Heisman Trophy in 2012. Soon after becoming the first college freshman to receive this top individual football award, Manziel began having trouble both on and off the field. In January of 2012, Manziel was arrested for disorderly conduct, using a fake ID, and fighting which resulted in a suspension from the Texas A&M team. Not long after, in June of 2013, Manziel posted on Twitter that he "couldn't wait to leave College Station" referencing his desire to enter the professional ranks of the NFL. At the start of the 2013 college football season, Manziel was under investigation by the NCAA for selling his autographs and profiting from the sales. Despite these issues, Johnny Manziel was drafted by the Cleveland Browns in the 2014 NFL draft.

The move to professional football did not seem to help Johnny or his troubles. In July of 2013 he left the Manning Football Camp early, citing illness and dehydration but leaving teammates and other players skeptical about his work ethic and commitment to the league. That same month, Manziel was caught partying and drinking while underage rather than focusing on his career efforts. In addition to Manziel's off-the-field antics, his on-the-field production as an NFL quarterback did not meet the industry expectations. In his preseason debut for the Browns, Manziel was fined $12,000 by the NFL for giving the middle finger to the Washington Redskins during the game. This and other factors related to his brand image may have been contributing factors to the Browns naming Brian Hoyer as the starter for the 2014 season. Manziel eventually saw play in a game on December 14, 2014 against the Cincinnati Bengals and threw two interceptions, resulting in a disappointing 30–0 loss.

Manziel's troubles and brand issues continued after his rookie season. His excessive partying and credibility issues led him to check into rehab in January of 2015. His 10-week stay resulted in a public apology regarding his actions and lack of respect for the game of football, yet only months later he was back in the news after a verbal altercation with a fan. He continued his partying ways and ended up being listed as the backup to Browns QB Josh McCown the following year. His second football season offered more playing time, but little was done to improve his image and change the public's perception of him.

By 2015 fans had grown disinterested in Johnny Manziel altogether. He continued to party, end up in the news, and disrespect authority. His NFL career was troubled when he missed a mandatory concussion protocol meeting and was fined by the NFL. This, coupled with an accusation of domestic violence, kidnapping, and an apparent threat to kill his then-girlfriend Colleen Cowley, may have been the final straw for the NFL. Manziel was released by the Cleveland Browns following the completion of the 2015 NFL season. Not long after his release, Manziel's father reported to the press that he believed his son would not live to see his 24th birthday.

After all his troubles, Johnny Manziel was released by his agent Erik Burkhardt in February 2016.

Burkhardt claimed that he and Manziel's family had worked tirelessly to try to help him and the future was now up to Johnny. Manziel was quickly picked up by NFL veteran agent Drew Rosenhaus. Top agent Rosenhaus took a chance on Manziel as it would be a clear challenge to find a team that would take Manziel. Only a few short weeks after the news of Manziel hiring Drew Rosenhaus, he was dropped by the 27-year agency veteran. Rosenhaus cited that it was time for Johnny Manziel to get it together and seek the treatment he needs to get better. Rosenhaus indicated that it was a "life and death situation."

CASE QUESTIONS

1. Ethical issues are a common occurrence on the part of the sport agent, but rarely does an agent have to fire a player. What were the key ethical issues in the case of Johnny Manziel?

2. How can a sport agent manage these types of ethical public relations problems?

3. The government regulates much of the behavior of agents; discuss your opinion about the league regulating the actions of the players in these types of situations.

4. Discuss your opinion about a player being dropped by an agent. Do you think it was appropriate for Burkhardt and Rosenhaus to drop Johnny Manziel?

5. What ethical decision-making criteria (Chapter 1) might be considered in this case?

6. Do you believe that policies should exist regulating the number of times a player can change agents? Why or why not?

7. Compare and contrast the situation of Johnny Manziel with another athlete you know who has had public relations or brand image issues in the past. What happened? How did the agent handle the problem?

GLOSSARY

Agent is defined as any person who represents a player or athlete or acts on behalf of that player or athlete.

Agent runners are those that provide simple services to agents.

American Baseball Guild (ABG) is an organization formed in 1946 to assist players in baseball to create a minimum salary and a players' pension fund. The ABG eventually became the Major League Baseball Players Association.

Authoritative power is power that appears legitimate and comes from a perceived expert.

Buying power allows athletes to dictate fees paid to an agent, create an environment for abuse, and create an atmosphere of tolerance for enticements such as money, trips, cars, women, club visits, game tickets, and more.

CC Pyle is the first recorded player agent.

Collective Bargaining Agreement is an agreement between the employer, players, and the union regarding pay, hours, and working conditions.

Conflict of interest refers to a situation in which an agent is faced with the competing demands of two or more clients.

Contract is the primary binding agreement between two persons or parties that is enforceable by law; negotiating contracts is a key role of the player–agent relationship.

Corruption is dishonest or fraudulent conduct typically by those in some power position.

Elam Model, which was named after Matt Elam, refers to when athletes dealing with fees and prospective agents choose to negotiate contracts without an agent.

Fiduciary duty is the legal duty to act solely in the best interest of another. Fiduciaries may not profit from their relationship with their principals unless they have the principal's informed consent.

National Labor Relations Act (NLRA) was enacted in 1935 by Congress to protect the rights of employees, to encourage collective bargaining, and to regulate labor and management practices in the United States economy.

Players associations are organizations (unions) created to represent player rights and serve to confront team owners about salaries and fair labor practices.

Poaching is the common practice of stealing or convincing players to change sport agents.

Reserve system was a restrictive system based on a gentleman's agreement between owners that bound players to their teams and ultimately gave the teams in the league the power to retain all players. This barrier to player movement kept salaries low and limited the ability of an agent to help a player.

Scott Boras, according to Forbes, is one of the top agents, with over 30 years of experience representing baseball players.

SPARTA, or the Sports Agent Responsibilities and Trust Act, is a federal statute instituted in 2004 to supplement the requirements of UAAA and prevent bribery and illegal gifts by agents.

UAAA, or the Uniform Athlete Agents Act, regulates the relationship between agents, student-athletes, and education institutions.

References

Abramson, M. (2015, August 1). Jay Z's Roc Nation Sports hit with $20 million lawsuit as boxing promoters claim agency tried to steal client. *NY Daily News*. Retrieved from http://www.nydailynews.com/sports/more-sports/20m-suit-claims-jay-z-agency-steal-client-article-1.2310751

Brandt, A. (2010, October 15). So you want to be an NFL agent? *Huffington Post*. Retrieved from http://www.huffingtonpost.com/andrew-brandt/so-you-want-to-be-an-nfl_b_764188.html

Brandt, A. (2013), December 19). Football's other recruiting. *Sports Illustrated (MMQB)*. Retrieved from http://mmqb.si.com/2013/12/19/nfl-agents-recruit-draft-prospects

CAA Sports. (2016. About CAA Sports. Retrieved from http://sports.caa.com/

Dave, P. (2013, December 25). Sport agents sometimes have a balancing act with clients. *Los Angeles Times*. Retrieved from http://articles.latimes.com/2013/dec/25/sports/la-sp-1226-same-agent-20131226

Dohrmann, G. (2010, October 18). Confessions of an agent. *Sports Illustrated*. Retrieved from http://sportsillustrated.cnn.com/2010/magazine/10/12/agent/

Edelman, M. (2013). Disarming the Trojan horse of UAAA and SPARTA: How America should reform its sports agents laws to conform with true agency principles. *Journal of Sports & Entertainment Law, 4*(2), 145–189.

Evans, S. B. (2010). Sport agents: Ethical representatives or overly aggressive adversaries. *Moorad Sports Law Journal*. 17: 1(3). Retrieved from http://digitalcommons.law.villanova.edu/cgi/viewcontent.cgi?article=1051&context=mslj

FitzGerald, T. (2007, October 20). A tempting business. Retrieved from http://www.sfgate.com/sports/article/A-TEMPTING-BUSINESS-2495622.php

Forbes. (2016). Sports agents. Retrieved from https://www.forbes.com/sports-agents/list/

Fusfeld, A. (2010, November 23). Baseball agent Scott Boras accused of giving improper loans to Dominican prospects. *Business Insider*. Retrieved from http://www.businessinsider.com/baseball-agent-scott-boras-accused-of-giving-improper-loans-to-dominican-prospects-2010-11

Heitner, D. (2011, October 27). Michael Beasley v. Joel Bell Inc. exposes dark side of youth basketball recruiting. *Sports Agent Blog*. Retrieved from http://sportsagentblog.com/2011/10/27/michael-beasley-v-joel-bell-inc-exposes-dark-side-of-youth-basketball-recruiting/

Heitner, D. (2014, February 20). Hakeem Nicks retains Jay Z's Roc Nation Sports and Creative Artists agency. *Forbes*. Retrieved from http://www.forbes.com/sites/darrenheitner/2014/02/20/hakeem-nicks-retains-jay-zs-roc-nation-sports-and-creative-artists-agency/#5fad51641975

Heitner, D. (2014, March 10). Jay Z has 99 problems but is being a sports agent one. *Forbes*. Retrieved from http://www.forbes.com/sites/darrenheitner/2014/03/10/jay-z-has-99-problems-but-is-being-a-sports-agent-one/#1668137975d1

King Jr., V. E. (1989, March 5). Do agents hurt or help? *New York Times*. Retrieved from http://www.nytimes.com/1989/03/05/sports/views-of-sport-do-agents-help-or-hurt-dependency-leads-to-abuse.html

Mason, D. S., & Slack, T. (2003). Understanding principal–agent relationships: Evidence from professional hockey. *Journal of Sport Management, 17*(1), 4–5.

Masteralexis, L. P., Barr, C. A., & Hums, M. A. (2012). *Principles and practice of sport management* (4th ed.). Sudbury, MA: Jones & Bartlett Publishing.

Masteralexis, L. P., Masteralexis, J., & Snyder, K. (2013). Enough is enough: The case for federal regulation of sports agents. Retrieved from http://digitalcommons.law.villanova.edu/cgi/viewcontent.cgi?article=1283&context=mslj

Neff, C. (1987). Den of vipers: A sports scourge: Bad agents. *Sports Illustrated Vault*. http://www.si.com/vault/1987/10/19/116409/den-of-vipers-a-sports-scourge-bad-agents

NHLPA. (2017). Inside NHLPA. Retrieved from http://www.nhlpa.com/inside-nhlpa

Roc Nation. (2012). About Roc Nation. Retrieved from http://rocnation.com/about/

Ruxin, R. H. (2010). *An athlete's guide to agents* (5th ed.). Sudbury, MA: Jones & Bartlett Publishing.

Sharp, L. A., Moorman, A. M., & Claussen, C. L. (2007). *Sport law: A managerial approach*. Scottsdale, AZ: Holcomb Hathaway.

Shropshire, K. L., & Davis, T. (2008). *The business of sports agents* (2nd ed.). Philadelphia, PA: University of Pennsylvania Press.

Staudohar, P. D. (1991). *The business of professional sport*. Chicago, IL: University of Illinois Press.

Staudohar, P. D. (1996). *Playing for dollars: Labor relations and the sport business*. Ithaca, NY: Cornell University Press.

Willenbacher, E. (2004). Regulating sports agents: Why current federal and state efforts do not defer the unscrupulous athlete–agent and how a national licensing system may cure the problem. *Saint Johns Law Review, 78*(1225).

ETHICAL ISSUES IN SPORT MARKETING AND PROMOTIONS

CHAPTER 7

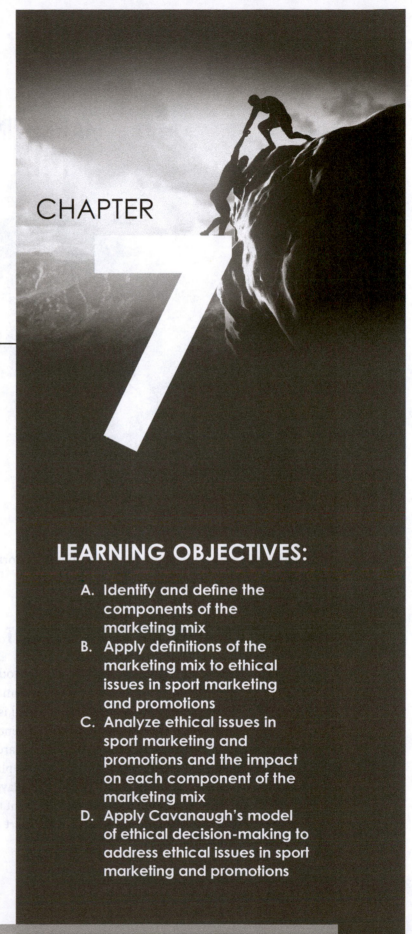

The sport industry is unique in that it not only acts as an entertainment outlet for consumers, but also serves as a promotional vehicle beyond the field of play. As such, sport organizations may engage in the marketing of the sport, while also providing an outlet for outside organizations to market through sport. The competitive, and oftentimes crowded, marketplace requires sport marketers to be exceptionally creative when marketing the products of their organization to ensure they attract and engage consumers with many options on how and where to spend their discretionary income. While unethical marketing practices can and do occur, the hope is that marketers will incorporate marketing ethics into the marketing process to promote the products of the organization in a socially responsible manner.

In an effort to achieve organizational goals and objectives, sport marketers rely on the controllable variables in the marketing mix: product, place, price, and promotion. To be successful, sport organizations must market the right product, at the right price, in the right place, using the right promotion to successfully reach the target market. This chapter will address ethical issues

LEARNING OBJECTIVES:

A. Identify and define the components of the marketing mix

B. Apply definitions of the marketing mix to ethical issues in sport marketing and promotions

C. Analyze ethical issues in sport marketing and promotions and the impact on each component of the marketing mix

D. Apply Cavanaugh's model of ethical decision-making to address ethical issues in sport marketing and promotions

THE MARKETING MIX

PRODUCT

PLACE

TARGET MARKET

PRICE

PROMOTION

Petr Vaclavek/shutterstock.com

sport marketers must understand in the competitive sport marketplace with respect to each component of the marketing mix, beginning first with the product.

THE MARKETING MIX: PRODUCT

A **sport product** can be a tangible, physical good pre-produced in a factory such as a basketball, or intangible services such as those associated with an event or game-day experience. Regardless of whether a particular sport product is a physical good or service, the goal is to satisfy the needs of consumers. Furthermore, the sport product includes both the **core product**, or central product offered, and **product extensions**, including amenities and other related products (Mullin, Hardy, & Sutton, 2015). The core product refers to the game itself and whatever is essential for the game to take place, including apparel and equipment, game form (the rules and techniques associated with the game), players, fan behavior, venue, personnel, and process. The extensions, on the other hand, include coaches, print materials, programs, videos, music, memorabilia, mascots, cheerleaders, and the organization itself. Sport marketers must take each into consideration in their decision-making processes.

When making decisions on how to market a sport product, sport marketers rely on the primary benefits sought by consumers (Fullerton, 2009). One segment may desire escape from the stress of their everyday lives through entertainment, while another segment may view attending an event as a socialization opportunity in which they can interact with their friends and family without being overly invested in the core product. Based on the particular motives sought by the targeted segment, sport marketers can make decisions on which elements of the core product and which types of product extensions to emphasize in their messaging to consumers.

Outsourcing

There are many ethical issues with respect to the product component in the marketing mix. One such issue is with the tangible, physical sporting goods produced in a factory setting. Many organizations outsource the manufacturing of their sporting goods in order to save money. **Outsourcing,** or contracting out of the business process to another party, provides benefits such as savings on labor costs and overhead expenses, flexibility, and focus (Hamlett, n.d.). Labor cost reductions include savings on competitive wages and health benefits. Overhead cost reductions include savings on utilities, equipment maintenance, and indirect labor. With respect to flexibility, outsourcing allows organizations to meet increased production requirements faster. Finally, focus refers to allowing the organization to focus on marketing and sales efforts and trusting the outsourced company to deal with the production of the products.

In the sport industry, one company that has been notorious for outsourcing the manufacturing and production of its products is Nike. In the 1970s, a majority of Nike products were manufactured in South Korea and Taiwan. However, with the formation of unions and rising wages, Nike chose to move the manufacturing of its products to countries where protective labor laws are not enforced and the formation of independent trade unions is prohibited (Global Exchange, n.d.). Nike's success as an organization coupled with the out-

patpitchaya/shutterstock.com

sourcing of its labor led to the organization being seen as a global symbol for **abusive labor practices** (Lutz, 2015). Allegations of poor working conditions and child labor have tainted the reputation of the Nike brand for decades. Nike co-founder and chairman Phil Knight admitted many issues existed with respect to the outsourced manufacturing of the company's products. To Knight, the most disappointing of the issues surrounding Nike involved the reports of children as young as 10 years old producing Nike products in Pakistan and Cambodia (Boggan, 2001). Knight responded to the issue by stating that the Nike organization has high standards with respect to appropriate working age for the company, with employees expected to be 18 in footwear manufacturing and 16 for apparel and equipment manufacturing. Unfortunately, in some countries in which Nike products are manufactured, it is nearly impossible to verify the age of employees because records of birth do not always exist and those that do can easily be forged (Boggan, 2001).

Team Names, Logos, and Mascots

A second ethical issue associated with the product component of the marketing mix involves team names, logos, and mascots. Each of these represents an important component of the overall image of a brand. The name, logo, and mascot are oftentimes the first associations that individuals have with a sport brand. As such, each is heavily present in the branding efforts of sport marketers. There have been a number of controversial team names, logos, and mascots in the sport industry, Some of which are still present today. For the purposes of this textbook and the consideration of ethical issues with the product components of the marketing mix, attention will be placed on the following organizations: Washington Redskins, Washington Bullets, Cleveland Indians, New York Red Bulls, and Zulu Cannibal Giants.

Washington, D.C., is home to two of the most controversial team names in U.S. sport history, the Redskins of the National Football League (NFL) and the Bullets of the National Basketball Association (NBA). The Redskins name is perhaps the most contentious as it is considered a racial slur by many, who equate its use with the skin color of Native Americans. Opponents to the Redskins name have expressed their disbelief in its use by comparing the Redskins name to having a team called the Blacks or the Whites. The Redskins organization, on the other hand, has defended its use of the name by stating its intentions are honorable and the organization is celebrating the Native American culture. Following the cancellation of the franchise trademark by the Trademark Trials and Appeal Board in 2014 (Munguia, 2014), the Redskins organization argued that a ban on their trademark was not constitutional as it burdened content and viewpoint-based speech (O'Dell, 2015). Support for the Redskins, opinion was recently found in a Supreme Court case in which Simon Tam, an Asian-American frontman of his band, brought a lawsuit after trademark examiners refused his trademark application for the band name, The Slants. Tam originally won at the United States Court of Appeals for the federal circuit and the Supreme Court affirmed this decision. The Supreme Court struck down the rule against disparaging trademarks under the notion that one cannot ban speech based on the grounds that ideas may be offensive (Liptak, 2017). This ruling may help to support the Redskins' position that their trademark is an idea and cannot be banned by the Trademark Trials and Appeals Board.

The Washington Wizards, formerly known as the Washington Bullets, are also located in Washington D.C., which is infamous for violent crime. The Bullets organization was the target of much criticism for the violent connotation of the team name. In 1997, Abe Pollin, the owner of the team, heeded the criticism and changed the organization's name from the Bullets to the Wizards. Posthumously, the Wizards organization credited the changing of the organization's name as a way in which Pollin could express his abhorrence of gun violence in the D.C. community (Steele, 2010). Following the death of Pollin, a locker room gun incident occurred between NBA players Gilbert Arenas and Javaris Crittenton, which seemingly illustrated the gun violence Pollin was trying to overcome. The violence depicted in the Bullets name was present in the organization's own locker room. While the gun incident occurred following the name change, the media referenced the Wizards' prior name in some of the reporting of the incident.

Photo Works/shutterstock.com

Another organization that has received criticism for its name, logo, and mascot is the Cleveland Indians. The Indians' name is obviously associated with Native Americans, but it is the mascot of the organization, Chief Wahoo, that has caused the most controversy. The Chief Wahoo logo has been regarded as the most offensive sports logo as it caricaturizes an entire race of people with its red face appearance. In response to disparagement for the use of the Chief Wahoo logo and mascot, the Indians changed their primary logo to a block letter "C"; however, Chief Wahoo is still featured on team caps and jersey sleeves (Brown, 2014).

While racism and violence are the criticisms of the other teams' names, logos, and mascots mentioned thus far, the New York Red Bulls' name has been denigrated for another reason: corporate greed. Jersey sponsorships, in which a corporate organization pays for advertisement space on team jerseys, have been commonplace internationally for years. In the United States the four major professional leagues, Major League Baseball (MLB), the NBA, NFL, and National Hockey League (NHL), have allowed corporate logos on practice jerseys for years. Furthermore, the Women's National Basketball Association (WNBA), Major League Soccer (MLS), and NASCAR also feature corporate logos on jerseys (Garcia, 2016). The NBA will be the first of the four major professional leagues to sell ad space on the jerseys worn during the regular season through a three-year pilot program during the 2017–2018 season (Harper, 2016). The New York Red Bulls, however, take it a step further than jersey sponsorship. The organization has been criticized for allowing Red Bull to egregiously advertise its brand through the actual name of the team. This platform ensures that any fans of the team who purchase licensed merchandise will not only be walking billboards for the team, but for the Red Bull corporation as well.

A final example of ethical issues surrounding a team name, logo, and mascot is the Zulu Cannibal Giants. The Giants were an all African American baseball team based in Louisville, Kentucky from 1934 to 1937. Although most games would start seriously, the team would eventually break into comedic routines pandering to the worst attitudes and most stereotypical views of Blacks in America (Lanctot, 2004). The comedic effort on the field has since been compared to the work of the Harlem Globetrotters, which is no surprise since one of the team's previous owners, Abe Saperstein, went on to found and be the first owner of the Globetrotters (Serchuk, 2014). Unlike the comedy of the Globetrotters, the Giants seemingly relied on feeding into

negative stereotypes of African Americans, which was depicted by the team playing barefoot, wearing grass skirts, headdresses and war paint, and using bats shaped like war clubs (Serchuk, 2014).

Changing of Team Colors, Uniforms, and Logos

Another product-related ethical dilemma involves the changing of team colors, uniforms, and logos (Laczniak, Burton, & Murphy, 1999). This concept was omnipresent in the 1990s when more than 25 professional teams announced redesigned logos and uniforms (Mullin et al., 2015). Logo changes have been rationalized by a number of reasons. Name changes, as discussed in the previous section, obviously warrant logo changes. However, other reasons include the basic goal of change and the desire for increased team merchandise sales (Ahn, Suh, Lee, & Pedersen, 2012).

One reason that may incite a logo change is when organizations have a shift in ownership. This was evidenced in 2003 when the Atlanta Falcons introduced a meaner and more aggressive appearing logo than what they had used in the past (Foster, Greyser, & Walsh, 2006). The desire to transition from unsuccessful seasons also provoked a logo change for the Baltimore Orioles. A third change that has prompted a new logo is the opening of a new facility. This particular change influencer was seen when the Florida Marlins changed their name to the Miami Marlins and also changed their logo and color scheme. The change was accompanied by a move from

Sun Life Stadium, which they previously shared with the Miami Dolphins, to Miami Ballpark (Knapel, 2011). In each of these incidents, the logo change was intended to improve the reputation and perceptions of the organization in the eyes of consumers.

Rebranding a sport organization also occurs with the goal of increased licensed merchandise sales. This might occur through a complete name and/or logo change, a change in colors or the addition of alternate jerseys in addition to the traditional home and away versions.

STUDENT ACTIVITY
Why would teams change their logo? What does the relationship with major merchandise brands have to do with ethical decision making?

THE MARKETING MIX: PLACE

The place component of the marketing mix typically refers to the distribution component of the marketing process. **Place** involves the transfer of goods and services from the producer to final buyers and users. In the sport entertainment industry, where marketers do not have control over the core product (the game itself), emphasis must be placed on product extensions and the event experience. This can be accomplished by emphasizing the place ensemble, which includes the following elements: landscape, artifacts, history and memories (nostalgia), ideologies, aesthetics, experiences, and problems (Mullin et al., 2015). With respect to marketing the place ensemble, think of Wrigley Field, home of the Chicago Cubs.

- Landscape—Wrigleyville is the nickname of the Chicago neighborhood directly surrounding Wrigley Field. The area features low-rise brick buildings and houses, and some of Chicago's best sports bars and restaurants.
- Artifacts—As the second-oldest ballpark in baseball, historic Wrigley Field is known for three key artifacts: the ivy covering the brick outfield walls; the iconic, red marquee sign on the outside of the stadium; and the hand-operated scoreboard.
- History and memories (nostalgia)—Statues of Ernie Banks, Harry Caray, Ron Santo, and Billy Williams greet fans as they arrive at Wrigley Field. Each statue is a representation of history and evokes memories for fans. Kerry Wood's 20-strikeout game in 1998 made history at Wrigley Field; however, one of the greatest pieces of baseball history also occurred at Wrigley Field when Babe Ruth allegedly pointed to the bleachers and "called his shot" during Game 3 of the 1932 World Series.
- Ideologies—Although Wrigley Field does not necessarily evoke political or social ideologies, it has emphasized the importance of simplicity and history in the game of baseball by maintaining its roots despite a series of renovations.
- Aesthetics—Former *Chicago Tribune* columnist Jerome Holtzman described the aesthetics of the Friendly Confines when he stated, "All of the new parks were the same . . . If you've been to one, you've been to them all." Wrigley, on the other hand, provides close proximity to the field, a cozy neighborhood setting with views of the Chicago skyline, the ivy, manual scoreboard, and clean sightlines (Peterson, 2005).
- Experiences—The experiences of attending a game at Wrigley Field highlight the aesthetics described above from the atmosphere of the ballpark, including the ivy on the outfield walls, the brick backstop, marquee board, manual scoreboard, 7th inning stretch, and smells from the concession stands, to the experiences surrounding the venue in Wrigleyville before, during, and after the game.

Nagel Photography/shutterstock.com

- Problems—Without close, on-site stadium parking, attendees are forced to find off-site parking. This can lead to traffic issues surrounding the stadium. Although the Cubs provide shuttle services from different lots, parking can still be troublesome to attendees.

1-MINUTE REFLECTION

With the place ensemble in mind, marketers must think about their messaging to consumers. Is it ethical to only emphasize the positive, or should consumers also be informed of the bad images and issues in the messaging?

Advertising

An issue surrounding the place component of the marketing mix involves advertising, more specifically the types of advertising displayed in sport venues and through sport broadcasting. Questions arise as to whether or not certain types of businesses, namely alcohol, gambling, and adult entertainment, should be associated with sport brands. The issue arises from the fact that certain relationships may tarnish the reputation of the sport organization.

This notion was put to test in 2012 when a struggling Los Angeles-based Little League organization received a surprise $1,200 donation from Jet Strip Club. Prior to the surprise donation, league officials said they were experiencing financial difficulties following increased rental fees and not being allowed to sell hot dogs during games. Although the league was in dire need of financial assistance, they chose to reject the donation. This was likely attributed to the possibility of the Jet Strip Club using the Little League brand in future advertisements, posters, brochures, newsletters, etc., as the Little League website states those sponsoring an organization have the right to do (Mohney, 2012).

Sport marketers must also consider the impact of advertising tobacco products in their marketing strategies. The following situation depicts the impact of tobacco advertising in the sport industry. In the 1997 Super Bowl in New Orleans, Marlboro maker Phillip Morris Companies was pressured to remove Marlboro brand signage in the Superdome before the telecast of the game. The reason for the removal of the signage was the United States Cigarette Labeling and Advertising Act of 1965, through which tobacco advertising is prohibited on television (Laczniak et al., 1999).

DAILY FANTASY SPORTS

Keith Bell/shutterstock.com

A second ethical issue associated with advertising is false advertising (also referred to as deceptive advertising). **False advertising** occurs when a marketer utilizes an advertising platform and gives an incorrect understanding about a product or service. False advertising is considered deceptive, misleading, and illegal. Because of the illegal nature of the practice and the impact it can have on stakeholders, marketers must take appropriate steps to ensure they are not utilizing false advertising. The Federal Trade Commission (FTC) is responsible for the enforcement of advertising laws. The FTC monitors the marketplace and files actions in federal court when cases of fraud or deception are discovered (FTC, n.d.).

In the sport setting, there have been a number of lawsuits filed based on false advertising. One example involves a class action lawsuit filed against daily fantasy sports sites DraftKings and FanDuel. The case claimed the misrepresentation of fairness in the games on the two sites (Rovell, 2015). In other words, although the sites were advertised as fair, they were not fair. The rationale for the case is employees of each organization were allowed to enter fantasy contests on the other's sites for cash and prizes, but analytics on strategies of how to win were potentially available to the participating employees because of their jobs and access to information. Following the suit, DraftKings and FanDuel said they would prohibit employees from the other organization competing on the competitor's site (Rovell, 2015). While this seemingly addressed the issue, was it ethical to originally advertise the games and competitions as fair?

Another example of false advertising claims in the sport setting can be found in FTC charges faced by TicketNetwork, the third largest online ticket exchange in the United States. TicketNetwork, along with two of its sales partners, Ryadd, Inc. and Secure Box Office, LLC, used misleading advertising techniques to convince people they were buying event tickets at face value directly from the venue of the event (Tressler, 2014). According to Tressler, the organizations designed search engine advertisements and websites using names and URLs mimicking the venue names of the events. Their actions were considered deceptive, misleading, and illegal.

Ambush Marketing

Piggybacking on the concept of false advertisement is the notion of ambush marketing. **Ambush marketing** occurs when companies that are not official sponsors seek to associate themselves with a sport organization.

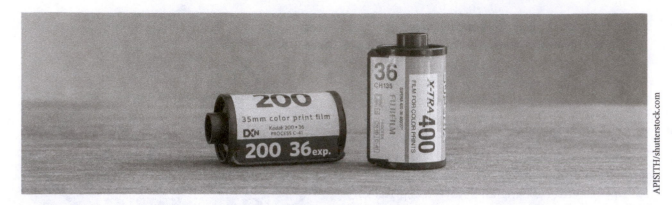

The intent is to capitalize on the goodwill of a sport organization or event without having to pay the requisite sponsorship fees (Mullin et al., 2015). Organizations that practice ambush marketing typically imply an association without actually stating one exists. It is this implication, rather than actual assertion of a relationship between the two entities, that leads to ambush marketing's distinction from false advertisement. There are a number of tactics commonly employed by ambush marketers including sponsoring media coverage of an event, sponsoring a subcategory within an event, using themed advertising, having a presence in and around the event venue, and employing consumer promotions (Crompton, 2004).

Ambush marketing has a long history in the sport industry, beginning first in the 1984 Los Angeles Olympics. Rather than focusing on the number of sponsorships sold, the emphasis was placed on "official sponsorships" in which organizations received exclusive rights for fairly exorbitant costs. This led to competition before the games, as direct competitors were forced to contend for the sponsorship rights. In the camera category, Fuji beat rival Kodak for the title of "official camera of the Olympics." Rather than accepting defeat and retreating, Kodak signed a deal to sponsor broadcasts of the games. This tactic allowed Kodak advertisements to be seen by far more viewers than Fuji advertisements at the live events.

Four years later, in somewhat of a payback, Fuji pulled an ambush on Kodak. Kodak became the official camera category sponsor of the Olympics, while Fuji chose to invest in a sponsorship with the U.S. swimming team (Meenaghan, 1996). Although the sponsorship did not provide Fuji with the exclusive category rights Kodak received, the tactic of sponsoring a subcategory within an event allowed the event association at a reduced cost (Bayless, 1988).

SMALL GROUP ACTIVITY:
With the use of your computers, phones, tablets, etc., find three additional examples of ambush marketing in sport. The examples should differ from those discussed in this chapter. In addition to finding other examples of ambush marketing, answer the following questions:
1. Is ambush marketing desperate or smart business? Explain your answer.
2. Should ambush marketing be illegal? Why or why not?
3. Is ambush marketing ethical or unethical? Explain your answer.

Ticket Restrictions

Since the place component of the marketing mix also involves the distribution of tickets, the implementation of ticket restrictions is another ethical issue that must be considered. **Ticket restrictions** refer to limitations placed on potential consumers with respect to tickets to sport events. The rationale for the use of the restrictions is to protect the home-court/home-field advantage of the hosting team, particularly in big games, such as championships.

Mega Pixel/shutterstock.com

One example of the implementation of a ticket restriction policy occurred in 2014 when the Seattle Seahawks refused to sell National Football Championship (NFC) tickets to residents of California. The Seahawks only sold tickets to customers using billing addresses in Washington, Oregon, Montana, Idaho, Alaska, Hawaii, British Columbia, and Alberta (Boren, 2014). This decision forced San Francisco 49ers fans not residing in one of those areas to purchase tickets from the secondary market.

In a similar situation, the Nashville Predators implemented a "keeping the red out" policy intended to not allow the traveling Chicago Blackhawks fans to attend games in Nashville. Much like the Seahawks, the Predators implemented a restricted sales area policy for the Blackhawks game at Bridgestone Arena based on zip code, in which only those in Tennessee, Kentucky, Mississippi, Alabama, and Georgia could purchase tickets. The difference between the Seahawks example and this situation is fans were not able to purchase tickets through the secondary market because the Predators enforced credit card rules in which the original purchaser had to be present with photo identification to get into the arena (Rosenbloom, 2016).

A third example can be seen through the Tampa Bay Lightning, who took the ticket restrictions policy a step further. During the Stanley Cup Finals in 2015, the Lightning required ticket purchasers to have a credit card with a Florida address to purchase tickets to the series against the Chicago Blackhawks. The Lightning's goal was to make it difficult for out-of-state fans to buy tickets in an effort to maintain the home-ice advantage. Much like the aforementioned examples with the Seattle Seahawks, fans outside of Florida could purchase tickets from the secondary market. The catch? Costs on the secondary market were triple face value. Beyond the zip code restrictions, the Lightning also implemented apparel restrictions in their club seating. Fans wearing logos from the opposing team were offered neutral colored shirts to wear or seating outside of the club area (Ryan & Thompson, 2015).

SMALL GROUP ACTIVITY:
In a small group (three or four students), use the preceding examples to answer the following questions.
1. Is it ethical for sport marketers to implement ticket restriction policies in an effort to somewhat control the home field/home court advantage in sport? Why or why not?
2. Is it fair to implement ticket restriction policies? Explain your answer.
3. Are ticket restriction policies discriminatory? Why or why not?

THE MARKETING MIX: PRICE

The price component of the marketing mix is oftentimes considered the most difficult component in the marketing process. Tickets are most often associated with pricing, but other factors of the event also impact the overall price of the event experience. The total amount of money spent by the consumer in the consumption of the sport product is referred to as the **cost of attendance** (Mullin et al., 2015). The cost of attendance typically includes pricing for factors such as tickets to the event, parking, concessions, and licensed merchandise and/or memorabilia. For consumers traveling to attend the events, hotel and transportation may be additional costs.

It is clear that the cost to attend events quickly adds up due to the ancillary revenue generated from additional products beyond tickets. Because of escalating costs, it is important to ensure consumers are having valuable experiences. **Value** refers to the ratio of benefits to money spent or, the worth of something as defined in Chapter 1. In other words, do consumers feel as though the benefits received are worth the money spent on the entire event experience? Because of the differences in consumers, it is important to remember that value is subjective and varies from one consumer to the next (Mullin et al., 2015).

There are many ethical issues associated with the price component of the marketing mix. One ethical decision that must be made by sport marketers is whether or not to increase prices after championship years. This decision is important, as the organization is likely to receive some backlash from consumers following the increases. Another example of an ethical decision with respect to price includes misleading price reductions. A **misleading price reduction** occurs when an organization advertises a sale, which in turn excites customers, as they do not want to miss out on the sale. However, the original price may have been increased prior to the "sale" so the organization does not lose additional revenue. FTC guidelines against deceptive pricing suggest a product can be advertised as being sold at a reduced price if the product was offered at the former price for a reasonably substantial period of time.

THE MARKETING MIX: PROMOTION

The **promotion** component of the marketing mix involves the vehicles employed by marketers to convey desired information about the other three components of the marketing mix (Mullin et al., 2015). In an effort to draw consumers to the product, marketers must be creative in their promotional strategy as the ultimate goal is to generate revenue. One concept in the achievement of this goal is the use of the AIDA approach. The **AIDA approach** is an acronym that stands for creating awareness/attention, increasing interest, generating desire, and producing action (Fullerton, 2009). The first "A" in the acronym refers to creating awareness of a product or service amongst potential consumers. The "I" represents the ability of an organization to generate or increase interest in a product or service. The "D" represents desire and refers to the ability of an organization to create a sense of desire amongst consumers to the point they want the product or service. The second "A" refers to action, which involves the actual purchasing of the product or service by consumers. Take a look at some examples of sport promotions below and determine whether or not each is ethical and whether or not each meets the components of the AIDA concept.

Examples of Sport Promotions

On the 10-year anniversary of Mike Tyson biting off a chunk of Evander Holyfield's ear during a rematch bout, the Fort Myers Miracle, a minor league baseball affiliate of the Minnesota Twins, hosted Mike Tyson Ear

Night. For the promotion, the first 1,000 fans in attendance received a fake ear. Additionally, there were ear decorating stations available throughout the stadium, as well as fake tattoo stations for patrons to get face tattoos like Mike Tyson's (Hill, 2007a). The New Britain Rock Cats, another affiliate of the Minnesota Twins, held a speed dating promotional night. During the evening, eligible bachelors and bachelorettes changed seats every inning to meet others. Their experiences were documented via scorecards and later sent to a dating company to set up participants on second dates (Pahigian, 2007).

The Altoona Curve, a minor league affiliate of the Pittsburgh Pirates, created and hosted a series of "Awful Nights" in the 2000s (Hill, 2007b). Some activities associated with the theme night included stadium employees singing bad karaoke during warm-ups, announcing each player's "failure average" in lieu of batting average, a cold SPAM eating contest, awful announcing, and a tighty-whitey underwear launch instead of the traditional t-shirt toss (Hill).

The career of Jose Canseco ended with the Long Beach Armada. Following the release of his book *Juiced*, the Fullerton Flyers hosted a Juice Box Night when Canseco's team visited Fullerton. As part of the promotion, the Flyers gave away 500 juice boxes (Rhodes, 2011). In another promotion focused on the tarnished reputation of an athlete, the Atlantic City Surf hosted Terrell Owens (T.O.) Appreciation Night. The theme night included two upper box tickets to fans that brought T.O. merchandise to the game, which would be burnt on the field after the game. There was also a contest for the fan who gave the best reason to hate T.O. The prize included 40 suite tickets. Additionally, the event included 81-cent hot dogs dedicated to the "greasiest number 81" ever to play for the Eagles (Pumerantz, 2012).

In yet another promotional night in which the focus was on a former athlete, the Utah Flash of the NBA D-League hosted a theme night in which they promoted a halftime one-on-one game between Michael Jordan and former Utah Jazz guard Byron Russell. Jordan, however, never responded to the request to attend the game. This led the owner of the Flash to hire a Jordan-lookalike for the event. The fans, many of whom came to the game for the sole purpose of seeing the one-on-one game, were furious when they realized Jordan was not actually there. Fans threw T-shirts from a T-shirt toss onto the court and stormed out of the game. Flash owner Brandt Andersen apologized to those offended by the promotion and explained it was done in fun. He also offered free tickets to a future Flash game (Bartosik, 2009).

Finally, one of the most prominent promotions in the history of sport is Disco Demolition Night hosted by the Chicago White Sox in 1979. Admission to the game was only 98 cents for fans who brought a disco record to be blown up in centerfield after the game. The White Sox organization anticipated 35,000 fans for the event and hired 50 off-duty policemen for security. To their surprise, 60,000 fans showed up and were climbing the walls and using ladders to enter the stadium. With chants of "Disco sucks" many fans rushed the field and tore down the batting cage, ripped up the pitching mound and home plate, and lit signs on fire in centerfield (Mastropolo, 2015).

DVARG/shutterstock.com

> **SMALL GROUP ACTIVITY**
> In a small group (three or four students), create a promotion you believe will sell tickets without compromising the ethical integrity of the organization. Identify the components of the promotion and the target market.

ETHICAL DECISION MAKING IN MARKETING

It is clear from the preceding examples in this chapter there are a myriad of ethical decisions facing sport marketers. Within each component of the marketing mix (product, place, price, and promotion) sport marketers must weigh the pros and cons of alternatives associated with potential decisions. In determining whether or not a sport marketing decision is ethical, one can utilize an ethical analysis decision-making model such as Cavanaugh's model. As discussed in Chapter 1, Cavanaugh's model employs three considerations in the ethical decision-making process: utility, rights, and justice. After gathering the facts for the situation, one should answer the three questions in Table 7.1 prior to making a decision about an ethical issue.

TABLE 7.1 *Questions to Ask When Using Cavanaugh's Model of Ethical Decision-Making*		
Consideration	**Emphasis**	**Question to Answer**
Utility	The aim of the organizational goals is satisfying the constituencies of the organization	Does the choice optimize benefits?
Rights	Individual rights regarding life and safety, truthfulness, privacy, freedom of conscience, free speech, and private property	Does the choice respect the rights of those involved?
Justice	Fair treatment, fair administration of rules, fair compensation, fair blame, and due process	Is the choice fair?

CONCLUSION

Ethical issues in sport marketing occur at all levels of the marketing mix. As a sport manager, students will be faced with a variety of decisions with respect to the product, place, price, and promotion. Given the impact decisions can have on stakeholders, it is important that sport managers consider the ethical issues surrounding each component of the marketing mix and the consequences of those decisions. It is also important to understand how to implement marketing decisions to maximize revenue generation while maintaining the integrity of the sport organization.

DISCUSSION QUESTIONS

Using Cavanaugh's model for ethical decision making, run the following ethical marketing questions through the *utility, rights, and justice* framework illustrated in Table 7.1.

1. Was it ethical for Nike to outsource the manufacturing of its products? Why or why not? What portion of the framework most influenced your ethical decision? What overwhelming factors did you consider?

2. Is it ethical for sport teams to use Native American names, logos, and symbols in the branding of their organizations? Why or why not? What portion of the framework most influenced your ethical decision? What overwhelming factors did you consider?

3. Is it ethical for sport organizations to change colors, uniforms, and/or logos in an effort to profit? Why or why not? What portion of the framework most influenced your ethical decision? What overwhelming factors did you consider?

4. Is it ethical for sport organizations to engage in ambush marketing? Why or why not? What portion of the framework most influenced your ethical decision? What overwhelming factors did you consider?

5. Is it ethical for sport organizations to implement ticket restrictions? Why or why not? What portion of the framework most influenced your ethical decision? What overwhelming factors did you consider?

6. Is it ethical for sport organizations to employ outlandish promotions to increase attendance? Why or why not? What portion of the framework most influenced your ethical decision? What overwhelming factors did you consider?

7. Is it ethical for the NBA to sell ad space on the jerseys? Why or why not? What portion of the framework most influenced your ethical decision? What overwhelming factors did you consider?

CASE STUDY: BECKMAN ON-FIELD EXPERIENCE

Russell Beckman is a high school social studies teacher that lives in Mount Pleasant, Wisconsin, which is about an hour north of Chicago. He is a diehard Green Bay Packers fan who happens to have season tickets to both the Packers and the Chicago Bears. He has owned a Personal Seat License at Soldier Field, the home of the Bears, since 2003. One of the perks of being a Bears season ticket holder involves an on-field experience for fans before a game. Beckman participated in the pre-game experience at Soldier Field before the Packers and Bears played in both 2014 and 2015. For each experience, he went onto the field decked out in his Packers gear. In 2016, however, the Bears implemented a policy that prohibited participants of that experience from wearing the opposing team's gear. The team communicated the new policy via email with Beckman less than a week before the scheduled event. He called the front office and asked them to reconsider the policy, but was denied. Beckman decided to still show up to the on-feild pre-game event at Soldier Field wearing his Packers gear and was denied entrance for failing to adhere to the new policy.

After being denied his on-field experience, Beckman filed a federal lawsuit against the Bears. He is representing himself in the case, and is not suing for financial damages except to recoup legal fees. Instead, he simply wants the Bears to change their policy since he is a paying customer, despite him being a fan of both NFL teams (Ryan, 2017).

CASE QUESTIONS

1. What do you think is the major ethical issue with this case?

2. Using Cavanaugh's model for ethical decision making, determine if it is ethical for the Bears to not allow Beckman on the sideline in his Packers gear. What portion of the framework most influenced your ethical decision? What overwhelming factors did you consider?

3. Do you think that fans have more rights if they are longtime season ticket holders? Why or why not?

4. Do you think that the Bears should have changed their policy? Why or why not?

5. What do you anticipate the outcome of the lawsuit will be?

6. How might an organization such as the Bears better promote season ticket holder benefits to avoid situations similar to this?

GLOSSARY

AIDA approach is an acronym that stands for creating awareness/attention, increasing interest, generating desire, and producing action.

Ambush marketing occurs when companies that are not official sponsors seek to associate themselves with a sport organization with the intent to capitalize on the goodwill of a sport organization or event without having to pay the requisite sponsorship fees.

Core products are the central products offered, including the game itself and whatever is essential for the game to take place, including apparel and equipment, game form (the rules and techniques associated with the game), players, fan behavior, venue, personnel, and process.

Cost of attendance refers to the total amount of money spent by the consumer in the consumption of the sport product.

False advertising occurs when a marketer utilizes an advertising platform and gives an incorrect understanding about a product or service.

Misleading price reductions occur when an organization advertises a sale, which in turn excites customers, as they do not want to miss out on the sale; however, the original price may have been increased prior to the "sale" so the organization does not lose additional revenue.

Outsourcing is the contracting out of a business process to another party.

Place typically refers to the distribution component of the marketing process and involves the transfer of goods and services from the producer to final buyers and users.

Product extensions include amenities and other related products, such as coaches, print materials, programs, videos, music, memorabilia, mascots, cheerleaders, and the organization itself.

Promotion is the component of the marketing mix that involves the vehicles employed by marketers to convey desired information about the other three components of the marketing mix.

Sport products are tangible, physical goods pre-produced in factories or intangible services such as those associated with an event experience.

Ticket restrictions refer to limitations placed on potential consumers with respect to tickets to sport events.

Value refers to the ratio of benefits to money spent.

References

Ahn, T., Suh, Y., Lee, J., & Pedersen, P. M. (2012). Sport fans and their teams' redesigned logos: An examination of the moderating effect of team identification on attitude and purchase intention of team-logoed merchandise. *Journal of Sport Management, 27*, 11–23.

Bartosik, M. (2009, December 8). Utah Flash fans duped by Michael Jordan hoax. NBC Chicago. Retrieved from http://www.nbcchicago.com/news/sports/Nowhere-Jordan-Utah-Fans-Duped-by-Michael-Jordan-Hoax-78793047.html

Bayless, A. (1988, February 8). Ambush marketing is becoming a popular event at Olympic Games. *The Wall Street Journal*.

Boggan, S. (2001, October 20). 'We blew it': Nike admits to mistakes over child labor. Retrieved from http://www.commondreams.org/headlines01/1020-01.htm

Boren, C. (2014, January 13). Seahawks won't sell NFC championship tickets to fans from California. *The Washington Post*. Retrieved from https://www.washingtonpost.com/news/early-lead/wp/2014/01/13/seahawks-wont-sell-nfc-championship-tickets-to-fans-from-california/

Brown, D. (2014, January 9). Cleveland Indians demote Chief Wahoo logo. Big League Stew. Retrieved from http://sports.yahoo.com/blogs/mlb-big-league-stew/cleveland-indians-marginalize-chief-wahoo-logo-081024357--mlb.html

Crew, J. (2016, April 29). Here's how much NFL draft pick Laremy Tunsil lost because of 1 tweet. *Fortune*. Retrieved from http://fortune.com/2016/04/29/laremy-tunsil-tweet-video/

Crompton, J. L. (2004). Sponsorship ambushing in sport. *Managing Leisure, 9*, 1–12.

Federal Trade Commission (FTC). (n.d.). Truth in advertising. Retrieved from https://www.ftc.gov/news-events/media-resources/truth-advertising

Foster, G., Greyser, S. A., & Walsh, B. (2006). The business of sports: Text and cases on strategy and management. Mason, OH: Thomson South-Western.

Fullerton, S. (2009). Sports Marketing (2nd ed.). New York, NY: McGraw-Hill.

Garcia, A. (2016, April 15). NBA becomes first major US sports league to allow ads on jerseys. CNN Money. Retrieved from http://money.cnn.com/2016/04/15/news/nba-jerseys-corporate-sponsors/

Global Exchange. (n.d.). Nike FAQs. Retrieved from http://www.globalexchange.org/sweatfree/nike/faq

Hamlett, K. (n.d.). Reasons for outsourcing in a manufacturing industry. Retrieved from http://smallbusiness.chron.com/reasons-outsourcing-manufacturing-industry-1292.html

Harper, Z. (2016, April 15). It's official: NBA approves jersey sponsorships beginning in 2017–18. CBS Sports. Retrieved from http://www.cbssports.com/nba/eye-on-basketball/25555978/its-official-nba-approves-jersey-sponsorships-beginning-in-2017-18

Hill, B. (2007a, June 26). Top 10 upcoming promotions. Minor League Baseball. Retrieved from http://www.milb.com/news/article.jsp?ymd=20070626&content_id=265465&fext=.jsp&vkey=news_milb

Hill, B. (2007b, August 3). Promo review: Altoona's awful night V: Curve pays tribute to all that is bad. Minor League Baseball. Retrieved from http://www.milb.com/news/article.jsp?ymd=20070803&content_id=284032&fext=.jsp&vkey=news_milb

Kellenberger, H. (2016, May 12). Laremy Tunsil admits to taking money from Ole Miss coaches. The Clarion-Ledger. Retrieved from http://www.clarionledger.com/story/sports/college/ole-miss/2016/04/28/laremy-tunsil-admits-taking-money-ole-miss-coaches/83683484/

Knapel, R. (2011, July 23). Florida Marlins to be renamed Miami Marlins next season. Bleacher Report. Retrieved from http://bleacherreport.com/articles/777336-florida-marlins-to-be-renamed-miami-marlins-next-season.

Laczniak, G., Burton, R. H., & Murphy, P. (1999). Sports marketing ethics in today's marketplace. *Sport Marketing Quarterly, 8*(4), 43–53.

Lanctot, N. (2004). Negro league baseball: The rise and ruin of a black institution. Philadelphia, PA: University of Pennsylvania Press.

Liptak, A. (2017, June 19). Justices strike down law banning disparaging trademarks. *The New York Times*. Retrieved from https://www.nytimes.com/2017/06/19/us/politics/supreme-court-trademarks-redskins.html

Lutz, A. (2015, June 6). How Nike shed its sweatshop image to dominate the shoe industry. Business Insider. Retrieved from http://www.businessinsider.com/how-nike-fixed-its-sweatshop-image-2015-6

Mastropolo, F. (2015, July 12). 'It was like a riot': The history of disco demolition night. Retrieved from http://ultimate-classicrock.com/disco-demolition-night/

Meenaghan, T. (1996, October 15). Ambush marketing: A threat to corporate sponsorship. Sloan Management Review. Retrieved from http://sloanreview.mit.edu/article/ambush-marketing-a-threat-to-corporate-sponsorship/

Mohney, G. (2012, March 13). LA area Little League rejects strip club donation. ABC News. Retrieved from http://abcnews.go.com/blogs/headlines/2012/03/little-league-team-rejects-strip-club-donation/

Mullin, B., Hardy, S., & Sutton, W. (2015). *Sport Marketing* (4th ed.). Champaign, IL: Human Kinetics.

Munguia, H. (2014, September 5). The 2,128 Native American mascots people aren't talking about. Retrieved from http://fivethirtyeight.com/features/the-2128-native-american-mascots-people-arent-talking-about/

O'Dell, L. (2015, November 3). Washington Redskins defend controversial name by citing other 'offensive' trademarks. Associated Press. Retrieved from http://www.boston.com/sports/football/2015/11/03/washington-redskins-defend-controversial-name-citing-other-offensive-trademarks/d0CUulArqCVlFPEDMsaCiI/story.html

Pahigian, J. (2007, July 11). Baseball's top-10 minor league publicity stunts. ESPN. Retrieved from http://espn.go.com/travel/news/story?id=2931344

Patterson, C. (2016, April 28). After Instagram hack, Laremy Tunsil admits to taking money at Ole Miss. CBS Sports. Retrieved from http://www.cbssports.com/collegefootball/eye-on-college-football/25570474/after-instagram-hack-laremy-tunsil-admits-to-taking-money-at-ole-miss

Peterson, P. M. (2005). *Chicago's Wrigley Field*. Charleston, SC: Arcadia Publishing.

Pumerantz, Z. (2012, September 13). The craziest promotions in sport history. Bleacher Report. Retrieved from http://bleacherreport.com/articles/1331719-the-craziest-promotions-in-sports-history/page/2

Rhodes, C. (2011, May 5). Crazy promotions all part of minor league baseball lore. Patch. Retrieved from http://patch.com/california/lakeelsinore-wildomar/crazy-promotions-all-part-of-minor-league-baseball-lore

Rosenbloom, S. (2016, January 12). Predators wonks are at it again, Blackhawks fans. *Chicago Tribune*. Retrieved from http://www.chicagotribune.com/sports/rosenblog/ct-blackhawks-fans-predators-tickets-rosenbloom20160112-column.html

Rovell, D. (2015, October 9). Class action lawsuit filed against DraftKings and FanDuel. ESPN. Retrieved from http://espn.go.com/chalk/story/_/id/13840184/class-action-lawsuit-accuses-draftkings-fanduel-negligence-fraud-false-advertising

Ryan, S. (2017, June 20). Season ticketholder sues Bears over ban on wearing Packers gear on sideline. *Chicago Tribune*. Retrieved from http://www.chicagotribune.com/sports/football/bears/ct-packers-fan-sues-bears-spt-0620-20170619-story.html

Ryan, S., & Thompson, P. (2015, June 2). Lightning impose apparel, ticket restrictions on Blackhawks fans. *Chicago Tribune*. Retrieved from http://www.chicagotribune.com/sports/hockey/blackhawks/ct-lightning-fan-restrictions-spt-0603-20150602-story.html

Serchuk, D. (2014, October 14). Foul ball: The Zulu Cannibal Giants, Louisville's most disturbing team. Insider Louisville. Retrieved from http://insiderlouisville.com/lifestyle_culture/zulu-cannibal-giants-louisvilles-disturbing-sports-team/

Steele, A. (2010, January 27). Wizards statement on Arenas, Crittenton. *The Washington Post*. Retrieved from http://voices.washingtonpost.com/wizardsinsider/2010/01/wizards-statement-on-arenas-cr.html

Tressler, C. (2014, July 24). Ticket resellers settle misleading advertising charges. Retrieved from https://www.consumer.ftc.gov/blog/ticket-resellers-settle-misleading-advertising-charges

ETHICAL ISSUES WITH TECHNOLOGY IN SPORT

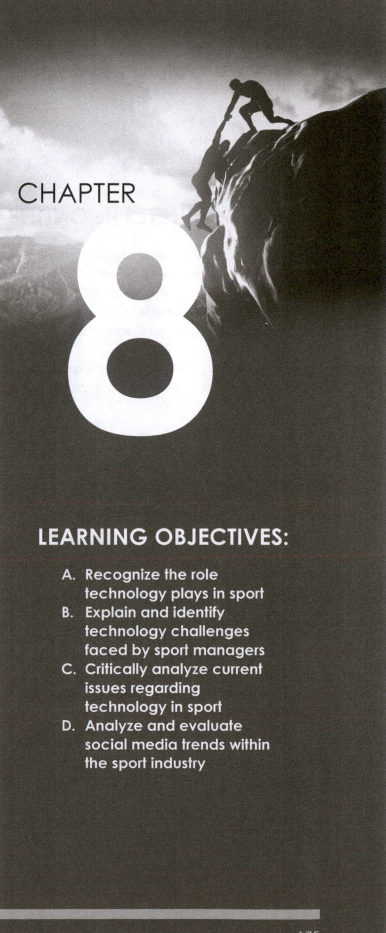

CHAPTER

8

LEARNING OBJECTIVES:

A. Recognize the role technology plays in sport
B. Explain and identify technology challenges faced by sport managers
C. Critically analyze current issues regarding technology in sport
D. Analyze and evaluate social media trends within the sport industry

Technology, specifically technology in sport, has been constantly improving over the past several years. On the playing field, athletes have sought to improve overall performance with the potential use of technology. One example could include how the tennis racket has been updated from wood to laminated wood, to steel, to aluminum, to titanium. These changes allow for the tennis rackets to be lighter to reduce athlete fatigue, but also include stronger material for better performance. Quarterbacks for the National Football League (NFL) organizations use technology in the form of virtual reality to assist them to recognize the movements of receivers from the QB view, instead of a bird's-eye view. Outside of the playing field, sport managers have been using technology to make better decisions about ticket pricing strategies, new marketing approaches, fan engagement, nutrition, facility upkeep and many other industry specific necessities. Social media websites like *Snapchat* and *Twitter* allow sport organizations to develop relationships with their followers, for little to no cost. Even though technology may seem to be making this world more complicated, it has helped maximize resources for athletes and sport organizations alike.

This chapter seeks to identify and elaborate on a variety of new technologies and the role technology plays in sport. **Technology in sport** can refer to the use of scientific knowledge to improve an athlete's performance in sport or technology that can add to the improvement of athletic performance and the game day experience. Technology has become very useful for sport organizations, but it can also bring about perils. First, this chapter looks at technology in sport at the college level, the impact and influence of technology on athletic performance, and future trends in technology that sport managers need to consider.

STUDENT-ATHLETES IN ONLINE COURSES

Online courses provide a tremendous amount of benefits for their users. The ability to do the coursework on one's own time, the ability to be outside of a specific city to learn from a professor, or having the freedom to listen to the lecture at one's leisure are all benefits for students when it comes to online learning. Online classes have grown in popularity in recent years, which allows for greater flexibility with students in the sport realm, but can also lead to some dangers.

Student-athletes can benefit from online courses in several ways, but most specifically they can benefit from the flexibility online courses provide their schedules. No longer are students required to be "in class," but

Rawpixel.com/shutterstock.com

instead can take courses online that fit their academic schedule without conflicting with their sport schedule. Further, student-athletes can do their coursework, listen to lectures, and post on discussion boards when they are traveling to compete, without having to miss a class. However, student-athletes could also be having their coursework completed for them. Such was the case at the University of Southern Mississippi with the basketball team. The head basketball coach for the Golden Eagles, Donnie Tyndall, was directing two of his graduate assistants and two of his assistant coaches to complete homework assignments for potential recruits from junior college institutions. In this instance, hundreds of assignments were completed by the staff, including over 30 psychology assignments submitted from Jamaica, when the student-athlete was attending a two-year institution in Florida (New, 2016). The National Collegiate Athletics Association (NCAA) banned Tyndall from coaching for 10 years in order to help prevent this type of behavior in the future. **Ghostwriting,** the practice of writing something for another or hiding credit from the real author, or taking tests for other students is a common example of issues in online courses and can make cheating efforts even easier for student-athletes (Rothschild, 2011).

What should the NCAA do about online courses and student-athletes? Online courses, as stated before, have a tremendous amount of benefits for student-athletes as they give them flexibility in their classes and with their time. However, should there be a cap on the number of online classes a student can take? For instance, Johnny Manziel, while attending Texas A&M University, took only online classes during his sophomore year (Fowler, 2013). He was only required to come to campus once a month, and could spend the rest of

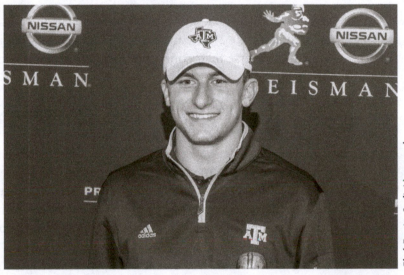

Black Russian Studio/shutterstock.com

his time outside of an academic classroom. As the number of students taking online courses continues to increase (Haynie, 2015), the concern for the NCAA has become greater. The NCAA currently has policies related to nontraditional courses, but the rules on the number of online courses or the number of athletes completing correspondence, distance learning, independent studies, and individualized instruction courses remain unclear.

The NCAA can implement policies to ensure that student-athletes do not abuse the system, but the NCAA cannot treat a student-athlete any differently than a non-student-athlete. If the NCAA did so, it could be considered discrimination and subject to legal penalty. The NCAA should have legitimate concern related to the current climate of student-athletes taking online courses. The NCAA claims to have seen an increase in the number of student-athletes enrolled in online courses, yet official numbers are not available. As more and more athletes are recognizing the freedom and flexibility of this option, it may become a more common problem for the NCAA and its member institutions. Both universities and the NCAA will likely need to revise the monitoring of student-athlete activity in online and all nontraditional campus classes.

SOCIAL MEDIA AND SPORT

Over the past decade, social network sites have become a growing trend in modern-day society. **Social network sites** are defined as

> "web-based services that allow individuals to (1) construct a public or semi-public profile within a bounded system, (2) articulate a list of other users with whom they share a connection, and (3) view and traverse their connections and those made by others within the system" (Boyd & Ellison, 2008, p. 211).

As of June 2017, Facebook is the largest social network website with over 2 billion active users worldwide. YouTube, Instagram, Twitter, and Reddit follow Facebook with over 250,000,000 users for each site (Maina, 2016; Kallas, 2017). The social networking is not limited to websites but also includes apps like SnapChat which measure videos and pictures sent, instead of by the number of users. SnapChat is an app that allows the user to send a temporary photo or video to another user. Over 8,500 photos are sent every second through SnapChat and users collectively watch 6 billion videos daily (Mediakix, 2016). Social networking sites have become extremely popular worldwide and have found a comfortable home within sport.

Social networking sites have flourished with fans, sport managers, student-athletes, and professional athletes. Most research on sport and social networking sites involves Twitter, due to it being the dominant social networking site used in sport (Browning & Sanderson, 2012). Witkemper, Lim, and Waldburfer (2012) found that sport fans follow athletes for information, entertainment, to pass time, and for fanship. However, accessibility to the social networking sites and the ability to use the social networking sites, known as skill, were the largest constraints to athletes. Not only do fans use social networking sites, but athletes do as well. At the collegiate level, student-athletes use Twitter for keeping in contact with friends, family, and peers, communicating with followers, and accessing information. When faced with critical tweets, student-athletes respond in a number of ways: not letting the tweets bother them, using the tweets as motivation, deleting the users who sent out mean tweets, and even responding to their critics (Browning & Sanderson, 2012). Professional athletes use Twitter to interact with fans the most, followed by talking about their personal lives and their business lives (Pegoraro, 2010). Researchers are starting to understand why athletes use Twitter and other social network sites and the benefits the sport world can gain from these social platforms. However, ethical issues still persist when it comes to sports and the use of social network sites. For instance, 45% of student-athletes who use Snapchat have posted something inappropriate (profanity, racial discrimination, sexual conduct, drugs/alcohol, or violence) and over half had no social media training (DeShazo, 2016).

While social networking sites can offer an outlet for student-athletes to build their brands, they can also offer opportunities for student-athletes to damage their brands. An example of the latter is Laremy Tunsil, former offensive tackle from the University of Mississippi. Tunsil was considered a top pick for the NFL draft in 2016. Hours before the draft started, a video of Tunsil in a gas mask, smoking marijuana, surfaced on Tunsil's Twitter account. Further, Tunsil's Instagram account was hacked and photos of text messages between athletic director John Miller and Tunsil discussing paying rent and electricity bills for Tunsil's mother were made public. Instead of being selected potentially number one overall, Tunsil slid down to being drafted number 13. Tunsil lost an estimated $8 million from the leaked tweet and Instagram post (Crew, 2016). While Tunsil acknowledged that the video was of him in the mask and the text messages were valid, he denied the social network posts were from him. His accounts were hacked and the photos were leaked by someone who had the ability to abuse his social networking accounts. Tunsil has become the poster child for how media can harm an athlete's reputation or image (See Case Study at end of this chapter).

Currently, there is no one best social networking site policy for athletic departments. On one hand, allowing complete freedom of social networking could end up in a Laremy Tunsil situation where the athlete not only hurts his/her own image, but the associated university. However, having complete control of a student-athlete's social networking activity could create tension between the student-athletes and the athletic department. There is a delicate balance that athletic departments must maintain to ensure all parties use social networking sites correctly. As stated previously, there is not one way to achieve the delicate balance. Different athletic departments have developed different social networking site policies. A few universities have no social networking site policy, therefore trusting the student-athletes to represent themselves and the university appropriately. Most universities ban certain content from social platforms, including content containing drugs, guns, alcohol, sex, and other content perceived as harmful to the athlete, team, or university. Other universities take an active approach and require all student-athletes to follow an administrator or coach during their time at the university or subscribe to a program called UDiligence. **UDiligence** is a third-party website that monitors an account's activity and sends a red flag to the athletic department if certain inappropriate words or phrases are used, as determined by an athletic department. For example, the athletic department could flag the words "bomb," "gun," and "marijuana" and any post from their student-athletes using those words will be sent to the athletic department (Santus, 2014). Other athletic departments or coaches require student-athletes to shut down all social networking sites during the season, so no posts, damaging or otherwise can be made during the season.

rvlsoft/shutterstock.com

Most of the aforementioned policies are **ambiguous**, or open to interpretation, in nature (Sanderson & Browning, 2013). With ambiguous policies like "A student-athlete may be punished, suspended, kicked off the team, or lose their scholarship if they post content that hurts the image or reputation of the athlete, team, athletic department or university," student-athletes may not know exactly what would be considered detrimental to the image or reputation of the athlete, team, athletic department, or university. Therefore, the athletic department can impose any punishment on the student-athlete for any post deemed inappropriate. It is impossible to think of everything that would be considered inappropriate content, but by making general, ambiguous statements like the one above, the athletic departments can loosely cover all posts they may consider inappropriate content. With ambiguity in their social media policies, athletic departments hold all the power over student-athletes.

Social media does not just affect student-athletes. In May 2016, a tweet from Texas A&M assistant football coach Aaron Moorehead caused a highly touted high school recruit to decommit from Texas A&M. After Tate Martell, the third-ranked dual-threat quarterback of the 2017 class, decommitted from Texas A&M through a tweet, Moorehead took to Twitter to voice his frustrations. The assistant coach tweeted, "I feel sorry for ppl who never understand loyalty. I can't really even vibe with u. At the end of the day trust is (100 emoji) & everything else is BS." He then followed up with another tweet, "People act like the truth is all of a sudden a bad thing. Society is too sensitive. Y'all boys soft. #texastough" (Khan, 2016). That same day, receiver Mannie Netherly, the 181st overall player in the ESPN 300 recruiting measurement, tweeted his decommitment from Texas A&M due to the coach's tweets. Other recruits chimed in, saying they were reconsidering their commitment to Texas A&M. The assistant coach, not a student-athlete, was responsible for harming the program's image.

Sport managers are also not immune from the perils of social media. In October 2015, the Texas Rangers' verified Twitter account tweeted "Fire Charlie, #bye." The tweet was a reference to Charlie Strong, who had been hired as the University of Texas at Austin football coach. Strong was having a down year with a 1–4 record in his second season when the Twitter account tweeted the message. An hour after the tweet was sent out, the Rangers employee responsible for the tweet was fired (Andro, 2015).

Social networking sites have the opportunity to grow an athlete, coach, or organization's image if used correctly. If used incorrectly, social network sites can harm the image of the athlete, coach, or organization. As a sport manager, understanding how to utilize social network platforms for the betterment of the entire organization is necessary. As the sport industry continues to learn about social networking sites, those who can utilize the platforms effectively will be the leaders of the future.

IS TECHNOLOGY A COMPETITIVE ADVANTAGE?

Over recent years, technology has been invented to assist athletes to become bigger, faster, and stronger. Technology can come in the form of actual equipment that intends to improve athlete performance, like a tennis racket or a new Nike shoe. Tennis rackets have been evolving since the days of the wood racket. New materials were used year after year to help improve the sport of tennis. Titanium allows for the racket to be lighter weight, but remain sturdy and last a longer period of time. Not all technology comes in the form of sporting equipment or wearable technology. For instance, when Ray Allen was on the Miami Heat, the organization had a machine called Noah (Haberstroh, 2012). The machine was designed to track a player's shooting arc during drills for analysis. The machine also verbally announces the exact degree and angle in which a shot comes off a player's hand. The technology helped Allen make his three-point-shot motion constant, thus improving his shooting percentage. Allen, considered the best three-point shooter at the time, used technology to help him improve his shot.

A good example of technology in sport going too far was seen during the 2008 Olympics through the full body suits used by swimmers. To gain a competitive advantage, swimmers wear swim caps or shave off all body hair to compete for faster swim times. In 2008, however, a whole-body polyurethane swimsuit, called the LZR suit, caused a large controversy in the sport. The full body suit included a thin layer of foam-like material with little pockets of gas around the fabric. This allowed the swimmers to be a little more buoyant and float a little closer to the top as they swam (Barrow, 2012). As a result, they were up against less resistance and could swim faster. This may not seem like a huge competitive advantage, but in the 2008 Beijing Olympics, the LZR suit won 98% of the medals (Morrison, 2012). In the 2009 world championships, 20 new world records were set from individuals wearing the suits (Barrow, 2012). The race was unequal from the start as only a few athletes with the resources to purchase a LZR suit could wear it. The effectiveness of the suits led them to be banned from competitive meets in 2010. One of the beneficiaries of the suits, Michael Phelps, applauded the decision as he was threatening to sit out competitions because he believed the suits were unfair and changed the sport of competitive swimming.

The use of the LZR suits by only athletes with resources to purchase them begs the question of whether or not technology only helps those with the available resources. The best and newest equipment can be extremely expensive. Not all athletes were provided the resources to purchase a LZR suit in swimming, so many believe those without the suit had a considerable disadvantage. As sport managers, it is important to think about the consequences of introducing new technology into the sport world. The LZR suits were introduced and may have denied victories to those who

Paolo Bona/shutterstock.com

trained the hardest, simply because they did not have the resources to afford the newest suits. Further, the records broken because of the suits may never be reached again. Sport managers of today have to think critically about the impact of technology.

Another example is the recent trend of organizations like Nike and Under Armour sponsoring high school athletic teams, specifically football, with the best uniforms and equipment. Under Armour specifically has been actively pursuing many high schools for sponsorship deals. Having Nike or Under Armour provide up to $12,000 in sleek new uniforms and equipment is a desirable benefit for most high schools (Barker, 2015). Nike and Under Armour, however, are not interested in sponsoring every high school in America. Therefore, some schools are left without a sponsorship and have to pay for their own equipment. Sport managers will face decisions related to fairness and equality, as many situations are complex due to varying rules, state regulation, and the public versus private issues related to capitalism and secondary education in the US.

Technology has provided sport with great equipment, but technology can lead to an unfair competitive advantage for some athletes and teams. Sport is built on **competitive balance**—the thought that when the athletes hit the field, all things are equal and those who try the hardest and outperform others will win. However, competitive balance is severely threatened when one athlete or team has the resources to buy the latest and greatest technology, but others do not.

IS TECHNOLOGY TAKING THE HUMAN ASPECT OUT OF SPORT?

As with the LZR suits, sometimes technology can take the human element out of sport. Take, for instance, replay in sport. **Instant replay** is a recording of an action in sport that can be shown immediately after the original play transpires (Instant replay, 2016). Instant replay helps improve the accuracy of the calls made on the field. It is common for most fans to have experienced a game in which their favorite team has either benefited or been hindered by the reversal of a call. More often than not, the referees using instant replay confirm that the referees on the field got the call correct. However, some of the most iconic moments in sport could have been prevented had instant replay been used. "The Play," as it is known, was the famous kickoff return by the University of California, Berkeley Golden Bears against the Stanford Cardinals in the closing seconds of the 1982 Big Game between the two schools. With four seconds left, Stanford had a 20–19 lead and kicked the ball off to the Bears. The Bears proceeded to lateral the ball five times and scored a touchdown, while the Stanford band was on the field. It was truly a miracle that has been replayed every year since that game. However, there is controversy surrounding The Play. A review of the footage reveals multiple illegal laterals and that at one point a player's knee was down, which was missed by the referees. The Play would never have existed in today's age because of the use of technology and instant replay.

The NFL has popularized instant replay in North American sport. As early as the 1970s, the game of football was being introduced to instant replay (History of Instant Replay, 2016). Art McNally, director of officiating for the NFL at the time, wanted to implement instant replay for important plays, but the technology was too expensive to install at every venue and the calls remained inconclusive after lengthy reviews. Any attempt to introduce instant replay was futile until the 1980s when technology started to improve. Owners did not want a playoff game decided by a bad call, so in 1986, the owners agreed to implement limited use of instant replay. Plays up for review in the press box by the replay official included plays of possession or touching, plays governed by the sidelines, goal lines, end lines, and line of scrimmage, and easily detectable infractions (like too many players on the field). Coaches were not allowed to challenge; the officials had to decide when to use the technology. The owners were slightly concerned it would alter the game too much, so instant replay was only implemented for one year. The next year, it was barely passed for implementation and there were a few tweaks, including an upgrade in the review monitors from nine inches to twelve. There were some issues with the technology when it was first implemented, giving critics of instant replay ammunition for their arguments. For instance, in the Kansas City Chiefs and Oakland Raiders game in 1986, the Raiders threw a pass into the corner of the end zone late in the first half. On the field, officials called the play a touchdown, but the booth disagreed. The replay official used his walkie-talkie and told the head umpire "pass incomplete." However, the head umpire heard "pass complete" and the play stood, despite being wrong. Oakland would win the game by a touchdown. Mistakes like this ended up costing instant replay a home in the NFL after six consecutive years from 1986 to 1991.

Instant replay made a return in the mid-1990s, at the request of then-commissioner Paul Tagliabue. In 1996, instant replay was used in 10 preseason games. This time, coaches were allowed to challenge the rulings on the field on plays involving out of bounds, number of players on the field, and scoring. Each coach could **challenge** three plays per half, but each challenge cost a timeout, whether the team won or lost the challenge. Additionally, instead of having someone in the press box look at the monitor, the head umpire viewed the play on the field and was allowed 90 seconds to make a ruling, to speed up the game. Owners did not approve of implementing instant replay in 1997, mainly because the cost of a timeout for a challenge was too high for the coaches. However, in 1999, compromises were made on the technology and the owners agreed to implement instant replay again. Coaches were only allowed two challenges per half, only unsuccessful challenges cost a timeout, and the officials automatically reviewed any play in the last 2 minutes of the half that was reviewable, so the coaches could concentrate on the game. It was not until 2007 that the owners voted to allow instant replay to be a permanent fixture in the league, coincidentally, the same year the NFL switched to high-definition review systems costing each team $300,000 to install. Instant replay has been an increasing practice in the league for the past 40 years. In 1999, 44% of all games were played without a review, while in 2013, only 17% of games were played without replay (History of Instant Replay, 2016). The NFL boasts of its ability to incorporate and revolutionize instant replay in its games. However, the NFL understands it is not a perfect system and it may never be a perfect system. For example, the Green Bay Packers were recently

a victim of a wrong call known as the "Fail Mary." In 2012, the NFL referees and the NFL were in a **lockout** (when owners determine a work stoppage in professional sport) due to disagreements on compensation and other benefits. The NFL proceeded to use replacement referees from high school and lower college level divisions. In a regular season game between the Green Bay Packers and Seattle Seahawks, the Packers were winning 12–7 with eight seconds left. The quarterback of the Seattle Seahawks, Russell Wilson, threw a Hail Mary pass from behind the Packers' 30-yard line on

Lori Sparkia/shutterstock.com

4th and 10. The pass went into the corner of the end zone where Packers safety M. D. Jennings intercepted the pass; but Seahawks wide receiver Golden Tate barely grasped a small portion of the ball. Simultaneously, one official called the play incomplete, while the other official signaled a touchdown. The play went to review and the official could not find evidence to reverse the touchdown signal. Outrage over the call ensued and the play was dubbed the Fail Mary (McTigue, 2014). Several days later, the lockout between the original NFL referees and the NFL ended (Garafolo, 2012). The replacement referees were relieved after the missed call. While the NFL has achieved a nice balance of replay in its leagues, other leagues like Major League Baseball (MLB) are still trying to find their comfort level with replay in their sport.

While instant replay in the NFL dates back to the 1970s, MLB has been reluctant to introduce the system. The reason the MLB was the last of the four major leagues to introduce instant replay was the human error that dictates the game. Umpires determined every aspect of a baseball game, including balls, strikes, outs, and home runs. The MLB did not want to answer the question of what should be reviewed and what should not be reviewed. If every pitch was to be subject to instant replay, baseball games would last a long time. In 2008, MLB decided to introduce limited instant replay for disputed home run calls, fair or foul, in or out of the ballpark, and fan interference (Bloom, 2008). If the crew chief determined a call was necessary for instant replay, an MLB.com technician transmitted the necessary footage to the chief and umpires for the call. In 2014, MLB organizations unanimously voted to expand instant replay with the success of the program. The tweaks in the system made instant replay in baseball unique. For example, all instant replay will go to a set of full-time umpires in New York instead of just happening on the field, like in the NFL. Each manager begins with one challenge to use before the first six innings. After the sixth inning, the umpires decide to challenge the call, similar to the last two minutes of the NFL. If the managers win their initial challenge, they get a

Aspen Photo/shutterstock.com

ISSUES AND ETHICS IN SPORT

second one, but no more than two challenges per game. Managers can challenge anything except for checked swings, balks, infield flies, balls, and strikes, the "neighborhood play" at second base, and tagging up to score on fly balls. All other plays are available for review (Hagen, 2014).

Each league and sport is finding its balance with instant replay. The MLB, which boasts itself as America's pastime, has a conservative instant replay policy, trying to ensure the human element remains in the game. In contrast, the NFL was the first to implement instant replay and has been expanding ever since. It is important for sport managers to listen to key stakeholders when trying to find the balance for using instant replay. Bill Belichick, head coach for the New England Patriots, loves replay and would prefer all plays become reviewable. Jon Gruden, ESPN analyst, wants to eliminate it all because it takes the energy out of the stadium and could cause all plays to be reviewed. Both sides of the argument are valid, so it comes down to the decision making of the sport manager to determine the balance between too much instant replay and just enough.

STUDENT ACTIVITY:
How does replay differ across the four major professional sport leagues in the United States (NFL, NBA, MLB, and NHL)? Does any league have too much instant replay? Does any league have too little instant replay? How does this compare with other major professional sport leagues and competitions (La Liga, World Cup, Olympics, Premier League, etc.)?

FUTURE OF SPORT?

Athletes and Virtual Reality

Technology offers exciting possibilities for sport and sport performance in the future. Every day, it seems, a new piece of technology is introduced ready for the sport industry to take advantage of, like virtual reality. According to the virtual reality society, virtual means near, while reality is what we as humans experience in our world. Put those together and **virtual reality** (VR) means near-human experience (Virtual Reality Society, 2016). VR allows the user to get as close to real-life experiences as possible. It is currently popular with video games,

betto rodrigues/shutterstock.com

where VR allows the users to put themselves in the characters' point of view. VR has the potential to change the game of sport completely.

Athletes and coaches currently use VR in the sport of football. In the past, quarterbacks have relied on birds-eye views of the defenses they were scouting. They could see the movement of the defensive line, defensive backs, linebackers, and safeties through four or five slides. This was designed to help them recognize what formation the defense was in and react when the time was right. However, they were getting a birds-eye view from the press box, so they would have to translate the birds-eye view into what they would see on the field. Today the programs with the most resources and willingness to think outside of the box are using VR. The quarterback can use Oculus Rift Goggles, which allow the user to see the VR happen in front of them, and see the same plays from a personal vantage point. The quarterback snaps the ball and sees the exact same play being run, except this time he gets to see it from the point of view he would see in a game. The quarterback sees the live action players moving instead of flipping through slides, and is able to see the defense in the exact same uniforms as the opponent the following week. NFL teams like the Dallas Cowboys are using this technology to help quarterbacks and other positions train in VR while tricking the brain to think it is real (Dent, 2015). The Tampa Bay Rays use VR during batting practice to reduce wear and tear on the body (Alvarez, 2016). Even certain colleges, the NFL, and the Women's National Basketball Association (WNBA) are using this technology to their advantage (Zorowitz, 2015).

STUDENT ACTIVITY:
Stanford University developed a technology called STRIVR to assist the football team in drill training. This virtual reality software has recently partnered with Learfield (an organization that manages sponsorships for over 20 college institutions) to increase their access and reach to national college programs. STRIVR seeks to engage more athletes, fans, and programs in the VR offerings. What type of competitive advantage does this offer these institutions? Is this ethical? Why or why not?

Technology Growth in Sport

Marketers of an organization can also benefit from the use of VR. In the future, VR will be used to give potential donors a realistic look at their seats. For example, a development or ticket director could bring a donor in and find out that he or she is considering courtside seats, but have a hard time closing the sale. The development director could have the donor put on VR goggles and transport them to the middle of a game against a rival with 28,000 fans cheering on the home team. The experience could allow the donor to feel what the game would be like if there were little time on the clock and the donor was sitting in the exact seats he or she is considering. Another use of VR, still in the early stages, is potentially selling tickets using VR. Organizations could potentially film the games and live-stream them into homes using Oculus Rift. Assuming the individual owned the equipment, they could purchase the streaming rights (similar to a ticket) and be put on the 50-yard line of their favorite team. Parking, traffic, lines, and overpriced food would all be eliminated with this technology, but the spectator would still seemingly be at the game enjoying the best seats in the house. This would be particularly useful for organizations like the Green Bay Packers, as it can be nearly impossible to acquire season tickets. Instead of submitting for the lottery system, where it could take three generations to get the tickets, the Packers could sell VR tickets and allow those unable to get tickets to the games at Lambeau Field.

A more recent technology seen on ESPN is a new tech competition called drone racing. **Drone Racing** is a high-speed competitive racing sport. Individuals put on VR goggles and race drones (quad-helicopters) through an obstacle course as if they were actually flying a helicopter from the cockpit (What is FPV drone racing, n.d.). The drones go up to 120 miles per hour and make hairpin turns on a dime throughout an empty Miami Dolphins stadium. The new phenomenon has become so popular, ESPN reached an agreement with the Drone Racing League (DRL) to air 10 one-hour episodes of the drone-racing competitions. The DRL became immensely popular due to a $12 million investment from Miami Dolphins owner Stephen Ross and Cleveland owner Dan Gilbert (Rovell, 2016).

Technology Growth in Analytics

Virtual reality in sport is not the only way sport will be influenced by technology in the future. Big data and analytics are becoming more popular with teams and management every day. Analytics was made popular by the Oakland Athletics and the book and movie *Moneyball*. **Analytics** refers to using a large amount of statistics to measure something or someone. Billy Beane used the tactic to find the best players he could afford as General Manager of the Athletics by analyzing their batting, fielding, and other statistics.

Professional organizations have started to use VR to track statistics on their own players and opponents. In the 2013–2014 NBA season, some of the teams used a SportVU tracking system. The system had six cameras in the arena and would measure every move a player made and every move the ball made. Instead of just points, rebounds, or assists per minute as judgment of a player's efficiency, the camera allows organizations to see the player's productivity per touch and defensive effectiveness (Mooney, 2014). The SportVU system helps organizations determine, which player is being the most efficient on the court. Players can use the technology as well to study their opponent's movement patterns or defensive tendencies.

For sport managers within ticketing sales, analytics can track when an individual ticket holder comes most often to games and use that to customize ticket packages for their spectators. The database can gather big data on a ticket holder to help personalize the experience for the fan. Further, corporations and potential sponsors can understand who exactly will be in the stadium at certain points of the year. For instance, big data can track what demographic attends which games. If there is a weekday, day game in the MLB where the majority of attendees are college students, the MLB organization can approach sponsors who associate with college students for that specific game.

Smart arenas will also be built in the sport industry in the near future. Over 70% of fans attending games bring their mobile device to a game and use it, so organizations are looking to exploit mobile phones. The new Sacramento Kings arena, which opened in October 2016, is a smart arena. Before the game, the accompanying application will make parking easier with a map showing the available open spots. Once inside the game, the application will usher the individuals with smartphones to their seats so they do not have to waste time looking for their seats. Fans will be able to use their phones to determine the shortest bathroom lines and concession lines. Even after the game, the phone may invite the user to get a live look into the post-game conference of the star players. The trend of turning traditional arenas into smart arenas is providing easy access to the fans to boost fan engagement and experience.

Another trend of sport organizations includes globalization of their product. While the team may be based in Houston, the Rockets organization has a strong following in China. All-Star center Yao Ming helped the Houston Rockets enter into a market that was once considered unreachable. The Rockets have done a great job capitalizing on this opportunity as they have made their website available in two languages: English and Chinese. They also wear Chinese New Year jerseys to connect with their fan base overseas. The Sacramento Kings owner, who is Indian American, created a team website in Hindi and has hosted multiple international Google+ Hangouts during games. Technology allows fans and owners to come together from outside of the immediate vicinity to experience the game. As sport managers attempt to find new target markets for their product, seeking international markets may be a great place to start.

Technology Growth in Esport

Another increasingly popular trend is the rise of a sport created and used by technology. **Esports** are defined as professional and competitive video gaming. Currently, video games like *League of Legends, Dota 2, Hearthstone, Overwatch, Super Smash Brothers*, and *Counter Strike: Global Offensive* are the most popular competitive esports. Esports athletes practice and compete against other professional teams or athletes in competitions and tournaments. The industry has boomed over the past five years and only continues to grow in popularity. A report from Newzoo, a video game and esports marketing firm, revealed there were 235 million esports viewers in 2015. In 2016, there was a 36.6% increase to 323 million viewers. The number is expected to increase to 385 million viewers in 2017 and 589 million viewers in 2020. Roughly 50% of esports enthusiasts are from the Asia-Pacific region, but Europe (18%) and North America (13%) hold a large number of viewers as well. Not only are the viewership numbers for esports impressive, but so is the revenue. In 2015, esports total revenues (media rights, sponsorship, game publisher fees, merchandise and tickets) equated to $325 million. The number would increase to $493 million in 2016. The exponential growth is expected to continue to grow in 2017 to $696 million and $1,488 billion by 2020 (Warman, 2017).

One of the primary reasons for esports' success is Internet streaming. **Internet streaming** is placing one's content online for others to view live or pre-recorded. With the industry based in technology and aided by the invention of the Internet, the majority of the viewership comes online through websites like Twitch. tv. Anyone with Internet access and a phone can watch free live esports content on Twitch.tv. In fact, Twitch.tv brought in 100+ million unique monthly viewers in 2016 and 292 billion minutes of content watched

(Takahashi, 2017). Twitch.tv actually became so popular that Amazon purchased the company for $970 million in 2014 (MacMillen & Bensinger, 2014).

Esports spectating has resulted in these impressive numbers for a few reasons. First, the esports industry decided to stay away from television and stick to streaming on the Internet when it was beginning to take form. Once again, since the Internet gave birth to the boom in esports, it only makes sense that the Internet is the home to esports. This allowed esports to learn how to perfect live-streaming of events on an Internet platform and appeals to younger generations who favor Internet streaming services over cable television. Second, esports is a global sport, not just limited to a few countries. Twitch.tv is the main source of esports viewership, so anyone in the world who wants to consume esports would use that website. Therefore, most viewership of esports is streamlined into that one website.

Every major esports competition can be promoted on a global scale, instead of just a national scale. Oftentimes, esports entities, like *League of Legends*, will host multiple international competitions. Four times a year, the best esports organizations from North America, Europe, China, Korea, South America, and other countries are competing against each other to determine who is best. This brings together the global community of fans of the game to watch events. Imagine if the NBA played its season, and then the winner of the NBA Finals represented North America against the other best teams in the world in a two-week world championship every year. Perhaps the NBA team would consistently win the tournament, similar to the Olympics, but the yearly competition would promote continent rivalries and increase the level of play for every other region, making the global presence of the NBA stronger. The esports industry has already implemented this, and it helps the industry grow and thrive.

Syda Productions/shutterstock.com

Not only is esports growing with spectators, it is growing with legitimacy as well. The United States government began recognizing esports athletes on equal footing as mainstream sport athletes when they started to award foreign esports athletes athletic visas to come to America to play (Makuch, 2013). This meant that Big Papi, Thierry Henry, and Yao Ming were considered equal with Nicolaj "Jensen" Jensen and Lee "Rush" Yoonjae. The United States government made this decision because it saw the potential of an esport athlete to make a career. In addition, athletic departments are beginning to offer athletic scholarships to esport athletes. Robert Morris University in Illinois started offering 50% tuition for top *League of Legends* players in 2014 (Tassi, 2014). Even former mainstream professional athletes are buying into esports, literally. Former Los Angeles Laker Rick Fox, an avid esports fan, invested in a few esports organizations, and in *League of Legends* and *Counter Strike: Global Offensive*. His organizations are known as Echo Fox and he has a large role in their operations. Shaquille O'Neal, Alex Rodriguez, Jimmy Rollins, and Dallas Mavericks owner Mark Cuban are also investors in esports organizations, understanding the possibilities esports has as a major industry moving forward. Esports has a tremendous amount of potential in the future, and it is all because of technology. Twenty or thirty years ago, the esports industry would not have even been thought of as gaining legitimacy, but technological advancements in the electronic equipment used for professional gaming and the ability to bring the global audience together on platforms like Twitch.tv has grown the esports industry into an estimated multi-billion dollar industry in 2018 (SuperData Research, 2015).

STUDENT ACTIVITY:
Split into small groups and research the following esports. Each group can report on the major teams/players involved with the esport, type of esport (first-person shooter, card, massive multiplayer online, etc.), governing structure of the esport, major tournaments within the esport, and the game designer for the esport:
1. *League of Legends*
2. *Counter Strike: Global Offensive*
3. *Hearthstone*
4. *Dota 2*
5. *Call of Duty*

CONCLUSION

The technological influences on sport mentioned in this chapter are just a small portion of what is available for fans, athletes, and sport organizations. Fans have greater connectivity and access to organizations and athletes through social media. While social networking can bring the fan, organization, or athlete closer to improve the fan relationship, it also puts the sport organizations and athletes in the spotlight. Athletes have equipment to improve their abilities with Fitbits and apps that are able to track performance. While this technology can help improve athletic performance, it can interfere with the integrity of the sport, as with blood doping and cycling (discussed in Chapter 3). Sport organizations can use technology to improve stadiums and facilities for their fans and athletes. However, this trend has caused concern related to the original or natural parts of sport. The main point is that technology has the opportunity to improve sport, but it also can harm sport. Using the ethical decision-making model in Chapter 1, sport managers should analyze decisions on including new technology in sport for fans, athletes, and sport organizations.

DISCUSSION QUESTIONS

1. What are some examples of technology impacting sport equipment? What are some examples of technology impacting sport itself?

2. What are benefits of new technology in sport? Drawbacks?

3. Is there a "best" social networking site policy for athletic departments? Explain your answer.

4. Should the NCAA cap the number of online classes a student-athlete can take per semester? Why or why not?

5. Does technology take too much of the human element out of the game with instant replay? Explain your answer.

6. Does technology only aid those with the resources to acquire new technology (the rich get richer concept)? Why or why not?

7. What are some future trends in technology in sport?

8. Why is it important for sport managers to know the future trends of technology in sport?

9. Other than the examples discussed in this chapter, how can VR be used in sport?

10. What puts the "sport" in esports? Is an esports athlete a real athlete?

CASE STUDY: SOCIAL MEDIA GETS HACKED

Social media marketing provides many benefits to organizations and personal brands. For instance, social media platforms allow immediate, 24/7 access to brands and athletes without first being filtered through a public relations department. The platforms also allow brands to communicate with consumers to develop and foster relationships that lead to increased brand loyalty. While the benefits of social media platforms are plenty, the negative consequences of the use of platforms must also be considered.

Unfiltered exposure is a double-edged sword. Yes, it is great for consumers to get an inside look into the lives of their favorite athletes directly from the athletes themselves. However, the immediacy and unfiltered nature of social media can also cause severe backlash toward the personal brand of an athlete and associated organizations. Perhaps this was never truer than during the 2016 NFL draft when Laremy Tunsil's social media accounts were hacked, leading to a media firestorm and absolute nightmare for Tunsil.

Tunsil, who played football at Ole Miss, was projected to be a top six draft pick in the 2016 draft. His fate took a turn for the worse when an anonymous hacker used Tunsil's Twitter account to post damaging information the night of the draft. The first post was a video of Tunsil smoking out of a bong fashioned out of a gas mask (Kellenberger, 2016). This video, although two years old, seemingly damaged the personal brand of Tunsil enough to move him not only from the top six draft slots but also out of the top 10 entirely to the number 13 spot. The drop in draft spots cost Tunsil more than $8 million in lost wages (Crew, 2016).

The social media nightmare for Tunsil did not stop there. The hacker then went to Tunsil's Instagram account where screenshots of text messages between Tunsil and John Miller, assistant athletic director for football operations, were posted with the caption "Coach Freeze and the Ole Miss program are snakes." The screenshots of the text conversation illustrated Tunsil asking Miller for money to pay rent and his mother's $305 electric and water bills (Kellenberger, 2016).

In a post-draft press conference, Tunsil admitted the picture smoking marijuana from the gas mask was him. He also admitted to taking money from a coach while at Ole Miss, a blatant violation of NCAA rules. Perhaps this was not surprising since he was suspended for the first seven games of the 2015 Ole Miss season for accepting impermissible benefits (Patterson, 2016). The individual responsible for the hacking has not been identified.

While Tunsil obviously did not intend to share the information that was leaked through his hacked accounts, his previous actions hurt his personal brand. In addition to costing him at least $8 million in NFL contract money, his potential for endorsement deals has also decreased, as companies are less willing to take a risk on an individual with controversy surrounding him. Tunsil's personal nightmare illustrates the concept that one's actions off the field can impact his personal brand as much as his actions on the field. This is particularly true in today's digital age when information can be shared with the click of a button.

CASE QUESTIONS

1. Are the risks associated with social media worth the benefits at the collegiate level? Why or why not?

2. Are the risks associated with social media worth the benefits at the professional level? Why or why not?

3. What are steps athletic departments can take to avoid the risk of a Laremy Tunsil-type situation?

4. Make a list of all the stakeholders in the Tunsil case. How was each impacted?

5. Pretend you are the agent for Tunsil. What steps can you take to help improve Tunsil's image?

6. Should athletic departments limit social networking site usage by student-athletes?

CASE STUDY: ADVANCES IN TECHNOLOGY IN SPORT

Sport analytics is a growing field in which decision makers are employing technology and data to make evidence-based decisions. In terms of athlete performance, video has been the predominant source of data. Advances in technology have led to improvements in the type of data produced from videos. Traditional video has been used to study the film of an organization's opponents. What is the opponent most likely to do in certain situations? How can we respond to the opponent's weaknesses and overcome their strengths?

Further advances in video technology have led to more detailed types of data produced from videos. The NBA and MLB are two leagues at the forefront of data analytics in terms of league-wide adoption of technology. For instance, PITCHf/x is used in every MLB ballpark to capture data on the game's pitching. Some MLB teams are taking it a step further and also incorporating data from HITf/x and FIELDf/x to capture data from hitting and fielding (Davenport, 2014). Similarly, every NBA arena utilizes SportVU, which is a six-camera system used to track the real-time positions of players and the basketball 25 times per second. SportVU is particularly effective in producing analytics based on speed, distance, player separation, and ball possession. While the data produced from these video formats is plentiful and helpful, it is fairly basic in terms of descriptive analytics. For more complex analytics, a human analyst is necessary to further analyze the relationships between different variables identified within the data.

In terms of individual athlete performance, locational and biometric devices, such as GPS devices, radio frequency devices, and accelerometers, are being adopted by many organizations (Davenport, 2014). These types of devices assess the amount of physical activity the athletes undertake and allow decision makers to tailor training plans to ade-

quately fit the needs of the individual athlete. Rather than relying on participants using gym equipment in an unnatural environment, the wearable technology behind the biometric devices allows athletes to physically exert themselves the same way they would during competition (Catapult, n.d.). The data produced from the devices provides insight into athlete readiness, risk, and return to play.

The data produced from the technology from both the video format and wearable technology format can be combined to assist in the decision-making processes of an organization. This is proven by the Golden State Warriors, as their director of athletic performance Keke Lyles uses a combination of the two formats by using SportVU during games and wearable technology from Catapult Sports in practice (Berger, 2015). The data provided from the technology allows Lyles to develop pre-set parameters for each athlete's danger zone, which includes a combination of player fatigue and proof of diminished load capacity. The technology also allows the coaching and training staffs to monitor every player's movement patterns and physiological responses in real-time to illustrate how the athlete is moving and how the body is responding to the movement (Berger, 2015).

Practice and game plans can be modified based on the data produced from the technology. For instance, during the 2014–2015 NBA season, Steve Kerr decided to rest four players in mid-March. At the time of the decision, the team had already won 51 games and had the best record in the Western conference (Berger, 2015). Fans who had spent money to see the NBA's best team and league all-stars Stephen Curry and Klay Thompson were angry. The organization received backlash for Kerr's decision in the form of complaints on social media and e-mails sent to the team. What fans did not understand at the time was the decision to rest the athletes was a data-based decision. If Kerr had not allowed the players to rest with the information he had and they were injured, who would have been at fault?

As technology continues to improve, more leagues will incorporate data-driven decisions into their organizations. With technology like PITCHf/x, HITf/x, FIELDf/x, and SportVU, managers and coaches will be able to make optimal decisions with the generated data. In the near future, every decision in sport may be influenced by technology and the data that can be provided to the decision makers in sport.

CASE QUESTIONS

1. At the NBA level, wearable technology such as Catapult's GPS device can only be used in practice. The use of it during games would need to be collectively bargained with the National Basketball Players Association. Is this something NBA players, coaches, and trainers should pursue? Why or why not?

2. Is it ethical to charge fans money to see star athletes play and then sit them out because of the data produced from sport analytics technology? Explain your answer.

3. Could too much generated data diminish the manager's or coach's role for a team? Why or why not?

4. Is there a scenario where too much technology can take the human element out of sport? Explain your answer.

5. In what ways could leagues like the NFL, NHL, or English Premier League utilize sport analytics for their specific sport?

GLOSSARY

Ambiguous means open to interpretation.

Analytics is examining data with the purpose of drawing conclusions from the data.

Competitive balance is the thought that when the athletes hit the field, all things are equal, and those who try the hardest and outperform others will win.

Drone Racing is a high-speed competitive racing sport.

Esport is professional and competitive video gaming.

Ghostwriting is the practice of writing something for another or hiding credit from the real author, or taking tests for other students.

Instant replay is a recording of an action in a sports event that can be shown on television after the original play happens.

Internet Streaming is broadcasting an individual's content online for an audience.

Lockout is when owners determine a work stoppage in professional sport.

Social Network Sites are web-based services that allow individuals to (1) construct a public or semi-public profile within a bounded system, (2) articulate a list of other users with whom they share a connection, and (3) view and traverse their connections and those made by others within the system.

UDiligence is a third-party website that monitors an account's activity and sends a red flag to the athletic department if certain inappropriate words or phrases are used, as determined by an athletic department.

Virtual Reality (VR) is a near-human experience through the use of technology.

References

Alvarez, E. (2016, April 17). *Major League Baseball team uses VR for batting practice*. Retrieved from http://www.engadget.com/2016/04/07/tampa-bay-rays-mlb-virtual-simulator/

Andro, A. (2015, October 3). Rangers fire employee after offensive tweet directed at UT coach. *FoxSports.com*. Retrieved from http://www.foxsports.com/southwest/story/texas-rangers-texas-longhorns-tweet-fire-charlie-strong-100315

Barker, J. (2015, August 14). Under Armour makes high-school push in its 'backyard.' *The Baltimore Sun*. Retrieved from http://www.baltimoresun.com/business/under-armour-blog/bs-bz-under-armour-high-schools-20150814-story.html

Barrow, J. D. (2012, July 25). Why ban full-body Olympics swimsuits? A scientist explains polyurethane. *The Daily Beast*. Retrieved from http://www.thedailybeast.com/articles/2012/07/25/why-ban-full-body-olympics-swimsuits-a-scientist-explains-polyurethane.html

Berger, K. (2015, June 3). Warriors 'wearable' weapon? Devices to monitor players while on the court. *CBS Sports*. Retrieved from http://www.cbssports.com/nba/writer/ken-berger/25203846/warriors-wearable-weapon-devices-to-monitor-players-while-on-the-court

Bloom, B. M. (2008, August 26). Limited instant replay debuts Thursday. *MLB.com*. Retrieved from http://m.mlb.com/news/article/3370519/

Boyd, D. M., & Ellison, N. B. (2008). Social network sites: Definition, history, and scholarship. *Journal of Computer-Mediated, 13*, 210–230.

Browning, B. & Sanderson, J. (2012). The positives and negatives of Twitter: Exploring how student-athletes use Twitter and respond to critical tweets. *International Journal of Sport Communication, 5*, 503–521.

Casselman, (2015, May 22). Resistance is futile: esports is massive . . . and growing. *ESPN*. Retrieved from http://espn.go.com/espn/story/_/id/13059210/esports-massive-industry-growing

Catapult USA. (n.d.). *Wearable technology for elite athletes*. Retrieved from http://www.catapultsports.com/

Crew, J. (2016, April 29). Here's how much NFL draft pick Laremy Tunsil lost because of 1 tweet. *Fortune*. Retrieved from http://fortune.com/2016/04/29/laremy-tunsil-tweet-video/

Davenport, T. H. (2014). Analytics in sports: The new science of winning. *International Institute of Analytics*. Retrieved from http://www.sas.com/content/dam/SAS/en_us/doc/whitepaper2/iia-analytics-in-sports-106993.pdf

Dent. S. (2015, June 8). Dallas Cowboys become the first NFL team to go all-in on VR. *Engadget.com*. Retrieved from http://www.engadget.com/2015/06/08/dallas-cowboys-strivr-vr-tech/

DeShazo, K. (2016, April 25). 2016 social media use of student athletes. *Field House Media*. Retrieved from http://www.fieldhousemedia.net/2016-social-media-use-of-student-athletes-infographic/

Dubois, L. (2015, June 24). Artificial turf controversy a constant in backdrop of Women's World Cup. *SportsIllustrated.com*. Retrieved from http://www.si.com/planet-futbol/2015/06/23/womens-world-cup-artificial-turf-canada

Fowler, J. (2013, March 1). Jonny Manziel won't be Johnny Online for long. *CBSSports*. Retrieved from http://www.cbssports.com/collegefootball/writer/jeremy-fowler/21791629/johnny-manziel-wont-be-johnny-online-for-long

Garafolo, M. (2012, September 27). NFL, referees end lockout after reaching new labor deal. *USA Today*. Retrieved from http://usatoday30.usatoday.com/sports/nfl/story/2012/09/27/nfl-referees-end-lockout-after-reaching-new-labor-deal/57846906/1

Haberstroh, T. (2012, October 27). Ray Allen meets Noah for first time. *ESPN*. Retrieved from http://espn.go.com/blog/truehoop/miamiheat/post/_/id/15552/ray-allen-meets-noah-for-first-time

Hagen, P. (2014, March 26). Instant replay review FAQ. *MLB.com*. Retrieved from http://m.mlb.com/news/article/70189582/instant-replay-review-faq

Haynie, D. (2015, February 15). Study shows sluggish online learning growth for second year. *US News*. Retrieved from http://www.usnews.com/education/online-education/articles/2015/02/05/study-shows-sluggish-online-learning-growth-for-second-year

History of Instant Replay. (2016). *NFL.com*. Retrieved from http://operations.nfl.com/the-game/history-of-instant-replay/

Instant replay. 2016. In *Merriam-Webster.com*. Retrieved from http://www.merriam-webster.com/dictionary/instant%20replay

Kallas, P. (2017, July 1). Top 15 most popular social networking sites and apps. Retreived from https://www.dreamgrow.com/top-15-most-popular-social-networking-sites/

Khan, S. (2016, May 5). A&M assistant's tweets add fuel to fire of No. 3 QB's decommitment. *ESPN*. Retrieved from http://espn.go.com/college-football/recruiting/story/_/id/15465600/texas-aggies-lose-second-recruit-night-coach-tweets

MacMillen, D., & Bensinger, G. (2014, August 24). Amazon to buy video site Twitch for $970 million. *The Wall Street Journal*. Retrieved from http://www.wsj.com/articles/amazon-to-buy-video-site-twitch-for-more-than-1-billion-1408988885

Maina, A. (2016). 20 popular social media sites right now. *Small Business Trends*. Retrieved from http://smallbiztrends.com/2016/05/popular-social-media-sites.html

Makuch, E. (2013, July 12). US government recognizes League of Legends players as pro athletes. *GameSpot*. Retrieved from http://www.gamespot.com/articles/us-government-recognizes-league-of-legends-players-as-pro-athletes/1100-6411377/

McTigue, J. (2014, September 8). MNF moments, No. 1: The Fail Mary. *ESPN*. Retrieved from http://espn.go.com/blog/nflnation/post/_/id/138835/mnf-moments-no-1-the-fail-mary

Mediakix. (2016, April 13). How many people use SnapChat? *Mediakix*. Retrieved from http://mediakix.com/2016/04/how-many-people-use-snapchat-2016/

Mooney, L. (2014, April 28). Five key trends that are driving the business of sports. *Stanford Business*. Retrieved from https://www.gsb.stanford.edu/insights/five-key-trends-are-driving-business-sports

Morrison, J. (2012, July 27). How Speedo created a record-breaking suit. *Scientific American*. Retrieved from http://www.scientificamerican.com/article/how-speedo-created-swimsuit/

New, J. (2016, April 11). 'This thing has tentacles.' *Inside Higher Ed*. Retrieved from https://www.insidehighered.com/news/2016/04/11/ncaa-finds-southern-mississippi-basketball-staff-committed-academic-fraud

Pegoraro, A. (2010). Look who's talking—Athletes on Twitter: A case study. *International Journal of Sport Communication*, *3*, 501–514.

Rothschild, D. (2011, August 17). Can ghostwriting be considered plagiarism? *iThenticate*. Retrieved from http://www.ithenticate.com/plagiarism-detection-blog/bid/64034/Can-Ghostwriting-Be-Considered-Plagiarism#.WVVWFYjyvIU

Rovell, D. (2016, September 14). Drone Racing League, ESPN reach broadcasting agreement. *ESPN*. Retrieved from http://www.espn.com/moresports/story/_/id/17544727/drone-racing-league-espn-announce-broadcasting-agreement

Sanderson, J., & Browning, B. (2013). Training versus monitoring: Examination of athletic department practices regarding student-athletes and Twitter. *Qualitative Research Reports in Communication*, *14*(1), 105–111.

Santus, R. (2014, March 26). Colleges monitor, restrict athletes on social media. *American Journal Review*. Retrieved from http://ajr.org/2014/03/26/social-media-monitoring-widespread-among-college-athletic-departments/

SuperData Research. (2015). *Esports: The market brief*. New York City, New York: Stephanie Llamas.

Takahashi, D. (2017, February 15). Twitch viewers watched 292 billion minutes of live streams in 2016. *Venture Beat*. Retrieved from https://venturebeat.com/2017/02/15/twitch-viewers-watch-292-million-minutes-of-livestreams-in-2016/

Tassi, P. (2014, June 20). Illinois College Makes 'League of Legends' A Varsity Sport, Offers Scholarships. *Forbes*. Retrieved from http://www.forbes.com/sites/insertcoin/2014/06/20/illinois-college-makes-league-of-legends-a-varsity-sport-offers-scholarships/

Virtual Reality Society. (2016, January 9). What is virtual reality? *Virtual Reality Society*. Retrieved from http://www.vrs.org.uk/virtual-reality/what-is-virtual-reality.html

Warman, P. (2017, February 14). Esports revenues will reach $696 million this year and grow to $1. Billion by 2020 as brand investment doubles. *Newzoo*. Retrieved from https://newzoo.com/insights/articles/esports-revenues-will-reach-696-million-in-2017/

What is FPV drone racing? (n.d.). *DRL*. Retrieved from https://thedroneracingleague.com/learn-more/

Witkemper, C., Lim, C. H., & Waldburfer, A. (2012). Social media and sports marketing: Examining the motivations and constraints of Twitter users. *Sport Marketing Quarterly*, *21*, 170–183.

Zorowitz, J. (2015). It just got real. *NBC Sports*. Retrieved from http://sportsworld.nbcsports.com/virtual-reality-sports-arkansas-kentucky/

ISSUES IN SPORT MEDIA AND PUBLIC RELATIONS

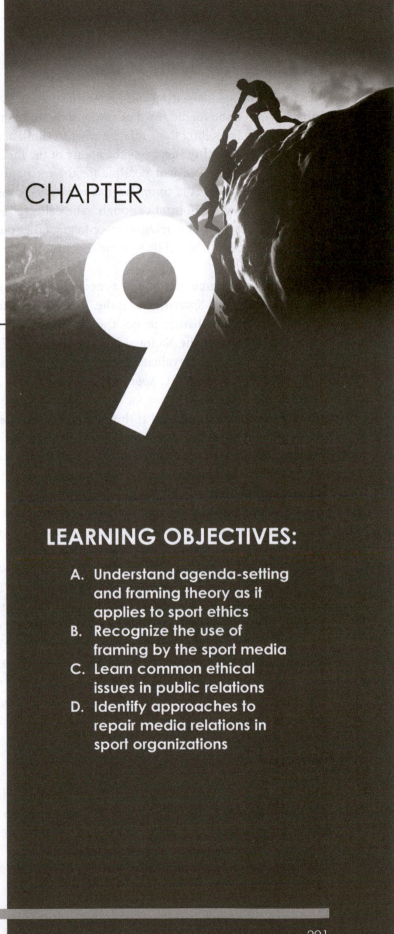

CHAPTER

9

This chapter is dedicated to ethical issues in sport media and public relations. For students who want to get into sport media/communication, this chapter should provide an opportunity to reflect on the incredible power of communication. For the others that may not want a career in sport media/communication, this chapter may still be useful as it may provide a look into some ethical dilemmas in the media. For example, how are Black athletes and White athletes reported in the media? Are the descriptors or images used for female athletes the same as male athletes in promotional materials? By the end of this chapter, students should be able to recognize the power of media to influence the public. To start, this chapter will begin by looking at significant theories that drive a vast majority of the discussion around media and public relations issues and ethics. Focus will be placed on agenda-setting theory and framing theory. These two theories are used in this chapter to investigate what the media reports and what aspects of stories the media and public highlight in an ethical context in the sport industry.

LEARNING OBJECTIVES:

A. Understand agenda-setting and framing theory as it applies to sport ethics
B. Recognize the use of framing by the sport media
C. Learn common ethical issues in public relations
D. Identify approaches to repair media relations in sport organizations

Agenda-setting by the Media

The concept of agenda-setting was first introduced in 1972 by Maxwell McCombs and Donald Shaw. These authors claimed the media was not responsible for telling an individual what to think, but the media may be responsible for telling the audience what to think *about*. McCombs and Reynolds (2002) most recently defined **Agenda-setting theory** as the ability of the media "to influence the salience of topics on the public agenda" (p. 2). However, is it possible for the media to tell an individual (or its audience) what to think about? In short, the media controls what messages it considers most important as the news for the day. They choose what news is important enough to be delivered to the masses, and what is not important enough to be discussed on air, in the newspaper, or in any other outlet for media members. It is the media that gets to select the agenda for the public to view and interpret.

SportsCenter is a prime example of a media outlet that selects the agenda for its viewers. One of the most popular segments on *SportsCenter* is the "Top 10 Plays" of the week or day. Two researchers, Saks and Yanity (2016) investigated whether or not the top 10 plays had any sort of agenda-setting by *SportsCenter*. The researchers compared the National Hockey League (NHL) and the National Basketball Association (NBA), two similar leagues, and evaluated which league had more highlights. The NBA had almost triple the number of highlights of the NHL. *SportsCenter*, a product of ESPN, has the network rights for the NBA, but not the NHL. It makes more sense for *SportsCenter* to showcase NBA plays, as it may garner people to watch the NBA more often on ESPN if they see it on *SportsCenter*. The NHL may receive less interest, as people watching the NHL on other channels does not increase the number of viewers on ESPN. Note, however, that ESPN is not telling the consumer *what* to think about the NBA or NHL, but it wants the consumer to think about the NBA more often. This is a prime example of how the media can subconsciously, or deliberately, influence the audience.

While the above example of *SportsCenter* showing mostly NBA clips instead of NHL clips is harmless, agenda-setting is important to study because it can influence people's realty. A study by Cynthia Frisby revealed that the media focused more on the criminal actions of Black athletes, while focusing on overwhelmingly positive stories about White athletes. The study examined 155 news articles from online and print news stories and noted more stories were about White athletes (43%) than Black athletes (39%). Over 50% of the stories had a negative tone towards Black athletes, but 27% were negative about White athletes (Hurst, 2015). The overexposure of negative stories and comments about Black athletes, in this example, is dangerous. Imagine being subjected to negative stories about Black athletes constantly, individuals might perpetuate negative stereotypes about Black athletes. The role of the media is important in this regard. They have the power to set the agenda, to push certain stories or hold back certain stories. And it is not just Black and White athletes. Male and female athlete stories oftentimes have different tones, just like stories about athletes with a disability and athletes without a disability.

Framing Theory

Framing theory is derived from multiple backgrounds, including sociology and psychology. Goffman (1974) has been credited most often with his essays on framing from a sociological standpoint. Goffman states that people live in their own "frame" of reference. The **frame**, as Goffman defined it, is the mental schemas facilitating quick processing of information in everyday life. As humans, we accomplish the rapid processing of information through frames by selecting and emphasizing certain aspects while eliminating others (Entman, 1993). Goffman uses a literal picture frame to help explain the concept. The picture frame holds the picture in place; it is the structure supporting the image. The painting, image or picture, in turn, represents the context. Changing the picture frame can alter how one views the picture, just as changing the "frame of reference" can change how individuals perceive a situation. It is extremely important to understand that primary frameworks are derived from the social or cultural context of the individual. For example, a thumbs-up in Germany represents the number one (1), but a thumbs-up in Japan represents the number five (5) (Cotton, 2013). The same image can have two completely different meanings depending on the culture or social construction of the image/word.

LiliGraphie/shutterstock.com

A simplistic example of a frame can be found in a baseball play. Imagine a baseball game between two professional teams. It is the bottom of the ninth, with two outs, and the home team at bat is down by one run with a runner on second base. The batter hits a ball to the outfield and it soars to the wall. The outfielder jumps and tries to grab the ball, but it tips the top of his glove and falls past the wall for a homerun. The news may show the highlight and frame the play as an amazing hit by the batter to win the game. Conversely, the news could frame the clip as a mistake by the outfielder who touched his glove to the ball, but could not quite catch it. The play is the same, but the media can frame it as two different outcomes. Each perspective can change the fans' view of the situation. If the play is viewed as the batter hitting the game-winning run, the outfielder may not even make the highlight reel. The same can be said for the game being portrayed as a catch that got away. The media, along with our interpretation of the way the media is presenting the play, could alter how we view sport history.

This example, although basic, represents the key framing elements that are often used by the media. Frames typically invite people to view something in a particular way (Tewksbury & Scheufele, 2009). Frames are particularly great at influencing individuals when they can link issues to particular beliefs. Logos are useful at framing objects as they link the individual to the specific products through the "lens" of a favorite logo. As fans get excited or feel a sense of familiarity or pride with a team, they too may feel that pride or loyalty to a said product. The intense feeling is what the media or sporting goods producer want the audience to experience. They, in turn, capitalize on the goodwill of the logo through their content and products.

This chapter will make reference to several agenda and framing examples. While reading, consider how agendas are set or the way frames are produced. For instance, when reading about the Olympics and how the Games are portrayed by the media, think about how often the Olympics are on the agenda for NBC. Pretty often considering the Games are hosted by NBC, so it makes sense for NBC to push the Olympics. Think about *how* the Olympics are portrayed right before, during, and after the Olympics conclude.

Media framing of the Olympics

The Olympics are oftentimes subject to investigation by researchers and journalists on how the Games are framed. The examples below show different ways the Olympics are framed before and during the Olympic Games. Discussions surrounding Olympic framing include: framing of ambush marketing (see Ellis, Scassa, & Séguin, 2011), the degree to which gender, ethnic, and national biases influence prime-time telecasts of the Games (see Billings & Eastman, 2003), how female athletes were portrayed by journalists (see Kian, Bernstein, & McGuire, 2013), a comparison of how social media and traditional media framed the 2014 Sochi Olympics (see Frederick, Pegoraro, & Burch, 2016), and many more. This chapter focuses on a few studies that provide prolific examples of framing of the Olympic Games.

Tibetan-China/US

A recent case study by Huang and Fahmy (2013) discusses the framing of the Olympics by different countries. The 2008 Olympics in Beijing, China, were surrounded by controversy for the home nation because of China's treatment of Tibet, a region of China. China, in fact, was denied the Olympics in 2000 because of its human rights abuses and brutal suppression of dissent, most obviously with Tibet (Dorning, 2008). After China was denied the 2000 Olympics, the Beijing 2008 Olympic Committee improved their human rights concerns and built their Olympic bid around the improved treatment of humans. Despite their improvements, athletes from around the globe were considering boycotting the 2008 Olympics for recent violent attacks toward Tibet by China (Dorning, 2008). While athletes were warned against protesting, civilians of the United States were more than willing to protest during the Olympic torch relay as it passed through San Francisco (McKinley, 2008).

Researchers Huang and Fahmy (2013) investigated how the United States and Chinese press visually framed the journey of the 2008 Olympic torch. From an agenda-setting viewpoint, the Chinese press included a total of 272 photos of the Olympic torch relay, while the United States only included 85 photographs. The stark difference shows the relative importance of the relay for each country. Since the Olympic Games were held in Beijing, the Chinese press wanted to emphasize the importance of the relay and Games for the country. Perhaps the increased media attention was to garner support and excitement for the Games and downplay the controversy surrounding Tibet and the Chinese. The United States media agenda was better suited for other issues, not the torch's relay. From the framing standpoint, the researchers investigated whether the photos from the Chinese and United States press were either of harmony or protest. Photos of harmony were welcoming of the torch relay process without any protest interruption. Protest photos portrayed interruptions of the torch relay process and/or protests caused by the torch's journey (Huang & Fahmy, 2013). Overwhelmingly, the United States press photos were of the protests (roughly 67%). An individual subjected to only United States press would be made to believe the torch relay was mostly fielded with protest and conflict. The photos from the Chinese press consisted primarily of images of harmony (above 65%). An individual subject to only the Chinese press saw frames showing peace and welcoming around the torch, with little visual images of protests in China. Why would there be a difference? Why wouldn't the photos and narratives of the torch's relay be the same? The answer can be found in each country's political views toward Tibet. The American press was sympathetic toward the human rights groups and was happy to showcase the protests of the relay. Conversely, the Chinese press did not want to showcase the protestors as they would bring the Tibetan issue to the forefront of the public's attention and delegitimize the government's author-

ity. Instead, the press focused on the peaceful frames of the torch's journey to inspire nationalism and, perhaps, distract the public from the human rights concerns brought up by the rest of the world. The Tibetan-China/US case is a real-life example of how nations can use the media to influence their messages towards the public. The Chinese pushed peaceful photos to ensure their audience is thinking positively towards the torch's relay, but not about the treatment of Tibetans. The United States wanted its audience to see a different side of the Chinese Olympics as they opposed the way the Chinese were treating Tibet.

Sam DCruz/shutterstock.com

Agenda-setting and Framing in the Olympics

An opportunity to look at both agenda-setting and framing in the Olympics was presented by Angelini, Billings, and MacArthur (2012). The researchers investigated how NBC, an American broadcast company, covered the 2010 Vancouver Olympics. There were two main components to the study: (1) The frequency that NBC employees mentioned American versus non-American athletes and stories (agenda-setting) and (2) The rhetoric NBC employees were saying about the successes and failures of the American and non-American athletes (framing).

The findings related to agenda-setting considered first the number of athlete mentions by country. A total of 42.3% of the 9,867 mentions were American athletes, while 57.7% were from every other country involved in the Olympics. Additionally, 8 of the top 10 most mentioned athletes were American athletes. Only two athletes, Charles Hamelin (Canada #6) and Lee Ho-Suk (South Korea #9), were non-Americans (Apolo Anton Ohno was the most mentioned athlete with 558 mentions). The researchers speak to the notion that the American telecast was focused on highlighting American athletes compared to non-American athletes. The example of NBC's favoritism toward American athletes is a prime example of agenda-setting. There were plenty of other stories from foreign athletes that were not subject to a large amount of news coverage, but most were spurned for American athlete coverage. Why focus the majority of attention on American athletes when a vast amount of athletes were non-American? Perhaps American audiences favor news about their own athletes and do not care about non-American athletes. Regardless of the reason, NBC chose to spend the majority of their agenda on American athletes, excluding their audience from opportunities to see the impactful stories from around the world (Angelini, Billings, & MacArthur, 2012).

The other focus of the study investigated the *way* successes and failures were framed regarding the American and non-American athletes. For Americans, the rhetoric surrounding their performance was commitment, good luck, bad luck, intelligence, and outgoing/extroverted personalities. For non-Americans, athletes were likely to receive comments about their athletic strength and skill, and their size and parts of the body. There was a clear difference between the descriptions of American versus non-American athletes. American successes and failures were framed in a way of non-tangible or interior factors, while non-American athletes were framed in a way of observable and exterior factors. An individual cannot see the level of commitment, intelligence, or luck, but they can see athletic strength, skill, and size of the body. The authors indicate the reason there is such a stark difference between the two descriptions of American and non-American athletes could stem from how much more familiar the employees (reporters) were with American athletes than non-American athletes. Another reason may include the fact that NBC intentionally set an agenda to focus on American athletes. NBC reporters were more familiar with and probably learned more information about the athletes they knew they would be covering (Angelini, Billings, & MacArthur, 2012). This example indicates how agenda-setting theory can influence framing. Angelini et al. (2012) make a strong case for the frames set out by NBC being influenced from agenda-setting theory.

Sergei Bachlakov/shutterstock.com

Should NBC set the agenda to highlight mostly American athletes? Should NBC frame the stories of American athletes in a more athletically positive manner than non-American athletes? On one hand, the NBC audience will be mostly American as it is an American-based company. It makes sense to pander to the audience, especially during the Olympics when patriotism is high. On the other hand, there are so many more amazing, inspirational, and impressive stories of non-American athletes. The debate has valid points on both sides, but think about the potential social benefit for NBC to highlight the stories of all athletes from the Olympics. NBC can help usher in a new age of a global community by regularly exposing its audience to foreign athletes. Instead of promoting a U.S.-against-everyone-else mentality by only promoting American successes, NBC could help build goodwill towards foreign countries and people. The major drawback could be a decline in viewership during the Olympic highlights, initially. NBC did pay the Rio Olympics $1.2 billion for the right to broadcast the Games, so the media company is probably not hurting for money (Tam, 2016).

ISSUES AND ETHICS IN SPORT

Media and the Sport Manager

The media portrays stories in a variety of ways. Sport managers, especially those in sport information positions, will also have the ability to frame a story to best fit the organization. In a sport position choices will often be presented, and it will be essential to determine the importance, necessity, and validity that should be passed on to the fans and stakeholders. When highlighting or framing stories in certain ways, stereotypes can be perpetuated. One way to ensure stories are appropriately covered and framed in an appropriate way is to diversify the workforce. Providing a variety of personalities and ethic backgrounds in the office can assist in eliminating common stereotypes. Diversifying the staff allows for fair and accurate reporting of the news, and provides opportunities for perspectives, ideas, or news stories not previously considered.

PUBLIC RELATIONS

The topic of public relations is the second part of this chapter as it oftentimes requires the individual or organization to work with media. According to the Public Relations Society of America, **public relations** is the "strategic communication process that builds mutually beneficial relationships between organizations and their publics" (About public relations, n.d., para. 3). A manager has to be proactive and reactive with the public (oftentimes through the media) to garner goodwill.

Positive Public Relations

Public relations are meant to garner goodwill between an organization and the community. A great sport manager will be proactive about sending out media stories or campaigns about the positive influence of a player, coach, administrator, or the affect a team may have on a city. Many athletes or teams engage in the community, simply to benefit the community. A prime example of positive public relations is the NBA Cares and WNBA Cares campaigns. Both organizations have websites specifically dedicated for the campaigns, specific logos, television and online commercials before, during, and after games, frequent media stories, social media accounts, and strong mission statements. The organizations want to push those stories about their Cares campaigns to build the goodwill between the community and the NBA/WNBA. It is not uncommon to see NBA and WNBA players and teams out in public helping their community build homes, teach youth, or support the military. The public and sport fans may be more likely to view these organizations more favorably. It is important, as a sport manager, to build relations with the community and educate fans about participation that is a benefit to the community.

Being proactive about positive stories to the media and public are essential for any good public relations manager, but it is important to remember there will likely be some pitfalls of reporting positive stories to the media and public. For instance, it may be tempting to stretch the truth or lie to the media to build goodwill. Such was the case for Lance Armstrong. Lance Armstrong was an American cyclist who beat cancer to win seven straight Tour de France races from 1999–2005. As early as 1999, the year of his first Tour de France victory, there were claims that Armstrong was using PEDs during the races. Armstrong shunned those claims off as witch-hunts and continued racing under the inspirational story of a man who beat testicular cancer to win the toughest cycling event in the world. Armstrong even created the Livestrong Foundation, an organization dedicated to helping people affected by cancer. The organization, amidst Armstrong's dominance, created yellow rubber bracelets with the words Livestrong to promote awareness and fundraise for the organization. As he gave his speech after the record breaking seventh Tour de France in 2005, Armstrong stated, "I'm sorry you don't believe in miracles" (Cycle of deceit, 2012, para. 1) to those who doubted the legitimacy of his races. He reached out to the public, through numerous channels, to promote this positive image and build goodwill. It led to a tremendous fall from grace as Armstrong was revealed to have used doping techniques to assist him during the Tour de France. His fall from grace was even larger and more shameful because of his dishonest statements towards the press and public. Public relations are supposed to build goodwill through proactive measures of showcasing the positive interactions between athlete, coach, or organization and the public.

Negative Public Relations

Sometimes, however, public relations are reactionary, as in the case of an athlete, coach, or an organization making a mistake. Mistakes happen, but sometimes a mistake is worse than others. In the case of an issue, it is best to be quick to correct the mistake, issue an apology, and take disciplinary action if needed. On June 3rd, 2017, the Ogden Raptors, Class A affiliate of the Los Angeles Dodgers, announced an Hourglass Appreciation Night. Women, dressed in bikinis, were going to the broadcast booth during the game. The Raptors were going to video-stream the broadcast and allow fans to pose with pictures with the women whose "curves rival those of any stud pitching prospect" (Mandell, 2017, para. 3). This promotion was termed "sexist" and was short lived. The promotion was rescinded two days later as the Raptors issued an apology. The issue will likely tarnish the organization in the short term, but the organization avoided long-term negative consequences by quickly rescinding the promotion. For bigger organizations, the news may continually cover the story, putting pressure on the organization to respond to their misdoings. In that case, it is best to know some image repair strategies to use when organizations are faced with an issue.

STUDENT ACTIVITY:
Steve McNair, former NFL quarterback for the Baltimore Ravens and Tennessee Titans, was arrested in 2003 for driving under the influence of alcohol and illegal possession of a handgun. Surprisingly, there is little information online about the then star quarterback getting in trouble with the law. Read the article *McNair apologies for DUI, gun charges* by Teresa M. Walker. How does it paint someone convicted of a DUI and illegally owning a gun? Is it positive or negative? How is Steve McNair and the Titans organization viewed throughout the article? The article is a prime example of public relations in a reactionary sense, but doing it in the right way.

ISSUES AND ETHICS IN SPORT

IMAGE REPAIR STRATEGIES

Oftentimes players on athletic teams will transgress, hurting the image and goodwill of an organization. It falls upon the sport managers of an organization to enact image repair strategies when an employee misbehaves, transgresses, or disobeys organizational demands. If an employee does so, Benoit (2006) offers 14 image repair strategies divided into five general strategy headings to help. The repair strategies offered by Benoit (1995, 1997, 2000, 2006) have been used for political, business, and even sport-related case studies. When an individual or organization is caught within a transgression or alleged transgression, the entity may use one or a combination of strategies to help their public relations images. The transgressor must pick and choose correctly, however, as using the wrong strategy can actually hurt an organization or individual's public image. The five strategies are: denial, evade responsibility, reducing offensiveness, corrective action, and mortification.

Denial

Denial is split into two sub-categories: simple denial and shifting blame. **Simple denial** is just claiming the transgression never happened. **Shifting blame** is denial in the sense that the individual accused of the wrongdoing blames another party, thus shifting blame to a different person or organization. For an example, two Olympic sprinters compete in a 100-meter dash and in the final 10 meters the two sprinters are ahead of the pack. All of a sudden, both sprinters get their legs tangled up and fall before the finish line. One sprinter may be accused of purposely tripping the other player. The runner accused may claim that it was an accident and the attempted trip never happened (simple denial), or that the other sprinter was the one that tripped the accused runner (shifting blame).

> **QUICK RECALL EXERCISE**
> First, select a level of play—youth/interscholastic, college, or professional (including international competitions). Next, in a small group (three or four students), come up with two events in which simple denial or shifting blame happened in sport. Be prepared to share these experiences or examples with the class.

Evade Responsibility

Evading responsibility is split into four groups. First, the accused may evade responsibility through provocation. **Provocation** is the claim that the transgression was a response to another, prior, wrongful act. Next, **defeasibility** evades responsibility by the assertion that the wrongdoer had no control or information over the offensive act. Third, the wrongful act can be framed in a way that it was an accident or mishap. Finally, the transgressor can argue the wrongful act was an act of good intentions. Think of a head basketball coach who is getting blamed for one of his/her assistant coaches illegally paying players to come to their college when they were on a recruiting trip. The head coach may claim the money was actually reimbursement for travels. In the past the NCAA did not pay for the entire cost of a recruit prior to 2016 (provocation; VanHaaren, 2016). The head coach may choose to state that he or she had no control over the actions of the assistant coach (defeasibility). One strategy a head coach could attempt to use is to acknowledge the money accidentally fell out of the assistant coach's hand into the recruit's hands (accident). Finally, the head coach could claim the assistant coach was just trying to be a friendly person and the player really needed the cash to survive (good intentions). Each of these strategies are commonly used in the sport industry.

Reducing Offensiveness

Reducing offensiveness is split into six categories. **Bolstering** is stressing the positive traits of the transgression. **Minimization** tries to minimize the bad consequences of the act. Next, one could use **differentiation**, where the transgressor portrays the act as less harmful than similar acts. **Transcendence** tries to appeal to values or more important ends. The accused could attempt to switch the script and attack the accuser and reduce their credibility. Finally, an individual could always use compensation by reimbursing the victim(s). An example that showcases the different strategies within reducing offensiveness could be an athletic director cutting at least one male sport team due to non-compliance with Title IX. The athletic director could claim that by cutting at least one men's team, more resources would be made available for the rest of the teams (bolstering). Another strategy the athletic director could claim is that there is only one men's team that needs to be cut, not multiple teams (minimization). The athletic director could bring up other instances where men's teams were cut due to less severe circumstances (differentiation). The athletic director, in desperation, could always attack the media or accuser by claiming the cut was not related to Title IX and that the accuser had incorrect facts (transcendence). Alternatively, the athletic director could always express his/her desire to honor the student-athlete's scholarships and offer the remainder of the money for the student-athlete to complete their education regardless of the cuts (compensation).

Corrective Action

Another strategy an accuser could utilize is corrective action. **Corrective action** is the plan to repair the incident and/or prevent recurrence. A YMCA youth sport director could alter policy after a young child gets hurt at a coaching camp. An NBA organization could replace their entire sales staff if the ticket sales were the lowest in organizational history. There are multiple ways to take corrective action; all include actions by the organization, not words.

Mortification

Finally, **mortification** involves apologizing and acting remorseful for the acts. An important part of mortification is how genuine the accuser is when they apologize. Being disingenuous can be disastrous as it seems like the accuser is not remorseful and did not care. However, offering a sincere apology may help turn around the poor public image. Andy Pettitte, a three-time all-star and five time World Series champion, who had his number (46) retired by the Yankees, offered a heartfelt apology when he admitted to using steroids in the early 2000s (Lapointe, 2008). Pettitte used mortification, along with other strategies, to help restore his image and help the New York Yankees' image.

Dennis Ku/shutterstock.com

Other Repair Strategies

The aforementioned image restoration strategies are from Benoit's typology. The idea of image repair is ever-expanding and, therefore, has expanded to include more strategies that do not fall under Benoit's typology. For instance, Smithson and Venette (2013) noted a stonewalling strategy. **Stonewalling** is the use of superficial responses, refocusing, or redirecting the attention, while denying the accuser specific information. A star player accused of cheating on his or her spouse may focus on other facts of the case other than the details of the extra-marital affair. Another strategy, detailed by Sanderson (2008), is victimization. **Victimization** is the accused outlaying their suffering as a self-defense tactic. A marketing director accused of using a racially insensitive term may claim that he/she is the victim of society taking his/her words too seriously. **Conforming** is blaming the culture for the action, similar to Tour de France cyclists who used blood doping or performance enhancing drugs because everyone else was using the illegal tactics. Additionally, **retrospective regret** is the remorseful reflection and proclaiming the accuser would never do the wrongful act again (Hambrick, Frederick, & Sanderson, 2015). The aforementioned strategies in this section are just some of the other strategies outside of Benoit's typology that can be used in public relations and should be recognized by sport managers.

If an athlete or organization finds themselves accused of a transgression, the athlete or organization must successfully use multiple strategies to repair their image and prevent any harmful damage to the organization. For instance, Frederick, Burch, Sanderson, and Hambrick (2014) investigated how Manti Te'o used different image repair strategies after it was revealed he had a fake girlfriend. During the 2012–2013 college football season, Manti Te'o was the star linebacker for the Notre Dame football team and led the Irish to a berth in the national championship. Te'o also used a late-season emotional surge to finish runner-up for the Heisman Trophy (Fortuna, 2013). The player, who was known for being emotional on the field, saw his grandmother pass away and, just a few hours later, the death of his long-distance girlfriend late in the season. Te'o seemingly used his late-girlfriend, Lennay Kekua, as motivation for his play. He tweeted out condolences and pictures of his deceased girlfriend throughout the late months of 2012. News broke a month before the national championship game that Kekua (the girlfriend) was not a real person, but Te'o was **catfished** (an individual impersonating another individual) by an acquaintance of Te'o, Ronaiah Tuiasosopo (Burke & Dickey, 2013). According to the *Deadspin* report by Burke and Dickey, Tuiasosopo's friend was confident Manti Te'o was aware Kekua was fake and used the story to garner national attention (Burke & Dickey, 2013). Regardless if Te'o was in on the ordeal, Te'o's image was in need of severe repair.

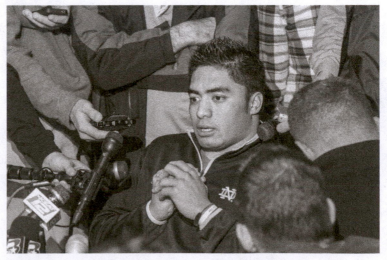

To begin to repair his image, Te'o went on live television in an interview to explain his side of the story. Researchers Frederick et al. (2014) analyzed his words to determine which of the above image repair strategies Te'o used. During his interview, Te'o used eight different image repair strategies: defeasibility, victimization, stonewalling, good intentions, retrospective regret, bolstering, shifting blame, and simple denial. Frederick and his colleagues determined simple denial, shifting blame, bolstering, good intentions, and retrospective regret were the most useful strategies that should be emphasized by other athletes or individuals in a catfish situation. The useful strategies helped Te'o's image by showing he was an innocent bystander in the whole ordeal. Conversely, the researchers noted defeasibility, victimization, and stonewalling were inappropriate image repair strategies. These strategies made Te'o look like he did not have an explanation for the ordeal and blamed others. Te'o's story should showcase how an individual can use multiple repair strategies. Additionally, one should understand that there are good strategies and poor strategies to use in certain situations.

CONCLUSION

Communication through and with the media and the public is essential for sport managers. The media is a powerful mechanism that can influence the way managers, the community, and the fans think or feel about a person, culture, or society. The media has the ability to influence the perception of many, especially in game-winning or game-losing plays involving close outcomes. Agenda-setting or framing, although simplistic, can have a powerful impact on sport. There are more examples of agenda-setting and framing within sport that have detrimental effects on society over time. As researchers investigate the difference between male athletes and female athletes on *Sports Illustrated* or *ESPN Magazine* covers, the differences are clear. Male athletes are more likely to be in athletic poses or active roles. Female athletes are more likely to be sexualized, featured in ways that emphasize conventional female norms, and in passive poses (Martin & McDonald, 2012). This has detrimental effects on generations of men and women who see these pictures as the norm. It has become common to see women being stripped of their athletic accomplishments to highlight their bodies and see men as active, masculine, and celebrating athletic success. The importance of understanding the power of the media and how one can influence the agenda or narrative is essential in a sport career.

A career in sport communication or the public relations is not required to have a deep understanding of how the media can depict sport. Every sport organization has great moments where they benefit the surrounding community outside the field, stadium, or arena. It is up to the sport manager, in any position within the organization, to be proactive and tell the media, community, or friends about the positive stories of the organization. This can help build goodwill to the community and increase the organization's brand. There may be times, however, that the organization will make poor ethical decisions and the sport manager will need to be swift and decisive with a response. Sport managers must know image repair strategies to help the organization survive the transgression and come out looking favorable once again. The repair strategies, as outlined above, can help with that process.

The role as a sport manager is crucial to making ethical decisions related to and with the public and the media. By diversifying, being cognizant of the social trends, and continuing to maintain high ethical and moral practices, sport managers will assist the media in leading positive change in sport communication, media, and public relations.

DISCUSSION QUESTIONS

1. Describe agenda-setting and give an example.

2. Describe framing and give an example.

3. How were media frames different for the Olympic torch relay by the Chinese and American Media?

4. How did NBC show examples of agenda-setting theory and framing in the 2010 Olympics?

5. What is the goal of public relations?

6. When should a sport manager use proactive public relations? When should they use reactive public relations?

7. What are the different image repair strategies an accused individual could use?

8. Using Cavanaugh's model for ethical decision-making from Chapter 1, determine if it was ethical for Manti Te'o to continue to use a fake girlfriend to help his potential career. Be sure to consider the *utility, rights, and justice* framework to support your answer.

CASE STUDY: CAUCASIAN HERITAGE NIGHT

In 2015, the Orem Owlz, a minor league team for the Los Angeles Angels in Utah, created a promotion based off Wonder Bread for burger buns, a vertical leap contest, watching the television shows *Friends* and *Seinfeld* (two shows with predominantly White casts), and watching Mixed Martial Arts (MMA). The night was called "Caucasian Heritage Night" and was set for August 10th (Alter, 2015). The organization announced the promotion on June 19th.

Two days before the promotion, a White supremacist, Dylann Roof, went into Emanuel African Methodist Episcopal Church in South Carolina and killed nine Black parishioners. Roof, who was 21, committed the act in hopes of starting a race war (Mosendz, 2015). The mass shooting sent shock waves across the US as race tensions between White and minority Americans were tense.

Immediately after the Owlz released their "Caucasian Heritage Night" promotion to the public, Twitter erupted with commentary about the planned night. One Twitter user stated, "Caucasian Heritage Night?! I must be misinformed, isn't Caucasian Heritage Night every day/holiday/history lesson???" Another replied to the Owlz Twitter account stating, "@OremOwlz terrible. Seriously. An embarrassment to the entire state of Utah. Cancelled what never should've been planned". The president of the National Association for the Advancement of Colored People Tri-State Conference of Idaho, Nevada, and Utah went to the press and expressed concern over the promotion, especially given the timing of the South Carolina shooting (Zdanowicz, 2015).

Others came to the defense of the promotion. One individual claimed that every other race received their promotional night, so Caucasians should too. Another Twitter user explained "Is grilling hot dogs and then watching @BellatorMMA a shameful #CaucasianHeritageNight thing of me to do?" Another supporter of the night hoped the organization would reschedule the night, commenting, "Please in the future have a bigger backbone. Or at least schedule this for later. Blaming you or other Whites for what one White did in South Carolina is racist and caucasiaphobic."

CASE QUESTIONS

1. Identify three ethical dilemmas in this case. Explain the components of each dilemma.

2. Should the organization cancel the 'Caucasian Heritage Night'? Why or why not?

3. Let's assume the organization believes it should cancel the event. Make a plan as to how you would announce the cancellation of the promotion. What channels would you use? What would you say? Would you take any disciplinary action?

4. The following statement was issued as a result of the backlash from the 'Caucasian Heritage Night':
Minor League Baseball, and the Orem Owlz, is about baseball, togetherness and family fun for all fans of all races, religions, and orientations. Our goal in this promotion, like any of our promotions, is to have fun and make fun of everyday normalcies. Our night was to include wonder bread on burgers with mayonnaise, clips from shows like Friends *and* Seinfeld *and trying to solve the vertical leaping challenge. We understand, in light of recent tragic events, that our intentions have been misconstrued. For that, we sincerely apologize. The Owlz are committed to all its fans, families and all fans of baseball alike—no matter who you are. The event has been removed from our promotional schedule effectively immediately* (Owlz, 2015, para. 2–3). Was this a sufficient response? Outline the positives of this response and the negatives.

5. Make a list of the image repair strategies utilized by the Orem Owlz.

6. How can situations like this one, and the 'Hourglass Appreciation Night', be avoided? What steps can a sport manager take to avoid making insensitive promotions?

GLOSSARY

Agenda-setting theory is the ability of the media "to influence the salience of topics on the public agenda" (McCombs & Reynolds, 2002, p. 2).

Bolstering is stressing the positive traits of the transgression.

Catfishing is when an individual impersonates another individual.

Conforming is blaming the culture for the action.

Corrective action is the plan to repair the incident and/or prevent recurrence.

Defeasibility evades responsibility by the assertion that the wrongdoer had no control or information over the offensive act.

Differentiation involves the transgressor portraying the act as less harmful than similar acts.

Framing is the mental schemas facilitating quick processing of information in everyday life.

Minimization tries to minimize the bad consequences of the act.

Mortification involves apologizing and acting remorseful for the acts.

Public relations: is the strategic communication process that builds beneficial relationships between organizations and the public.

Provocation is the claim that the transgression was a response to another prior, wrongful act.

Retrospective regret is the remorseful reflection and proclaiming the accuser would never do the wrongful act again.

Simple denial is just claiming the transgression never happened.

Stonewalling is the use of superficial responses, refocusing, or redirecting the attention, while denying the accuser specific information.

Shifting blame is denial in the sense that the individual accused of the wrongdoing blames another party, thus shifting blame to a different person or organization.

Transcendence tries to appeal to values or more important ends.

Victimization is the accused outlaying their suffering as a self-defense tactic.

References

About public relations. (n.d.). Retrieved from https://apps.prsa.org/AboutPRSA/PublicRelationsDefined/index.html#.WKo6w_nyvIU

Angelini, J. R., Billings, A. C., & MacArthur, P. J. (2012). The nationalistic revolution will be televised: The 2010 Vancouver Olympics games on NBC. *International Journal of Sport Communication, 5,* 193–209.

Alter, C. (2015, June 19). Utah baseball team cancels 'Caucasian Heritage Night'. *Time.* Retrieved from http://time.com/3929063/utah-baseball-cancels-caucasian-heritage-night/

Benoit, W. L. (1995). *Accounts, excuses, and apologies: A theory of image restoration strategies.* Albany, NY: State University of New York Press.

Benoit, W. L. (1997). Image repair discourse and crisis communication. *Public Relations Review, 23,* 177–186.

Benoit, W. L. (2000). Another visit to the theory of image restoration strategies. *Communication Quarterly, 44,* 463–477.

Benoit, W. L. (2006). President Bush's image repair effort on *Meet the Press:* The complexities of defeasibility. *Journal of Applied Communication Research, 34*(3), 285–306.

Billings, A. C., & Eastman, S. T. (2003). Framing identities: Gender, ethnic, and national parity in network announcing of the 2002 winter Olympics. *Journal of Communication, 53*(4), 569–586.

Brazeal, L. M. (2008). The image repair strategies of Terrell Owens. *Public Relations Review, 34,* 145–150.

Burke, T., & Dickey, J. (2013, January 16). Manti Te'o's dead girlfriend, the most heartbreaking and inspirational story of the college football season, is a hoax. *Deadspin.* Retrieved from http://deadspin.com/manti-teos-dead-girlfriend-the-most-heartbreaking-an-5976517

Cotton, G. (2013, June 13). Gestures to avoid in cross-cultural business: In other words, 'keep your fingers to yourself!' *Huffingtonpost.* Retrieved from: http://www.huffingtonpost.com/gayle-cotton/cross-cultural gestures_b_3437653.html

Cycle of deceit: A timeline of the fall of Lance Armstrong (2012, October 11). *New York Daily News.* Retrieved from http://www.nydailynews.com/sports/i-team/cycle-deceit-timeline-fall-lance-armstrong-article-1.1179861

Dorning, A. M. (2008, March 24). Beijing boycott? Don't tell Olympic athletes. *ABC News.* Retrieved from http://abcnews.go.com/Sports/story?id=4501952&page=1

Ellis, D., Scassa, T., & Séguin, B. (2011). Framing ambush marketing as a legal issue: An Olympic perspective. *Sport Management Review, 14,* 297–308.

Entman, R. M. (1993). Framing: toward clarification of a fractured paradigm. *Journal of Communication, 43*(4), 51–58.

Fortuna, M. (2013, January 9). Te'o's ND career ends, legacy will live on. ESPN. Retrieved from http://www.espn.com/blog/ncfnation/post/_/id/76020/teos-nd-career-ends-but-legacy-will-live-on

Frederick, E. L., Burch, L. M., Sanderson, J., & Hambrick, M. E. (2014). To invest in the invisible: A case study of Manti Te'o's image repair strategies during the Katie Couric interview. *Public Relations Review, 40,* 780–788.

Frederick, E., Pegoraro, A., & Burch, L. (2016). Echo or organic: framing the 2014 Sochi Games. *Online Information Review, 40*(6), 798–813.

Goffman, E. (1974). *Frame analysis: An essay on the organization of experience.* New York, NY: Harper & Row.

Hambrick, M. E., Frederick, E. L., & Sanderson, J. (2015). From yellow to blue: Exploring Lance Armstrong's image repair strategies across traditional and social media. *Communication & Sport, 3*(2), 196–218.

Huang, Y., & Fahmy, S. (2013). Picturing a journey of protest or a journey of harmony? Comparing the visual framing of the 2008 Olympic torch relay in the US versus the Chinese press. *Media, War & Culture, 6*(3), 191–206.

Hurst, N. (2015, June 2). Black athletes stereotyped negatively in media compared to White athletes. *School of Journalism: University of Missouri.* Retrieved from https://journalism.missouri.edu/2015/06/black-athletes-stereotyped-negatively-in-media-compared-to-white-athletes/

Kian, E. M., Bernstein, A., & McGuire, J. S. (2013). A major boost for gender equality or more of the same? The television coverage of female athletes at the 2012 London Olympic Games. *Journal of Popular Television, 1*(1), 143–149.

Lapointe, J. (2008, February 19). Pettitte apologizes to Yankees and his fans. *New York Times.* Retrieved from http://www.nytimes.com/2008/02/19/sports/baseball/19yankees.html

Mandell, N. (2017, June 6). Minor league team pulls 'hourglass appreciation night' promotion, blames 'unauthorized press release'. *USA Today.* Retrieved from http://ftw.usatoday.com/2017/06/ogden-raptors-hourglass-appreciation-night

Martin, A., & McDonald, M. G. (2012). Covering women's sports? An analysis of Sports Illustrated covers from 1987-2009 and ESPN the magazine covers from 1998-2009. *Graduate Journal of Sport, Exercise & Physical Education Research, 1,* 81-97.

McCombs, M. E., & Shaw, D. L. (1972). The agenda-setting function of mass media. *Public Opinion Quarterly, 26*(2), 176–187.

McCombs, M., & Reynolds, A. (2002). How the news shapes our civic agenda. In Bryant, J., & Oliver, M. B. (Eds.), *Media effects: Advances in theory and research* (1–17). Mahwah, NJ: Lawrence Erlbaum Associates.

McKinley, J. (2008, April 8). As torch reaches San Francisco, it runs for cover before its run. *New York Times.* Retrieved from http://www.nytimes.com/2008/04/09/us/09torch.html

Mosendz, P. (2015, June 19). Dylann Roof confesses: Says he wanted to start 'race war'. *Newsweek.* Retrieved from http://www.newsweek.com/dylann-roof-confesses-church-shooting-says-he-wanted-start-race-war-344797

Owlz, O. (2015, June 19). Owlz cancel event. *Minor League Baseball.* Retrieved from https://www.milb.com/owlz/news/owlz-cancel-event/c-131690108/t-196096846

Saks, J., & Yanity, M. (2016). The not-so-neutral zone?: ESPN, agenda setting, and the National Hockey League. *Journal of Sports Media, 11*(1), 81–100.

Sanderson, J. (2008). "How do you prove a negative?": Roger Clemens' image repair strategies in response to the Mitchell Report. *International Journal of Sport Communication, 1,* 246–262.

Smithson, J., & Venette, S. (2013). Stonewalling as an image-defense strategy: A critical examination of BP's response to the Deepwater Horizon explosion. *Communication Studies, 64,* 395–410.

Tam, D. (2016, August 5). Let's do the numbers: The money spent on the Rio Olympics. *Marketplace.* Retrieved from https://www.marketplace.org/2016/08/05/world/let-s-do-numbers-what-has-been-spent-rio-olympics

Tewksbury, D., & Scheufele, D. A. (2009). News framing theory and research. In Bryant, J., & Oliver, M. B. (Eds.), *Media effects: Advances in theory and research* (17–33). Mahwah, NJ: Lawrence Erlbaum Associates.

VanHaaren, T. (2016, April 19). NCAA allows schools to pay for two guardians to accompany recruits on official visits. *ESPN.* Retrieved from http://www.espn.com/college-sports/recruiting/story/_/id/15271513/ncaa-passes-rule-allowing-institutions-pay-two-guardians-accompany-recruits-official-visits

Zdanowicz, C. (2015, June 22). Pro baseball team cancels 'Caucasian Heritage Night'. *CNN.* Retrieved from http://www.cnn.com/2015/06/20/us/caucasian-heritage-night/index.html

DIVERSITY AND INCLUSION IN SPORT: CURRENT TRENDS AND POLICY

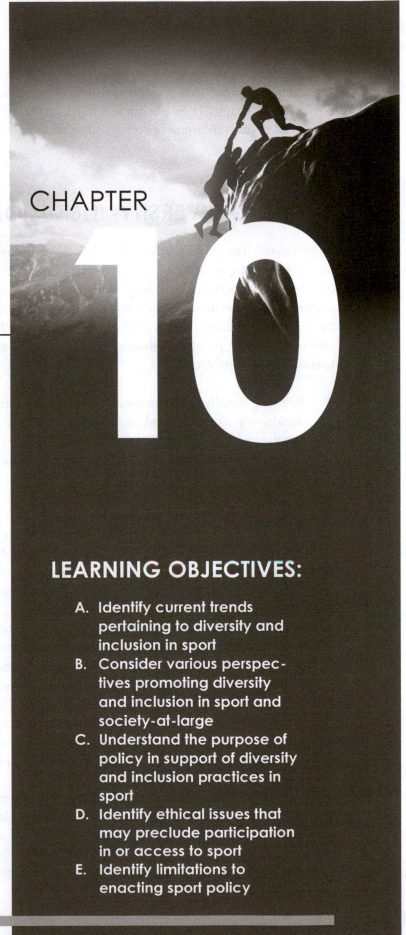

CHAPTER

10

This book provides the opportunity to learn about ethics and reasoning, the role of power and politics in ethical decision-making strategies, and ethical leadership in the context of sport. This chapter will explore the tangible results of ethical reasoning, decision making, and leadership policy. Policy in the context of current trends will be discussed pertaining to diversity and inclusion in sport. This chapter will also examine how sport might promote or inhibit diversity and inclusion for participants, fans, and sport administrators. Think about the following questions addressed in this chapter:

- Why are men more likely to coach women's teams than women?
- What is the impact of transgender athletes in sport?
- How can sport be more inclusive for people with disabilities?
- Why is sexual orientation an issue in sport?
- What role does race/ethnicity play when hiring coaches and administrators?
- How has sport promoted or inhibited diversity and inclusion in society at large?
- Why is Title IX relevant today?

LEARNING OBJECTIVES:

A. Identify current trends pertaining to diversity and inclusion in sport
B. Consider various perspectives promoting diversity and inclusion in sport and society-at-large
C. Understand the purpose of policy in support of diversity and inclusion practices in sport
D. Identify ethical issues that may preclude participation in or access to sport
E. Identify limitations to enacting sport policy

Each of the questions above do not have a "yes" or "no" answers. Instead, they imply various aspects of diversity and inclusion are, in fact, important and relevant to today's participant, spectator, and sport administrator. Thus, this chapter examines current trends in diversity and inclusion and how sport organizations have developed policies to promote access and equality to diverse populations in the United States and around the world.

DEFINING DIVERSITY, INCLUSION, AND EQUITY

To get started, it might be helpful to first define and discuss the terminology we used in this chapter. Whether on a college campus or in a business setting, the term diversity is used in a context to improve the student learning experience or to help an organization achieve its objectives. While that is no doubt true, it is important to understand what diversity really means. For the purposes of this chapter, **diversity** means all the ways people differ (Jordan, 2017)—sex, gender identity, race and ethnicity, socio-economic status, education, geography, political affiliations, sexual orientation, religious beliefs, life experiences, and opinions. **Inclusion,** then, involves:

> bringing together and harnessing these diverse forces and resources in a way that is beneficial. Inclusion puts the concept and practice of diversity into action by creating an environment of involvement, respect, and connection—where the richness of ideas, backgrounds, and perspectives are harnessed to create business value (Jordan, para. 2).

So why discuss diversity and inclusion in the context of sport? First and foremost, sport is a global phenomenon. From young boys and girls kicking around a ball made of rags on a dirt lot, to multi-billion-dollar sport organizations and millionaire professional athletes, sport is a common language for people and cultures around the world. Sport, however, has dualistic qualities. On one hand, sport has been used as a device to divide people and countries by promoting racism, discrimination, corruption, and violence (Chalip, 2006; UN, 2003). On the other hand, sport has also been identified as a tool for resolving social problems, including deficiencies in education, the spread of disease, poverty, inter-ethnic conflict, and gender inequities (UN, 2003). Research has also found that sport fosters social integration, teaches coping mechanisms, increases knowledge, contributes to education, and creates social relationships by building connections and improving communication between individuals and groups (UN, 2003). Furthermore, sport and physical activity promote fitness, reduce stress and anxiety (Allender, Cowburn, & Foster, 2006; Seefeldt & Ewing, 1997), and provide opportunities for peer-to-peer social interaction beyond family networks (Meier, 2005). When individuals and groups of people are denied access to sport and physical activity, they are also denied the benefits. Denial of benefits has the potential to further marginalize people and create deficits in health, education, economic status, equality, and environmental sustainability.

National and international sport organizations have attempted to create rules or policies to prevent aspects of sport (e.g., discrimination, racism, sexism, homophobia, and violence) from dividing people and communities. Further, advocates recognize the benefits of sport to an individual's health and well-being. Therefore, policies have been created to help make sport more accessible to people around the globe. Sport managers will be asked to develop and support existing policies that promote diversity and are inclusive, equitable, and fair.

ISSUES AND ETHICS IN SPORT

So, what is a policy? A **policy** is a standard or course of action that defines how an organization conducts business affairs. Thus, it is important that the policy aligns with the goals and mission of the organization. Because a policy offers a guideline for action within the context of an organization's mission and goals, it also aids managers in making decisions that are in the best interests of their sport, organization, and stakeholders (e.g., players, fans, sponsors). Most importantly, an ethical policy has the potential to not only change sport or a sport organization; it may also have far-reaching positive consequences for a group of people. For example, one of the most important, yet little known, policies to affect sport and participation in physical activity was the 1978 International Charter for Physical Education and Sport, which declared sport as a basic human right (UNESCO, 1978). Despite the Charter's declaration of sport as a human right and the recognition of benefits for all people, access to and equal participation in sport and physical activity is still often limited to certain groups of people.

CURRENT TRENDS IN DIVERSITY AND INCLUSION

As a sport manager, it is important to consider *why* access and participation are still limited to certain groups of people, as well as *how* history and context influence access and participation. More importantly, how can you, as a sport manager support and develop policies that are inclusive and equitable? Thus, it is important to understand concepts of equality and equity. In doing so, one can begin to understand how historical contexts and current social climates impact not only sport participation, but how sport is managed. **Equality** is about sameness. That is, everyone gets the same thing. **Equity** is about fairness and ensuring people have access to the same opportunities. As you read definitions of diversity, inclusion, and equity, you have likely already identified individual people or groups of people who have been excluded from participation in sport or treated differently simply because they were or are . . . different. This section explores demographics of difference that impact decision making for sport managers.

Race and Racism in Sport

> *"Sports and athletic competition in the 21st century are subject to many of the same racial prejudices and beliefs that have come to consume daily American life"* (Kerr, 2011, p. 19).

IN THE UNITED STATES. Though Kerr's statement limits observations of race and racism in sport and competition to the current century, such prejudices have plagued sport in the United States and around the world for hundreds of years. In the United States, we can recall sport icons like Jesse Owens (1936 Olympian, track and field), Jackie Robinson (Brooklyn Dodgers, baseball), and Althea Gibson (Wimbledon champion, women's tennis) for breaking color barriers in their respective sports. One familiar photograph is of John Carlos and Tommie Smith at the 1968 Olympics on the podium with raised gloved fists in the Black Power salute after receiving their medals. The gesture was intended to raise awareness about the discrimination and abuse African American people experienced as part of their

Popperfoto/Contributor/Getty

daily lives in the United States. Two days later, Carlos and Smith were stripped of their medals for violating the Olympic Charter, which prohibits athletes from participating in political activities during the Games.

While Owens, Robinson, Gibson, Smith, and Carlos (among other African Americans) broke color barriers in sport, the triumphs only further exposed the racial tensions between Blacks and Whites in the United States. African Americans were barred from entering stores and restaurants through the front doors. Bathrooms, swimming pools, water fountains, and transportation were segregated and separate facilities were used for "whites only" or "colored people." The public education system in the United States was segregated until 1954. When landmark legislation *Brown v. Board of Education* integrated school systems, African American students were integrated into White schools. Because White students were not integrated into African American schools, many closed; teachers and coaches lost their jobs. When African American students attempted to participate in sports at their new schools, they were not given playing time by the White coaches.

In college settings, African American players endured poor treatment from White teammates. Despite efforts of integration, many still slept and ate in segregated facilities. Whether home or away, African American athletes endured physical and verbal abuse from opponents and fans. Many teams from Southern colleges and universities refused to play historically Black colleges and universities (HBCU), thus reducing opportunities for competition. However, when an all-Black Texas Western team defeated all-White basketball powerhouse University of Kentucky in the 1966 NCAA national basketball championship, the Black athlete became a commodity for traditionally White colleges and athletic programs.

Though positive in some respects, integration also left lasting legacies that continue to impact the experiences of African American athletes and coaches. African American athletes often experience a phenomenon called "stacking" in which they are over- or under-represented in particular positions on teams. The NFL has been widely criticized for this practice. For example, African American athletes are often put in to positions on the field that demand power and speed (e.g., wide receiver, running back). While this could be perceived as a positive, relegating African American athletes to specific positions perpetuates the notion that African American players are intellectually inferior and not equipped for "thinking" positions like quarterback (Coakley, 2010). In 2010, the *Racial and Gender Report Card* (Lapchick, 2010) found that, despite African American players making up only 19% of quarterbacks, stacking "in the NFL is no longer a major concern" (Lapchick, 2015a, p. 14). In Major League Baseball, African American players are also severely under-represented in "thinking" positions such as pitcher, catcher, and infielder (Lapchick, 2015b). A mere 3.1% of pitchers and 7.9% of infielders in MLB are African American.

Both historical and present-day data suggest racism exists in sport. Though there is evidence that supports more inclusion, non-White athletes may still experience violence, discrimination, and unfair treatment. As a sport manager, it is important to work toward inclusion and equity for all athletes.

GLOBAL PERSPECTIVE. In South Africa, Whites and Blacks were segregated for nearly 50 years (1948–1994) during apartheid. Similar to racial segregation in the United States (late 1880s to 1964), **apartheid** subjected non-White individuals (e.g., Black people, people of color, South Asians) to separate and unequal medical, educational, housing, and recreational opportunities (Baldwin-Ragaven, London, & De Gruchy, 1999). Under apartheid, interracial contact in sport was also discouraged. As a result, four separate football (soccer) leagues were created and distinguished by race. Not surprisingly, three of the four leagues—those comprised of non-White athletes—nearly folded due to financial inequities. The financial inequities spurred the non-White athletes to combine forces from three leagues into one—the South African Soccer Federation (SAHO, 2012). Apartheid also prevented South Africa from competing in international competitions, including the World Cup of soccer and the Rugby World Cup. Just prior to and after the fall of apartheid in 1994, international soccer and rugby federations allowed South Africa to compete internationally.

While South Africa is only one example of racism in sport, concern about racism from international sport organizations, including FIFA, the Australian Football League, European Soccer Leagues, and major professional sport organizations in the United States (e.g., NFL, MLB, NBA, etc.), continues to grow. As a result, some sport organizations have developed policies to combat racism in the field of competition and in the stands. In 1995, the Australian Football League (AFL) introduced "Rule 30: A rule to combat racial and religious vilification." Specifically, Rule 30 prohibited action or language that vilified, threatened, or insulted another person "on the basis of that person's race, religion, color, descent, or national or ethnic origin" (AFL, 1995, p. 7). It was passed after White players taunted non-White players with derogatory language and racial slurs. This also led the AFL to create a Vilification Framework, which provides a structured protocol for addressing social issues through education, awareness campaigns, support services, and research (AFL, 2016).

SUMMARY AND ADDITIONAL APPLICATION. While this section focused primarily on African American athletes, consider the experiences of other racial and ethnic minorities in sport. For example, sport teams at every competitive level continue to use demeaning, disrespectful, and racist images of Native Americans to promote their teams and brands. Such images not only perpetuate negative stereotypes about Native Americans, but are also likely to enforce stereotypes about other racial and ethnic minorities (e.g., African Americans, Hispanic/Latino) (Pearson-Wharton, Garland, & MacDonald-Dennis, 2012). Hispanic/Latino athletes, particularly baseball players, immigrate to the United States to pursue dreams of professional careers. They often face language and cultural barriers that can make them vulnerable to sport agents seeking to take advantage of "cheap talent" (Zirin, 2005). While salaries for professional baseball players have increased, just over a decade ago Hispanic and Latino players often signed contracts worth only 10% of their US counterparts (Zirin).

Despite efforts to quell racism in sport, athletes, coaches, and fans still endure discrimination and derogatory language; racial minorities (most often non-Whites) are subject to negative environments, prejudice, and violence due simply to the color of their skin. Sport organizations are creating policies to aid in safer environments for all people, but considerable work at the societal level must occur before conditions improve.

GENDER

Quite often, the terms "sex" and "gender" are used interchangeably. Without delving too much into science, **sex** is determined by biological traits (e.g., chromosomes, genitalia), while **gender** is the "social construction of roles, attributes, and behaviors that a society considers appropriate for men and women" (WHO, 2016, para. 1). Thus, social roles are applied to men and women based on shared beliefs of "masculinity" and "femininity." For example, women possess (or are expected to possess) feminine characteristics such as kindness, submissiveness, and compassion. Men, on the other hand, are expected to be assertive, dominant, and aggressive. Based on these social conventions of gender, sometimes girls and women are discouraged from playing sport, they are sometimes deemed too weak for physical activity, and sometimes medical doctors have suggested that sport participation will harm women's reproductive health (UN, 2007). Moreover, traditionally, sport has been hailed as a male domain through which boys and young men learn to be aggressive, tough, dominant, and even violent. For women, often, participating in sport and physical activity has been considered deviant because female athletes fail to conform to culturally appropriate domestic roles of passivity, submission, and fragility (Dowling, 2000). Pierre de Coubertin, founder of the modern Olympics, underscored this perspective by excluding women from the first modern Olympic Games because he wanted to promote masculine values and social male dominance (Carpentier & Lefèvre, 2006). Both society and popular institutions like sport have contributed to gender inequities and discrimination.

GENDER EQUITY

IN THE UNITED STATES. In the United States, most boys and girls born after 1972 have grown up participating on a youth soccer team or in a basketball league with team members of the opposite sex. Prior to 1972, however, the opportunity for girls to participate in organized sport did not exist. In other words, girls and women in the United States were often denied the right to participate in sport simply based on their sex. In 1972, the federal government passed **Title IX** which stated, "No person in the United States shall, on the basis of sex, be excluded from participation in, be denied the benefits of, or be subjected to discrimination under any education program or activity receiving federal financial assistance" (U.S. Department of Education, 2015, para. 1). The intention of Title IX was to provide girls and women equal opportunity, equal access, and fair treatment in educational settings. Did you notice the word "sport" or "athletics" is not mentioned in Title IX? So how did Title IX impact sport? Pay particular attention to the phrasing in Title IX that reads "education program or activity." Athletic programs (e.g., varsity sports, intramurals, club sports) from elementary schools to colleges and universities are considered educational activities. Thus, girls and women who are students in these educational environments have the right to equal opportunity and access when it comes to physical activity and sport participation.

Title IX is a U.S. law, which means it is subject to enforcement by a federal entity, the Office for Civil Rights. Educational institutions must comply with Title IX in three areas. First, Title IX prohibits discrimination in athletic financial assistance, including interscholastic, intramural, and intercollegiate participation. The financial assistance must be in proportion to the number of students participating in athletics (Figure 10.1). Second, each sex participating in athletics must receive fair treatment in opportunities and benefits. This is also known as the "laundry list" (NCAA, 2012) (Figure 10.2). Third, institutions must provide the effective accommodation of student interests and abilities. Effective accommodation is measured by a three-pronged test:

1. Provide participation opportunities for women and men that are substantially proportionate to their respective rates of enrollment;
2. Demonstrate a history and continuing practice of program expansion for the underrepresented sex;
3. Fully and effectively accommodate the interests and abilities of the underrepresented sex (U.S. Department of Education, 2015).

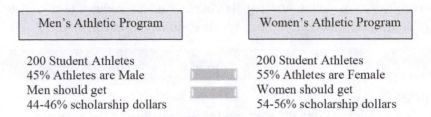

FIGURE 10.1. EXAMPLE OF ATHLETIC FINANCIAL ASSISTANCE

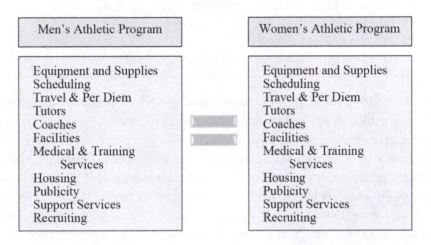

FIGURE 10.2. BENEFITS "LAUNDRY LIST" (NCAA, 2012)

According to the Office for Civil Rights, "The three-part test is intended to allow institutions to maintain flexibility and control over their athletic programs consistent with Title IX's nondiscrimination requirements" (U.S. Department of Education, 2015, p. 11). Flexibility and control means that educational institutions must meet only one of the three prongs to meet the requirement of effective accommodation of student interests and abilities.

In April 2011, the U.S. Department of Education reiterated the importance of keeping an educational environment free from sex discrimination, including freedom from sexual harassment and sexual violence (Office for Civil Rights, 2011). Since the clarification of Title IX in 2011, multiple Title IX lawsuits pertaining to sexual violence have been filed against colleges and universities. Lawsuits include sexual violence allegations against high-profile athletes including Peyton Manning (while at the University of Tennessee) and Jameis Winston (Florida State University). In 2015 and 2016, similar suits were filed at Baylor University, Kent State University, the University of Iowa, and the University of Minnesota; all pending suits involve allegations of sexual assault, sexual harassment, and/or sex discrimination by a student-athlete, coach, or athletic administrator (Buzuvis & Newhall, 2016).

Even though increased access to sport was not explicitly stated in Title IX, the participation of girls and women in organized athletics in schools, colleges, and universities has increased 900% since the implementation of Title IX. Think about it this way: prior to 1972 fewer than 300,000 girls participated in interscholastic sport when compared to 3.6 million boys (NFHS, 2016). Today, over 3.2 million women participate compared to 4.4 million young men (NFHS). Still, female athletes in high school receive 1.3 million fewer participation opportunities than males, and female college student athletes receive $183 million less in scholarships than male student athletes (Women's Sports Foundation, 2016).

TITLE IX ACTIVITY:
Is your school in violation of Title IX? Visit the following website, http://projects.chronicle.com/titleix/, which shows how many and which schools were in violation of Title IX. Do some more research on what a Title IX violation looks like:
1. Pick a university who has had a Title IX violation.
2. What was the violation?
3. Is the violation active or resolved?
4. What should the university do to remedy the situation?

The passage of Title IX in 1972 resulted in the exponential growth of women's participation in interscholastic and intercollegiate athletics. An unintended consequence of Title IX has been the precipitous decline of female coaches and female athletic administrators. In 1972, the percentage of female head coaches of women's teams was nearly 90% (Acosta & Carpenter, 2014). Women also served as Athletic Directors for 90% of women's intercollegiate athletic programs (Acosta & Carpenter, 2014). Today, women represent only 42.6% of head coaches for women's teams, while the percentage of female Athletic Directors has fallen to 19.1%—a decline of 2.2% since 2008 (Acosta & Carpenter, 2014). The most recent *Racial and Gender Report Card* (RGRC; Lapchick, 2013) reported that between 2001 and 2013, the representation of women in executive management positions declined in five of the six North American professional sport organizations (i.e., NFL, MLB, NHL, NBA, MLS). The WNBA was the only exception reporting an increase of women in senior and executive administration.

Women in various sport settings and organizations often face hostile, antagonistic, and discriminatory work environments. Women are more likely to be in professional staff or lower managerial positions (Burton, Barr, Fink, & Bruening, 2009; Burton, Grappendorf, & Henderson, 2011; Whisenant, Pedersen, & Obenour, 2002) and may encounter personal and professional barriers to career progression (Grappendorf & Lough, 2006; Grappendorf, Lough, & Griffin, 2004; Hancock & Hums, 2016; Hoffman, 2010), because sport organizations are environments where men and men's activities are valued and rewarded (Cunningham, 2008).

GENDER EQUITY ACTIVITY:
Gender equity is not just an issue on the playing field. Sport managers, like yourself, also see the pitfalls of gender inequity in athletic departments. Research the number of athletic directors that are female at NCAA Division I institutions. Next, investigate the number of female athletic directors across all division levels of the NCAA. Answer the following questions:
1. Why are there so few female athletic directors?
2. What is the cause of the lack of female athletic directors at the Division I level?
3. Was there any difference between Division I and Divisions II and III?
4. As you sit in your classroom, what is the gender breakdown? What does the ratio of males to females say about the sport management discipline?

GLOBAL PERSPECTIVE

In many societies around the world, cultural and social norms limit access to and opportunities to participate in sport and physical activity for girls and women. When girls and women cannot participate in sport, they cannot access the benefits provided by sport. Thus, girls and women may occupy weaker social, political, economic, legal, and educational positions in most countries (Meier, 2005). To help solve this problem, the International Working Group on Women and Sport crafted the Brighton Declaration (1994). The Declaration aimed to afford girls and women opportunities to participate in sport in a safe and supportive environment, as well as access to the positive benefits (e.g., physical, mental, and emotional well-being; improved body image and self-esteem; access to education). The Brighton Declaration also requested that governing bodies and institutions responsible for the implementation of sport comply with equality provisions set forth by other international policies, including the Universal Declaration on Human Rights (1948) and the UN Convention on the Elimination of All Forms of Discrimination against Women.

Despite the numerous international policies advocating the use of sport in promoting women's development and empowerment, enacting policies of this magnitude across nations and cultures can be difficult. First, organizations like the UN (2003) acknowledge sport as a human right, but rarely is sport a priority for countries besieged by poverty, disease, and violence. The same can be said for gender equity—it's important, but not a priority. In fact, a 2007 United Nations report found limited progress in achieving gender equality and the "relative neglect of women and girls continues to prevail in most countries" (UN, 2007, p. 5). Second, neither the International Charter on Physical Education and Sport nor the Brighton Declaration provide practical recommendations for implementing programs that forward sport as a human right or enhance the development of girls and women. The Windhoek Call for Action, the United Nations, and the World Health Organization offer suggestions for items to consider when planning a program, but these recommendations are vague and may prove inaccessible (e.g., time, financial expense, human capital) for field practitioners. There has been a proliferation of sport and physical activity programs for girls and women around the world backed with considerable resources (e.g., financial, intellectual, human). Therefore, it is important to consider if and how these programs are contributing to women's development, empowerment, and equity.

muzsy/shutterstock.com

SUSAN LEGGETT/shutterstock.com

Karves/shutterstock.com

GENDER IDENTITY

As noted, sex and gender have often been at the root of discriminatory practices and policies in sport (Sykes, 2006). In recent years, gender identity—more specifically, athletes who identify as transgender—has become an important topic of conversation for national and international sport organizations. **Transgender** is an umbrella term used to describe individuals whose gender identity does not match their assigned birth gender (Griffin & Carroll, 2011). For example, a transgender male (female-to-male or FTM) may have a competitive advantage over other women when he begins taking hormones such as testosterone. Conversely, a transgender female (male-to-female or MTF) may be viewed as having a competitive advantage because she is perceived to have physiological characteristics (e.g., height, weight, strength) that are male. Recently, trans-athletes have gained more media attention though, they have been competing at all levels for decades. To illustrate:

- Balian Buschbaum (FTM). Prior to transitioning, Buschbaum competed in the women's pole vault for Germany in the 2000 Olympic Games.
- Keelin Godsey (FTM). A 16-time NCAA Division III All-American and two-time national champion in track and field.
- Kye Alums (FTM). First openly trans-athlete in NCAA Division I. He played on the George Washington University women's basketball team in 2010.
- Lana Lawless (MTF). In 2010, Lawless petitioned the Ladies Professional Golf Association (LPGA) to compete following sex reassignment surgery in 2005.
- Chris Moser (FTM). Founder of TransAthlete.com, Moser won a spot on the men's sprint duathlon for Team USA in 2015.
- Fallon Fox (MTF). First openly transgender athlete in Mixed Martial Arts. She had sex reassignment surgery in 2006.
- Caitlyn Jenner (MTF). Earned an Olympic gold medal for Team USA in the 1976 Montreal Games.
- Renee Richards (MTF). Formerly known as Richard Raskin, a professional tennis player, Renee Richards had sex reassignment surgery in 1975. She also sued the United States Tennis Association to compete as a woman after being barred. Her case helped pave the way for other transgender athletes.

- Mack Beggs (FTM). Won the Texas Class 6A girls' state high school wrestling championship in 2017. Mack was forced to compete against other girls because Texas state high school wrestling rules stipulate athletes must compete according to their sex at birth.

As such, much of the controversy surrounding trans-athletes in competition at any level is grounded in maintaining a level playing field (Coggon, Hammond, & Holm, 2008; Sykes, 2006; Teetzel, 2006). Nationally and internationally, administrators working in sport organizations at every level from youth to elite must now reconsider conceptualizations and policies pertaining to gender in order to address ethics of fair play, access, and inclusion (Sykes, 2006).

PARTICIPATION POLICIES IN THE UNITED STATES

National Collegiate Athletic Association

In the United States, the National Collegiate Athletic Association (NCAA) adopted a new policy regarding the participation of transgender athletes in intercollegiate sport competition (Lawrence, 2011). The policy allows transgender student-athletes the opportunity to compete "in accordance with their gender identity while maintaining the relative balance of competitive equity among sports teams" (Lawrence, 2011, para. 2). The NCAA has also defined policies to clarify the participation of trans-athletes undergoing hormonal treatment for gender transition:

- A trans-male (FTM) student-athlete who has received a medical exception for treatment with testosterone for diagnosed Gender Identity Disorder or gender dysphoria and/or transsexualism, for purposes of NCAA competition, may compete on a men's team, but is no longer eligible to compete on a women's team without changing that team status to mixed team.
- A trans-female (MTF) student-athlete being treated with testosterone suppression medication for diagnosed Gender Identity Disorder or gender dysphoria and/or transsexualism, for the purposes of NCAA competition, may continue to compete on a men's team but may not compete on a women's team without changing it to a mixed team status until completing one calendar year of testosterone suppression treatment (NCAA, 2011, p. 13).

The NCAA's policy further states, "Any transgender student-athlete who is not taking hormone treatment related to gender transition may participate in sex-separated sports activities in accordance with his or her assigned birth gender" (p. 13). Additionally, trans-male (FTM) student-athletes who are not taking testosterone may choose to participate on a men's or women's team. A trans-female (MTF) trans-athlete, however, cannot compete on a women's team when she is not taking hormone treatments because the athlete is perceived to have a competitive physiological advantage (NCAA).

Youth Sport and High School Athletics

In the United States, policies regarding trans-athlete participation vary by state and school district. Middle schools often follow policies set forth by high schools if middle schools do not have an existing policy

(Transathlete.com, 2017). According to TransAthlete.com (2017), four types of policies governing transgender participation in sport exist:

- Inclusive: No medical hormones or surgery required
- Needs modification: Case-by-case or individual review
- Discriminatory: Requires birth certificate or surgery and hormone wait period
- No policy exists (State: AR, DE, HI, LA, MS, MT, ND, SC, TN, WV)

Trans-athletes have little to no chance of participating in high school sport in "discriminatory" states.

The Transgender Law and Policy Institute (TLPI; 2017) recently published "Guidelines for Creating Policies for Transgender Children in Recreational Sport." The TLPI suggests:

> All young people should have the opportunity to play recreational sports and have their personal dignity respected. Transgender young people are no different. In fact, because transgender young people often must overcome significant stigma and challenges, it would be particularly harmful to exclude them from the significant physical, mental and social benefits that young people gain by playing recreational sports. The impact of such discrimination can be severe and can cause lifelong harm. In contrast, permitting transgender children and youth to participate in recreational sports in their affirmed gender can provide an enormous boost to their self-confidence and self-esteem and provide them with positive experiences that will help them in all other areas of their lives (Transathlete.com, 2017, para. 3).

The Guidelines for Creating Policies for Transgender Children in Recreational Sport set forth by the TLPI offer sport managers suggestions for developing policies that will ensure the inclusion of trans-athletes at every age and in varying stages of transition. Still, most youth sport organizations and school systems have yet to develop any policies that promote the inclusion of trans-athletes.

INTERNATIONAL PARTICIPATION POLICIES

International Olympic Committee

In 2004, the International Olympic Committee (IOC) introduced the Stockholm Consensus, which defined the **trans-athlete** as someone who has undergone sex reassignment surgery and is being treated with sex hormones to adopt the physiology of the opposite sex (IOC, 2003). In 2015, however, the IOC revised the guidelines for trans-athlete participation eligibility as follows:

1. Those who transition from female to male are eligible to compete in the male category without restriction;
2. Those who transition from male to female are eligible to compete in the female category under the following conditions:
    a. The athlete has declared that her gender identity is female. The declaration cannot be changed, for sporting purposes, for a minimum of four years.

b. The athlete must demonstrate that her total testosterone level in serum has been below 10 nmol/L for at least 12 months prior to her first competition (with the requirement for any longer period to be based on a confidential case-by-case evaluation, considering whether or not 2 months is a sufficient length of time to minimize any advantage in women's competition).

c. The athlete's total testosterone level in serum must remain below 10 nmol/L throughout the period of desired eligibility to compete in the female category.

d. Compliance with these conditions may be monitored by testing. In the event of non-compliance, the athlete's eligibility for female competition will be suspended for 12 months (IOC, 2015).

The Stockholm Consensus (and subsequent updates to the policy) is a template for international sport organizations interested in developing policies to regulate the participation of trans-athletes in an effort to maintain an ethic of fair play.

TRANSGENDER POLICY ACTIVITY

Policies governing high school sport participation by a trans-athlete vary from state to state. Find your state on the list and visit TransAthlete.com to find your state's specific policy. Answer the following questions:

- If your state is "inclusive," should the policy be modified in any way? Why or why not? If so, how?
- If your state "needs modification" or is "discriminatory," would you recommend a more inclusive policy? Why or why not? What changes would you make?
- If your state has no policy, would you recommend a policy that is discriminatory or inclusive? Provide evidence for your policy decision.

As sport administrators, developing and cultivating inclusive and safe environments for current and prospective athletes—youth to elite is a constant charge. The ethics of fair play and opportunities for access and inclusion are essential for success of all sport programs. Understanding the transgender athlete and the issues he/she may encounter in competition, in medicine, and in society can help managers think more critically about policy and implementation.

Sexual Orientation

In the United States and around the world, lesbian, gay, and bisexual (LGB) men and women have experienced discrimination in many forms, including policies that affect employment (hiring or being fired), access to medical care, and fair housing opportunities. LGB people are also more likely to experience physical violence, homelessness, lower socioeconomic earning power, alcohol and drug abuse, and higher levels of depression and suicide (CDC, 2016). Similarly, LGB men and women have experienced discrimination in sport—as athletes and employees.

ATHLETES. In terms of participation, before 1975 no athlete identifying as gay, lesbian, or bisexual dared to share his or her sexual orientation publicly (Griffin, 2012). The "cultural social consensus was that being

LGB was sinful, sick, and immoral, and publicly identifying oneself as LGB invited ridicule and discrimination" (Griffin, p. 2). After former NFL player Dave Kopay came out in a December 1975 *Washington Post* article, slowly LGB athletes began to discuss their sexual orientation publicly, but usually only after retiring from sport. In the mid-1970s, very few policies existed explicitly excluding LGB people from participating in sport; however, no policies actually prohibited discrimination based on sexual orientation. This meant that LGB athletes at every level could be subject to discrimination based on their sexual orientation.

Prior to and during the 2014 Winter Olympic Games in Sochi, Russia, groups protested the Russian government over the country's anti-LGB stance. In short, Russia passed a law in 2013 banning the promotion of "non-traditional sexual relations" among minors (Luhn, 2013). This ruling prompted a rise in anti-LGB violence and raised concerns of participating countries and their athletes. The Canadian Institute for Diversity and Inclusion launched a public service announcement in support of LGB rights during the Winter Olympics with the tag line "The Games have always been a little gay. Let's fight to keep them that way." An even larger campaign, Principle 6, allowed "athletes, spectators, and global supporters to celebrate the Olympic principle of non-discrimination" and support LGB athletes without "violating Russian anti-gay laws or violating the Olympic ban on political speech" (Principle 6, 2014, para. 3).

The public support of LGB athletes has resulted in an environment in which several collegiate and professional athletes have openly acknowledged their sexual orientation as gay, lesbian, or bisexual. For example, athletes including Liz Carmouche (mixed martial arts), Megan Rapinoe (U.S. Women's Soccer), Michael Sam (former NFL player), and Britney Griner (Women's National Basketball Association), all came out during their professional careers. However, a study by Campus Pride (2013) found that 25% of college LGB athletes were pressured to stay silent about their sexual orientation. Another 21% of LGB athletes experienced harassment on social media—that is double the reported harassment of heterosexual athletes (Campus Pride).

Now, many sport organizations have policies protecting the rights of their LGB athletes. In response to concerns that NFL prospects were asked about their sexual orientation during the scouting combine, the National Football League sent a memo reminding ownership, players, and coaches of the League's sexual orientation anti-discrimination and harassment policies (Patra, 2013). While the NCAA does not have a specific policy, they provide inclusive educational programming "to support equitable laws and practices, increase opportunities for individuals from historically underrepresented groups to participate in intercollegiate athletics at all levels . . . " (NCAA, 2016, para. 2) that specifically includes sexual orientation and gender expression.

EMPLOYMENT. Over time, laws in the United States and other countries became more inclusive and protective of LGB people. In terms of employment, Wisconsin passed the first state law prohibiting discrimination based on sexual orientation in 1982 (Griffin, 2012). Surprisingly, only 22 U.S. states have non-discrimination laws (mostly pertaining to employment) covering sexual orientation (ACLU, 2016). This means that in states where non-discrimination laws do not exist, people can be fired because they are gay, lesbian, or bisexual. According to the Women's Sports Foundation (2016), if women coaches are or are perceived to be lesbian or bisexual, they may be subject to termination or may be targeted for negative recruiting by other coaches. **Negative recruiting** is a strategy employed by some coaches that uses the real or perceived negative attributes of another coach, team, or school to lure prospective athletes away from the "bad" college or university. As noted in an article about negative recruiting in women's basketball, "Coaches aren't worried about getting fired for being lesbian, but they do worry about being fired for not being able to recruit successfully because of it" (Cyphers & Fagan, 2013, para. 14).

As societies evolve and become more inclusive of LGB people, policies will follow suit. Administrators are in a unique position to create and provide inclusive environments for athletes, coaches, and other employees who identify as lesbian, gay, or bisexual.

Persons With Disabilities

The World Health Organization (WHO) defines **disability** as:

> an umbrella term, covering impairments, activity limitations, and participation restrictions. An impairment is a problem in body function or structure; an activity limitation is a difficulty encountered by an individual in executing a task or action; while a participation restriction is a problem experienced by an individual in involvement in life situations. Thus disability is a complex phenomenon, reflecting an interaction between features of a person's body and features of the society in which he or she lives (WHO, 2016).

With support from the World Health Organization and United Nations, countries around the world have laws against discrimination against persons with disabilities. For example, the Disability Discrimination Act (DDA) was enacted in 1995 in Northern Ireland. England, Wales, and Scotland adopted the Equality Act of 2010. The United States enacted the Americans with Disabilities Act (ADA) in 1990. Not only do these laws protect people from discrimination, but they are also designed to make the world a more accessible place for all people.

Still, it is clear that people with disabilities face barriers that limit access to and participation in daily activities, including education, health care, transportation, and employment. Additionally, disabled people may have even less opportunity to participate in sport and physical activity (SportandDev.org, 2016a). However, as noted by the United Nations, sport has the potential to foster health and well-being and inclusive environments for people with disabilities.

As discussed earlier in this chapter, the International Charter of Physical Education in Sport (1978) declared that every person is entitled to participate in sport. Ten years later, the Council of Europe created "Sport for All: Disabled People Charter" (SportandDev.org, 2016b), which encouraged the use of sport as a conduit to connect the disabled person to his or her community. In 2006, the United Nations Convention on the Rights of Persons with Disabilities included Article 30.5. Article 30.5 granted people with a disability the right to equal participation in recreational, leisure, and sporting activities (SportandDev.org).

Through the work of national and international governing agencies, people with disabilities have more access to sport than ever before. However, it must be noted that competitive opportunities for people with disabilities only began in the early 20th century with the 1924 International Silent Games in Paris, France. The first Paralympic games took place in 1960 (Rome, Italy). Eight years later, the Special Olympics held its first World Games at Soldier Field in Chicago, Illinois. Today, opportunities exist for disabled persons to participate in organized sport competition as well as adapted recreational activities. However, more work is necessary to ensure access. The International Platform for Sport and Development offered considerations for including people with disability in sport:

- Treat people with disabilities who participate in sport as athletes;
- Focus on what the athlete can do and has the potential to do. A lack of skill does not necessarily indicate the lack of potential ability;
- Teaching or coaching style, rules, equipment, and the environment can all be adapted and modified to promote active participation from every person;
- Use the athlete as a resource of information on themselves, and ask them what they can do and how specific tasks may be modified to suit their skill level;
- Whether a disability is acquired from birth or later in life may have an impact on a person's basic skill level;
- Including people with disabilities is simply good coaching (SportandDev.org, 2016c, para. 2).

In addition to these considerations, The Platform for Sport and Development outlined future priorities for policy development, including more widely promoting the United Nations Convention on the Rights of Persons with Disabilities to developing countries.

DISABILITY POLICIES ACTIVITY
Persons with disabilities are not only impacted on the field, but in stadium seats as well. Research the ADA and its impact on stadium seating. Then, go to your school or your favorite professional team's website to find out the assistance given to persons with disabilities. Are the remedies for persons with movement-impairment disabilities only? What about those that are hard of hearing? Are there remedies for individuals with non-movement-impairment disabilities?

CONCLUSION

This chapter discussed policies that make sport more inclusive for women; lesbian, gay, and transgender individuals; racial minorities; and persons with disabilities. Despite the development of policies designed to make sport and physical activity accessible to all individuals, inequities still remain. Sport managers will be tasked with developing policies that are appropriate, fair, and inclusive of various populations. Thus, it is imperative to understand the historical and social contexts of a particular group. Additionally, the policies created should be in line with the goals of the organization, governing body (e.g., the NCAA, NFL, FIFA), and national or international legislation.

DISCUSSION QUESTIONS

1. Why was the 1978 International Charter for Physical Education and Sport important? In your opinion, how did it impact national and international sport policies?

2. What does Title IX have to do with the prevention of sexual assault and sexual violence? How has Title IX changed sport? Is Title IX still necessary? Should educational institutions be required to meet more than one prong of effective accommodation of student interest and abilities? Explain your answers.

3. Were the IOC's changes to the Stockholm Consensus necessary? Why or why not? Do the policies set forth by the IOC and NCAA allow for fair play, inclusion, access, and/or equity for all? Why or why not?

4. If it was meant to be inclusive of all people, why do the policies in the 1978 International Charter for Physical Education and Sport need to explicitly include certain populations?

5. What role can sport organizations play in changing racist behavior in sport? And in society?

6. As noted, when individuals and groups of people are denied access to sport and physical activity, they are also denied the benefits. Imagine you are advocating in front of city leaders for a youth basketball league for children with disabilities. Using information in this chapter, what would you include in your argument? Why?

7. A future policy area identified for the inclusion of persons with disabilities includes more widely promoting the United Nations Convention on the Rights of Persons with Disabilities to developing countries. Do you think this should be a priority for developing countries? Explain and defend your answer.

CASE STUDY: TRANSGENDER ATHLETES IN THE LOCKER ROOM: IS IT TIME FOR POLICY CHANGES IN PUBLIC SCHOOLS?

Throughout history, sport has provided individuals a platform to demand broad social change while acting as a moral compass for individuals and society as a whole. In recent years, a key social issue in sport participation has been the inclusion of transgender athletes in sport programs. In the past, the majority of the issues regarding transgender athletes have related to competitive balance and equality on the playing field (Coggon et al., 2008; Hancock & Hums, 2011; Sykes, 2006; Teetzel, 2006). Several researchers have examined transgender policies in sport, but little research has occurred as it relates to the rights of transgender athletes to be in the locker room of the gender in which they identify. Changes in the cultural acceptance of the transgender athlete have evolved in recent years. Transgender youth are "coming out" more frequently and at a much younger age. There is an increased need for the implementation of policies designed specifically for transgender athletes in the locker room. As transgender athletes have gained more access in their respective sport, one should only assume that inclusion of transgender athletes in the locker room should also exist.

In May 2016, President Barack Obama sent a directive to U.S. public schools that required them to allow transgender students to use the bathroom of their identified gender or be in jeopardy of losing federal assistance. This directive was issued in response to an ongoing debate in North Carolina over transgender laws and individual versus state rights. Obama defended his statements by claiming that his administration was interpreting federal statute and that he was seeking to offer "best practices" to U.S. schools. In April 2014, the United States Department of Education released a "significant guidance document" explaining a school's role in effectively responding to student violence and sexual harassment in accordance with the requirements of Title IX. This document discusses how access to restrooms and locker rooms of a student's identified gender may be considered a requirement or remedy for addressing transgender discrimination in schools. The Title IX law has not changed and still permits disparate treatment "on the basis of sex" through the creation of separate facilities— http://www2.ed.gov/about/offices/list/ocr/docs/know-rights-201404-title-ix.pdf

As the social acceptance of transgender athletes has gone from participation policy to now the discussion of transgender athletes in the locker rooms, the need for sport managers and administrators to understand federal and state laws becomes more important. Numerous participation policies at the youth, high school, college, national, and international levels have been implemented in recent years. The National Collegiate Athletic Association (NCAA) implemented a policy in 2010 allowing transgender athletes to participate in intercollegiate sports with a medical exception for treatment (Lawrence, 2011). This policy provides transgender students the opportunity to participate in the sport of the gender in which they identify. The International Olympic Committee (IOC) identifies a transsexual athlete as someone who has undergone sex reassignment surgery and has or is currently being treated with sex hormones to adopt the physiology of the opposite sex (IOC, 2003). In 2004, the IOC tightened the requirements to include those who have surgically undergone the anatomical change, gained legal recognition of their assigned sex, and undergone hormone therapy appropriate for the assigned sex (Hancock & Hums, 2011; IOC, 2003). Atherton High School in Louisville, Kentucky, allows transgender students to use the bathroom and locker room of their identified gender (Use of School Space, Policy 500). Atherton will maintain separate locker room facilities for male and female students. Students, upon prior approval and within parameters set by the administration, shall have access to the locker room facility that corresponds to their gender identity asserted at school. If there is a request for increased privacy, any student shall be provided access to a reasonable accommodation such as: use of a private area within the public area of the locker room facility (e.g., nearby restroom stall with a door or an area separated by a curtain), use of a nearby private area (e.g., nearby restroom), and/or a separate changing schedule.

A recent national poll on the issue showed that 33% of Americans support the decision of allowing transgender students to use the bathroom of the gender in which they identify, 51% were opposed and 16% were undecided. Americans with elementary age children were among the most opposed, arguing that this issue is not the place for federal government involvement (Rasmussen Report, 2016). The majority of the public schools in the United States lack any type of transgender inclusion policy related to participation and use of facilities. The current national debate and conversation around transgender students will continue to be an ethical issue regarding athletics.

The most recent involvement of this issue in sport involves the HB2 law passed in North Carolina. This legislative bill was passed to essentially ban transgender people from using the bathroom in which they identify in any "public building". This created a backlash from many event organizers that had scheduled events in the state. Specifically, the NCAA and the ACC pulled all events from the North Carolina venues. Currently, officials in NC are reworking the bill due to the backlash from the media, fans, and the LGBTQ community (Berman, 2017).

CASE QUESTIONS

1. Compare and contrast each position in this case. Who are the proponents and what is their position? Who are the opponents and what is their position?

2. What are the roles of the federal and state governments in this case? Why are they involved?

3. If you were a high school administrator, what might you do if you were faced with implementing a transgender participation and/or locker room policy?

4. Do you agree with the stance that the NCAA and the ACC took on the HB2 law? Why or why not?

GLOSSARY

Apartheid is a system of racial segregation that subjected non-White individuals (e.g., Black people, people of color, South Asians) to separate and unequal medical, educational, housing, and recreational opportunities in South Africa.

Disability is an umbrella term, covering impairments, activity limitations, and participation restrictions.

Diversity refers to all the ways in which people differ, including gender identity, race and ethnicity, socio-economic status, education, geography, political affiliations, sexual orientation, religious beliefs, life experiences, and opinions.

Equality is about sameness. That is, everyone gets the same thing.

Equity is about fairness and ensuring people have access to the same opportunities.

Gender is the social construction of roles, attributes, and behaviors that a society considers appropriate for men and women.

Inclusion involves bringing together and harnessing diverse forces and resources in a way that is beneficial to involved parties.

Negative recruiting is a strategy employed by some coaches that uses the real or perceived negative attributes of another coach, team, or school to lure prospective athletes away from the "bad" college or university.

Policy is a standard or course of action that defines how an organization conducts business affairs.

Sex is the biological traits (e.g., chromosomes, genitalia) one possesses.

Stacking is the phenomenon in which a particular race is over- or under-represented in particular positions on teams.

Title IX is an Act of 1972 stating, "No person in the United States shall, on the basis of sex, be excluded from participation in, be denied the benefits of, or be subjected to discrimination under any education program or activity receiving federal financial assistance."

Trans-athlete is someone who has undergone sex reassignment surgery and is being treated with sex hormones to adopt the physiology of the opposite sex.

Transgender is an umbrella term used to describe individuals whose gender identity does not match their assigned birth gender.

References

ACLU. (2016). Non-discrimination laws: State by state information map. Retrieved from https://www.aclu.org/map/non-discrimination-laws-state-state-information-map

Acosta, R. V., & Carpenter, L. J. (2014). Women in intercollegiate sport: A longitudinal study—thirty-seven year update, 1972–2014. Retrieved from http://www.acostacarpenter.org/

AFL. (1995, June). Racial and religious vilification rule, Article A. *Football Record, 84*(13).

AFL. (2016). Vilification framework. Retrieved from http://s.afl.com.au/staticfile/AFL%20Tenant/AFL/Files/Respect%20and%20Responsibility/AFL_Vilification_Policy.pdf

Allender, S., Cowburn, G., & Foster, C. (2006). Understanding participation in sport and physical activity among children and adults: A review of qualitative studies. *Health Education Research, 21*(6), 826–835.

Berman, M. (2017, April 14). Justice department drops federal lawsuit over North Carolina's 'bathroom bill'. *The Washington Post* Retrieved from https://www.washingtonpost.com/news/post-nation/wp/2017/04/14/justice-dept-drops-federal-lawsuit-over-north-carolinas-bathroom-bill/?utm_term=.4adc7878e236

Baldwin-Ragaven, L., London, L., & De Gruchy, J. (1999). *An ambulance of the wrong color.* Cape Town, South Africa: University of Cape Town Press.

Brighton Declaration on Women and Sport. (1994). Brighton: Sports Council.

Burton, L. J., Barr, C. A., Fink, J. S., & Bruening, J. E. (2009). "Think athletic director, think masculine?": Examination of gender typing of managerial subroles within athletic administration position. *Sex Roles, 61,* 416–426.

Burton, L. J., Grappendorf, H., & Henderson, A. (2011). Perceptions of gender in athletic administration: Utilizing role congruity theory to examine (potential) prejudice against women. *Journal of Sport Management, 25,* 36–45.

Buzuvis, E., & Newhall, W. (2016). Title IX blog. Retrieved from http://title-ix.blogspot.com/

Campus Pride. (2013). Score Card: Campus Pride 2012 LGBTQ national college athlete report. Retrieved from https://www.campuspride.org/resources/score-card-campus-pride-2012-lgbtq-national-college-athlete-report/

Carpentier, F., & Lefèvre, J. (2006). The modern Olympic movement, women's sport, and the social order during the inter-war period. *The International Journal of the History of Sport, 23*(7), 1112–1127.

CDC. (2016). Lesbian, gay, bisexual, and transgender health. Retrieved from http://www.cdc.gov/lgbthealth/

Chalip, L. (2006). Toward a distinctive sport management discipline. *Journal of Sport Management, 20,* 1–21.

Coakley, J. (2010). *Race and Ethnicity in the Sociology of Sport in the United States.* Colorado Springs, CO: University of Colorado.

Coggon, J., Hammond, N., & Holm, S. (2008). Transsexuals in sport: Fairness and freedom, regulation and law. *Sport, Ethics, and Philosophy, 2*(1), 4–17.

Cunningham, G. B. (2008). Creating and sustaining gender diversity in sport organizations. *Sex Roles, 58,* 136–145.

Cyphers, L., & Fagan, K. (2013, April). Unhealthy climate. *ESPN.* Retrieved from http://espn.go.com/ncw/news/story?page=Mag15unhealthyclimate

Dowling, C. (2000). *The frailty myth: Women approaching physical equality.* New York, NY: Random House.

Goorin, L. J., & Bunck, M. C. (2004). Transsexuals and competitive sports. *European Journal of Endocrinology, 151,* 425–429.

Grappendorf, H., & Lough, N. (2006). An endangered species: Characteristics and perspectives from female NCAA division I athletic directors of both separate and merged athletic departments. *The Sport Management and Related Topics Journal, 2*(2), 6–20.

Grappendorf, H., Lough, N., & Griffin, J. (2004). Profiles and career patterns of female NCAA division I athletic directors. *International Journal of Sport Management, 5*(3), 243–261.

Griffin, P. (2012). LGBT equality in sports: Celebrating our success and facing our challenges. In G. B. Cunningham (Ed.) *Sexual orientation and gender identity in sport: essays from activists, coaches, and scholars* (pp. 1–13). College Station, TX: Center for Sport Management Research and Education.

Griffin, P., & Carroll, H. (2011). *NCAA inclusion of transgender student-athletes.* Indianapolis, IN: NCAA.

Hancock, M.G., & Hums, M. A. (2016). "A leaky pipeline?" Perceptions of barriers and supports of female senior-level administrators in NCAA Division I athletic departments. *Sport Management Review.*

Hancock, M., & Hums, M. A. (2011). Participation by transsexual and transgender athletes: Ethical dilemmas needing ethical decision making skills. *Journal of the International Council of Sport Science and Physical Education (ICCSPE) Bulletin, 62.*

Hoffman, J. L. (2010). The dilemma of the Senior Woman Administrator role in intercollegiate athletics. *Journal of Issues in Intercollegiate Athletics, 3,* 53–75.

IOC. (2003). Statement of the Stockholm Consensus on sex reassignment in sports. Retrieved from www.olympic.org/Documents/Reports/EN/en_report_905.pdf

IOC. (2015). IOC consensus meeting on sex reassignment and hyperandrogenism, November 2015. Retrieved from http://www.olympic.org/Documents/Commissions_PDFfiles/Medical_commission/2015-11_ioc_consensus_meeting_on_sex_reassignment_and_hyperandrogenism-en.pdf

Jordan, T. H. (2017). Moving from diversity to inclusion. *Profiles in Diversity Journal.* Retrieved from http://www.diversityjournal.com/1471-moving-from-diversity-to-inclusion/

Kerr, I. B. (2011). The myth of racial superiority in sports. *The Hilltop Review,* 4(1), 19–27.

Lapchick, R. E. (2013). The complete racial and gender report card, 2013. Retrieved from http://nebula.wsimg.com/728474de65f7d28b196a0fbb47c05a91?AccessKeyId=DAC3A56D8FB782449D2A&disposition=0&alloworigin=1

Lapchick, R. E. (2015a). The 2015 racial and gender report card: National Football League. Retrieved from http://nebula.wsimg.com/b04b442e160d0ff65cb43f72ca2aa67e?AccessKeyId=DAC3A56D8FB782449D2A&disposition=0&alloworigin=1

Lapchick, R. E. (2015b). The 2015 racial and gender report card: Major League Baseball. Retrieved from http://nebula.wsimg.com/35d775f4b01264c377a96da7f616a3b8?AccessKeyId=DAC3A56D8FB782449D2A&disposition=0&alloworigin=1

Lawrence, M. (2011). Transgender policy approved. Retrieved from http://www.ncaa.org/wps/wcm/connect/public/NCAA/Resources/Latest+News/2011/September/Transgender+policy+approved

Luhn, A. (2013, September). Russian anti-gay law prompts rise in homophobic violence. Retrieved from http://www.theguardian.com/world/2013/sep/01/russia-rise-homophobic-violence

Meier, M. (2005). Gender equity, sport and development (Working paper). Biel/Bienne, Switzerland: Swiss Academy for Development.

NCAA. (2011). NCAA inclusion of transgender student-athletes. Retrieved from https://www.ncaa.org/sites/default/files/Transgender_Handbook_2011_Final.pdf

NCAA. (2012). Equity and Title IX in intercollegiate athletics. Retrieved from http://www.ncaapublications.com/productdownloads/EQTI12.pdf

NCAA. (2016). LGBTQ resources: NCAA inclusion initiative framework. Retrieved from http://www.ncaa.org/about/resources/inclusion/lgbtq-resources

NFHS. (2016). 2014–2015 High school athletics participation survey. Retrieved from http://www.nfhs.org/ParticipationStatistics/PDF/2014-15_Participation_Survey_Results.pdf

Office for Civil Rights. (2011). Dear colleague letter. Retrieved from https://www2.ed.gov/about/offices/list/ocr/letters/colleague-201104.html

Patra, K. (2013, April). NFL reminds teams of sexual orientation, harassment policy. Retrieved from http://www.nfl.com/news/story/0ap1000000165220/article/nfl-reminds-teams-of-sexual-orientation-harassment-policy

Pearson-Wharton, S., Garland, J., & MacDonald-Dennis, C. (2012). Statement on Native American mascots. Retrieved from http://www.myacpa.org/sites/default/files/acpa_resolution_native_american_march2013.pdf

Principle 6. (2014). Principle 6. Retrieved from http://www.principle6.org/

Rasmussen Reports (2017). What American thinks about the transgender bathroom debate. Retrieved from http://www.rasmussenreports.com/public_content/lifestyle/general_lifestyle/may_2016/what_america_thinks_about_the_transgender_bathroom_debate

SAHO. (2012). Football in South Africa. Retrieved from http://www.sahistory.org.za/topic/football-south-africa-timeline-1862-2012

Seefeldt, V. D., & Ewing, M. E. (1997). Youth sports in America: An overview. *President's Council on Physical Fitness and Sports Research Digest, 2*(11), 3–14.

SportandDev.org. (2016a). Introduction. Retrieved from http://www.sportanddev.org/en/learnmore/sport_and_disability2/background___sport___disability/introduction/

SportandDev.org. (2016b). Policy development. Retrieved from http://www.sportanddev.org/en/learnmore/sport_and_disability2/policy__practice_and_future_priorities_in_sport_and_adapted_physical_activity/policy_development/

SportandDev.org. (2016c). Tools and practice. Retrieved from http://www.sportanddev.org/en/learnmore/sport_and_disability2/policy__practice_and_future_priorities_in_sport_and_adapted_physical_activity/tools_and_practice/

Sykes, H. (2006). Transsexual and transgender policies in sport. *Women in Sport and Physical Activity Journal, 15*(1), 3–13.

Teetzel, S. (2006). On transgendered athletes, fairness, and doping: An international challenge. *Sport and Society, 9*(2), 227–251.

TransAthlete.com. (2017). K–12 policies. Retrieved from https://www.transathlete.com/k-12

Transgender Law & Policy Institute (TLPI). (2017). Guidelines for creating policies for transgender children in recreational sports. Retrieved from https://media.wix.com/ugd/2bc3fc_6cd03b8e19147c71c0153c81e96babcb.pdf

United Nations (UN). (2003). *Sport for development and peace: Towards achieving the millennium development goals.* Report from the United Nations Inter-Agency Task Force on Sport for Development and Peace.

United Nations (UN). (2007). Women: 2000 and beyond. Retrieved from http://www.un.org/womenwatch/daw/public/Women%20and%20Sport.pdf

United Nations Educational, Scientific and Cultural Organization (UNESCO). (1978). International Charter on Physical Education and Sport. Retrieved from http://portal.unesco.org/shs/en/ev.php-URL_ID=9538&URL_DO=DO_TOPIC&URL_SECTION=201.html

U.S. Department of Education. (2015). Title IX resource guide. Retrieved from https://www2.ed.gov/about/offices/list/ocr/docs/dcl-title-ix-coordinators-guide-201504.pdf

WHO. (2016). Disabilities. Retrieved from http://www.who.int/topics/disabilities/en/

Windhoek Call for Action. (1998). Windhoek, Namibia: Ministry of Youth and Sport.

Whisenant, W. A., Pedersen, P. M., & Obenour, B. L. (2002). Success and gender: Determining the rate of advancement for intercollegiate athletic directors. *Sex Roles, 47*(9/10), 485–491.

Women's Sports Foundation. (2016). Title IX myths and facts. Retrieved from https://www.womenssportsfoundation.org/home/advocate/title-ix-and-issues/what-is-title-ix/title-ix-myths-and-facts

Zirin, D. (2005). Say it ain't so, big leagues. Retrieved from https://www.thenation.com/article/say-it-aint-so-big-leagues/

ATHLETE ACTIVISM

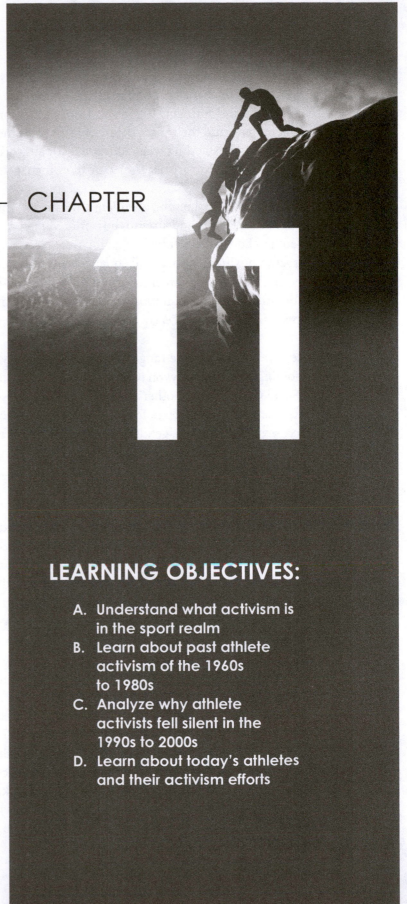

CHAPTER 11

Muhammad Ali once stated, "Service to others is the rent you pay for your room here on Earth" (Cork, 2013, p. 141). For the famous boxer, part of that service came in the form of activism. Ali understood the opportunity he had as one of the greatest boxers of all time to use his platform to fight the injustice and inequality around him. However, Ali's activism was met with backlash and disdain during his career, as is common with athlete activists. For refusing to fight in the Vietnam War, Ali was suspended from boxing for three of his prime fighting years. This did not deter Ali from speaking out against the injustices that plagued the United States and the world at the time. It took society far too long to realize this, but Ali's acts were courageous, worthy, tremendous, and powerful. Not only will Ali go down as one of the greatest athletes in history, but he will also go down as one of the greatest activists and humanitarians of the past 50 years.

LEARNING OBJECTIVES:

A. Understand what activism is in the sport realm
B. Learn about past athlete activism of the 1960s to 1980s
C. Analyze why athlete activists fell silent in the 1990s to 2000s
D. Learn about today's athletes and their activism efforts

This chapter examines athlete activism and what activism means in sport. Activism is important to study due to its ability to change people, societies, or even the world. The power of activism is tremendous, but it also comes at a cost for many in the sport world. As sport managers, it is important to recognize the power that athletes have and their place in society that gives them an elevated platform to protest perceived social inequalities. Understanding what activism is for athletes, what activism can do, and the positive and negative impacts of activism are necessary for sport managers and the future of sport.

To gain a better understanding of athlete activism, one must consider some of the most famous athlete activists in the United States and around the world. Muhammad Ali, perhaps the most famous athlete activist, has a museum in Louisville, Kentucky that focuses on equality, diversity, and improving humanity in addition to his career in boxing. To Ali, social equality was greater than boxing, as is evident in the fact that he gave up three years of his boxing career to protest the Vietnam War. Other athletes like Billie Jean King, John Carlos, and Tommie Smith are all important names worth noting. However, the athlete activist would seemingly disappear in the 1990s and early 2000s.

In recent years, with a wide range of tragedies in society, the athlete activist has resurfaced. The controversial shooting deaths of Trayvon Martin, Michael Brown, and Eric Garner, the human rights issues from the 2014 Sochi Olympics, and other societal events may have brought back the athlete activist. The resurgence of athlete activism is important for sport managers to recognize in today's world. Whether athletes stand up for race, sexual orientation, gender, age, ability, or other issues, athletes are recognizing the power they hold and are using it to positively impact the world with sport managers by their sides.

What Is Activism?

Outside of the sport management realm, **activism** is "extra-ordinary, extra-usual practices which aim, collectively or individually, institutionally or informally, to cause social change" (Bayat, 2005, pp. 893–894). However, the term activism in sport management literature has yet to be formally defined, which leads to this question: What exactly is activism within the athletic environment? In a study performed by Kaufman and Wolff (2010), the authors interviewed athletes and found athletes had used sport to promote progressive social change. Unfortunately, the meaning of "promote progressive social change" is subjective. Progressive social change may be one thing to one person and the opposite to another. A study conducted by Agyemang, Singer, and DeLorme (2010) of Black athletes' perceptions of activism maintained that social and political activism is "organized and collective forms of protest and conflict" (p. 420). This definition highlights the collective or groups of people coming together in the form of a protest, but does little to speak to the impact or the scale of the activism. Based on these limited definitions of athlete activism in sport management, **athlete activism** can be defined as an athlete's practices which aim to individually or collectively, institutionally or informally promote progressive social change. While this definition encompasses activism within an athletic realm, it fails to define the threshold between activism and non-activism. However, this might not be seen as an issue for most people, due to people thinking and formulating ideas on their own. Thus, the definition of activism comes down to allowing the individual who is trying to bring about social change to determine whether his or her actions constitute activism.

Impact of Athlete Activism

In the study mentioned earlier by Kaufman and Wolff (2010), 21 athletes who were activists were interviewed about why they were activists. These athletes were using their platforms to speak out against topics such as war, racism, sexism, sexual violence, and homophobia. The researchers noted four main links that the athletes drew as their inspiration for their activism: *social consciousness, meritocracy, responsible citizenship,* and *interdependence.*

Social consciousness refers to an individual's awareness of his/her societal presence and how it differs from everyone else. Athlete activists of the past were able to recognize their potential to affect social change due to the platform that sport gave them. Athletes and sport are often placed on a pedestal in American society. This in turn puts athletes in a unique position to use the sport platform to benefit others. Many athletes are also aware of the many injustices that are happening all around them. For example, one might recognize that their organization benefits from unjust working conditions of exploited workers, particularly related to athlete clothing. Two-time U.S. Olympian in the hammer throw, Kevin McMahon, was listening to a report about the terrible conditions of sweatshops in Central America that produced NBA jerseys. McMahon realized that he may not be in the NBA, but he was wearing free Reebok and Adidas clothing that was cut from the same cloth. He had been advertising for these companies that were exploiting people in other countries. McMahon and many of the athletes recognized this injustice and became more conscious and socially aware of the harm being done, as athletes often do when they are informed by societal expectations

Meritocracy is the belief that individuals succeed or fail due to the amount of work, skill, and attitude the individual puts into the task, sport, or life. Meritocracy is the belief that if one works hard and maintains a positive attitude, one will succeed. Conversely, if one is lazy and has a negative attitude, one will not succeed. While this may not be true outside the world of sports, this can be true inside the world of sports. Improbable upsets occur frequently and the notion of "any given Sunday" refers to the fact that the last place team could beat the first place team. Rules are created to ensure competitive balance on the field, so one team does not have success over another team solely because of its resources. Kaufman and Wolff (2010) note, "If sport represents an arena where individuals with fewer resources can compete fairly with individuals with great resources, and if we applaud this defining characteristic of sport, why not promote such a similar arrangement on a societal level?" (p. 165). Essentially, we expect our sports teams to have an equal chance to win when the whistle blows, but we do not expect that of society. These athletes, who identified as athlete activists, wanted to bring that fairness to society.

Responsible citizenship has another name in the athletic world: good sportsmanship. The authors note that good sportsmanship on the field is similar to being a responsible citizen within society. Good sportsmanship is usually the first lesson an individual learns from sport. When playing youth soccer, football, T-ball, or basketball, usually the teams line up to shake hands after the game, no matter the outcome. That is one of the simplest and earliest sport memories that individuals may have and remains a theme throughout all of sport. Now think about people who have participated in high-level sport their entire life. They are always being evaluated on their sportsmanship skills. Someone who wants to take their platform and use it to promote positive societal change would have those skills to be one of the greatest vehicles for change.

Finally, athletes recognized their **interdependence** with those around them. Many star athletes such as LeBron James, Derrick Rose, Serena Williams, and Megan Rapinoe did not become some of the best in their sport without the help of others. They needed support from their family, friends, coaches, opponents, administrators, medical trainers, and many more. For the athlete activist, it is easier to understand they can be the ones to help others. Athletes can use their voices to be the unified voice for those who are being discriminated against. Athletes have recognized the power of collaboration and how much it can accomplish. Just as the athlete cannot be a world champion on his or her own, the struggling worker cannot receive fair working conditions by himself or herself. It is the power of a group of individuals working toward achieving the same goal that can create positive results.

It is also worth noting the process of engaging in sport and the process of engaging in activism for positive social change are similar. It is not easy to be a champion or to champion an end to inequality. Discipline, goal setting, work ethic, determination, constant striving for improvement, and a long-term perspective are just some of the ways that athletics and activism are similar. Through *social consciousness, meritocracy, responsible citizenship, interdependence,* and the process, it is obvious that there are distinct links between athletics and activism. Athletes are able to use their teachings on the field to become agents of social change, just as Muhammad Ali, Billie Jean King, Tommie Smith, and John Carlos did.

SPORT ACTIVIST'S OF THE PAST

Muhammad Ali

Cassius Clay Jr. was born on January 17, 1942, in Louisville, Kentucky. At the age of 12, his bike, gifted to him by his father, was stolen. The upset Clay was determined to get his revenge on whoever stole his bike. While Clay was reporting the theft, a policeman named Joe Martin told Clay that he should learn to fight before he started running his mouth about getting revenge. Martin saw the passion in Clay and eventually trained him to become one of the greatest boxers in the history of the world. Six years later at the age of 18, Clay would win the gold

Joseph Sohm/shutterstock.com

ISSUES AND ETHICS IN SPORT

medal in the Light Heavyweight Boxing Division in the 1960 Rome Olympics, which would just be the start of his legendary career (Muhammad Ali, n.d.).

Shortly after claiming the Heavyweight Champion of the World title in 1964, Cassius Clay joined the Nation of Islam and changed his name to Muhammad Ali, doing away with his slave name. Ali would begin a long journey of activism that spanned multiple decades, countries, and social issues. Perhaps his most famous and controversial activism moment came in 1967, when Ali refused to be inducted into the United States armed forces to fight in Vietnam. For refusing to appear when he was drafted by the United States Army, Ali was arrested. As a result of his arrest, he was stripped of all his titles (including Heavyweight Champion of the World) and had his boxing license removed for three years, during his prime. Ali would be called unpatriotic, be criticized by the media and fans who loved him, and lose millions of dollars for his act. However, that did not stop him from standing up for what he believed. He was too concerned about the lives of those in Vietnam and the lives of those in his home state of Kentucky to be concerned with titles, boxing, and money. Unpopular and condemned by most of society, Ali never allowed public influence to discourage him even in a time where segregation was rampant within the United States. In 1971, Muhammad Ali's conviction was overturned by the Supreme Court. It took three years, but Ali would reclaim the World Heavyweight Champion title in 1974 (Muhammad Ali, n.d.).

Even though his boxing career concluded in 1981, Ali continued to fight. Ali's humanitarian efforts spread outside of the United States to Afghanistan, North Korea, Cuba, and South Africa. Whether it was a goodwill mission, delivering medical supplies, assisting with the release of 15 U.S. hostages in the first Gulf War, or meeting Nelson Mandela after he was released from prison, Ali used his platform for the benefit of the people of the world. Ali is considered one of the greatest athletes and activist athletes of all time for his activism during his boxing career and well after. Giving up the sport that introduced him to the world, Ali spurned boxing to stand against the violence that war brings. Being ridiculed by society for his refusal to enter the draft, Ali remained steadfast in his beliefs. Even after his boxing career was over, Ali still used his fame to benefit the world. When he was diagnosed with Parkinson's disease in 1984, Ali never wavered on who he was as an activist athlete. Today, years after his death, Ali serves as inspiration for many people around the globe. He took the best punches from everyone—Joe Frazier, George Foreman, the media, his fans and all of society—but always got back on his feet determined to be victorious.

Billie Jean King

Billie Jean Moffitt was born in California in 1943. A gifted athlete from a young age, King had to make a switch from playing softball to tennis to be more "lady-like." The move would turn out to be a smart one as Moffitt would go on to be one of the best women tennis players of all time. In 1961, Moffitt and her doubles partner, Karen Hantze Susman, became the youngest pair to win the Wimbledon doubles tournament. Shortly after, Billie Jean married a law student named Larry King. From that moment on, she would go by Billie Jean King. After early struggles, King would see a rise in the rankings and multiple titles in the U.S. Open, French Open, and Wimbledon, including a sweep of the three tournaments in 1972.

King's activism started when she noticed the pay difference between men and women. For instance, in 1968, Rod Laver won the men's bracket at Wimbledon and earned 2,000 pounds, while King accomplished the same feat on the women's side, but was paid only 750 pounds (Billie Jean King, n.d.). King knew she had to find a way to demand that tennis tournaments give equal pay for both genders. In 1973, King saw an opportunity. The male professional tennis players were talking about creating a tennis union to better serve the interests of tennis players at major tournaments. King assumed that the women professional players would be included in this association, but they were not. The men excluded the women, believing that no one would pay any money to go see women play, so it would not make sense to include them (Billie Jean King, n.d.). This decision did not sit well with the tennis star, so King created her own group, the Women's Tennis Association, which gave birth to the same professional women's tennis we see today. That same year, King was so determined to achieve equal pay for both sexes that she threatened to boycott the U.S. Open for not giving both sexes the same pay. After that act, the U.S. Open became the first major tournament to offer equal pay for men and women.

©Anthony Correia/shutterstock.com

King's work was not done. In May of 1973, Bobby Riggs, former number one male tennis player in the world turned self-promoter, openly claimed that a woman could never beat a man in tennis. He would start a spectacle called the Battle of the Sexes. Riggs was determined to play against King, who had made herself known as a champion tennis player and a champion of gender equality. If Riggs could beat the loudest voice for women's rights, he could make a great payday. He asked King multiple times, even offering her $10,000 to play him. Knowing what this could do for gender relations, she declined. Riggs went to the next best alternative: the number one female player at the time, Margaret Court. Despite King strongly recommending to Court that she decline, Court accepted, downplaying the impact this game would have on gender relations. Riggs, who was 55, crushed the multi-champion Court 6–2, 6–1 (Roberts, 2005). After that defeat, King realized that she had to accept Riggs' invitation to the Battle of the Sexes II.

This was a big match for women in American sport history. The Women's Tennis Association was just a few years old and in a very tenuous position. Equal pay for women and men in professional tennis had just been accomplished. A loss by King could undo everything that she worked hard for and "set women back 50 years." In front of an estimated worldwide television audience of 100 million, King and Riggs faced off in the Battle of the Sexes II (Popovich, 2015). King knew that she did not need to win by overpowering Riggs like Court thought. King knew she could win by using her intellect. Instead of trying to hit the ball as hard as she could, she ran Riggs all over the court. To the net, back to the baseline, from right to left, lob, drop shot. King outsmarted Riggs the entire match and won 6–4, 6–3, 6–3 (Schwartz, n.d.). By winning the Battle of the Sexes II, King showed the ability of women to thrive in pressure-filled situations and that society should rethink how women's physical activity was treated. However, King still had more work to do.

King was not only an advocate for women's rights. She was one of the first prominent athletes to come out as homosexual and has carried the flag for the LGBT community ever since. Her parents were homophobic;

she was homophobic, but never felt comfortable in her own skin. She came out in 1981, ten years after she knew she was homosexual. She recalled being tired throughout the 1970s—tired from having to live a lie about who she was. Fast-forward 40 years and she proudly and confidently stands tall knowing who she is. Many stand with her, including former President Barack Obama. In 2014, King was named one of two individuals to go to Sochi, Russia, for the 2014 Winter Olympics as delegates by Obama. This move was powerful due to Sochi's strict anti-LGBT laws that were enacted before the Olympics. Obama wanted to send the message that we as a nation are proud of individuals like Billie Jean King and that discrimination against members of the LGBT community would not be tolerated. This was the first time since 2000 that the United States did not send a president, former president, first lady, or vice president as a delegate (Boren, 2013).

The combination of being told to act within her gender norms and her acknowledgment of the treatment of people based on gender started Billie Jean King on the path of being an athlete activist. King empowered every woman in athletics and let them know they deserved equal pay, they were just as athletically capable as the men, and they had every right to be proud of who they were. She showed that we as individuals need to be comfortable in our own skin, no matter what society says. Billie Jean King paved the way for many influential female athletes: Brandi Chastain, Mia Hamm, Serena Williams, and Mo'ne Davis, among many, many others.

Tommie Smith and John Carlos

Tommie Smith and John Carlos will be names that are linked forever as athlete activists. In 1968, the United States was still stuck in segregation and racial tensions. Issues were so bad in America that Black athletes who qualified for the Olympics were threatening a boycott. They questioned if it was fair to an athlete to be labeled a second-class citizen by society, yet train and compete for his or her nation. The Black athletes did not, however, boycott. They let their actions speak for them.

The 200-meter dash was the Olympic race to shine for Smith and Carlos, and shine they did. Taking first and third respectively, Smith and Carlos won the gold and bronze medals. Smith even set a world record: 19.83 seconds (Olympic protestors, n.d.). As they crossed the finish line, they knew a decision was to be made. Should they remain silent and enjoy their moment on the podium, or take a stand and make a statement about the social inequalities that plagued their lives with the certainty of backlash? The latter was the decision the two sprinters made. During the United States national anthem, both Smith and Carlos raised a black-gloved fist into the air in a silent protest against the racial discrimination which was taking place in their home country. Smith raised his right fist to represent Black power, while Carlos raised his left fist to represent Black unity. While the raising of the fist was noticeable, the two men also had more subtle acts on the podium. Both sprinters wore black socks, but did not wear their shoes on the podium to symbolize racial poverty in America. Further, Smith wore a scarf and Carlos wore beads around their necks in memory of the victims who were lynched simply due to their race (Davis, 2008).

© John S. Quinn/shutterstock.com

The moment the men stepped off the podium they were booed by the crowd. The next day, they were forced to return their medals by the International Olympic Committee, who had also threatened to expel the entire American team for the actions of Smith and Carlos. Back in America, society was outraged at what they had done. They received death threats for their actions of solidarity. The backlash for these two men was terrible, but they endured, never apologizing for their actions.

Nearly 50 years later these two men are celebrated for their actions. The athletes mentioned in this chapter, Ali, King, Smith, and Carlos, were not the only athletes to have used their sports to enact social change. There have been thousands of athletes from around the globe who could not stand for the social injustices that plague our world. Individuals like Kareem Abdul-Jabbar, Jackie Robinson, Jim Brown, Babe Didrikson Zaharias, Gertrude Ederle, and many others deserve their own sections within this chapter for their great accomplishments in making our world a better place. Being stripped of their athletic accomplishments, told they were not worth anything, and the verbal abuse they received were not enough to convince these athletes to stop their activism efforts.

STUDENT ACTIVITY:
Break into groups and research the following athlete activists who were not mentioned in this chapter. What was the social issue they were trying to conquer and how did they do it?
1. Bill Russell
2. Arthur Ashe
3. Brandon Marshall
4. Brandi Chastain
5. Jason Collins

THE FALL OF THE ACTIVIST ATHLETE AND SOCIAL RESPONSIBILITY

As activism thrived in the civil rights era, the activist athlete disappeared in the late 1980s. The work of Ali, King, Smith, and Carlos, as well as many other athletes, should have shown the world that athletes can use their status and platform to invoke social change. The late 1980s, 1990s, and 2000s saw very little athlete activism by the most prominent sport stars. This left many to ask, why?

Scholar Kwame J. A. Agyemang, a researcher who studies how athletes use their platform to benefit society, offers Michael Jordan as one of the reasons that athlete activists, specifically among Black athletes, fell silent (2011). Agyemang noted that Michael Jordan was the epitome of a sports hero in the 1990s. The athlete had tremendous power on and off the court around the entire world, let alone the United States. Jordan was a movie star, commercial star, and had his image on Nike shoes. Gatorade even had a commercial with a song titled "Be Like Mike."

Despite this tremendous platform, Jordan was silent on many social issues. Within his home state of North Carolina, a right-wing conservative Jesse Helms was running for a Senate position against a Black candidate Harvey Gantt in 1990. Helms was known to be a racial segregationist. Asked why Jordan never endorsed Gantt to help change the social climate of his home state, Jordan declined and later stated to a friend that "Republicans buy shoes too" (Granderson, 2012). Further, Jordan claimed he was not aware of the Rodney King riots in Los Angeles and never once spoke up about Nike's treatment of sweatshop labor when he was practically living the brand. Agyemang contends that there were multiple times Jordan could have stood up against a social injustice, but chose not to do so.

While Michael Jordan was rarely criticized for not standing up against social inequalities, other athletes, such as Kareem Abdul-Jabbar (another activist athlete), have been critical of Jordan.

Abdul-Jabbar even stated that Jordan cared more about his brand than his conscience (Howard, 2015). The argument is that Jordan cared so much about his brand, being liked and being famous, that he did not want to upset anyone with controversial statements or actions. By making a controversial statement, Jordan could risk his brand being negatively impacted. A loss of sales, then sponsorship, and ultimately money would plague Jordan if he made comments about Helms, the treatment of Rodney King, or Nike's treatment of sweatshop labor. This led to a silent generation of Black male athletes who followed in Jordan's footsteps because they were literally told to "Be Like Mike." Is it fair to place the blame for the silence of the athlete activist solely at Jordan's feet (or his Nikes)?

Other scholars point to the economic differences between yesterday's and today's athletes as the main reason for the decline in the activist athlete. In the 1960s, when athlete activism started to take off, athletes were barely making $100,000 a year, and only if they were one of the best players in the entire league. In fact, the MLB Players Association had to negotiate raising the minimum wage of professional baseball players from $6,000 to $10,000. The 1970s saw the first ever million-dollar contract as Bobby Hull of the Winnipeg Jets signed a 10-year, 1 million dollar contract. Then, the 1980s and 1990s brought a boom in multimillion dollar contracts on the court and field. Off the court, athletes were recognizing the appeal of endorsement and sponsorship deals that could increase their earning power. This growth in endorsement earnings could potentially garner higher income than what could be made playing for the team. In 2009, Tiger Woods was the first athlete to make $1 billion in earnings and endorsements (Stephenson, 2014). That type of money was unfathomable for an athlete in the 1960s. So, is that the reason why athletes did away with their activist ways? Yesterday's athletes had less to lose if there was backlash for their activism. Today's athletes have to worry about having a clean image for endorsements and their team. In fact, Agyemang and his colleagues asked collegiate Black male athletes about activism and their views on it. While they were cognizant of the activism by Ali, Smith, and Carlos, the athletes were unwilling to engage in activism themselves. The interviewees stated that they would not engage in activism because today's athletes are being caught up in their sport due to the extreme competitive nature of sport and the ability to have an important contract taken away from the athlete due to speaking up (think about an athlete endorsed by Nike speaking out against the working conditions in Asia).

Interestingly enough, researcher George B. Cunningham spearheaded a study to determine if being a social activist had an impact on an athlete's brand (2012). The researchers noted that there was not a negative impact on an athlete's brand if they were a social activist. Yet, an athlete's reasoning for not being a social activist is oftentimes the fear of the negative consequences for their brand. Whatever the reason, whether it is the brand, the potential monetary loss, the sense of entitlement by today's athletes, or any other reason, there was a sharp decline in athlete activism during the 1990s and early 2000s.

STUDENT ACTIVITY:
Research and review Steve Nash and his activism efforts. In 2003, when the athlete activist was relatively silent, Nash tried to be an athlete activist, but received considerable backlash. Why did he receive backlash and from whom? Why do you think athletes did not actively address social issues in the 1980s, 1990s, and 2000s?

CURRENT SPORT ACTIVISM

Events in the 2010s changed the game for athlete activists. The deaths of Trayvon Martin, Eric Garner, and Michael Brown made a huge impact on athlete activists inside the United States. It was not a sudden onset of events that led athletes to speak up against social inequality, but a series of events started years before. There were so many events and it had happened for so long that prominent athletes could no longer idly stand by and watch the social inequalities taking place around them.

In early 2012, the death of Trayvon Martin shook America. George Zimmerman, a neighborhood watch captain in Sanford, Florida, called into the local police a report of a suspicious person in his neighborhood. The suspicious person was Trayvon Martin, a 17-year-old Black male who was walking home from the convenience store with a bag of Skittles and iced tea. The police advised Zimmerman to stay in his car and not approach the teen. Zimmerman did not listen to those instructions and approached Martin. Moments later, Martin was shot dead by Zimmerman. While Zimmerman admitted to shooting Martin, Zimmerman claimed he shot Martin in self-defense. Zimmerman was not charged at the time because his story could not be disproven, according to the Sanford Police Chief Bill Lee. However, Christopher Serino, Sanford Police Department's homicide detective, investigated the incident and recommended that Zimmerman be tried for manslaughter because the wounds on Zimmerman's head were not from deadly force or a deadly weapon and Zimmerman had failed to identify himself as a neighborhood watch member several times throughout the night. Later, evidence would come out of several 911 calls from the incident where the words "help, help" could be heard in the background, followed by a gunshot. Zimmerman was tried on second-degree murder, but found not guilty (Trayvon Martin, 2015).

Prominent athletes, specifically within the National Football League (NFL) and National Basketball League (NBA) were in an uproar. LeBron James and members of the Miami Heat wore sweatshirts with hoods with the hashtag #WeAreTrayvonMartin and #WeWantJustice. Stephen Curry, Michael Vick, Adrian Peterson, Shaquille O'Neal, and many others took to Twitter to protest the verdict or express their sadness or condolences over the death of Martin. Social media was the catalyst that led players to express their views on the event. This led to academics (Annelie Schmittel and Jimmy Sanderson) noticing a trend with athletes involved in activism on Twitter. The researchers investigated what exactly NFL players were tweeting about during and after George Zimmerman's trial. The researchers collected 465 tweets from 125 NFL players and noted that players talked about the case in (1) anticipation of the verdict, (2) disbelief of the events, (3) critiques of the American justice system, (4) social commentary,

(5) condolences, (6) any tweet responding to the tragedy, and (7) freedom of speech arguments (Schmittel & Sanderson, 2014). The researchers noted that social media gave these athletes a tool to speak out about the racial injustice that was happening around them. Twitter was more personal than traditional media for the athlete. The tweets came directly from them with less filtering from members of the organization they worked for, their sponsors, or traditional media. These authors also thought that having social media in one's pocket could encourage more athletes to speak their minds and partake in social activism. Unfortunately, Martin's controversial death was not the only one in the mid-2010s.

A year and a half later, the deaths of two more Black males, Eric Garner and Michael Brown, occurred. Eric Garner, a 46-year-old Black male, was selling untaxed cigarettes when the New York City police were preparing to arrest him. Anticipating resistance from Garner, the police officer Daniel Pantaleo put Garner in a chokehold. As he held the chokehold, Garner could be heard saying, "I can't breathe." Garner would die shortly after due to the chokehold (Newman, 2014). In Ferguson, Missouri, an 18-year-male named Michael Brown was leaving a market and liquor store when he was approached by police officer Darren Wilson in his car. Wilson was confronting Brown as there was surveillance video of Brown stealing cigarillos from the store. An altercation happened between the two and Wilson shot twice from inside his car at Brown. Brown ran off and Wilson followed him on foot. Brown stopped and either put his arms straight up in the air or charged at Wilson. Wilson fired 10 shots at Brown with 6 hitting him in the forearm, chest, and face. Brown died shortly after sustaining those injuries (Robles & Bosman, 2014). Months later, the Pantaleo and Wilson grand juries declined to indict either police officer.

a katz/shutterstock.com

As with Martin's death, society was outraged by these events. Riots occurred in Ferguson, Missouri; New York; and other places around the nation. The sport world chimed in as well. Many athletes took to Twitter to discuss the events, just as they had done with the death of Trayvon Martin. This time, however, prominent athletes also used their platforms during the games to let their views be heard. NBA players such as LeBron James and Derrick Rose wore "I Can't Breathe" shirts during warm-ups. This move broke NBA rules as the shirts were not Adidas shirts. However, NBA Commissioner Adam Silver did not fine the players for their acts. In the NFL, players of the St. Louis Rams raised their hands in a do-not-shoot manner, similar to Michael Brown, as they were walking onto the field (Murray, 2014). The St. Louis Police Department demanded the players be fined for their acts. Neither the NFL nor the St. Louis Rams punished the players. Athletes this time were not only using Twitter to voice their concerns about the social climate, but they were actively breaking rules and making demonstrations against the social injustice. They were aware that they were going to upset people with their acts, but they still performed them. The sports world saw prominent athletes taking a stand against the socially unjust actions in this country.

Other Activism Efforts by Today's Athletes

But the athlete activism was not just tied to prominent athletes in high-profile sports over the issue of race. Many of the best professional women soccer players banded together and pushed back on FIFA and the Canadian Soccer Association for using artificial turf instead of grass during the 2015 FIFA Women's

ISSUES AND ETHICS IN SPORT

World Cup. The coalition of soccer players sued on the basis of gender discrimination, stating that men would never have to play World Cup games on artificial turf (Das, 2014). NCAA collegiate players, spearheaded by members of the Northwestern University football team, attempted to form a union within intercollegiate athletics to look out for their well-being (Farrey, 2015). The 2014 Sochi Olympics were protested by athletes all over the world as Russia's strict anti-LGBTQ laws were in place. The athletes displayed special rainbow pins, flags, and clothes in celebration of LGBTQ rights.

The year 2014 was special because it showed prominent athletes starting to push back on the societal injustices that plague this world. These athletes seemed to care little about their sponsorships, league rules, or governing bodies as they decided to act. LeBron James, Megan Rapinoe, and Kain Colter were among the few who used their platform to encourage others to bring back activism to the athletic world.

Tyler McKay/shutterstock.com

STUDENT ACTIVITY:
Research an athlete. How are they involved in activism? What are they doing to make change in society?

Activism and Social Change in the Sport Industry

While much of the discussion has been focused around athletes, it would be inappropriate to ignore those who are not athletes, but still are members of the athletic world who strive for social change. Activism or acts for social change can come in many different forms by many different individuals or organizations. One such organization is Athlete Ally. Athlete Ally is a non-profit organization dedicated to fostering inclusive sports communities, with an emphasis on LGBT inclusiveness. Hudson Taylor, founder of Athlete Ally, was once a high school and collegiate athlete who noticed extreme homophobia, especially in the sport world. In an environment that is built on masculinity and toughness, Taylor became disgusted at the way athletes discriminated against those in the LGBT community. Taylor wore an equality sticker from the Human Rights Campaign on his wrestling headgear. Like most athlete activists, he received backlash from his peers for his acts. Despite the critics, many sent him e-mails and personal messages that showed support and gratefulness for his act of solidarity with the LGBT community. Taylor decided to commit himself to this cause after his playing days were over and founded Athlete Ally. Today, Taylor fights for allyship in athletic environments around the United States. Taylor employed the help of individuals who were from far outside the athletic environment to help run the organization. Mike Balaban, an international finance veteran, and Andrew Ward, a legal and compliance consultant, agreed to be co-chairs of Athlete Ally and serve on the Board of Directors. They reached out to hundreds of athletes to serve as board members, both athletes and non-athletes, for Athlete Ally and to help run the organization. Former NHL star Sean Avery, Super Bowl winner Brendon Ayanbadejo, and former Executive Vice President of Nike Brands Frances Boller are just a few of the board members dedicated to the success of this organization (Our Story, n.d.).

Athlete Ally understands it cannot do its job alone without the help of current athletes. Their name, after all, is Athlete Ally. The organization enlists the help of collegiate, professional, and international ambassadors to help expand their cause. Hundreds of athletes from all over the world have dedicated themselves to fostering allies and fighting for members of the LGBT community. These athletes come from the NBA, MLB, NFL, quidditch leagues, Rugby, MMA, WWE, fencing, squash, and a host of other sports. Athlete Ally may be one of the best examples of an organization that was created by an athlete and enlists the help of athletes willing to use their platform to stand against social inequalities.

STUDENT ACTIVITY:
You are a general manager for an NBA team. A highly prominent athlete on your team approached the coach about spending a few hours a week trying to champion a social issue. The athlete does not mind the financial risks, but wants to wear shoes with activism messages, send out Twitter messages in support of the movement, and use press conference time to talk about the social issue. The coach is not a fan of this idea as he is worried about the potential backlash from teammates and media, which could lead to a distraction on the team. As the sport manager, how do you handle this tense situation?

RETURN OF THE ACTIVIST ATHLETE

The return of the activist athlete has been aided substantially by one thing: social media. When the Miami Heat wore sweatshirts with hoods and tweeted the message #WeWantJustice, many praised the NBA team for speaking out on the issue. However, others were critical, thinking that just sending out a tweet will not make the major changes needed to right the injustice. Debate continues on whether slacktivism is real activism or not, but it is important to understand what the term is and its impact.

Slacktivism is defined as "a willingness to perform costless, token display of support for a social cause, with an accompanying lack of willingness to devote significant effort to enact meaningful change" (Kristofferson, White, & Peloza, 2013, p. 1149). Some of the more popular slacktivism examples include wearing a ribbon, changing a profile picture on Facebook, or retweeting a tweet about social activism on Twitter, to name a few. A unique example of a past slacktivist activity included a bucket of ice cold water and Twitter. In 2014, there was a popular fad called the Amyotrophic Lateral Sclerosis (ALS) Ice Bucket Challenge. Someone on Twitter would be nominated to be part of the ice bucket challenge. They had two options: have a frozen bucket of ice poured on them or donate money to ALS research. Once either of those two steps was completed, the person would nominate three other individuals to take the challenge. The Ice Bucket Challenge spread across the nation and seemingly everyone was participating, including star athletes like LeBron James, Dikembe Mutombo, and Caroline Wozniacki. There was pushback toward this gesture as many people noted individuals pouring buckets of ice on themselves, but not donating toward ALS research. It seemed some people were doing it because it was the popular thing to do, but not helping benefit ALS research. The ALS Association, however, noted that $110 million was raised for ALS for research, services, and education from the Ice Bucket Challenge (Putting your dollars to work, n.d.).

Slacktivism can be seen as a token display of support; simply hitting the retweet offers little cost to the individual. The athlete is risking little when they change their profile picture or retweets someone else's tweet. Some may say that there is little to gain by tweeting a specific hashtag. However, Twitter and other social media websites have been shown to create and foster cultural conversations (Brock, 2012). Changing one's Facebook picture to a picture that says Black Lives Matter may not be as impactful as the activism of Tommie Smith and John Carlos, but it shows support for that cause. The athlete can make that change and encourage his or her followers to do the same to help mobilize a marginalized voice or foster conversation that can be beneficial.

Slacktivism could also be the first step to helping athletes gain more confidence and willingness to become activists. With the death of Trayvon Martin and the non-conviction of George Zimmerman, athletes took to Twitter to voice their outrage. Then Michael Brown and Eric Garner died and athletes used Twitter and displayed their activism on the court and field. With the "I Can't Breathe" pregame shirts from LeBron, Rose, and others and the Rams players holding their hands up signifying "Don't Shoot," these athletes showed they were not afraid to take a stance on the field. If these athletes feel it is their responsibility to help positively change society, what could their next act be?

STUDENT ACTIVITY:
Research the following hashtags related to sport and social issues. What issues were the hashtags in reference to? What events started the hashtags? Which athletes used these hashtags? What was the result (if there was one) of this hashtag movement?
1. #EveryFan
2. #WomenInFIFA
3. #BlackLivesMatter
4. #LoveWins

CONCLUSION

One of the reasons athlete activism and social responsibility is so intriguing is because it is happening right before our eyes. The 1960s and 1970s saw activism by some of the greatest athletes. Muhammad Ali, Billie Jean King, Tommie Smith, and John Carlos were among some of the most prominent athletes who understood how their platforms could be used. These athletes took a tremendous risk pushing back on society for the injustices around them. Their brand, potential earnings, legacy, career, and safety were in jeopardy. However, this did not concern these athlete activists as there were bigger issues surrounding them. Issues bigger than money and even themselves. They withstood death threats, discrimination, and the loss of participation and awards to fight for a cause in which they believed. Today, Ali, King, Smith, and Carlos are a few of the many athletes who have solidified their identities as champions both on and off the court.

What will this generation's athletes bring? The 1990s and 2000s saw athletes silent on controversial social issues. Perhaps Michael Jordan can take some of the blame for this, but does he deserve it? Does Jordan have the *responsibility* to speak for those who are discriminated against or does he have the *choice* to, given the platform he had? Regardless of what society believes, the athlete activist did not die, but fell silent. With the 2010s, society is seeing the resurgence of the athlete activist or the socially conscious athlete. LeBron James and others have shown that they will use their personal brands to stand against the social inequalities in our society.

Sport managers may encounter a situation with an activist athlete like Adam Silver of the NBA or the St. Louis Rams of the NFL encountered when their athletes resisted social norms to send a message. Should a sport manager encounter this situation, it is best to listen to the athlete and understand exactly what the message is. The sport manager can help him/herself by understanding what the social inequality is they are pushing back on and then educate him/herself on the issue.

ISSUES AND ETHICS IN SPORT

DISCUSSION QUESTIONS

1. Who were some of the athlete activists that championed social issues in the past?

2. Why did the athlete activist fall silent during the 1990s?

3. When did the athlete activist make a resurgence and why?

4. How are today's athletes fighting social injustices and how does that compare to the athlete activists of the past?

5. What are some of the societal issues that today's athletes are fighting against?

6. In what ways can social media help athletes be activists?

7. How should society value slacktivism? Does slacktivism equate to activism?

8. What are some societal issues that are not talked about, but should be discussed?

9. Do athletes have a responsibility to be athlete activists? Why or why not?

10. What are some of the risks to an athlete of engaging in activism?

CASE STUDY: ATHLETES RESPOND TO SHOOTING OF PHILANDO CASTILE

On July 6, 2016 Philando Castile was shot and killed by a St. Anthony, Minnesota police officer during a traffic stop. Dashcam video of the shooting of Castile was released to the public nearly a year later. The video showed that when the officer approached the vehicle, he told Castile his brake lights were out. He asked for Castile's driver's license and insurance. Castile then began to tell the officer he had a firearm on him. The officer repeatedly told him to not reach for it or pull it out. Castile claimed he wasn't reaching for it, but the next thing the video shows is the officer reaching for his gun and firing seven rapid shots into the car, five of which hit Castile. The traffic stop and shooting lasted just 40 seconds. The shooting came just one day after a video went viral of police in Baton Rouge shooting and killing Alton Sterling (Croft, 2017).

Diamond Reynolds, Castile's girlfriend, and her 4-year-old daughter were in the car at the time of the shooting. Reynolds began recording the encounter and streaming to Facebook Live during the traffic stop. Prior to the release of the dashcam video, Reynold's video was the only live recording of a shooting on Facebook. Her Facebook Live video illustrated Yanez yelling, "I told him not to reach for it!" and Castile, who had been shot, saying, "I wasn't reaching." Reynolds and her daughter were instructed to exit the car. During the Facebook livestream, Reynolds can be heard saying, "They threw my phone, Facebook. Please, Jesus, no…don't let him be gone, Lord" (Croft, 2017).

On Friday, June 16, 2017, nearly a year after the shooting, a Minnesota jury acquitted the police officer of second-degree manslaughter and two felony counts for intentionally discharging the gun (Berman, 2017). Response to the shooting from the initial Facebook Live post to the releasing of the dashcam video and acquittal ranged from disbelief to outrage as evidenced by the number of social media posts and protests.

Athletes, both at the collegiate and professional level, were amongst those that shared their reactions to the shooting. Immediately following the shooting, National Football League (NFL) athlete Reggie Bush tweeted, "When will this stop I don't see any difference they still killing our people for no reason! Scared trigger happy cops with no training <sad face emoji>." National Basketball Association (NBA) athlete Jabari Parker also responded the day after the shooting posting the following on Twitter, "I know all police officers aren't bad but personally I just don't feel safe anymore. All our tax dollars go to them just to kill us! Why?" At the collegiate level, University of Minnesota football player Rodney Smith tweeted, "Cousin text me telling me to be safe. Being a black young man is scary sometimes." In response to the fatal shooting, athletes on Women's National Basketball Association (WNBA) teams wore black warm-up shirts. Three WNBA teams and their athletes were fined by the league for the wearing of the shirts because they didn't comply with WNBA guidelines (Moreno, 2016).

In each of the aforementioned situations, the athletes responded with opinions and positions on the situation. These high-profile athletes used their social media presence and platforms to address the shooting of Castile. Answer each of the following questions in response to the situation.

CASE QUESTIONS

1. Do you believe athletes have an ethical responsibility to use their platforms to speak out on social issues? Why or why not?

2. As evidenced in the case, both collegiate and professional athletes responded to the shooting of Castile. Should the NCAA place restrictions on student-athletes with respect to athlete activism? Why or why not?

3. Beyond the slactivism efforts of tweeting in response to the shooting and the WNBA teams wearing the black warmup shirts, research the response of other athletes to the situation. What did you find?

4. In what other ways can athletes use their platforms to respond to a situation such as the shooting of Philando Castile?

GLOSSARY

Activism is extra-ordinary, extra-usual practices which aim, collectively or individually, institutionally or informally, to cause social change.

Athlete activism is an athlete's practices which aim, individually or collectively, institutionally or informally, to promote progressive social change.

Interdependence is relying on others to help an individual succeed.

Meritocracy is the belief that individuals succeed or fail due to the amount of work, skill, and attitude the individual puts into the task, sport, or life.

Responsible citizenship is being a reasonable individual within society; it is akin to good sportsmanship.

Slacktivism is defined as "a willingness to perform costless, token display of support for a social cause, with an accompanying lack of willingness to devote significant effort to enact meaningful change."

Social consciousness is an individual's awareness of his/her societal presence and how it differs from everyone else.

References

Agyemang. K. J. (2011). Black male athlete activism and the link to Michael Jordan: A transformational leadership and social cognitive theory analysis. *International Review for the Sociology of Sport, 4*(47), 433–445.

Agyemang, K. J., Singer, J. N., & DeLorme, J. (2010). An exploratory study of Black male college athletes' perceptions on race and athlete activism. *International Review for the Sociology of Sport,* 419–435.

Bayat, A. (2005). Islamism and social movement theory. *Third World Quarterly, 26*(6), 891–908.

Berman, M. (2017, June 17). Minn. officer acquitted in shooting of Philando Castile during traffic stop, dismissed from police force. *The Washington Post.* Retrieved from https://www.washingtonpost.com/news/post-nation/wp/2017/06/16/minn-officer-acquitted-of-manslaughter-for-shooting-philando-castile-during-traffic-stop/?utm_term=.41511458d25e

Billie Jean King. (n.d.). In *Makers.* Retrieved from http://www.makers.com/billie-jean-king

Boren, C. (2013, December 18). Obama names openly gay athletes to Sochi Olympic delegation. *The Washington Post.* Retrieved from https://www.washingtonpost.com/news/early-lead/wp/2013/12/18/obama-names-openly-gay-athletes-to-sochi-olympic-delegation/

Brock, A. (2012). From the blackhand side: Twitter as a cultural conversation. *Journal of Broadcasting & Electronic Media, 56,* 529–549.

Cork, T. (2013). *G3: The gift of you, leadership, and netgiving.* Toronto, Canada: BPS Books.

Croft, J. (2017, June 21). Philando Castile shooting: Dashcam video shows rapid event. *CNN.* Retrieved from http://www.cnn.com/2017/06/20/us/philando-castile-shooting-dashcam/index.html

Cunningham, G. B., & Regan, M. R. (2012). Political activism, racial identity and the commercial endorsement of athletes. *International Review for the Sociology of Sport, 47,* 657–669.

Das, A. (2014, October 1). Stars sue organizers of Women's World Cup over use of turf. *The New York Times.* Retrieved from http://www.nytimes.com/2014/10/02/sports/soccer/womens-soccer-stars-sue-world-cup-organizers-over-artificial-turf.html

Davis, D. (2008, August). Olympic athletes who took a stand. *Smithsonian Magazine.* Retrieved from http://www.smithsonianmag.com/people-places/olympic-athletes-who-took-a-stand-593920/?no-ist

Farrey, T. (2015, August 17). Northwestern players denied request to form first union for athletes. *ESPN.* Retrieved from http://espn.go.com/college-football/story/_/id/13455477/nlrb-says-northwestern-players-cannot-unionize

Granderson, L. (2012, August 14). The political Michael Jordan. *ESPN.* Retrieved from http://espn.go.com/nba/story/_/id/8264956/michael-jordan-obama-fundraiser-22-years-harvey-gantt

Howard, A. (2015, November 5). Kareem Abdul-Jabbar: Michael Jordan chose 'commerce over conscience.' *MSNBC*. Retrieved from http://www.msnbc.com/msnbc/kareem-abdul-jabbar-michael-jordan-chose-commerce-over-conscience

Kaufman, P., & Wolff, E. (2010). Playing and protesting: Sport as a vehicle for social change. *Journal of Sport and Social Issues, 34*(2), 154–175.

Kristofferson, K., White, K., & Peloza, J. (2013). The nature of slacktivism: How the social observability of an initial act of token support affects subsequent prosocial action. *Journal of Consumer Research, 40*, 1149–1166.

Moreno, M. (2016, July 21). The WNBA is sending mixed messages on players' social activism. *3 News Now*. Retrieved from http://www.3newsnow.com/newsy/the-wnba-is-sending-mixed-messages-on-players-social-activism

Muhammad Ali. (n.d.). Retrieved from http://muhammadali.com/

Murray, R. (2014, December 9). How the sports world is reacting to Mike Brown, Eric Garner protests. *ABC News*. Retrieved from http://abcnews.go.com/US/sports-world-stoking-mike-brown-eric-garner-protests/story?id=27475409

Newman, A. (2014, December 2). The death of Eric Garner, and the events that followed. *New York Times*. Retrieved from http://www.nytimes.com/interactive/2014/12/04/nyregion/04garner-timeline.html?_r=0#/#time356_10550

Olympic protestors stripped of their medals. (n.d.). *History*. Retrieved from http://www.history.com/this-day-in-history/olympic-protestors-stripped-of-their-medals

Our Story. (n.d.). *Athlete Ally*. Retrieved from https://www.athleteally.org/about/

Popovich, N. (2015, September 11). Battle of the sexes: Charting how women in tennis achieved equal pay. *The Guardian*. Retrieved from https://www.theguardian.com/sport/2015/sep/11/how-women-in-tennis-achieved-equal-pay-us-open

Putting your dollars to work. (n.d.). *ALS Association*. Retrieved from http://www.alsa.org/fight-als/ibc-progress.html

Roberts, S. (2005, August, 21). Tennis's other 'Battle of the Sexes,' before Kings-Riggs. *New York Times*. Retrieved from http://www.nytimes.com/2005/08/21/sports/tennis/tenniss-other-battle-of-the-sexes-before-kingriggs.html?_r=0

Robles, F., & Bosman, J. (2014, August 17). Autopsy shows Michael Brown was shot at least 6 times. *New York Times*. Retrieved from http://www.nytimes.com/2014/08/18/us/michael-brown-autopsy-shows-he-was-shot-at-least-6-times.html

Schmittel, A., & Sanderson, J. (2014). Talking about Trayvon in 140 characters: Exploring NFL players' tweets about the George Zimmerman verdict. *Journal of Sport and Social Issues, 39*(4), 1–14.

Schwartz, L. (n.d.). Billie Jean won for all women. *ESPN*. Retrieved from https://espn.go.com/sportscentury/features/00016060.html

Stephenson, D. (2014, June 24). When did athletes start getting rich? *The Deal Room*. Retrieved from http://www.firmex.com/thedealroom/when-did-athletes-start-getting-rich/

Trayvon Martin Shooting Fast Facts. (2015, February 11). *CNN*. Retrieved from http://www.cnn.com/2013/06/05/us/trayvon-martin-shooting-fast-facts/

DEBATE IN SPORT

Classroom debates provide forums for discussion that may not otherwise occur. Students are provided the opportunity to express their opinions using facts and statistics on sensitive topics and work in groups to inform and persuade others about the topic at hand. It is undeniable that the ability to think critically and communicate effectively are essential skills to possess as future sport managers. For this reason, debates provide the platform to develop and practice these skills in the classroom. The chapter will begin with a general explanation of debates and the recommended format before getting into specific debate topics from within the sport industry.

WHAT IS A DEBATE?

Simply put, a debate is a structured discussion about an issue in which there are two sides, one supporting an affirmative outcome and a second supporting an opposing outcome. Debates are beneficial in the classroom as they allow students to express their opinions on real-world topics and issues while also learning from their classmates. While there are a variety of ways to conduct a classroom debate, we have suggested the following guidelines.

LEARNING OBJECTIVES:

A. Think critically about prominent ethical issues in the sport industry
B. Synthesize information to construct an argument
C. Develop communication skills required of effective sport managers

STUDENT PREPARATION

- Research the topic to ensure that you have prepared logical arguments supporting your assigned stance on the topic. Your arguments should use some form of evidence (i.e., facts and statistics) to support your claim.
- While supporting evidence for your topic is necessary, understanding the opposing view is also important in the formulation of effective arguments. Understanding the opposing viewpoint beforehand will also aid in your anticipation of counterarguments.
- Create a set of questions to ask the members of the opposing side during the debate.
- Meet as a group to formulate a strategy on the order of speaking and the arguments that will be emphasized by individuals within the group.
- Remember: A debate is not you against the other student/group. Structured debates should be focused on the issue and the other side's argument and NOT who is arguing the other side.

DEBATE FORMAT

It is suggested that the debates be completed in groups of six. The groups will work together to research their assigned stance prior to the debate. Two individuals from each will be assigned speakers during the actual debate while the other two group members will be responsible for asking questions of individuals on the other side of the issue. The format below is for a 32-minute debate. The time can be adjusted accordingly to fit the needs of the particular class in which the debate is occurring.

- The first person to speak (Person A) will be from the affirmative side of the issue. In the presentation of his or her case, the first speaker's goal is to illustrate that the affirmative side of the issue is true and provide support for that claim. The recommended time for this speaker is 5 minutes.
- The second speaker (Person B) will be from the opposing side of the issue. This speaker will ask the opening speaker (Person A) questions about what he or she said. Person A will then be provided an opportunity to answer these questions. The suggested time for this sequence is 3 minutes.
- The third speaker (Person C) will be from the opposing side of the issue. The main goal of this speaker is to demonstrate that the opposing viewpoint of the issue is true. The recommended time for this speaker is 5 minutes.
- The fourth speaker (Person D) will be from the affirmative side of the issue. This speaker will ask the opposing speaker (Person C) questions about what he or she said. Person C will then be provided an opportunity to answer these questions. The suggested time for this sequence is 3 minutes.
- The fifth speaker (Person E) will be from the opposing side of the issue. The goal of this speaker is to refute the affirmative position presented by the first speaker (Person A). The recommended time for this speaker is 5 minutes.
- The sixth speaker (Person F) will be from the affirmative side of the issue. This speaker will ask the previous speaker (Person E) questions about what he or she said. Person E will then be provided an opportunity to answer these questions. The suggested time for this sequence is 3 minutes.
- The seventh speaker (Person G) will be the final speaker from the affirmative side of the issue. The goal of this speaker is to overcome the objections presented throughout the debate by those on the opposing side of the argument. The recommended time for this speaker is 5 minutes.

- The final speaker (Person H) is the final speaker for the opposing viewpoint. This speaker will be responsible for raising any final questions to the affirmative side. The affirmative side will be provided with one last opportunity to address these questions. The suggested time for this speaker is 3 minutes.

The other two members of each group can participate in answering questions throughout the debate, but should lead the organization and preparation of debate materials before debate day. This might include leading group meetings, creating talking points for the speakers, and/or creating documents for the team to use during the debate. Following the debate, it is recommended that the rest of the class be given an opportunity to ask questions. The class and professor can also provide feedback to debate participants during this time.

DEBATE TOPIC #1 – THE USE OF NATIVE AMERICAN MASCOTS AND LOGOS IN SPORT

Sport brands often include team names, logos, and symbols associated with their products to differentiate themselves from other brands. Mascots are one element of the sport brand that are typically used as symbolic figures to rally team spirit and identification. The prominence of the mascot as an emblematic representation of the sport organization makes it an exceptionally important component of the sport brand.

miker/shutterstock.com

The use of Native American mascots by American sport organizations, at all levels, has occurred for more than a century. The use of the Native American mascots is often accompanied by the incorporation of fight songs, tribal dances, and traditional Native American attire (i.e., buckskin dresses, loincloths, feathered headdresses, moccasins, etc.) into the sport experience. The implementation of Native American traditions and practices into the sport realm has been explained as a celebration in which those who are doing the impersonating are impersonating the Native Americans' fighting prowess and bravery (Staurowsky, 2007). The question arises as to whether or not the use of Native American mascots is in fact honorable or just racist.

Formal Effort to Change

In 1968, the National Congress of American Indians (NCAI) created a campaign to eliminate negative stereotyping through the use of Indian names and mascots in sports. Their argument emphasized that the use of names, mascots, and logos was not only offensive, but also demeaning to Native Americans (Hylton, 2010). In the 1970s many colleges and universities responded to the pressures from the NCAI and Native Americans and took the initiative to change their nicknames. Five success stories from these actions are illustrated in Table 12.1.

TABLE 12.1 *Changing of Mascots in the 1970s*

College/University	Year	Previous Mascot	Current Mascot
University of Oklahoma	1970	Little Red	Boomer & Sooner
Marquette University	1971	Willie Wampum	Golden Eagle
Stanford	1972	Indians	Cardinals
Dartmouth College	1974	Indians	Keggy the Keg
Syracuse University	1975	Saltine Warrior	Otto the Orange

In 2005, the National Collegiate Athletic Association (NCAA) took action to disallow the use of Native American mascots by banning schools that use Indian names and symbols from post-season play, unless the teams secured permission for the use of the name from the tribe itself (NCAA, 2005). At the time of the NCAA's implementation of this policy, 18 colleges and universities continued to use Native American imagery or references. Since then, 10 of the colleges and universities have changed their nicknames (see Table 12.2).

TABLE 12.2 *Colleges and Universities Impacted by 2005 NCAA Ruling*

College/University	Nickname in 2005	Nickname in 2017
Alcorn State University	Braves	Braves
Arkansas State University	Indians	Red Wolves
Bradley University	Braves	Braves
Carthage College	Redmen	Red Men & Lady Reds
Catawba College	Indians	Indians
Central Michigan University	Chippewas	Chippewas
Chowan College	Braves	Hawks
Florida State University	Seminoles	Seminoles
Indiana University-Pennsylvania	Indians	Crimson Hawks
McMurry University	Indians	War Hawks
Midwestern State University	Indians	Mustangs
Mississippi College	Choctaws	Choctaws
Newberry College	Indians	Wolves
Southeastern Oklahoma State University	Savages	Savage Storm
University of Illinois-Champaign	Illini	Illini
University of Louisiana-Monroe	Indians	Warhawks
University of North Dakota	Fighting Sioux	Fighting Hawks
University of Utah	Utes	Utes

More recently, adidas announced an initiative to financially assist high schools in transitioning from potentially harmful Native American mascots to new mascots, names, and logos. Through the initiative, adidas is encouraging approximately 2,000 of the nation's 27,000 high schools that currently use names that cause concern for tribal communities to use its design resources to change their logos or mascots (adidas, 2015). In the press release announcing the initiative, Eric Liedkte, who is an adidas group executive board member, stated:

> Extraordinary things happen because of sports. Today, we can add another story on how sports bring people together and provide common ground to ignite change (adidas, 2015, para. 7).

While it is clear that organizations such as the NCAI and the NCAA believe that the use of Native American mascots is disparaging to Native Americans, proponents of the use of Native American mascots believe that the practice honors Native Americans and supports nostalgic feelings associated with Native American imagery. This viewpoint also suggests that keeping Native American imagery is preferable because it would be expensive to undergo the rebranding of sport organizations to change the mascots, logos, and other organizational images associated with Native Americans.

This sentiment is supported by others, such as Ivan Dozier who portrayed Chief Illiniwek at the University of Illinois and believes that the use of Native American mascots is a way to educate those who would not normally be knowledgeable or informed about Native American culture and history (Munguia, 2014). This is particularly important when we consider the unique nature of the sport consumer, as sport fans are unlike consumers of any other product. Sport fans are typically highly attached and loyal to their favorite organizations and their passion and reverence toward their favorite organizations illustrate their appreciation for the organizations that they follow.

Examples of Some of the Most Visible Native-American-Named Sport Franchises

UNIVERSITY OF ILLINOIS ILLINI. Perhaps the most controversial mascot change occurred at the University of Illinois in 2007 when Chief Illiniwek danced his final official dance at halftime of the last men's basketball game of the season, concluding his 81 years at the university (Klatell, 2007). Although the change came after the NCAA's 2005 ruling, the university's board of trustees had been considering a mascot change since 2001 (Munguia, 2014). Controversy surrounded Chief Illiniwek, who was portrayed

Jonathan Street/shutterstock.com

by buckskin-clad students who would perform tribal dances during athletic events. The NCAA deemed the use of Chief Illiniwek an offensive use of American Indian imagery (Klatell, 2007).

Following the NCAA's 2005 ruling, the University of Illinois could not host postseason events if it continued to use Chief Illiniwek as a mascot. The Fighting Illini appealed the NCAA's decision. Through that appeal, they were able to keep the team name, but not the mascot itself (Munguia, 2014). This ruling was attributed to the fact that Illini is short for Illinois, and the Fighting Illini signify a reference to the team's competitive spirit (Klatell, 2007). Although the mascot was officially retired in 2007, those who portrayed Chief Illiniwek were allowed to continue the tradition as long as there was no official affiliation with the university (Munguia, 2014).

WASHINGTON REDSKINS. The name of the Washington Redskins has been the subject of debate and legal battles since 1999. George Preston Marshall, the owner of the Redskins, changed the team name from the Braves to the Redskins in 1937. His explanation for the change of the name was that it was to honor the head coach at the time, William Henry Dietz, who claimed to be part Sioux (Munguia, 2014).

Opponents to the Redskins name consider it a racial slur, as it explicitly refers to the color of the skin of Native Americans. In 2014, the Trademark Trials and Appeal Board cancelled the franchise's trademark

mikermaker/shutterstock.com

and cited a substantial number of complaints regarding the disparaging connotations associated with the term Redskins (Munguia, 2014). U.S. District Judge Gerald Bruce Lee affirmed this ruling when he cancelled the organization's federal trademark registrations in July 2015 (Shapira, 2015).

The Redskins organization has filed court papers to defend their federal trademark registration, stating that the government has registered plenty of companies with disparaging or offensive names. The organization cited Aunt Jemima products, Uncle Ben's rice, and Red Man tobacco as other products with racially tinged trademarks that have not been challenged. Furthermore, the Redskins argued that a ban on registering disparaging trademarks is not constitutional as it burdens speech based on content and viewpoint (O'Dell, 2015). This argument was supported in a 2017 Supreme Court decision, which struck down the rule against disparaging trademarks under the notion that one cannot ban speech based on the ground that ideas offend (Liptak, 2017). The debate regarding the Redskins is ongoing as team owner Dan Snyder opposes the change, while Native American organizations, Congress members, and former President Barack Obama encourage a change.

CLEVELAND INDIANS. The Chief Wahoo logo has been regarded as the most offensive sport logo in the Western world as it is the only one that caricatures a race of people (McGraw, 2015). Native American poet and activist Suzan Shown Harjo described Chief Wahoo as the graphic equivalent of the Washington Redskins name (Wulf, 2014). In other words, the toothy grin, red skin, stretched cheeks, triangular eyes, and feather are believed to be just as offensive as the racial slur "redskin." Disdain toward Chief Wahoo was also evident when the Indians began their 100th season with the Indians logo and Chief Wahoo mascot in 2015. The organization's 100th season was accompanied by protests criticizing the racist nature of the organization's logo and its donning of red face apparel (McGraw, 2015).

Robert J Daveant/shutterstock.com

Although steps were taken to marginalize the presence of the Chief Wahoo logo when the Indians moved to a block letter "C" as the primary logo in 2014, the home uniform continues to feature him on caps and jersey sleeves (see image above), despite the racial associations with his appearance (Brown, 2014). While the organization appears to be open to change with respect to Chief Wahoo, a poll taken by Cleveland.com found that 70% of respondents wanted to keep him (Wulf, 2014). This puts the organization in a tricky predicament as they must work to satisfy their fan base in which a majority of Clevelanders wants to keep the traditions associated with Chief Wahoo, while addressing the claims of racism being thrown at them.

FLORIDA STATE SEMINOLES. The Florida State Seminoles have truly imbedded the university into the Seminoles' culture and history creating a unique relationship between the university and the Seminole Tribe of Florida. Following the NCAA's 2005 ruling, Florida State University received an endorsement of support from the Seminole Tribe of Florida and the Seminole Nation of Oklahoma (Powell, 2005). Following the ruling, administrators consulted the Seminole Tribe of Florida to alter the sport team's logo and fashion, leading to the creation of the costume for the Chief Osceola mascot and approval of the face paint, flaming spear, and Appaloosa horse despite its lack of connection to Seminole history (Powell).

The mutually beneficial relationship between the two organizations is demonstrated in educational opportunities afforded by the university as students are provided the opportunity to learn more about the Seminole Tribe by taking "History of the Seminoles and Southeastern Tribes, Pre-Contact to Present" as an elective (Culpepper, 2014). Furthermore, Florida State University collaborates with the tribe to include participation by tribal members in the university's most meaningful events and continued advice and direction to ensure the tribal imagery is authentic (Florida State University, n.d.). If an organization is granted tribal permission for the use of a tribe name, such as the case with the Florida State Seminoles and the Seminole Tribe of Florida, does it make it okay for fans to dress in traditional Native American garb with feathers in their hair, doing war chants and the Tomahawk chop? An old adage suggests that imitation is the best form of flattery, but is it ethical to participate in behaviors mimicking an entire race or ethnicity? Should an agreement with the Seminole Tribe of Florida speak for the entire Seminole Tribe and all Native Americans? Is it acceptable and flattering that others celebrate what they love most, sport, by acting in a manner that they view is representative of Native Americans? These are some questions to consider as you start to format your debate strategy.

Central Question: Should sport organizations be allowed to use Native American mascots and logos?

Affirmative View: Yes, sport organizations should be allowed to use Native American mascots and logos.

Opposing View: The use of Native American mascots and logos should not be allowed.

Ruth Peterkin/shutterstock.com

DEBATE TOPIC #2 – THE USE OF PERFORMANCE ENHANCING DRUGS IN SPORT

In 1927, Babe Ruth became the first professional baseball player to hit 60 home runs in a season. His record stood until Roger Maris broke it 34 years later when he hit 61 home runs (Baseball-reference.com, n.d.). In 1998, Sammy Sosa and Mark McGwire were in a home run race throughout the entire MLB season. McGwire ended up winning the home run battle, setting a new record of 70 home runs, while Sosa finished the season with 66. Yet again, the record was broken in 2001 when Barry Bonds hit an astounding 73 home runs throughout the season (Baseball-reference.com, n.d.). When McGwire and Sosa were battling it out in the 1998 season, fans intensely followed. However, by the time Bonds set the record in 2001, fans had become skeptical and the significance of the modern-day records was controversial.

The skepticism surrounding the home run records proved to be warranted. After originally being shy and evasive about the allegations, McGwire acknowledged using steroids in his record-setting season (Leach, 2010). While many current and former professional baseball players continued to deny the use of performance enhancing drugs (PEDs), the Mitchell Report, authored by former senator and diplomat George Mitchell, stated that anonymous tests conducted during the 2003 baseball season suggested that 5 to 7% percent of MLB athletes were using anabolic steroids (Mitchell, 2007). This percentage, however, may have been even higher had the anonymous tests had the capability to deduct human growth hormone, which they did not.

Aspen photo / shutterstock.com

MLB instituted its first steroid policy in 2003 (CNN, 2015). This initial steroid policy received criticism for being too lenient and was later updated in 2005 with its current testing policy for PEDs (Gehring, 2015). Since the updated policy has been in place, 39 MLB players have been suspended through the 2014 season (see Table 12.3).

TABLE 12.3   Major League Baseball Players Suspended for PEDs Since 2005

Athlete	Year (Length of Suspension)	Team
Eliezer Alfonzo	2008 (50 games)	San Francisco Giants
	2011 (48 games)	Colorado Rockies
Carlos Almanzar	2005 (10 days)	Texas Rangers
Antonio Bastardo	2013 (50 games)	Philadelphia Phillies
Ryan Braun	2013 (65 games)	Milwaukee Brewers
Marlon Byrd	2012 (50 games)	Free Agent
Everth Cabrera	2013 (50 games)	San Diego Padres
Melky Cabrera	2012 (50 games)	San Francisco Giants
Mike Cameron	2007 (25 games)	San Diego Padres
Francisco Cervelli	2013 (50 games)	New York Yankees
Bartolo Colon	2012 (50 games)	Oakland Athletics
Nelson Cruz	2013 (50 games)	Texas Rangers
Ryan Franklin	2005 (10 days)	Seattle Mariners
Freddy Galvis	2012 (50 games)	Philadelphia Phillies
Jay Gibbons	2007 (15 games)	Baltimore Orioles
Yasmani Grandal	2012 (50 games)	San Diego Padres
Jason Grimsley	2006 (50 games)	Arizona Diamondbacks
Jose Guillen	2007 (15 games)	Kansas City Royals
Felix Heredia	2005 (10 days)	New York Mets
Matt Lawton	2005 (10 days)	New York Yankees
Cameron Maybin	2014 (25 games)	San Diego Padres
Agustin Montero	2005 (10 days)	Texas Rangers
Mike Morse	2005 (10 days)	Seattle Mariners
Guillermo Mota	2006 (50 games)	New York Mets
	2012 (100 games)	San Francisco Giants
Rafael Palmeiro	2005 (10 days)	Baltimore Orioles
Troy Patton	2013 (25 games)	Baltimore Orioles
Jhonny Peralta	2013 (50 games)	Detroit Tigers
Neifi Perez	2007 (25 games)	Detroit Tigers
	2007 (80 games)	Detroit Tigers
Jorge Piedra	2005 (10 days)	Colorado Rockies
Manny Ramirez	2009 (50 games)	Los Angeles Dodgers
	2011 (100 games)	Tampa Bay Rays
Juan Rincon	2005 (10 days)	Minnesota Twins

Alex Rodriguez	2013 – 2014 (162 games)	New York Yankees
J.C. Romero	2009 (50 games)	Philadelphia Phillies
Carlos Ruiz	2012 (25 games)	Philadelphia Phillies
Juan Salas	2007 (50 games)	Tampa Bay Rays
Alex Sanchez	2005 (10 days)	Tampa Bay Rays
Dan Serafini	2007 (50 games)	Colorado Rockies
Jamal Strong	2005 (10 days)	Seattle Mariners
Miguel Tejada	2013 (105 games)	Kansas City Royals
Edinson Volquez	2010 (50 games)	Cincinnati Reds

Note: Table 12.3 is derived from the work of Gehring (2015)

The use of PEDs is not unique to baseball. There have been many other documented cases of their use in other sports. For instance, Arnold Schwarzenegger admitted to using PEDs while a professional bodybuilder. His explanation for their use was that they were legal at the time (ABC, 2005). Professional wrestler Hulk Hogan and NFL defensive end Lyle Alzado also conceded their use of PEDs (Delgado, 2014). In 2007, Marion Jones, one of the most decorated female track and field athletes, admitted to steroid use. After denying the allegations for years, she admitted to lying to federal prosecutors (Wright, 2009). More recently, in 2013 Lance Armstrong admitted in an interview with Oprah Winfrey that he used steroids in his professional career as a cyclist. When asked if he thought using them was wrong, he said that he viewed it as leveling the playing field (Calamur, 2013). Of all of the situations in which athletes admittedly used PEDs, Armstrong's perhaps was the most notorious because of his association with cancer research and his LIVESTRONG brand.

While it is clear that many professional athletes have admittedly taken PEDs, the question of whether or not they should be banned is a hot topic. As evidenced in the case of Arnold Schwarzenegger, they used to be legal; however, now they are not. There are many angles from which one can position an argument on this topic.

One argument for the use of PEDs involves the manner in which use is detected. Many intercollegiate athletes have supported their opposition toward mandatory drug testing with the backing of constitutional law (Lumpkin, Stoll, & Beller, 2002). The Fourteenth Amendment guarantees all citizens privileges and immunities of citizenship, due process, and equal protection. The argument put forth by these intercollegiate athletes is that they are being singled out by having to be tested in comparison to the rest of the student body that does not have to be tested, thereby eliminating the equal protection component of the Fourteenth Amendment. Similarly, the methods of testing for PEDs can be seen as an invasion of privacy. The expectation of privacy while using the restroom is one that most people have. When testing for PEDs through urine, privacy is not granted. While these two reasons may not support the use of PEDs, they do bring into question the respect and privacy of athletes.

Some, such as Lance Armstrong, believe that the use of PEDs levels the playing field. In other words, one individual might begin taking PEDs because he or she thinks that everyone else is taking them. Rather than attempting to gain a competitive advantage, that individual is actually just looking to keep up with his or her competition. This then turns into a never-ending cycle where athletes who did not consider using in the past

are forced to use to enhance performance and keep up with others. Should everyone be allowed to choose whether or not they want to use PEDs to keep up with the competition and excel, or should they be illegal altogether?

One argument against the use of PEDs is that they are not natural. It has been stated that the use of PEDs, especially at the high dosages believed necessary to actually enhance performance, can be considerably harmful (Effects of PEDs, n.d.). The Mitchell Report suggests that psychiatric problems, cardiovascular and liver damage, damage to reproductive systems, and musculoskeletal injuries can occur as a result of taking PEDs (Mitchell, 2007). While these risks associated with the use of PEDs are very serious, should the decision to take the risk be up to the individual athlete or governed by the leagues and federal government?

Another argument against the use of PEDs involves the idea of equalizing competition. If PEDs are banned, then everyone operates on an equal playing field. This will eliminate the peer pressure or coercion that would be associated with the use of PEDs if they were legal. However, does the imposition of such a rule disregard the personal decision-making capabilities and liberties of individual athletes?

There are obviously many issues associated with the use of PEDs. There is support for their legality and support for their ban. The discussion should and will continue. For the purpose of this text, consider the following central arguments and stances.

Central Question: Should the use of performance enhancing drugs in sport be legalized?

Affirmative View: Yes, the use of performance enhancing drugs should be legal in sport.

Opposing View: No, the use of performance enhancing drugs should not be legal in sport.

DEBATE TOPIC #3 – THE LEGALITY OF FANTASY SPORTS

The rising popularly of fantasy sports followed the exodus of online sportsbooks and poker when Congress passed the Unlawful Internet Gaming Enforcement Act (UIGEA) in 2009 (Kilgore, 2015). The UIGEA also had a section on fantasy sports, outlining three conditions to ensure legality. These conditions were the following: (1) All prizes had to be established before the contest and not be influenced by the number of participants. (2) The outcome of the contest must demonstrate the knowledge and skill of participants through statistical

Steve Cukrov/shutterstock.com

results. (3) The contest could not be based on the score, point spread, or performance of a single team or individual athlete in a single real sporting event (Kilgore). If one were to simply bet one team would win a game or the score of the game would be a particular score, this would violate the third condition. However, as a whole, the UIGEA seemingly protected fantasy sports because of the necessary skill and knowledge requirement. One issue with the interpretation of the UIGEA is that when it was written it was with traditional, season-long fantasy sports in mind.

The growth in fantasy sport is illustrated in the number of fantasy users. It is estimated that roughly 57 million Americans pay money to participate in fantasy sports even though sport betting is illegal in most states (Phillips, 2015). Traditional fantasy sports typically operate in a manner in which users pay a fee to enter and compete against each other. Users operate as managers of their teams and draft, trade, and set the rosters with real-world athletes. What is unique about fantasy sports is that the athletes on the different rosters who are competing with one another in the weekly matchups are not usually competing with each other in real-world games (Rose, 2015). However, the accomplishments that the real-world athletes achieve in their games are statistically tracked to see which fantasy user has won the matchup.

Daily fantasy sports operate under similar guidelines as those that regulate traditional fantasy sports. However, rather than competing against family, friends, and colleagues throughout the course of a season, daily fantasy sport competitions involve strangers in contests that can be as short as a few hours. Two of the most popular daily fantasy sports websites are DraftKings and FanDuel. Each of these websites further altered the traditional methods of playing fantasy sports by giving participants a salary cap from which they can choose real players. This differs from the draft process that occurs in a traditional fantasy sports competition. The changes seem to be working, as DraftKings, which began in 2011, illustrated exponential growth from 200,000 registered users in 2014 to over 2 million registered users in 2015 (Kilgore, 2015). With the changes that have been made from the traditional fantasy sports structure, the question arises as to whether or not the UIGEA still protects participation in daily fantasy sports websites.

Many professional leagues are supportive of daily fantasy sports sites, which was proven in 2006 when the top lawyers from the NCAA, NFL, NBA, NHL, and MLB asked Congress members to co-sponsor UIGEA, including the protection afforded to fantasy sports in the Act (Kilgore, 2015). The support for collaboration between the leagues and fantasy sports can also be seen in the partnerships that have begun in recent years. For instance, MLB became the first professional league to enter the daily fantasy business in 2013 when it purchased a stake in DraftKings (Kilgore, 2015). The relationship between the league and the fantasy sport website was further strengthened in 2015 through a multi-year deal making DraftKings MLB's "Official Daily Fantasy Game," which allowed co-branded and market-specific experiences (Heitner, 2015). In 2014, the NBA signed as an equity investor with FanDuel (Belson, 2014). Likewise, the NHL has an endorsement deal with DraftKings (Edelman, 2016). If the support is there from the league level, why is there so much controversy?

The question of whether or not participation in fantasy sports is illegal exists because of its association with gambling. Participants pay a fee to enter leagues. Typically, there is no limit on the cost of entering (Rose, 2015). With the fees ranging from a quarter to thousands of dollars, the payouts for winning are varied as well. In order for fantasy sports to be considered illegal gambling, the law states that the activity must meet the state-specific definition for three factors: consideration, reward, and chance (Edelman, 2014). Consideration and reward are present in most fantasy sports, so the legality usually comes down to the notion of whether or not chance or skill is involved with the participation.

Some have argued that there is a legal difference between illegal gambling and daily sports leagues. While illegal gambling involves putting your money on an entire game and the outcome being up to chance, daily fantasy sports involves skill in which participants bet on the individual players whom they have drafted (Buxton, 2015). The skills involved often include mathematical modeling in the appropriate selection of players for the roster (Edelman, 2016). Opponents to this stance suggest there is no difference between one team to win a game and roster full of players each week to come out statistically strong than those athletes on the roster of your opponent. For these reasons, two of the most popular daily fantasy sport sites, FanDuel and DraftKings, have found themselves on the receiving end of many lawsuits. There have been more than 30 class-action suits filed against the two sites, alleging that the participants were duped into illegal gambling operations in which the employees of the fantasy sport sites also participated (Bernstein, 2016). Is it skill or is it chance?

The argument against daily fantasy sports became even more complex when Vantiv Entertainment Solutions, a payment processing company that handles transactions for FanDuel and DraftKings, told the companies that beginning February 29, 2016, they would suspend all processing for payments related to daily fantasy sports (Drape, 2016). The reason for their decision was the growing number of state attorneys that have determined that daily fantasy sports constitute illegal gambling. There are seven states that identify daily fantasy sports as a form of gambling or illegal activity under current state laws (Drape). In other words, although the UIGEA provided somewhat of a loophole to protect fantasy sports, many current state laws say that daily fantasy sports are illegal. Should the laws be rewritten since fantasy sports are embraced by sport leagues, funded by Wall Street, and protected by federal law? Or should we accept and abide by the current interpretations of the state laws? These questions will guide this debate.

Central Question: Should fantasy sport be legal?

Affirmative View: Yes, fantasy sport should be legal.

Opposing View: Fantasy sport should be illegal.

DEBATE TOPIC #4 – PAY FOR PLAY

As revenue continues to rise in college sport, athletic departments across the nation are making millions every year from the athletes who are attending college to earn a degree and play for the university sport team. In 2015 alone, 28 college sport programs reported having grossed over $1 million in annual revenue (Solomon, 2015). The top college program in 2014 was Texas A&M bringing in over $192 million (NCAA finances, n.d.). In basketball alone, the University of Louisville was ranked the highest in estimated value among all schools at $38.3 million in 2014 (Smith, 2014). The growth and commercialization of the college sport product has been a topic of debate for decades. Since the inception of the NCAA in 1912, member institutions have been awarded a variety of financial benefits to contribute to the arms race in college sport. This commercialization has led academics, researchers, and fans of college sport to question whether or not college athletes should be paid. Athletes across the United States assist in generating universities larger sums of financial revenue from star performances, brand recognition, and merchandise and ticket sales. Many believe these athletes, who commit to practice, travel, and high levels of competition, deserve the opportunity to be fairly compensated for their actions and athleticism on and off the court or field.

The concept around pay for play (P4P) is simply a debate about paying athletes to play in college sport. The negative reality of P4P is that many of these star athletes are in college to generate money for the program rather than to get an academic degree. The continued dispute about how college athletes should be paid for their athletic accomplishments while they are in school is ever-changing. Some argue student-athletes are not professionals, and therefore should not be paid. Student-athletes are in school to get an education, and playing sports for the university is a privilege that is earned by effort and perseverance. Others may debate college athletes receive little financial assistance and have little time to get jobs outside of their commitment to schoolwork, team meetings, practices, workouts, games, and study halls.

Proponents

Proponents of P4P support athletes getting paid by the university or others affiliated with the university programs. Many fans of sport agree that the student-athletes are the labor as they provide the product on the field or on the court. Researchers and fans suggest that the athletes are not only bringing in ticket sales but also donations, grants, sponsorships, and public awareness of the university or program. College athletes are provided the opportunity to gain a college education, while playing sport and gaining experience at the same time. When a student-athlete has signed a National Letter of Intent, they are signing away their rights to allow the university to use their image and likeness for advertising or publicity. This is true; however, student-athletes should be able to make money off of the intellectual property that by constitutional right belongs to them. Many student-athletes complain of having little money to buy food and basic necessities.

If the student-athlete is provided pay, the athlete can live more comfortably, perform at a higher level, and devote their attention to college academics.

Opponents

Those that are opposed to P4P also have strong arguments about why student-athletes should not be paid. Andrew Luck said it well when he suggested "college sports are 'tethered' to education and everything surrounding it should have an educational purpose, if not, then it should not be allowed" (Ridpath, 2015, p. 2). Simply put, if an institution was to start paying student-athletes as employees, it would diminish the educational mission of most institutions. College athletic directors, university presidents, and the NCAA will claim that these student-athletes are amateurs and by the nature of that definition, they participate for the love of the sport and not to get paid. The term amateur is "someone who has not profited above his/her actual and necessary expenses or gained any competitive advantage in his/her sport" (NCAA, n.d., para. 2). Student-athletes participate for the enjoyment and involvement and not to receive compensation. Some argue that athletes already receive a free education, which includes tuition scholarship, housing, meal plans, and stipend. With all of the costs included in their scholarship, student-athletes arguably are already "getting paid." The college athletes also could potentially be considered an employee if they are paid outside of a scholarship. In addition, many professionals and economists in the industry are challenged by the ability for a P4P model to be fair across all sports at all levels. Many argue that a separate "Super Division" where the top power schools participate and pay college athletes might be a better solution. Others believe "there is no system of payment that can be put in place that is fair across the board to all students, all sports, and all schools that participate in college athletics" (Jackson, 2013, para. 2). Every student who signs that national letter of intent agrees to receive a stipend or scholarship of some kind, in order to continue playing their sport with the assumption they are fully aware that the university is going to be the one who reaps all the benefits.

P4P Issues in College Sport

Cam Newton, Heisman Trophy winner and No. 1 NFL draft pick in 2011, was involved with many investigations into whether or not he violated pay for play allegations (Associated Press, 2011). While Newton was in the process of changing schools and rising as a football star, his father allegedly asked Mississippi State University for $180,000 in order for his son to play football (Associated Press, 2011). Several recorded documents shed light on the many motivations that may exist regarding athletes seeking payment. This case in particular supported argument that many families of student-athletes could benefit from additional revenue or payment of players. It also brought up the common debate related to the potential financial struggles that many families of student-athletes face. Another issue

cpreiser000/Shutterstock.com

that has come up in recent years is top candidates in football and basketball accepting benefits or gifts from boosters, donors, coaches, or others associated with the university program. "Many players over the years who have accepted money or gifts, most likely did so because they believed that they deserved additional benefits" (Steak, 2010, para. 2). One familiar example is when Reggie Bush forfeited his Heisman Trophy in 2010 after he allegedly received improper benefits in the form of cash and gifts.

In 2014, Kain Colter and his Northwestern University football team filed a petition with the National Labor Relations Board (NLRB) to be recognized as potential employees of the university and gain basic "union rights" (Farrey, 2014). The Chicago regional office of the NLRB claimed the football players did have the right to unionize, and bargain collectively; however, the NLRB eventually denied their claim (Burch, 2014). This case gave athletes at private institutions a little power and raised the eyebrows of many university athletic departments. If athletes are allowed to collectively negotiate for insurance and other benefits, the current system will change dramatically. Student-athletes could be known as "employees" in the organizational context, receiving benefits outside of their already free education, housing, books, and meals.

The P4P debate is an ongoing challenge for many managers in the sport industry. There is support for payment for athletes and support for those opposed to any P4P model. For the purpose of this debate, consider both sides of the position to direct your debate.

Central Question: Should college athletes receive any portion of the money earned by athletic departments while they are playing at a university?

Affirmative View: College athletes should be paid as employees for their time and commitment to their sport and to the university.

Opposing View: College athletes should not receive compensation for their time and commitment to their sport and to the university.

DEBATE TOPIC #5 – ATHLETE ACTIVISM

Sport can be a powerful force for change, be it individual change or collective social change for the greater good (Kaufman & Wolff, 2010). The uniqueness of sport is further seen in its potential to promote greater human rights through its liberal-democratic ideals (Giulianotti, 2005). Professional athletes are in a unique position in which they are in the public eye and have a platform on which to speak on social and political issues if they so choose. Because of their status as professional athletes and the distinctive nature of the attachment that fans have to professional athletes, they are able to function as "agents of social change" (Pelak, 2005, p. 59).

Proponents of Athlete Activism

Cassius Clay, who changed his name to Muhammad Ali in 1964, is regarded as one of the first professional athletes to speak out on political or social issues. Ali was born in 1942 during a time in which African Americans were the servant class. It was only after his bike was stolen when he was 12 years old that he took up boxing. His popularity as an athlete grew during the 1960s, while political and social issues were exceptionally tumultuous. With his position as an extraordinary boxer, Ali began to use his platform as an athlete to voice his dissent on racial and political issues in America. In perhaps his most notable stance, Ali refused induction in the United States Armed Forces during the Vietnam War. This was a stance for which he was later jailed (Hauser, n.d.). Ali explained his viewpoint with the following quote:

Suzanne Tucker/shutterstock.com

> Why should they ask me to put on a uniform and go ten thousand miles from home and drop bombs and bullets on brown people in Vietnam while so-called Negro people in Louisville are treated like dogs? . . . I have nothing to lose by standing up and following my beliefs. So I'll go to jail. We've been in jail for four hundred years. (Marquesee, 1995, p. 18)

In the years after Ali's refusal to enter the United States Armed Forces draft, further dissent toward social issues was illustrated through sport. During the 1968 Olympics in Mexico City, Tommie Smith and John Carlos used the Olympic platform to demonstrate their dissatisfaction with equality in the United States. The Olympic Project for Human Rights leader had requested that African American Olympians either boycott the Olympics altogether or protest their displeasure with the state of equality in the United States (Radar, 1999). Smith and Carlos chose to compete, and compete they did. Smith won the gold medal, while Carlos won the bronze medal. During the medal ceremony, the two bowed their heads and raised their gloved fists. This motion was indicative of the Black Power salute.

Panom/shutterstock.com

More recently, LeBron James has demonstrated athlete activism. James, along with then-teammate Dwayne Wade, organized the first athlete protest following the killing of Trayvon Martin. In their protest of the fatal shooting of the unarmed teenager, James and his Miami teammates posed for a picture wearing hoodies over their heads similar to the final images of Trayvon Martin portrayed in the media. On his Facebook posting of the picture, which has been liked by nearly 370,000 people and shared over 23,000 times, LeBron wrote, "We are Trayvon Martin. Hoodies. Stereotyped. We Want Justice."

WE ARE ALL TRAYVON MARTIN

NFL players echoed the sentiments of James and his teammates through Twitter. The rise of social media and the ability of athletes to communicate through their accounts without first filtering information through a public relations department has further solidified the capability of athletes to not only participate in, but to lead social movements. This was illustrated through the five million tweets sent in the 24 hours following the George Zimmerman not-guilty verdict (Jurkowitz, 2013). In a study of 125 NFL players' tweets regarding the verdict, Schmittel and Sanderson (2014) found that the athletes used the social media platform to discuss the verdict in the following ways: (1) anticipation, (2) disbelief, (3) critiques of the American justice system, (4) social commentary, (5) condolences and support, (6) responding to fans, and (7) freedom of speech arguments. The researchers suggested that, given the personal nature of Twitter and its accessibility, athletes may be willing to engage in activism and social movements through the digital realm.

Perhaps the most noteworthy stance that James has taken thus far was in response to the Donald Sterling situation in 2014. After years of legal troubles for discrimination against minorities, Sterling's negative behavior toward minorities made national headlines when his ex-girlfriend V. Stiviano released an audio recording of a private conversation between the two of them during which Sterling made several racist statements (TMZ, 2014). The story spread quickly through the Internet and social media and James was one of the first professional athletes to respond. He expressed his disgust in Sterling's bigoted remarks by vowing not to play in the NBA if Sterling still owned a team (Schwartz, 2014). In response to the incident, NBA Commissioner Adam Silver fined Sterling $2.5 million and instituted a permanent life ban from the Clippers and the NBA (Shelburne, 2014). Whether or not James' stance influenced this decision is unknown. Finally, in response to the Black poverty rate being at 28% in his hometown of Akron, Ohio, James pledged $41 million to send up to 2,000 at-risk kids to college (Bryant, 2015).

Opponents to Athlete Activism

Not all athletes choose to operate as agents of social change. Cunningham and Regan (2012) suggested three potential reasons why contemporary athletes may choose not to participate in social and political

ISSUES AND ETHICS IN SPORT

movements. The first reason is that social issues are perceived to be less prevalent than they used to be. This is credited to social norms and legal mandates that have decreased, but have not eliminated, the social issues of the 1960s and 1970s. The second reason for contemporary athletes to choose not to participate in social and political movements is that athletes are concerned about their athletic achievements rather than social movements. The third reason that athletes may choose not to operate as agents of social change is that they may fear the financial implications of speaking out on controversial topics. Some are instead motivated by market forces and would prefer to focus on the development of themselves and their talents in their sports. The choice not to speak out on social issues could also be attributed to the backlash and criticism that other athletes have received when attempting to advance social and political issues. Being a "jock for justice" is not without consequences (Candaele & Dreier, 2004), as athletes are expected to play, not to protest (Kaufman & Wolff, 2010).

landmarkmedia/shutterstock.com

Michael Jordan

One example of an athlete who chose not to use his position to speak on social or political issues is Michael Jordan. Jordan is often touted as the GOAT, or Greatest of All-Time. While he experienced exceptional success on the court, highlighted by six NBA championships, five NBA MVP awards, two Olympic gold medals, and 14 All-Star appearances (NBA.com, n.d.), he has often been criticized for not speaking out on social or political issues. In 1990, criticism arose when he declined to support Black Democrat Harvey Gantt in North Carolina's Senate race (Agyemang, 2011). Jordan's refusal to support Gantt was clearly market motivated, as he asserted, "Republicans buy shoes, too" (Granderson, 2012). Criticism continued in 1992 when Los Angeles was suffering from violence and racial tension. Rather than speak out on the circumstances, Jordan suggested he was not up to speed on the matter. Which viewpoint is correct, the proponent or opponent view? Do athletes have a social responsibility to speak out on social and political issues? These questions will guide this debate on athlete activism.

Central Question: Do athletes have an obligation to speak out on social or political issues?

Affirmative View: Yes, athletes should use their platform to speak out on social or political issues.

Opposing View: Athletes are not obligated to speak out on social or political issues.

DEBATE TOPIC #6 – THE USE OF PUBLIC FUNDS IN SPORT STADIUM CONSTRUCTION

The use of public funds to build new sport venues and stadiums has dramatically increased over the past quarter century. It has become common for stadium renovation projects and new venue builds to use public money or taxpayer dollars for the changes. A recent Bloomberg report showed that over the course of the past 25 years, taxpayers have lost more than $4 billion in exemptions and taxpayer subsidies to support the build of new sport stadiums and sport venues (Kuriloff & Peterson, 2012). This situation has existed since the golden age of stadium construction (1907–1915), yet after the Tax Reform Act of 1986, a law that restricted stadiums from using more than 10% of direct stadium revenue to finance their facilities, the trend of using taxpayer money dramatically increased. The Tax Reform Act meant that sport owners and stadium builders could not use over 10% of the revenues from tickets, concessions, parking, or other areas to help to finance a renovation or a new build. The Act was not successful in its attempt to stop government spending, as it had the opposite effect. This Act required that stadiums and owners use other forms of funds to build their venues and stadiums. The other funds that owners sought out were the public monies available through tax bonds and subsidies from the government. According to Povich (2016) over 91 sport stadiums have been built or renovated since 1960 with the use of public funds.

Why Would a Facility Renovate or Build New?

The decision to build a new stadium can come from a variety of sources. The stadium decision makers (typically owners) want to generate new revenues to sell to fans. In the National Football League (NFL) for example, many of the stadium revenues must be shared with the league. This concept called "League Think" is designed to create a competitive balance among all NFL teams. In the NFL there are a limited number of monies that a team owner can keep and not share with the rest of the league. These revenues include a percentage of ticket sales, luxury box or suite ticket sales, Personal Seat Licenses (PSLs), and naming rights money. If an NFL owner wants to try to capitalize on the amount of money they keep, building a new venue with more luxury boxes and garnering a new naming rights deal may be the answer. New stadiums, or stadium renovations, are essential to create new revenues for sport teams. Another common reason for a new venue is stadium capacity. The number of tickets and "butts in seats" is a pivotal front-end decision that has dramatic effects on fan experience and the financial viability of a team.

meunierd/Shutterstock.com

What Is Public Funding Anyway?

There are several ways in which a stadium is publically funded. The most common is the use of government issued bonds and tax increment bonds. Bonds are simply promissory notes that are a promise by the

borrower to pay back the lender a specified amount of money with interest within a specific period of time. A General Obligation Bond (GOB) is a municipal bond "backed by the full faith and credit of the issuing body (state, local, or regional government)" is the most common in public stadium financing (Walker & Stotlar, 1997, p. 44). These bonds are secured by the taxes that the government collects from tax revenue to guarantee the repayment of the bondholders. General Obligation Bonds issued with full financial backing of the issuer (usually government or municipality) in the case of a sport facility are usually backed by taxes. A Revenue Bond is a bond that is repaid solely by revenue from stadium or from specific government fund. Revenue bonds are often issued based on the potential financial support of the proposed project. The issuer must evaluate if the project will produce enough revenue to repay the bond interest. Revenue bonds typically carry higher interest rates, have an increased risk, use potential financial support of proposed project, and use tax from revenue specific sources. The public use of government funds (taxes, borrowing) has played an important role in many recent stadium construction projects. Public funding can take multiple forms as the public is often not willing to take on the increased taxes. Typically if the public agrees to increase taxes for a new build, it is taxes that do not directly impact the individual within the community, such as hotel-motel tax, car-rental tax, parking tax, entertainment tax, airport traveler tax, or sin taxes (taxes on alcohol and cigarettes). Stadiums can be funded by Tax Increment Financing (TIF), which is typically a subsidy for the redevelopment of an area that has recently experienced a loss or needs improvement (Ammon Jr., Southall, & Nagell, 2010). TIF uses an increase in the local property and/or sales taxes within a geographic area and is designed to help generate new business development. One example of a TIF is in Louisville, Kentucky, where the Louisville Arena Authority oversees the management and repayment of the bonds issued to build and manage the KFC Yum! Center. The initial TIF covered a six square mile radius in the downtown area of Louisville, until 2013 when the Louisville Arena Authority redrew the radius to two miles to include many more local businesses that will benefit from the repayment of the bonds (Kitchen, 2014). In some cases the Direct Financial Subsidy or Zoning Changes are offered as government assistance to the stadium build. These are indirect methods of funding major capital investments, especially those with perceived high earning potential.

Most stadium builds will use a combination of public and private funding to finance the new venue. Private financing includes personal or corporate loans, donations, fundraising, and corporate investment. This type of financing has become more common as the price of stadium build has dramatically increased over the past several years. Sports Authority Field in Denver, Colorado, is owned in part by several counties in the greater Denver area, who in turn lease the stadium back to the Broncos. The stadium was 72% publically financed and private investors paid the difference.

Proponents of Public Funding

Team owners, ownership groups, and proponents of public funding of new stadiums often present very strong cases for why the stadium or venue should be built with the assistance of government money or taxpayer dollars (public funds). Oftentimes a team will try to convince a city or community that a new stadium

Katherine Welles/Shutterstock.com

is necessary for the team to stay. It has also been common that a city will offer to build a new stadium to try to lure a team to relocate. This happened in Milwaukee when the city built a publically funded baseball stadium to lure a Major League team to the city in the 1950s (Abrams, 2013). Still today, stadiums are being used as tools to keep teams in their respective cities. According to Povich (2016) the city of St. Louis tried to convince Stan Kroenke, owner of the then St. Louis Rams to stay in the city with an offer of a new stadium for the NFL team in 2015. Kroenke instead decided to move his team to Los Angeles and spend his own money to build the Rams a new state-of-the-art venue. This type of enticement from teams and from cities has become very common in franchise movement and sport.

Another common position supporting public funding is that a new build creates new jobs during the construction and the operation of the stadium or venue. Proponents argue that jobs are created not only in building the stadium and the management of the stadium but also in local businesses, hotels, and restaurants surrounding the venue (Wilhelm, 2008). Building a new stadium or ballpark can mean new construction jobs as well as generating new spending from spectators and fans. According to a Policy Matters article by Christopher Diedrich (2007) a concept called the "multiplier effect" where an increase in money to the community is in direct correlation to an increase in spending can be a common economic argument for the addition of a new venue. This is a similar argument used by proponents who discuss the economic impact that a stadium will have on the city and its community. Many argue that public assistance will help the redevelopment of run-down areas of town or grow the economy in old or under-developed neighborhoods. This

Dick Ercken/Shutterstock.com

was the case in 2007 when a public investment of $300 million to build Petco Park in San Diego brought in over $4 billion in private investment and growth to the area (Hoyt, Davila, & Foster, 2008).

Many in support of stadium builds claim that new facilities bring in additional revenue from tourism and visitors to the city or enhance city status. In 2015, Chicago's Mayor Rahm Emanuel claimed that tourism in the city was at an all-time high. Emanuel indicated that tourism in 2015 was expected to exceed $52 million supporting new jobs and an increase in over 529,000 visitor rooms. This growth in tourism in the area was believed to be directly related to many events Chicago hosted in 2015, including the NFL Draft and America's Cup (Office of the Major, 2016). City officials and others also will typically support new builds as they can often attract mega-events to the city. Many cities attempting to attract large-scale events such as the Super Bowl, Olympic Games, and the World Cup will sell this premise to the community and the taxpayers they are requesting assist in the cost of the build. The same strategy has also been used to promote urban redevelopment of run-down communities within the city. The San Diego Padres used urban redevelopment and revitalization strategies to convince the public to invest $300 million in their 2007 PETCO Park build (Hoyt et al., 2008). The sense of community, the facility updates, and the increased amenities (such as seat capacity and luxury boxes and suites) are ways that teams and owners strategize to borrow public money for stadium and venue builds.

Opponents of Public Funding

Taxpayers and community lobbyists that are in opposition of the public funding present many valid and supported reasons that a stadium or venue should not be built with government or taxpayer support. One primary reason discussed by the opposition is the position that already wealthy owners capture high

Robert Pernell/Shutterstock.com

percentages of the value of the new build. Jerry Jones, owner of the Dallas Cowboys, is an example of the lavish amounts of money an owner has the potential to make from new builds. Not only did Jones have the public put up $444 million for AT&T Stadium in Arlington, Texas, he recently convinced the city of Frisco, Texas, to put up $261 million on a Dallas Cowboys practice facility in 2016 making Jones' Cowboys the most valuable team for the 10th straight year (Sports Money, 2016). Jerry Jones negotiated several opportunities to capitalize on his new facility as he collects revenue from an increased seat capacity, additional luxury boxes and suites, naming rights, and parking at the new venue (Hoyt & Foster, 2003). Jones bought the Cowboys for $150 million and according to a 2016 Forbes valuation the team is worth over $4 billion and growing (Sport Money, 2016).

Many opposed to public funding believe that stadiums rank low in community priorities. The argument is that communities prefer better schools, nicer hospitals, an increased police presence, better roads, and more community parks. According to a Policy Matters article by Christopher Diedrich (2007), economists that oppose public funding agree that public funds should not be used for stadiums to provide entertainment, but rather be used for education, healthcare, the environment, and effective job creation (2007). Many sport economists and opponents of public funding argue that the creation of jobs is temporary and stadiums rarely create full-time, permanent, or long-term positions (Abrams, 2013).

Richard Cavalleri/Shutterstock.com

Economists also often dispute the economic impact argument claiming that total city revenues are often overestimated, as it is revenue substitution rather than revenue creation. This means that there is no new revenue brought to the city, but that the same money is just reallocated to a different area. Many opponents claim that revenue is often decreased in one area of the city and simply redistributed elsewhere in the community.

As many believe that building a new facility will bring in new events, the city of New York has done so without using public or government money. New York City has recorded an increase in tourism in recent years and created a model for success hosting the 2013 Major League Baseball All-Star Game, the 2014 Formula 1 Grand Prix of America, and the 2014 NCAA Regional Finals in Madison Square Gardens. None of these mega-events were held in new venues that the city assisted to build. In fact, NYC also hosted the Super Bowl XLVIII at MetLife Stadium built in 2010, but this venue was 100% financed by private funds. This debunks the argument or myth that stadiums cannot be built in this day and age using 100% private funding.

Central Question: Should sport organizations be allowed to use public funds to build or renovate their sport facility?

Affirmative View: Yes, sport organizations should be allowed to use public money to build or renovate their sport facilities, venues, or stadiums.

Opposing View: The use of public money for the purpose of a new stadium build or renovation should not be the responsibility of the taxpayer.

References

ABC. (2005, February 27). Schwarzenegger has no regrets about steroid use. *ABC News*. Retrieved from http://abc-news.go.com/ThisWeek/Health/story?id=532456

Abrams, R. I. (2013). Hardball in city hall: Public financing of sport stadiums. *Sport & Entertainment Law Forum 3*(1), 8.

adidas. (2015). adidas announces support for mascot name changes ahead of White House Tribal Nations Conference [Press release]. Retrieved from http://news.adidas.com/US/Latest-News/ALL/adidas-Announces-Support-For-Mascot-Name-Changes-Ahead-Of-White-House-Tribal-Nations-Conference/s/7197ec89-d0fe-4557-b737-cd-27dc76aba1

Agyemang, K. J. (2011). Black male athlete activism and the link to Michael Jordan: A transformational leadership and social cognitive theory analysis. *International Review for the Sociology of Sport, 47*(4), 433–445.

Ammon Jr., R., Southall, R. M., & Nagell, M. S. (2010). Sport facility management: Organizing events and mitigating risk. Morgantown, WV: Fitness Information Technology.

Associated Press. (2011, November 5). Auburn releases Cam Newton docs. *ESPN*. Retrieved from http://www.espn.com/college-football/story/_/id/7190987/auburn-tigers-records-reveal-details-cam-newton-scandal

Baseball-reference.com. (n.d.). *Career leaders and records for home runs*. Retrieved from http://www.baseball-reference.com/leaders/HR_career.shtml

Belson, K. (2014, November 15). Will other leagues join the NBA? Don't bet on it. *New York Times*. Retrieved from http://www.nytimes.com/2014/11/15/sports/not-all-leagues-ready-to-go-all-in-on-legalized-gambling.html?_r=0

Bernstein, M. (2016, January 26). Lawsuit claims fantasy sports websites FanDuel, DraftKings violate Oregon law. *The Oregonian*. Retrieved from http://www.oregonlive.com/pacific-northwest-news/index.ssf/2016/01/lawsuit_claims_fantasy_sports.html

Brown, D. (2014, January 9). Cleveland Indians demote Chief Wahoo logo. *Big League Stew*. Retrieved from http://sports.yahoo.com/blogs/mlb-big-league-stew/cleveland-indians-marginalize-chief-wahoo-logo-081024357--mlb.html

Burch, E. (2014, March 27). Pay to play debate continues. Retrieved from http://abc3340.com/archive/pay-to-play-debate-continues

Buxton, R. (2015, October 5). Here's the difference between daily fantasy sports and illegal sports betting. *HuffPost Sports*. Retrieved from http://www.huffingtonpost.com/entry/difference-between-daily-fantasy-sports-illegal-betting_us_5612c479e4b0dd85030cd937

Bryant, H. (2015, September 2). By this measure, Michael Jordan can't touch LeBron James. *ESPN*. Retrieved from http://espn.go.com/nba/story/_/id/13530915/cleveland-cavaliers-star-lebron-james-michael-jordan-beat-area

Calamur, K. (2013, January 18). Lance Armstrong admits to using performance-enhancing drugs. *NPR*. Retrieved from http://www.npr.org/sections/thetwo-way/2013/01/17/169650077/lance-armstrong-to-admit-to-using-performance-enhancing-drugs

Candaele, K., & Dreier, P. (2004). Where are the jocks for justice? *Nation, 278*(25), 21–24.

CNN. (2015, December 28). Performance enhancing drugs in sports fast facts. *CNN*. Retrieved from http://www.cnn.com/2013/06/06/us/performance-enhancing-drugs-in-sports-fast-facts/

Culpepper, C. (2014, December 14). Florida State's unusual bond with Seminole Tribe puts mascot debate in different light. *The Washington Post*. Retrieved from https://www.washingtonpost.com/sports/colleges/florida-states-unusual-bond-with-seminole-tribe-puts-mascot-debate-in-a-different-light/2014/12/29/5386841a-8eea-11e4-ba53-a477d66580ed_story.html

Cunningham, G. B., & Regan, M. R., Jr. (2012). Political activism, racial identity, and the commercial endorsement of athletes. *International Review for the Sociology of Sport, 47*, 657–669.

Delgado, C. (2014, November 5). A list of famous performance-enhancing-drug using athletes. *CBS Local*. Retrieved from http://931jackfm.cbslocal.com/2014/11/05/a-list-of-famous-performance-enhancing-drug-using-athletes-not-named-lance-armstrong/

Diedrich, C. (2007). Homefield economics: The public financing of stadiums. *Policy Matters, 4*(2), 22–27.

Drape, J. (2016, January 29). Payment processor to stop working with daily fantasy sport clients. *The New York Times*. Retrieved from http://www.nytimes.com/2016/01/30/sports/draftkings-fanduel-vantiv-daily-fantasy.html?_r=0

Edelman, M. (2014, July 29). Will Robert Bowman become Major League Baseball's first daily fantasy sports commissioner? *Forbes.* Retrieved from http://www.forbes.com/sites/marcedelman/2014/07/29/will-robert-bowman-become-major-league-baseballs-first-daily-fantasy-sports-commissioner/#736d1ae51941

Edelman, M. (2016). Navigating the legal risks of daily fantasy sports: A detailed primer in federal and state gambling law. *University of Illinois Law Review,* 1–39.

Effects of PEDs. (n.d.). *U.S. Anti-Doping Agency.* Retrieved from https://www.usada.org/substances/effects-of-performance-enhancing-drugs/

Farrey, T. (2014, January 28). Kain Colter starts union movement. Retrieved from http://www.espn.com/espn/otl/story/_/id/10363430/outside-lines-northwestern-wildcats-football-players-trying-join-labor-union

Florida State University. (n.d.). Relationship with the Seminole Tribe of Florida [Press release]. Retrieved from https://unicomm.fsu.edu/messages/relationship-seminole-tribe-florida/

Foster, G., Greyser, S. A., & Walsh, B. (2006). The business of sports: text and cases on strategy and Forde, P. (2011, July 18). Myth of exploited, impoverished athletes. Retrieved from http://www.espn.com/college-sports/story/_/id/6779583/college-athletes-far-exploited

Gehring, C. (2015, March 17). 10 years later, a look at every MLB suspended for PEDs. *SportsNation.* Retrieved from http://www.sportingnews.com/mlb-news/4638886-baseball-players-suspended-steroids-peds-list-all-time-policy

Giulianotti, R. (2005). *Sport: A critical sociology.* Cambridge, UK: Polity Press.

Granderson, L. (2012, August 14). The political Michael Jordan. *ESPN.* Retrieved from http://espn.go.com/nba/story/_/id/8264956/michael-jordan-obama-fundraiser-22-years-harvey-gantt

Hauser, T. (n.d.). The importance of Muhammad Ali. *The Journal of the Gilder Lehrman Institute.* Retrieved from https://www.gilderlehrman.org/history-by-era/civil-rights-movement/essays/importance-muhammad-ali

Heitner, D. (2015, April 2). DraftKings and Major League Baseball extend exclusive partnership. *Forbes.* Retrieved from http://www.forbes.com/sites/darrenheitner/2015/04/02/draftkings-and-major-league-baseball-extend-exclusive-partnership/#10c1ef294588

Hoyt, D., Davila, A., & Foster, G. (2008). San Diego Padres: PETCO Park as a catalyst for urban redevelopment Stanford Graduate School of Business [Case SPM37-PDF-ENG].

Hoyt, D., & Foster, G. (2003). Dallas Cowboys: Financing a new stadium. Stanford Graduate School of Business [Case SPM6-PDF-ENG].

Hylton, J. G. (2010). Before the Redskins were the Redskins: The use of Native American team names in the formative era of American sports, 1857–1933. *North Dakota Law Review, 86,* 879–903.

Jackson, S. (2013, September 12). The myth of parity. *ESPN.* Retrieved from http://www.espn.com/college-sports/story/_/id/9666004/pay-play-answer-college-athletics

Jurkowitz, M. (2013, July 17). On Twitter: Anger greets the Zimmerman verdict. *Pew Research Center.* Retrieved from http://www.pewresearch.org/fact-tank/2013/07/17/on-twitter-anger-greets-the-zimmerman-verdict/

Kaufman, P., & Wolff, E. A. (2010). Playing and protesting: Sport as a vehicle for social change. *Journal of Sport and Social Issues, 34*(2), 154–175.

Kilgore, A. (2015, March 27). Daily fantasy sports website find riches in Internet gaming law loophole. *The Washington Post.* Retrieved from https://www.washingtonpost.com/sports/daily-fantasy-sports-web-sites-find-riches-in-internet-gaming-law-loophole/2015/03/27/92988444-d172-11e4-a62f-ee745911a4ff_story.html

Kitchen, S. (2014, August). Tax revenue for the KFC! Yum Center increases. *Courier-Journal.* Retrieved from http://www.courier-journal.com/story/news/politics/metro-government/2014/08/24/tax-revenue-kfc-yum-center-increases/14454775/

Klatell, J. (2007, February 16). Fighting Illini say goodbye to the chief. *Associated Press.* Retrieved from http://www.cbsnews.com/news/fighting-illini-say-goodbye-to-the-chief/

Kuriloff, A., & Peterson, D. (2012, September). In stadium building spree. US taxpayers lose $4 billion. *Bloomberg.* Retrieved from http://www.bloomberg.com/news/articles/2012-09-05/in-stadium-building-spree-u-s-taxpayers-lose-4-billion

Leach, M. (2010, January 11). McGwire opens up about steroid use. *Major League Baseball.* Retrieved from http://m.mlb.com/news/article/7900244

Liptak, A. (2017, June 19). Justices strike down law banning disparaging trademarks. *The New York Times*. Retrieved from https://www.nytimes.com/2017/06/19/us/politics/supreme-court-trademarks-redskins.html

Lumpkin, A., Stoll, S. K., Beller, J. (2002). *Sport ethics: Applications for fair play* (3rd ed.). New York, NY: McGraw Hill-Higher Education.

Marquesee, M. (1995). Sport and stereotype: From role model to Muhammad Ali. *Race & Class, 36*(4), 1–29.

McGraw, D. (2015, April 11). Native Americans protest Chief Wahoo logo at Cleveland Indians home opener. *The Guardian*. Retrieved from http://www.theguardian.com/sport/2015/apr/11/native-americans-protest-chief-wahoo-logo-at-cleveland-indians-home-opener

Mitchell, G. J. (2007). *Report to the commissioner of baseball of an independent investigation into the illegal use of steroids and other performance enhancing substances by players in Major League Baseball*. Retrieved from http://files.mlb.com/mitchrpt.pdf

Munguia, H. (2014, September 5). *The 2,128 Native American mascots people aren't talking about*. Retrieved from http://fivethirtyeight.com/features/the-2128-native-american-mascots-people-arent-talking-about/

NBA.com (n.d.). *Michael Jordan biography*. Retrieved from http://www.nba.com/history/players/jordan_bio.html

NCAA. (2005). NCAA executive committee issues guidelines for use of Native American mascots at championship events [Press release]. Retrieved from http://fs.ncaa.org/Docs/PressArchive/2005/Announcements/NCAA%2BExecutive%2BCommittee%2BIssues%2BGuidelines%2Bfor%2BUse%2Bof%2BNative%2BAmerican%2BMascots%2Bat%2BChampionship%2BEvents.html

NCAA. (n.d.). What is amateurism? *NCAA*. Retrieved from http://www.ncaa.org/student-athletes/future/eligibility-center/what-amateurism

NCAA finances. (n.d.) *USA Today*. Retrieved from http://sports.usatoday.com/ncaa/finances/

O'Dell, L. (2015, November 3). Washington Redskins defend controversial name by citing other 'offensive' trademarks. *Associated Press*. Retrieved from http://www.boston.com/sports/football/2015/11/03/washington-redskins-defend-controversial-name-citing-other-offensive-trademarks/d0CUulArqCVlFPEDMsaCiI/story.html

Office of the Major, City of Chicago (April 26, 2016). Major Emanuel and Choose Chicago announce record tourism in 2015. Press Release. Retrieved from https://www.cityofchicago.org/content/dam/city/depts/mayor/Press%20Room/Press%20Releases/2016/April/4.26.16MayorChooseChicagoAnnounceRecordTourism.pdf

Pelak, C. F. (2005). Athletes as agents of change: An examination of shifting race relations within women's netball in post-apartheid South Africa. *Sociology of Sport Journal, 21*, 59–77.

Phillips, A. (2015, September 21). Are daily fantasy sports even legal? *The Washington Post*. Retrieved from https://www.washingtonpost.com/news/the-fix/wp/2015/09/21/are-daily-fantasy-sports-even-legal/

Povich, E. S. (2016, July). Why should public money be used to build sport stadiums? PBS News. Retrieved from http://www.pbs.org/newshour/rundown/public-money-used-build-sports-stadiums

Powell, R. A. (2005, August 24). Florida State can keep its Seminoles. *New York Times*. Retrieved from http://www.nytimes.com/2005/08/24/sports/florida-state-can-keep-its-seminoles.html?_r=0

Radar, B. G. (1999). *American sports: From the age of folk games to the age of televised sports* (4th ed.). Upper Saddle River, NJ: Prentice Hall.

Ridpath, D. (2015, October 23). FIRE pay for play debate: Entertaining, informative and balanced. *Forbes*. Retrieved from http://www.forbes.com/sites/bdavidridpath/2015/10/23/fire-pay-for-play-debate-entertaining-informative-and-balanced/2/#524817484f4f

Rose, N. (2015). Are daily fantasy sports legal? *Gaming Law Review and Economics, 19*(5), 346–349.

Schmittel, A., & Sanderson, J. (2014). Talking about Trayvon in 140 characters: Exploring NFL players' tweets about the George Zimmerman verdict. *Journal of Sport and Social Issues*, 1–14.

Schwartz, N. (2014, May 13). *NBPA's Roger Mason Jr. says LeBron James won't play next season if Donald Sterling is still an owner*. Retrieved from http://ftw.usatoday.com/2014/05/lebron-james-boycott-donald-sterling

Shapira, I. (2015, July 8). Federal judge orders cancellation of Redskins' trademark registrations. *The Washington Post*. Retrieved from https://www.washingtonpost.com/local/judge-upholds-cancellation-of-redskins-trademarks-in-a-legal-and-symbolic-setback-for-team/2015/07/08/5a65424e-1e6e-11e5-aeb9-a411a84c9d55_story.html

Shelburne, R. (2014, April 30). Donald Sterling receives lifetime ban. *ESPN*. Retrieved from http://espn.go.com/los-angeles/nba/story/_/id/10857580/donald-sterling-los-angelesclippers-owner-receives-life-ban-nba

Smith, C. (2014, March 17). College Basketball Most Valuable Teams 2014: Louisville Cardinals on top again. *Sports-Money*. Retrieved from http://www.forbes.com/sites/chrissmith/2014/03/17/college-basketballs-most-valuable-teams-2014-louisville-cardinals-on-top-again/#105748226c91

Solomon, J. (2015, December 17). Inside College Sport: SEC, big Ten dominate $100M revenue club. *CBS Sports*. Retrieved from http://www.cbssports.com/college-football/news/inside-college-sports-sec-big-ten-dominate-100m-revenue-club/

Sports Money: 2016 NFL Valuations. (2016, October). *Forbes*. Retrieved from http://www.forbes.com/teams/dallas-cowboys/

Staurowsky, E. J. (2007). "You know, we are all Indian." Exploring white power and privilege in reactions to the NCAA Native American mascot policy. *Journal of Sport and Social Issues, 31*(1), 61–76.

Steak, C. (2010, November 13). Cam Newton, Reggie Bush and why college athletes should be paid. *Bleacher Report*. Retrieved from http://bleacherreport.com/articles/516653-cfb-cam-newton-reggie-bush-and-why-college-athletes-should-be-paid

TMZ. (2014, April 25). Clippers Owner Donald Sterling to GF—Don't bring black people to my games, including Magic Johnson. *TMZ*. Retrieved from http://www.tmz.com/videos/0_wkuhmkt8/

Walker, M. L., & Stotlar, D. K. (1997). *Sport facility management*. Sudbury, MA: Jones & Bartlett Publishing.

Wilhelm, S. W., (2008). Public Funding of sport stadiums. Center for Public Policy & Administration. Retrieved from http://gardner.utah.edu/_documents/publications/finance-tax/sports-stadiums.pdf

Wright, H. (2009, April 13). The 10 most notorious steroid users in sports history. *Bleacher Report*. Retrieved from http://bleacherreport.com/articles/155381-top-ten-notorious-steroid-users

Wulf, S. (2014, September 24). Change is happening in Cleveland. *ESPN*. Retrieved from http://espn.go.com/mlb/story/_/id/11574381/cleveland-indians-say-goodbye-chief-wahoo